**A Gift from the**
**Friends of the La Jolla Library**

# KISSING THE MASK

## ALSO BY WILLIAM T. VOLLMANN

# KISSING THE MASK

## BEAUTY, UNDERSTATEMENT AND FEMININITY IN JAPANESE NOH THEATER

*with some thoughts on*

**Muses (especially Helga Testorf),**

**Transgender Women,**

**Kabuki Goddesses,**

**Porn Queens,**

**Poets, Housewives, Makeup Artists,**

**Geishas,**

**Valkyries** *and*

**Venus Figurines**

# WILLIAM T. VOLLMANN

## ecco

*An Imprint of HarperCollinsPublishers*

HarperCollins books may be purchased for educational, business, or sales promotional use. For information, please write: Special Markets Department, HarperCollins Publishers, 10 East 53rd Street, New York, NY 10022.

FIRST EDITION

A version of "The Mask Is Most Important *Always*" was first commissioned in 2002 by *Time Asia,* but, being too arcane for that publication, actually appeared in *Tin House* magazine in 2005.

Part of "The Decay of the Angel" was presented in a speech to PEN in New York in 2002 or 2003.

"A Branch of Flowers" first appeared (in shorter form) in the *American Book Review* in 2006.

A portion of "Crossing the Abyss" first appeared in periodical form in 2004.

*Designed by Mary Austin Speaker*

Library of Congress Cataloging-in-Publication Data has been applied for.

ISBN: 978-0-06-122848-3

10  11  12  13  14    OV/RRD    10  9  8  7  6  5  4  3  2  1

*For Kawai Takako, interpreter, fixer,*
*sweethearted friend*

What am I to do with you,
semblance of the laurel in the moon,
you whom I see but cannot touch?
PRINCE YUHARA,
*poem to a young woman, middle Nara era*

Dresses make the lady,
if one has the figure.
CHARLOTTE VON MAHLSDORF
*(born Lothar Berfelde),*
*bef. 1992*

A woman never imitates herself.
ZEAMI MOTOKIYO,
*1428*

# CONTENTS

# ILLUSTRATIONS

[Part title.] Geisha at her makeup table, 2008. Detail.

[Frontis 1.*] The maiko Konomi-san, Gion quarter, Kyoto, 2006.

[Frontis 2.] The geisha Suzuka-san, Higashi quarter, Kanazawa, 2008. (For pictures of the process by which she took on this appearance, see the part title and pages 217–21.)

[Full title underlay.] Paints and palates for Noh masks. Atelier of the renowned Noh mask carver Ms. Nakamura Mitsue. Kyoto, 2004.

*Both frontispieces were originally photographed with color film specially for this book. Unfortunately, reproducing them in such a way as to show you the resplendence of geisha attire would have been too expensive for the publisher.

cloth at my request for illustrative purposes only, and does not represent any approved Noh gesture or movement. Photographed in Mr. Umewaka's studio in Tokyo, 2002.

81   The apprentice holds the mask to his face. (The same caveat applies.)

82   Detail of *ko-omote* on page 80.

83   Ms. Nakamura by her wall of masks. Kyoto, 2004.

99   Geisha festival dance, Ponto-cho. Kyoto, 2005.

104  Mr. Mikata in the mirror room of Junenji Temple, placing to his face the *ko-omote* he used in this place on the previous evening to perform "Michimori." Kyoto, 2006.

114  The late Mr. Kanze Hideo, during an interview on the day after a Takigi-Noh performance. Kyoto, 2005.

119  Comparison-sketch of facial proportions: Ms. Aya Kudo, S & M porn model, *vs.* a *zo-onna* carved by Ms. Nakamura Mitsue.

122  Sketch-diagram of the five main gender-specific measurements, simplified from a diagram in Heath, who (sourcing J-M. Fellous) actually shows us twenty-four indicators of "gender discrimination and prediction of the basis of facial metric information," but he singles out the most important five to be "substituted into the following masculinity index equation."

125  [Ms. Nakamura's sketch.] Comparison of facial proportions: Generalized Utamaro *bijin-ga* face vs. generalized Noh mask.

129  Vulva, eastern California, 2008.

144  "Kiss me, won't you?" Tokyo, ca. 2004.

179  The geisha Masami-san bangs the drum. Kanazawa, 2008.

181  Tortoise-shell hair ornament for sale at the inconspicuous little shop in Kyoto patronized by the Gion geishas mentioned in this book. It was shockingly expensive; few non-geishas could have

afforded it. Hence in the text I have taken the minor speculative liberty of captioning this object "geisha hair ornament." The same goes for the caption to page 189 (below, this page).

188 Facsimile of the lyrics to "Black Hair," written out for me by the ochaya-san, Ms. Imamura, in calligraphy of refined elegance, 2006. The words were so archaic that my interpreter, a highly educated woman of late middle age, had recourse to her mother for help.

189 More geisha hair ornaments.

194 The renowned geiko Kofumi-san. Gion, Kyoto, 2006.

195 The maiko Konomi-san. Kofumi-san is her teacher. Gion, 2006.

196 Two instants of Kofumi-san's dance. On this occasion (Gion, 2004) she was not wearing her wig and *oshiroi* makeup.

197 Konomi-san dances "Fan to You." At lower left in the first photograph we can see Danyu-san playing the shamisen. Gion, 2006.

198 Another instant of Kofumi-san's performance of "Black Hair," and of Konomi-san's of "Fan to You." In both photographs Danyu-san plays the shamisen on the left.

200 Sketch of Gion Shrine, also called Yasaka Shrine. Kyoto, 2006.

203 Masami-san bows after she has danced for me. Higashi, Kanazawa, 2008.

207 Mannequin legs displaying panty hose. Bogotá, Colombia, 1999.

210 Mannequin. Mexicali, Mexico, 2005.

217 The geisha Suzuka-san begins making up for the evening in tiny dressing room of her ochaya in Kanazawa's Higasha pleasure district. All photos of her were taken in 2008.

218 Now she has applied her white *oshiroi* and begun touching up her eyes and mouth. The condition under which I was allowed to photograph her was: no representations of her incompletely made-

up face could be published. I love this portrait very much and am very grateful to her for relenting.

219 Her makeup is finished. She has changed into her formal kimono. The obi-tier and the ochaya-san now pull her tight.

220 Suzuka-san lowers the heavy custom-made wig onto her head.

221 Now she is ready.

226 My two makeovers by Yukiko. Tokyo, 2008. See also page 239.

231 Sketch of onnagatas. Tokyo, 2008.

232a Facade of Kabuki theater showing actors currently performing. Kanazawa, 2008.

232b Mr. Ichikawa Shunen, onnagata. He is relatively young but already quite well known. Tokyo, 2008.

236 Basic Kabuki makeup for an onnagata.

239 My makeover by the T-girl Katy. Los Angeles, 2008. The immediately following portraits of her are from the same period.

240 Katy at her makeup mirror, in a relatively early stage of transformation.

241 Now she is further along. As I look over these images of that sweet and gentle person, I feel tender toward her. She had a very open smile.

242 Here she is in full femme mode, but on a different occasion (the previous night). It is about midnight and she is standing in front of the bar. As you can see, her makeup, like a Kabuki actor's, is especially effective in such low-light environments as theater, bar, street.

243 Katy's housemate, the lovely T-girl Jennifer.

252 Cross-dresser's prosthetic vulva. This is a basic model; another version can menstruate.

madwoman Sakagami, was played by Mr. Kanze Kiyokazu. This first drawing shows Semimaru being carried in his palanquin to the wilderness, where he will be abandoned.

361   Sakagami with her madness-signifying branch.

364   Sakagami and Semimaru (who is wearing the tall hat, sitting at her left). In this quick drawing the stage pillar, chorus and musicians can also be seen.

365   The Osaka Noh theater after a performance, 2004.

391   Four instants in Masami-san's dance. Higashi, Kanazawa, 2008.

394   Congolese beauty I. Near the Congo River, 2001.

395   American beauty I (the rock star Paula Keyth). Portland, Oregon, 1995.

396   American beauty II (G-girl). Eastern California, 2008.

397   Thai beauty. Bangkok, 2001.

398   Kazakh beauty. Her face always reminds me of a lovely Noh mask. Altamy, 2000.

399   Congolese beauty II. Goma, 2001.

400   Iraqi beauty. Baghdad, 1998.

401   Japanese beauty. Tokyo, 1998.

402   *Waka-onna* mask belonging to the Umewaka family. Tokyo, 2002. Ms. Nakamura notes that this mask would be used specifically for "Michimori."

# KISSING THE MASK

O:

# Understatements About This String-Ball of Idle Thoughts

His colleagues gave their leisure to various pastimes: some read novels, others took up the chants and No plays of the Kanzé School, and still others gathered to write haiku and make sketches illustrating the poems. Most of these diversions, however, served as pretexts for getting together to do some drinking.

MISHIMA YUKIO,
*RUNAWAY HORSES*

D eaf, dumb and illiterate in Japanese, innocent of formal study in any discipline of art, a graceless dancer afflicted with bad eyesight, I may not be the perfect author for·any essay on Noh drama. Fortunately, this is no essay, but a string-ball of idle thoughts.*

---

*Moreover, it's not precisely about Noh drama, either. Whatever mistakes of fact I make, few people will catch them, even should my ignorance someday be exposed by translation into Japanese. A taxi driver in Kyoto said: "My opinion is that Noh is the art form which eliminates and simplifies to the maximum. I am not interested myself, but I know what Noh is. If it enters your intuition, so that you don't even need to think, then you will instantly understand it." — Oh, he knew, all right! — In Tokyo, the old proprietor of the sushi restaurant (established by his family in 1910) where my interpreter and I occasion-ally ate dinner proudly informed us that one of his customers was an Intangible Cultural Treasure; he advised us that torchlit Noh performances occurred in the park across the way; he himself preferred karaoke. — And at so many Noh performances the theater was almost empty. Often my fellow spectators would nod off; I'd see the head drop, the shoulders seeming to expand even as the ghost onstage was stamping, all emerald and tan and gilded! So perhaps it was always that way. A seventeenth- or eighteenth-century

Rarely able to compose a short sentence, let alone a short book, I admit that this attempt of mine to extol the beauties of understatement may well approach the ludicrous. All the same, can't a man praise the woman he loves? Can't he describe her? Without presuming to be her, or to know her as she knows herself, can't he claim acquaintanceship with her moods and ways?

In brief, rather than a primer prepared by a Noh expert, this short book is an appreciation, sincere and blundering, resolutely ignorant, riddled with the prejudices and insights of an alien, a theatergoer, a man gazing at femininity. Sometimes the blankness of my understanding corresponds to the faded-tattoo blue of Hiroshige's skies and marshes. In his prints, snowcovered boats ride in a pale blue harbor enthralled by snowy trees, and I find many a pale white moon in a pale blue sky. All is tea- and tattoo-ink. Ladies view plum blossoms or maple blossoms in the snow; often they stand in meditative pairs at the base of some snow-outlined tree whose arms are as graceful as their hair.

On the Ginza subway line, a longhaired woman is removing a tiny, tiny digital device from her purse, while a dollfaced girl stands in the doorway, peering into the screen of her cell phone. Not far above their heads, hints of scattered cherry-blossoms and horned women enrich the stylized movements of white hands, the rapid graces of diamond-crowned, scarlet-cloaked Kabuki princesses. In snowy Kanazawa the moment has come when the geisha and the musician are giggling downstairs and I hear the shamisen being tuned. And on the Noh stage in Kyoto, a man has just now become a woman whose elegance is precisely modulated, in keeping with the way that the edge of her horizontally held fan cleaves the air. I watch them all, then write down what I see.

What a long line at the Kabuki-za tonight! Will there be time for a beer and a grilled eel over rice? How much will the tickets cost? Three hundred dollars apiece? I ought to save two thousand for an hour with just one more geisha, and seven hundred for my female makeover with Yukiko; then it's off to the porn shop. I can still afford my coffin hotel, if I eat potato chips for breakfast all week. Someday the dollar might tumble

---

snatch of light verse about illicit visits to the pleasure quarter runs: "His book of Noh lessons: a prop for lies to tell his father."

downstairs; then I'd have to declare victory and end this book! Someday I might even turn *elderly*. But why entertain such impossibilities? I'd rather count the orange stripes of the white carp I saw in the pond of that snowy garden. A few more dances from now, I'll be able to tell you with confidence when and how each gender unmasks itself to the other? For you and only for you, I peer into ancient picture-scrolls until it's time for another snack. I sure hope the geisha won't see the wrinkles in my suit. (Of course she will, but she'll pretend she doesn't.)

Why does the neurotoxin in this blowfish sashimi make my tongue tingle? I *like* it. How much more would be fatal? Never mind that; Mr. Kanze's performing tonight in half an hour; time to pay the check and find a taxi; I'm ignorant about this Noh; will he be a man or a woman tonight?

Meanwhile the geisha Masami-san is rushing and rustling down the stairs, her brocaded obi comprising a square of loveliness at her back. Soon she will dance for me: My heart will voyage through the interstellar darkness around a white mask. Fukutaro-san tunes the shamisen. The two performers sit together, tilting their heads toward each other. Their kimonos are the same sky-blue.

How I love my life in this floating world! If I go drinking with the go-between, tomorrow my eyes will be as red as the lamps at Gion Shrine; but for that there's always green tea, powdered and whisked to a froth, accompanied by a perfect little pistachio sweet. I'm a glutton, a plump middle-aged man now beginning to understand the old lechers who clutch at beauty, not that *I'll* do that; I'm proud, so I'll watch grace in theaters, bars, teahouses; I'll invent a book about representations of feminine beauty and write off every geisha dance on my taxes . . .

# I
# BLACK HAIR

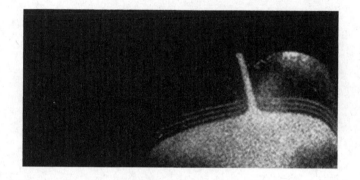

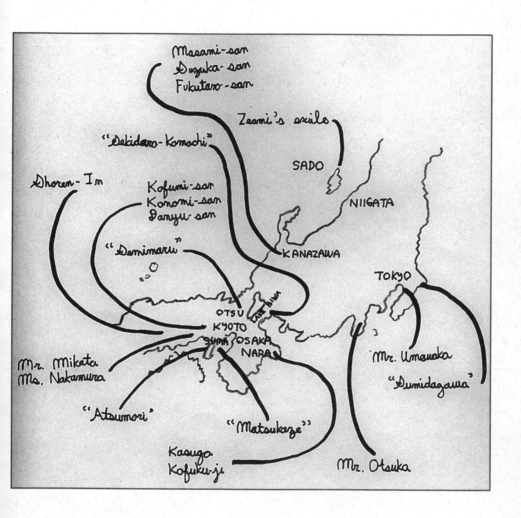

# "The Mask Is Most Important *Always*"

*The Noh Performances of Umewaka Rokuro*

A nd now, on the grounds of Yasukuni Shrine, the last few cherry blossoms shiver, as do the spectators, in this April evening's drizzly wind; and the *kyogen* skit about two servants who guzzle up their master's sake proceeds loudly, coarsely beneath the Noh stage's pagoda roof between the twin fires lit by Tokyo dignitaries an hour before, at the beginning of the entertainment; these wiggling jellies of light are, being theatrical adornments — a category which includes all earthly things — more show than substance; and I suspect that without the aid of the electric stagelights glaring in from either side of the court-yard, that painted pine on the Noh stage's mirror-board would remain no more than a faint and complex clot of darkness. The long stage-bridge glistens, potential and void; at its far end, the rainbow curtain twitches in the breeze, like the skirt of an impatient woman; and beyond this semi-permeable membrane — one of ever so many between "art" and "life" — in the mirror room, whose tatami mats feel warmly springy under one's stockinged feet, two apprentices in blue-and-black kimonos are slowly enwrapping Mr. Umewaka Rokuro in his various shrouds. So it must have been for the preceding fifty-five generations of the Umewaka family;* for there was an Umewaka dance troupe four centuries and more before Noh began. How did those ancientest actors prepare themselves? What masks did they wear, if any? I imagine each one taking his own silent interval, to dream upon his impending change. Thus a thousand years, fifty-five generations; this pleasant, broadfaced man marks the fifty-sixth. He is one of the most celebrated Noh actors in Japan, and has been called the best. His masked likeness appears on the cover of many a book; he performs about once a week, in Japan and out; in his spare time he sometimes reads mystery novels. The Noh corpus presently consists of about two hundred and forty plays. Mr. Umewaka keeps a hundred in his head. Standing in the doorway of this room, I can see that trembling rainbow curtain which will come to symbolize so much to me. To the right of it, a paper-windowed lattice glows in stagelight, overhanging a wall of long, horizontal slats between which the shouting actors flicker (*kyogen* is traditionally performed between Noh plays, for comic relief). But within the mirror room itself one gets no view of anything. This place is, as dressing rooms should be, womb and burial chamber, where an actor's day-to-day self gets ceremented away until the resurrection two hours hence; and another self, stranger, narrower, purer, unhurriedly germinates, preparing to come out at the appointed time, the end of the *kyogen*.

The apprentice who works on Mr. Umewaka from the front, kneeling at his feet, is the highest-ranking, most experienced of his kind — if he *is* an apprentice; for he might just as likely be a *koken*, a watcher-from-behind, the one who glides up to the actor as needed on stage to gather up a fallen prop or straighten his kimono.† He may be a prestigious actor

---

*A Noh expert comments here: "Rokuro is the direct descendant of Minoru I, who was his great-grandfather (and the teacher of Fenollosa). Minoru I was of merchant stock, and married into the Umewaka family. So while the Umewaka tradition does go back a thousand years, long before Noh was thought of, it was by no means a direct patrilineal transmission. The situation since Meiji, in which the Umewakas have had a master actor every generation, is probably extremely unusual."

†In Japanese usage the word "kimono" is in fact applied only to one of many kimono-like garments. Details may be found in the end note to this page. Rather than stiffen the text

who could continue the performance should Mr. Umewaka be incapacitated. In any event, one begins as an apprentice, and one commences the apprenticeship by learning which items to present at the appropriate instant; even this, like every other aspect of Noh, is said to be difficult. Mr. Umewaka stands erect and still, gazing straight ahead into the mirror. He has entered that objectified chrysalis when one can no longer live at will, nor yet give oneself over to the expression of art. What I see is not so much a person submitting to his helpers as a force consideredly drawing in upon itself, limiting, focusing, gathering, brooding. From his kimono the helpers snip gold threads unraveled by ancientness; this costume, like so many others, dates back to the Edo period (1600–1868).* The weaving of the old kimonos is finer than today's, not only visually but also structurally; in them Mr. Umewaka can move more freely, or I should say less constrictedly, thanks to some peculiar fashioning of the sleeves which would now cost millions of yen to reproduce. Moreover, he tells me, the artificial fertilizer ingested by the plants on which twenty-first-century silkworms feed weakens the silk. He laments: "Now they last only a hundred and fifty years — half as long as the old ones." Accordingly, these Edo kimonos are prized by Noh actors, and never, ever washed. They stink. The assistant at Mr. Umewaka's back has already presented a yellow-beige kimono which will frame the inner golden one; the lead apprentice kneels at Mr. Umewaka's feet once more, and the room roars with the faint rustling of cloth. Mr. Umewaka's face is so calm and old. I dare not say a word to him; I must not hinder his exit from this world. Now over the black skullcap goes the black horsehair wig, whose long tresses so cleanly glisten. But first they remove the yellow-beige kimono in honor of a green one; Mr. Umewaka is concerned that yellow-beige might express too great a contrast with his new black hair. Although the fourteenth-century Noh troupes which always performed together no longer exist, Mr. Umewaka frequently performs with the same persons. Moreover, he has long since mastered his particular part, whose gestures remain unalterable. Hence he forgoes Noh's

---

with more foreign words whose explication might distract, I have used "kimono" almost invariably throughout.

*For such dates, see Chronology.

customary day-before rehearsals. Whether he first puts his right or left foot forward, this too has been predetermined for each play — but in some respects Noh resembles a musical "jam" session, requiring certain nearly spontaneous decisions (for instance, in "Kinuta" the lead role of the ageing, perishing, abandoned wife will be played by Mr. Umewaka, who must take care not to be upstaged by the younger mask and costume of the actor who plays the ambiguously seductive maidservant) — and, since, moreover, venues vary so vastly, particularly in the quality of their stagelight, Mr. Umewaka always keeps several kimonos and wigs on hand for each part, so that he can choose and alter his beauty's skin up to the last moment. The helpers fluff out his hair as he looks into the mirror. Then they bring him a low stool, his wig coming off again as he silently sits. "At that point I don't think about what to do anymore," he told me later. "Up to the point where I'm dressing, I may still be planning. But at the mirror, well, I cannot be completely *nothing*, or at least I can think of *nothing* only for an instant, but at any rate, I am both relaxed and tense in front of the mirror." He replies briefly to their low-voiced question and they crown him with the other wig; now he exists alone before the mirror while the assistant behind him slowly unkinks each snarled hair, and he is so still while the *kyogen* bawls toward its boisterous end. The audience applauds. It is almost time. Five men attend him now, working at his wig, occasionally laughing very softly and gently together among themselves; and then at last the mask goes on, pale and unearthly against that black hair which they so carefully caress. They remove the mask, insert cushioning to increase its resonance for when he sings and, equally importantly, to move it farther forward, thereby widening its turning arc, and thus its expressiveness. (We will take up this subject later on.) Needless to say, the lowest objective in this fitting, if indeed it figures at all, is the actor's comfort. The man who last smoothed his hair now kneels behind him at a discreet distance, closes his eyes, and, so it seems to me, prays, although Mr. Umewaka expressed surprise when I questioned him about this later. Meanwhile, each member of the chorus enters in turn and bows to Mr. Umewaka, who slightly inclines his head in return as he gazes into the mirror. The padded mask returns to his face. They raise his beautiful hair and tuck it just so around the face of Shuntoku-maru, the blind temple-haunting vagrant of the uncertain step.

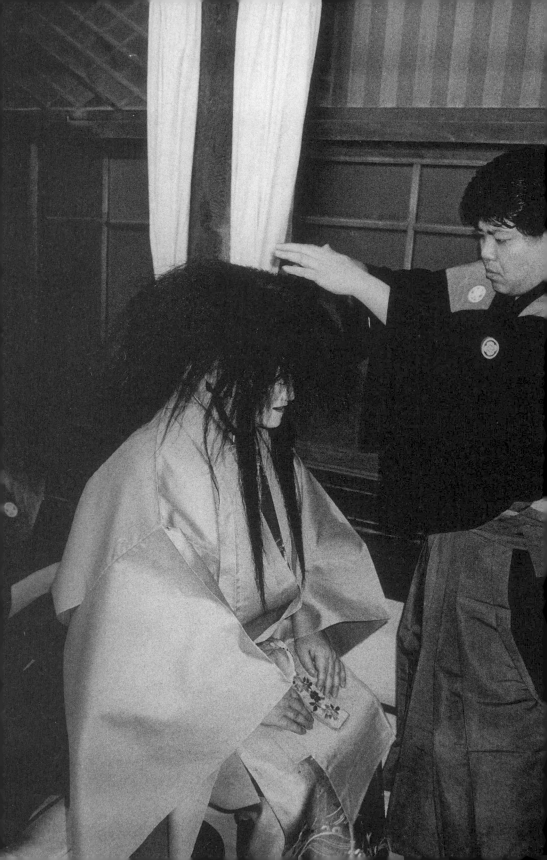

## WHAT IS NOH?

Opposing itself to the flickering of crowds across the wide white crosswalk-lines, the clatter of a million high heels through subway tunnels crammed with boutiques, the girls who dye their hair red, blonde or brown, the restaurant eels in crystalline tanks, the necktied salarymen rapt in their sadomasochistic comic books, the department stores excitingly bright with new electric goods, the clicking turnstiles, multistorey advertising screens, walkways and throughways, the vending machines so ubiquitous and diverse that they really ought to have their own Audubon field guide, the unending beeping and movement of Shinjuku Station at rush hour, the ball bearing music of pachinko parlors packed with gamblers all in rows, the breathlessly variable, deliciously novel, commercial, showy *now-ness* of urban life, Noh offers us long silences punctuated by a single chant, every instant as perfect as an ideally composed photograph; time stops in order to show us that fact. Outside the Noh theater, everything is present; inside, everything is long past even when it happens. Outside, we find so many things to see and hear that all we can do is gather armloads of them, dropping some as we go; later we'll remember just a few: a certain alley, face, toy, sign, price. Inside, Noh presents to us a single thing, which lives so slowly that we ought to be able to snatch it up and carry it off; frequently the performers fall inhumanly still; the electricity must have been turned off! The boredom which some people feel at Noh performances is in part self-defensive. If we can't comprehend this one thing — Mr. Umewaka's voice, half-spoken, half-sung, with its repeated patterns of cadence dwindling between silences — then what are we really coming away with? And why can't we comprehend it? In the beginning, it's easy to explain it away thus: Strangeness takes away all meaning. For example, a single voice moans: *Ohh!* and at intervals a drum strikes, and fingers flutter on it, then another mask, another ghost appears upon the bridge from elsewhere, and begins to chant, accompanied by perfect silence, with perfect silence between its own words: It's chanting in strophes. This pale figure invades the stage; then the orange-brocaded woman whom Mr. Umewaka has become slowly follows it. The two make a colloquy, kneeling, facing one another across a glittering wooden distance, and then the chorus begins, the shoulder-drum commences to shake, the fluttering arm strikes it from beneath as the flute screeches with inexpressible unearthliness, the chorus's voices rising and falling in almost wolflike fashion. What does this "mean"? What is being conveyed? I know the story; the abandoned wife in "Kinuta" is dying of loneliness and resentment; but were it a different, happier story, the music might still seem mournful to me. Mr. Umewaka himself, who first performed at age three, cheerfully acknowledged that his father and grandfather "just taught me the move, not the meaning. Later I tried to realize for myself what it meant." Geisha dancers tell me much the same. But in time we *do* begin to know, and even predict a trifle; we're taught what a certain gesture means, and these almost frozen figures on this nearly empty stage become larger, more complex, less explicable. Isn't that what "reality" is? I love to rush through Tokyo and I could spend hours adoring a Noh mask. Could Noh someday teach me to be equally exalted in contemplating an oval of white paper? Noh is contemplation. In the bygone centuries of its origin, Noh was the expression of sacred teachings; in the case of such spectacles as "Okina," which I'll describe later on, it's not inaccurate to speak of *Noh rites.*

"Is Noh secular or religious?" I once asked Mr. Umewaka.

"Of course it is closely connected to religious practice," he replied, "but this has now become very difficult for the audience to understand. So we remove that element" — and I was shocked to hear him say that he was prepared to remove anything. "We emphasize the theatrical. In the past we invoked the blessings of Buddha. Now we strive to be actors."

Indeed, to anyone lucky enough to attend a performance, Noh is a *theater* of upraised golden fans, shaken rattles, stone-faced, howling drummers, positional choreography (mark each performer's homing-spot on stage, and from this alone you'll know whether or not he's the protagonist), of mummy-faced demons in gorgeous kimonos, long silences, ceremoniousness. The noises of the drums, wooden and musical at the same time, mark time's spending of life and story as Mr. Umewaka raises his golden fan; the flute sounds; he slowly advances, then stamps, turns sideways, still more slowly traversing the stage, he and these other men expressing what at first seems to be the strictest, most severe stonefaced rigidity. Zeami, the fourteenth-century actor, composer and theoretician who with his father Kanami should be credited for much of Noh's present day form, states in the introduction to one of his secret treatises that "all the exercises must be severely and strictly done: there must be no self-assertion." It is precisely this which gives each performance what one observer labels "a religious and sober atmosphere of almost suffocating intensity, while the subtle and mysterious expression of the No mask reveals an extreme repression of joy and sorrow." After silence, one drum begins to beat again; then the tempo increases, the audience reverently murmuring and pointing out this or that subtlety to one another. The drummers chant: *"Yo — ho, yyyyyo!"* and their percussive representation of emotion and time grows ever more rapid, in time with the swirling of Mr. Umewaka's gilded fan, all sounds hollow and resonant, like life itself: significant, yet soon to be over. That fan's movements are as carefully conventionalized as each actor's place on stage. In Noh, as you might have realized by now, nearly *everything* is fixed, right down to the performers' order of entrances and exits: "There must be no self-assertion." When I asked Mr. Umewaka how it would be if I watched a Noh performance by two different masters, he insisted: "Well, they might do exactly the same thing but what the audience *feels* would be completely different." So it is with the fan. Held to the actor's temple, a fan can be a pillow; held lower, it might be a sake glass. At the end of "Yoro-boshi," the *waki*, the foil who plays Shuntoku-maru's father, opens his fan just before commencing to slowly glide after Shuntoku-maru on that long, pine-tree'd stage-bridge back to "reality's" curtain. This gesture expresses joy in the reconciliation of father and son. The widening fan emerging from the *waki*'s heart, rising up and out, this gesture *must* express joy; it always expresses joy. In "Yoro," which tells the tale of a magic spring, Mr. Umewaka manipulates the fan in such a way that any informed person will know that he is dipping water. And these various movements, like operatic motifs, can be combined, strung together: On the edge of the stage Mr. Umewaka kneels, gazing down through the fan into something far beyond "reality," which Noh continually defies anyhow (the chorus can express a single character's consciousness, and the lead actor may subdivide into different entities at any time). Slowly he rises, walking backward, raising the fan, momentarily covering his face with it; and the sound of the flute is like wind through a mountain gorge, the hollow, tuneful clanking of the shoulder-drum so "jungly" and "Asian," and just before the chorus begins its deep-voiced chant, *"Eeeoooooooooo-ooh!"*

howls the drummer as Mr. Umewaka slowly glides, his fan cutting the air like a knife. This is *Noh theater*, which especially stands out thanks to its *Noh rhythm*. Dr. Yokoyama Taro, formerly of the University of Tokyo, writes me that for him the following is paramount: "Unlike most other music/dance performances including jazz improvisation, Noh lacks any predetermined rhythmic concepts . . . Each Noh dancer (and musician) must be guided by some on-the-spot rhythmic agreement reached on the spot among themselves . . . Take away this free-flowing feature, try to arrest a Noh number on any constant rhythmic concept, and you will lose its essence."

"Oh, you mean *Noh dance?*" inquired my friend Reiko, who translates my novels, and I was sure that I didn't, because what I'd admired for a quarter-century now were the *"Noh plays"* in their various, variable and at times contradictory English translations. In short, I had read the librettos without going to the operas. And what librettos! Consider the play "Kagekiyo," one of my favorites. (I have never seen it performed; Mr. Umewaka, who's played the role four or five times, and remembers seeing both his father and grandfather perform it also, tells me that it possesses excellent music but remains difficult to bring alive because it has very little dancing, "just sitting.") When at the wish of his daughter, whom he has not seen since her babyhood and whom he'll never see again, the protagonist chants the tale of his bravery at the battle of Yashima long ago, his youth's rashness, strength and goodhumored generosity return to life in the telling, but only provisionally, even mockingly, for we cannot forget his present decrepitude. Just as darkness peeps out from within the deep wide sleeves of a Noh performer's kimono, so death flickers through that briefly recollected triumph, which is no more substantial than the reflections on that extremely polished yet unlacquered reddish stage-sea. The muscular pine tree of the mirror-board stands behind all, its arm twisted behind its wooden torso (it represents eternity, or, some say, divinity); and Kagekiyo's life is but one more dance in the larger dance of doom, after which Mr. Umewaka casts a golden fan upon the floor: Once the Heike clan reigned over all, but they overreached themselves, and the Genji family obliterated them. Kagekiyo fought on the losing side, the Heike one, and that is why he's been exiled. The destruction of the Heike gets told in one Noh play after another. (Not surprisingly, there are more

Heike than Genji stories in the repertoire, since whether or not they end peacefully, Noh plays tend not to end happily.)

As soon as his victory's danced out, Kagekiyo sends his daughter back home to the capital, the center of the world, from which he's been excluded for life. When I asked Mr. Umewaka why he committed such an act, which from a Western standpoint appears to be either cruel or almost insanely prideful, he replied, "That is according to the interpretation of the player, because the conclusion is not written. In my opinion, the situation is that he cannot expect a cheerful life since he is under *shura*, so even a family member could not help him. So it would be too sad for her." *Shura* is, if you like, damnation.\* "All the warriors, honorable or not, are sinful and enter a *shura* situation."

In my Judeo-Christian culture, it is impossible to be simultaneously honorable and damned. Even Dante's Ulysses, brave, alluring, glorious as he seems, has nonetheless convicted himself of prideful disobedience by transgressing the world's limits, set by God: the Pillars of Hercules. In effect, his sin is the same as Adam and Eve's. It was surely Dante's intention that I sympathize with him. But I am also supposed to condemn him (which I decline to do). Meanwhile, in the semi-fictive medieval war chronicle *Taiheiki*, immediately before the warrior brothers Masahige and Masasue, who have been defeated in battle, commit seppuku, they agree on wishing, even though it is "deeply sinful," "to be reborn again and again for seven lives in order to destroy the enemies of this court!" Not only does *Taiheiki*'s anonymous author command my sympathy on his heroes' behalf, but he also solicits my admiration for them. He gets it.

"Isn't it possible to be an honorable warrior and not be suffering and sinful?" I asked Mr. Umewaka.

"This is the sin of human beings," he replied. "But the point of Noh is that everyone can achieve peace of mind through Buddhism."

In several of the other warrior dramas, this does occur. For Kagekiyo,

---

\*The Noh expert Jeff Clark amplifies: "*Shura* is one of the six realms of . . . cyclic experience in Buddhism. It's a psychological state in which one returns to battle again and again, something like Post Traumatic Stress Syndrome. The battle is horrible, but also is the most intense experience in the warrior's life. It is what everything else in the warrior's life is directed toward. I think this is what Rokuro meant by speaking of 'under *shura*.' In Buddhism, hell is returning to the same experience again and again."

however, remission from *shura* appears far from certain. "The end is near," he tells the girl, "go to your home; pray for my soul departed, child, candle to my darkness, bridge to my salvation!" But will her prayers save him? The girl obeys his command to go away. Everything is over. She is more saddened than surprised. At the very beginning of the play, the playwright places this song on her lips: *Late dewdrops are our lives that only wait / Till the wind blows, the wind of morning blows.* To me that word "morning" is especially haunting. (As we Anglo-Americans would say, "life is but a dream.")

There we have one of the *Noh plays*. But one scholar who studied with Mr. Umewaka's great-grandfather writes that "in the time of Tokugawa (A.D. 1602 to 1868),* Noh became the *music* of the Shogun's court." Of course for all its chorus-chants, its shrill flute and triple drums, Noh isn't just music, either.

To be sure, Mr. Umewaka pays vigilant attention to the musical functioning of his performances — indeed, his selection of a mask for a given role depends in part on the music — and I often heard him make such remarks as: "If the bass of a chorus is not good, the whole thing will be ruined."

"How often will that happen?"

"Quite often!" he laughed.

Well, then, can't we say that in its combination of singing, music and story Noh resembles opera? I submitted as much to Mr. Umewaka, and he politely assented in a way that made it clear he didn't agree at all.

"In that case, what is the most important element — the singing, the dancing, the words?"

I expected him to say, as artists customarily do, "All of them!", but he replied: "Foremost the mask, *the expression of the mask.*"

"And how do you create expression with a mask?"

"Of course the masks are wooden," he said, "and they have no moveable parts, except for the Okina mask alone, whose mouth moves. But, depending on the angle, the mask *seems* to move! With the mask on, I cannot see myself in a mirror. I mean, the real angle of my mask cannot be seen. So you need a tutor. Normally you need eight years of tutoring . . ."

---

*Other sources say 1603 to 1867.

When Mr. Umewaka asked which of his hundred-and-fifty-odd masks I would like to see, I mentioned, among others, one appropriate to the role of Kagekiyo.

Because this old man, like Shuntoku-maru, has gone blind in his misery, in place of eyeballs the mask of Kagekiyo bears narrow eye-slits resembling upcurving fingernail-crescents. One of the apprentices told me that because the slits are so elongated, it is actually easier to see through this mask than through most others. In any other art form I can think of, the artist takes full advantage of his materials. This being Noh, many performers shut their eyes when they wear the Kagekiyo mask. Like poetry, Noh functions at least as much through exclusion as through mere selection. The blindness of Kagekiyo *sees*, in the fashion of Oedipus's blindness. And so inside this mask there is nothing but lacquered wood lacquered again with generations of sweat, a mouth-hole to sing through, two nose-holes to breathe through, and two minuscule apertures through which one locates one's place on the Noh stage; that is the inner side, the side of nothingness,* while the other side is a face, Kagekiyo's face, deeply stylized yet individuated, trollish, with a tuft of reddish-blond horsehair for a beard, the lean, angular cheeks grimacing in anguish.

## WHAT IS A WOMAN?

Although Zeami states that "the impersonation of old men is the most important thing in Noh," and although Mr. Umewaka prefers of all his dramas Heike stories, warrior stories, "the reason being the poetry," to me the most wondrous thing is when a Noh actor (who is often, after all, an old man) becomes beautifully female — one more way that Noh defies the tyranny of realism. Hence this book.

The unanswerable question, "What is a woman?" can be approximated, "What manifests a woman?" — in other words, how does somebody of either sex express, we might as well say, *herself* in such a way that we perceive or interpret her femininity? To Zeami the matter was as

---

*I have been told that to the extent which one's vision is limited by the mask, one's hearing and concentration will proportionately increase.

straightforward as anything can be in Noh: Get expert advice when playing court ladies, since their dress has been so carefully regulated and conventionalized; observe and emulate the costuming of the lowborn women who flourish all around us like weeds; mind a few general rules: "He must not bend too much at the waist or at the knees . . . He does not look like a woman when he holds his head too rigidly." Summing up, "in the impersonation of women the dressing is the fundamental thing for the actor." These maxims are still followed today in the red-light district of Kabukicho, where there is a bar especially for "new-halves," as transvestites are called in Japanese. One such sweet, shy, plump young lady, who happened to be dressed in white, whose curls were blonde, whose lips were richly red, and who kept ready any number of name-cards which bore her full-color likeness and e-mail address, was kind enough, after compensation had been arranged, to discuss this issue, which is, after all, of considerable aesthetic as well as sociobiological concern to us all.

"What does being a woman feel like, and how does that differ from being a man?"

She smiled, slowly lowering her hand through the air. "There's no difference," she said. "My heart feels the same."

As we have heard, Mr. Umewaka likewise feels nothing when he's a woman, or when he plays any other part, for that matter. He *strives* to feel nothing. He's a man-woman in a doll-perfect mask, facing forward, singsonging in a deep voice. From the back he is always wide and flat like a beetle, a paper cutout, with his black hair spilling perfectly down. Miss Tosaka,* on the other hand, is built for use. She has a rather nice bottom.

"What is the secret of being a convincing woman?"

"Ah," Miss Tosaka replied, slowly drawing a circle in the air, and my interpreter of the moment, the versatile Reiko, reported: "It seems that there's no secret."

"So how do you behave?"

"I act naturally. I don't care about how people regard me, how others look at me, as long as they are accepting. I do try to walk differently."

---

*I am informed that this name means "cockscomb," a double entendre which functions in both languages.

"How does one walk like a woman?"

"When I'm a woman, I try to keep my knees together. I take very short steps. When I sit down, I keep my legs together."

I had just interviewed one of the rare Noh actresses, a middle-aged lady named Yamamura Yoko, who has studied with Mr. Umewaka for twenty years and, of course, reveres him. She claimed that "mentally you're calmer in a kimono, and although your voice doesn't change, you sound more deliberate." — Miss Tosaka for her part had worn a kimono only once, for the very practical reason that "you have to pay some professional person to dress you in it, because so many Japanese can't do this ourselves anymore; that art is lost." (I thought of Mr. Umewaka surrounded by all his apprentice-helpers in the dressing room.) — "I also like dresses," she volunteered, but it seemed to me that she referred to her evening in the kimono with a certain wistfulness.

"Did it make you feel more feminine?"

"You know, it was very tight," she said, smiling sweetly and generously, "so I couldn't walk in long strides; it also kept my body very straight; so, yes, I did feel like a woman."

This certainly corresponds to Zeami's advice to hold one's body rigid, except for the head, when becoming a female; but Mr. Umewaka experienced a sense of confinement when he was being dressed for his various roles of *either* gender; and when I observe the quasi-mechanical action of Noh's dolls, whose faces so frequently downturn to express angelic sadness, without knowing the drama it can be difficult to distinguish male from female. Restriction is the very essence of Noh — or at least creates that essence. "Mentally I am comfortable," he remarked, "but physically it's not easy to move. The wig and mask hurt the head. It's difficult to breathe." (As we say in America, no price too great for beauty!) And yet he *seems* to move with a dreamy effortlessness. When he's the abandoned wife in "Kinuta," he rotates with remarkable slowness and sureness, never revealing any indication that his legs are moving beneath the long pale wings of the kimono. Once he's become her ghost, he bitterly touches his outstretched golden fan to the stage as he kneels . . .

"When you act in a female role, what, if anything, do you do differently?"

"Basically, it should be the same," he replied, which surprised me.* "But the steps are a little smaller, and the arm movements are a little narrower."

I relayed what Miss Tosaka had said about keeping one's legs together, and he remarked that such would be Kabuki style. Kabuki actors train for female roles by walking with a sheet of paper between the knees. "In Noh," he said, "originally it was like that, too. But as time passed, it became more abstract."

In other words, so it seemed to me, Zeami is now partially superseded. (Probably this means that I misunderstand Zeami. Mr. Umewaka makes a point of withholding from his apprentices for several years his family's Zeami manuscript, because "unless you master Noh to some extent, you interpret the instructions incorrectly.") Noh is not what it was. From a quasi-religious rite accessible to all,† to a leisure art explicitly restricted to nobles, to a resurrected tradition requiring either study or snobbery on the part of its audiences, Noh has grown ever more arcane (in the play "Miidera" the protagonist holds a bamboo branch over one shoulder. Why should this signify that the female character

---

*How would I do it? When I engrave a line into a block of wood, I know that the tool will cut precisely as I expect it to; I have damped down my own self-assertion in order to tune myself to what the tool best does, watching the groove it forms, as if I were its spectator, although of course it's I who's making it. Still, I am more or less asserting myself; no one artistic school has shaped me. Mr. Umewaka, on the other hand, has undergone a lifelong stringent training in the Kanze aesthetic, tuning himself accordingly to so many, many tools: a chorus whose members, most of whom must be familiar to him, nevertheless comprise ever new combinations; the peculiar geometry of the Noh stage, the masks and kimonos, the drums. Were I to set out to play a modern female part after such an education, I'd wear high heels, to be sure, but perhaps instead of today's machinegun clitterclacks of heels on concrete I might strive for something in harmony with the Noh drums, whose sounds are wooden, hollow, ancient, melodious; sometimes the drumbeats are almost like raindrops.

†I am taking Noh's historiographers at their word, and predicating Noh upon the ritual of "Okina." An expert comments here: "Until the Edo period, Noh was a popular art form patronized by the wealthy and powerful. Almost all the plays in the present repertoire were written during this period, and few of them can be described as quasi-religious rites, although they were often performed at temples or shrines . . . I believe that Noh has always required study; only an extraordinarily literate person could understand all the word play and classical allusions."

is deranged? Don't ask!), but the compensation for this lack of popular resonance is this very abstraction which Mr. Umewaka mentions. When one of his roles requires him to express sadness, he holds his hand before his face. If he's a man at that time, he uses the right hand; if a woman, then the left. Perhaps in Zeami's time this was in fact an observable behavioral distinction between the sexes. In present-day Japan it is not.* Therefore, both the actors and the spectators must learn it for it to convey anything.

In a sense, both Miss Tosaka and Mr. Umewaka are artists, but she has made herself what she is almost literally: a lovely lady of today;†

---

*Indeed, there are not so many distinctions now, at least not in Tokyo. On the stage outside the window of the coffee shop, men pass by in dark suits, some with clenched fists at their sides, most with a briefcase, most with their heads erect; and instead of seeing them either as individuals or as part of a swarm, I attempt to consider them as exemplars of a type to be stylized on stage, a type doomed to pass into the void as do all other types; all of us are the last few cherry blossoms falling in the drizzly wind at Yasukuni Shrine, each of us caught in the electric stage-lights like a mote of fire; if any of these salarymen would kindly freeze, with the black-sleeved knife-edge of his arm pointing ahead and down, then I would have the luxury of really looking at him; instead, it's incumbent on me as artist, journalist, idler, to generalize. (What would Zeami make of such a project? "As for the portrayal of high ranking officers and noblemen, or of natural things, such as flowers, birds, wind and moon, one must do it as realistically as possible. On the other hand, one must not copy the vulgar manners of common people." Let's hope that these office workers are sufficiently high ranking for me to model myself after.) And how do the women distinguish themselves from the men? Yamamura Yoko insisted that "there is not that much difference on the street that you can see, because mostly they wear Western clothes. If they wear kimonos, their steps are much shorter. Men wear *hakama*, so they can walk normally." — What about gestures? I asked. "Now men and women are the same in that regard; but, again, in kimonos, women's movements are more restricted." Looking out my coffee shop window, I see very few kimonos. The women do frequently constrain themselves into mincingness by wearing high heels, but they seem to keep pace with the men nonetheless; their miniskirts and bluejeans allow them to put one foot before the other as heartily as any male; fewer than ever carry their purses in that traditionally vulnerable feminine way, the strap dangling from the crook of the left elbow, the wrist accordingly compelled upward into soft vague blindness; no, they let their shoulderbags hang free now, so that their arms can fall naturally like men's; if they have purses, they tend to grip the handles in the left hand, just as would a man his briefcase.

†"What's your opinion of Japanese ladies of ancient times?" I asked her. — "They are beautiful, but I wouldn't want to be like them."

whereas Mr. Umewaka, in spite of his young woman's mask-face with its perpetual half-smile, is what he is *figuratively*, "abstractly" as he put it. As Ms. Yamamura said of him, "On the Noh stage, looking at him acting, you can see much more than is objectively there. In that sense, he's the best." In short, he does not merely imitate the mannerisms of a female. He stylizes that imitation in a manner which is archaic, non-representational, or both; and after decades of following that maxim of Zeami, *there must be no self-assertion*, he is an expressive vehicle for something greater than himself. Yes, he's aided by his mask and kimono. Every artist needs his tools. But I truly believe (no doubt he'd modestly deny it) that with no other attributes than his broad, kindly face, his thick grey eyebrows, his missing tooth, his whitehaired temples and slightly sunken eyes, his rotundity, his man's voice, he would still be able to make those bygone young women of the Noh dramas *live*, and gorgeously.*

And so, imagine what this man, with his perfect command of gesture, carriage and voice, can accomplish in a mask.

Which one will he choose? As I've said, it depends in part upon the music, in part upon his interpretation of the role. Regarding Shuntoku-maru, the blind vagrant with the uncertain step, he remarked: "There is a mask called Yoroboshi, but I did not use it. I used a mask for the blind man Semimaru[†] because it is more elegant . . ."

The wife of "Kinuta" stands in her brocaded splendor, uttering her sadness in a deep, musical male voice, chanting her own dying while the flute inhumanly, neutrally trills. The dull blows of the fulling block sound her dirge. She raises her hands to her face, meaning that she's crying; she's just learned that her husband will be away for another year; while the maidservant hovers eerily, half-smiling behind her; and later the striped curtain at the far end of the bridge will rise of its own accord as the sad woman glides out from behind it; she's died of anguish; she's a ghost now. Her hands clasp one another at the breast; her perfect face whitely gleams, peering and half-smiling as she impels herself toward

---

*So it used to be. "In the past," said Mr. Umewaka, "they only used masks for ghosts or dead characters. Black Jo for an old man, that's it. In Yoroboshi, that blind man Shunt-oku-maru, they didn't use a mask. They just closed their eyes."

†This play is discussed below, p. 357.

the stage, slowly swiveling toward us the fan tucked into the breast of her kimono. And her smile, her smile—

These masks are the Umewaka family's richest treasures. Certainly, their loveliness is almost indescribable.


## CLASSICAL BEAUTIES

The apprentice lays before me the mask of a young girl, most likely fifteen or sixteen, and a virgin. (Had she borne a child, a different mask would be required.) How strange I feel to see it in isolation from a dancer's rigid body, and likewise lacking both a splendid kimono and that spill of jet-black horsehair! It's called a *ko-omote*, a little mask, "little" referring to the age of the girl it portrays (she may be as young as thirteeen); and it's so real, so well-fashioned that it could almost be a real girl's decapitated head, except that it's not dead, nor gruesome; it could come alive at any instant. In a moment he'll show me a *waka-onna*, which is the mask of a woman who's a decade older and remains childless. Just as the kimonos for young women's roles all contain at least a splash of red, so these young women's masks have their teeth fashionably blackened in the style of classical Japanese beauties* — and, by the way, it is a wonder how these teeth, whose presence is in many cases not much more than hinted at between the half-smiling lips, glisten so translucently, as if each girl were truly alive and had just this second run her tongue across them. These masks also bear peculiarly high eyebrows, because in the Heian era (794–1185), aristocrats of both sexes depilated themselves there and painted surrogates far up upon their foreheads. It's said, although the apprentice disbelieves it, that these masks before me are five hundred years old. Two-thirds of the ones in the Umewaka family collection do come from the Edo period at least, so this sixteen-year-old girl, if she ever existed in life, has long since been dust. After her, dynasties burned out; the moat of Nagoya Castle is choked with grass — and within a few steps of it stands a Noh theater for Mr. Umewaka to perform in, acting

---

*In the olden days, the blackening was done with a lead-based pigment; for mask-teeth, *sumi* ink suffices.

out another dance of transience: "Late dewdrops are our lives." Since Noh is about karma and transience, how fitting it is that these ancient roles, these ancient beautiful faces, get brought to life by successive generations of actors who themselves become dust!

Once upon a time, in the long gone Muromachi centuries before Noh had become quite so codified, biological women did sometimes play Noh. I wonder what they looked like? Do these masks represent them? I remember a photograph of the mask called "Flower." I have gazed at an image of the mask called "Snow." I once saw a picture of the mask called "Moon." Thus the Three Treasures referred to by Edo mask makers as ideals for *ko-omotes*. In their teeth and eyebrows, in their bottom-heavy plumpness, too, these ladies do not in the least resemble the Japanese women of today. Every aspect of Noh is so antediluvian! Zeami writes that it is "really easy" for the Noh actor to "play the part of an ordinary woman . . . as he is accustomed to seeing them." I admit that on the train back from Yokohama, where I'd gone to study the exhibition of a renowned carver who'd faithfully copied her masks from six-hundred-year-old originals (Mr. Umewaka, who recommended her to me, had twice awarded her second place in the national competitions), I did finally see one woman whose face resembled a Noh mask: broad, flat, glossy, with sunken, upcurving eyes (she lacked the high-painted eyebrows, however), small and darkish teeth, a lower lip which protruded just as all the masks' did — so what? Miss Tosaka plays the part of a pretty lady of the twenty-first century. Mr. Umewaka can become a beauty of half a millennium ago — or should I say a beauty who never existed?*

---

*I own a book of photographs of the "last days of the Tokugawa Era," and these brownish or bluish images, whose originals seem to be decaying usually from the edges inward, do portray people whose heads appear wider than those of today; to some extent this derives from photography's standard trick of adding corpulence by forcing every visible feature of a head into one plane; flat maps of our round world suffer from kindred distortions. The flowing, cheek-hugging hairstyles of 1860 widen these faces somewhat further. Yet ladies' hair is equally often pulled back from forehead and temples. High foreheads must have been as valued under the Shogunate as in the Heian period. Indeed, as I browse through this volume, I seem to find more and more the Japanese face of *today*, whose photographed expression, to be sure, is more somber and dull than now, on account of the need to hold still for those long exposures. This stillness, and the high foreheads, yes, perhaps these faces are a trifle Heian, but it's mainly the faces of the children which

The best masks have been carved, very appropriately, from the endangered Kiso cypress,* a honey-colored, close-grained wood of middle weight whose scent resembles cardamom. Only about thirty professional Noh carvers continue the craft in Japan, and of course they all follow the same method, or what they have reconstructed of that method (during the Meiji Restoration, when Noh fell into decline, some details of this process were lost): smoothing and whitening the chiseled blankness of the newborn face with a mixture of hide glue and powdered oyster-shell — and, needless to say, this being Noh, several subtle finenesses of oyster-shell get employed in their season, these ranging in granularity from the coarseness of talcum powder to the silkiness of confectioner's sugar. As for the hide glue, that also comes in various grades, from a greenish-grey sheet resembling kelp (this was never used by the mask maker who brought me into his workroom in the mountain tea-fields overlooking Shimada; he considered the greenish sheets to be entirely inadequate) to higher-quality sticks of a dark amber, to candylike rods of a lighter amber, to astonishingly transparent honey-colored fragments which derive from deer and are purer and clearer than any of the various equivalents I myself have ever been able to find. The second-best glue, the kind which comes in slender rods, generally suffices at this stage. The mask maker showing these items (his name was Mr. Otsuka Ryoji) told me that if his carving has been exceptionally good, he can get by with five undercoats; often he requires as many as eight. I wish that you could see him there amidst his own beautifully handmade compasses and calipers of different woods, each tool lovingly stained; they sometimes resemble lobster-claws with blond spicules inset in their polished jaws; it takes him longer to fabricate them than it does the masks themselves. He sits there in a niche of

---

widen toward the chin. From the side, one adolescent girl of 1860 resembles the Heian stereotype: little black eyes in a white face, a tiny rosebud of a mouth (well, mask-lips part more widely than that, but what can you do?), puffy, delicious cheeks; her hair is tucked up behind her, and her kimono sports an elegantly striped sash.

*Kiso lies in what used to be the domain of the Tokugawa Shogun. Many of the cypresses were thought to be inaccessible because they grew on steep hillsides, but during the "bubble economy" of the 1980s a considerable number got carried away by helicopter. Their use is now more or less restricted to maintaining the shrine at Ise and making Noh masks.

his own design between the chisel-cabinet and the carving-bench, trying to work as slowly and quietly as possible, to control his breathing as he works, to be surrounded by the same natural sounds which the ancient carvers heard. It is in the individual painted hair-strands of his competitors' masks that he so often discovers the blemishes of haste. Try to see him there, carving and then ever so carefully undercoating. Compared to Mr. Umewaka, although far less so than I, he's infected with the disease of self-assertion; he likes to make fanciful mosquito masks, catfish masks, masks of modern Japanese faces; but what he possesses, what every artist must have to some degree, and anyone affiliated with Noh requires to the *nth* degree, is painstakingness. In the heart of the triple-storeyed Ume-

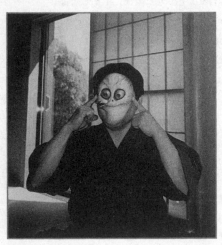

MR. OTSUKA.

waka family theater, which gazes down on its Japanese maples, keeps pace with its magnolias, and finds itself overshadowed by the apartment buildings whose flags are laundry hanging from their balconies, there is a darkened stage where Umewaka Rokuro sings in faraway resonance while his four-year-old granddaughter eagerly dances out a rudimentary pattern-square beside him, raising her fan when he does, lowering it, kneeling, coming and going at his word, his fan and her fan glistening; he chants, and she bustles obediently back and forth, kneeling, raising her fan, gazing at him adoringly. Once he was obliged to learn; now he must teach, lesson after lesson; fixing within the child the unalterable core of each gesture and position, so that Noh will live another generation, and the woman in the pale yellow kimono can once more outstretch her partially closed fan, her superbly, inexhaustibly beautiful face offering itself to the eye forever. As for Mr. Otsuka, in place of lessons, performances and exercises (although he encounters all those), he mainly confronts undercoats. Each layer must contain less hide glue than the one underneath, in order to avoid future cracking. Now for the outermost beauty itself. The basic color palette for a Noh mask is red, green and brownish-yellow, although, like the simplifications "hide glue" and "oyster-shell," this cannot do justice to the arrays of pigments in their labeled packets. Mr. Otsuka claims, and I lack the means to evaluate this, that the Japanese language possesses more words for color-shades than any other tongue; but I do see before me three different hues of, for instance, blood-red cinnabar. For the skin-tones of a Noh mask, a greenish-yellow mixed with fiery orange goes on first, this being lightened with layer after layer of glue and oyster-shell. I have read that these same whitened mercury pigments were used for both men's and women's cosmetics in the Heian era; Genji himself was known as "The Shining Prince" not only thanks to his charisma but also on account of his white complexion. How faithfully the Noh masks duplicate that makeup I doubt that anybody knows. At any rate, by this stage only the supreme grade of glue can be employed. "You use nice color," said Mr. Otsuka, "and then on top of it you put something else to make it look more subdued, so it doesn't look too shallow. After fifty or a hundred years, if you've used something unsubtle, it's really going to show; it'll start looking worse and worse." He applies a minimum of three such overcoats. Then come the eyes, the hair, the lips . . . Let's mention only the second of these. The lips of the *ko-omote* are colored with an orangish kind of cinnabar which he's enriched with one of its mid-scarlet cousins; next comes the glaze, which at the very end he partially removes, in order to bring out maximum brilliancy. The lips of his old-woman masks must be darker than those of the young girls. Every aspect of the making, in short, is flavored with distinctions and subdistinctions, guided by care, love, and skilled restraint. The most difficult part, he says, is "to have a clear image of the look and shape in my brain. First the mask forms in my mind. The physical work is relatively easy."

The words, music and choreography of a Noh drama cannot be changed.* The role is eternal. The mask is, practically speaking, nearly eternal: longer than a single human life. (Asked how long his collection would last, Mr. Umewaka very characteristically replied: "That is the concern. The new ones are weaker." Mr. Otsuka hoped and expected for his masks a minimum useful life of one hundred fifty to three hundred

---

*Still another of my oversimplifications, as you'll see.

years.) In a catalogue of selected masks from the Kanze School, which was made the official style of the Tokugawa Shogunate and to which the Umewaka family belongs (there are five schools of Noh,* and, just as you might imagine, it can be difficult to tell them apart), we find these captions: seventeenth century, sixteenth century, fifteenth century, eighteenth century . . . This *ko-omote* mask which Mr. Umewaka's apprentice has now unboxed for me might well have kept its virginity for four or five centuries. And five centuries from now, Noh may still be performed. In my discussion with the Noh actress Yamamura Yoko, when I brought up the melancholy fact that Shakespeare's language grows less intelligible to each English-speaking generation, she agreed that Noh suffers from the same wasting-sickness, but "the story itself is always simple, so it could happen in any age or country: a love affair, or sin, or conflict between parent and child." In effect, she thought that as long as we remain human (which, come to think of it, may not be much longer), Noh would live, and therefore so would this sixteen-year-old girl of the *ko-omote*, I mean this mask, this scratched wooden object whose paint has begun to scale and whose faceless side is salted with the sweat of many dead men.

In comparison to her older *waka-onna* sister, the *ko-omote*'s cheeks are plumper; in fact, the face actually widens toward the chin. The mask which Mr. Umewaka prefers for the warrior Atsumori, who like Kagekiyo fought against the Genji but came to a different end — slain at age fifteen — resembles hers in its high-eyebrowed,† pallid delicacy, but like the *waka-onna* it tapers at the chin; it's more spade-shaped. (Some performers do in fact play Atsumori with a female mask. Hide the eyebrows with a white sweatband, and you've indicated preparation for war.) The story is typically Noh: Atsumori's killer, having overcome his pity and decapitated the boy, discovers a bamboo flute upon the corpse. This revelation of an artistic spirit makes him so remorseful that he becomes a

---

*Distinguished below, p. 63.

†Eyebrow depilation was more typical of Heike than of Genji aristocrats. For this reason, Genji roles require more masculine-looking masks. Why were high eyebrows considered beautiful then? Perhaps for the same reason that they are today. One zoologist who has turned his attention to women's bodies believes that raised eyebrows remind us of a surprised child's, and may thereby connote just-ripe nubility.

priest in order to pray for Atsumori's soul — assistance which the victim surely needs, being under the same statutory damnation as Kagekiyo. At the end the antagonists are reconciled. Knowing this story, one looks upon the vulnerable, almost effeminate beauty of the Atsumori mask with new eyes. Effeminate, yes, but not female. How subtle these masks are! And this subtlety, like all great art, creates its own world which, like the world of nature, we need to survey from one fixed perspective but can walk around in, discovering ever finer details, as if we were to admire the beauty of a fern first by approaching and touching it, then by viewing it through a hand lens, and finally by using a microscope to observe its cellular organization.* To many people, such a minuscule appreciation is pedantry. Let them think so. I know that I will never tire of gazing at Noh masks.

The particular *ko-omote* which I have been describing is used in Mr. Umewaka's theater to play the beautiful young ghost in "Izutsu" — no matter that she is actually of *waka-onna* age; "our school does this because we have the original mask," said the other apprentice. This drama, written nearly six centuries ago and still frequently performed, expresses the same sadness about the transitory nature of life as "Kagekiyo," although the latter story was about valor-attachment and this one deals with love-attachment: "A frail dream breaks awake; the dream breaks to dawn." This mask is a frail dream, to be sure; it crowns a brocade kimono with a man inside it. And now the apprentice has laid it face up on the floor.

As I bend down toward it, my eyes not yet at chin level, it begins by looking upward and through me. How alive it truly is! The mask-carver in Yokohama had said: "When I feel some *existence* in them, I'm happy." If I were this girl's lover, my head would now be level with her breast. At this angle, the pallid, surprised beauty of her face, fit company for the

---

*"Mr. Umewaka, how far away do you think that someone in your audiences can sit and still appreciate the differences between masks?" — "In my theater," he replied, "you can be at the very rear. I think that's the limit. In the past, however, the place where the seating *began* was as far as it is from the stage to the very back of my theater! As you know, the stage was part of a shrine, and the audience had to sit some distance from it. In such a situation, over-acting is appropriate." — It seemed to me that he might have given our collective discernment too much credit here. Whenever I attended his performances I used my binoculars and I still longed to be closer.

slick, smooth-lacquered feel of the mask, seems wrapped up in itself; by classical standards she has already become a woman;* she lives in the narcissism of her fresh new beauty. I draw almost even with her face, and the expression becomes more intense, more aware of me, almost lustful; and then, when my face is right over hers, as if to kiss her, she gazes straight up into my eyes. I go on past; she looks up at me and is smiling.


## BECOMING OKINA

"The mask is most important *always*," Mr. Umewaka kept reminding me, which is why I will tell you whatever I can about the masks; but my best efforts can help you envision the *living* mask about as much as my descriptions of each instrument in the orchestra could help you hear Beethoven's Ninth. When the mask comes alive, one feels awe. Yamamura Yoko said of him: "The air of the stage changes when he comes! The *ki,* the energy that goes through your body, in his case, if he extends his arm, the *ki* goes beyond his arm." How can I convey to you the sense of an actual Noh performance? Even if I knew the Japanese language (and anyhow most Japanese cannot understand Noh's words when they are chanted, just as Germans cannot parse the syllables which the Wagner soprano sings); even if I possessed a connoisseur's knowledge, which I never shall, to relate to you what happened from start to finish one evening on that Noh stage with its triple-pine-tree'd bridge and the painted pine tree on the mirror-board, I'd be forced to rely on footnotes, parentheses, destructive translations. And since I'm not capable of executing that bad compromise, I'll fall back on relating what I see and hear — actually, I *don't know* how to describe what I hear; please imagine for

---

*In *The Tale of Genji,* from which so many Noh plays derive, the exact age when Genji deflowers his ward Murasaki is not stated, but she seems to have been quite young: "'How tall you have grown since last I saw you!' he said and pulled up her little curtain of honor . . . she had indeed grown up into as handsome a girl as you could wish to see; nor was she any longer at an age when it was impossible for him to become her lover. He constantly hinted at this, but she did not seem to understand what he meant." After he forces himself on her, "he understood that her distress was due merely to extreme youth and inexperience, and was not at all put out."

yourself the chorus's kneeling ranks and crested kimonos, their profiles as they gaze into the nothingness beyond the rainbow curtain. "It's all drums, mostly," explained Mr. Umewaka. "As for the voices, they should make you feel the situation. This is very simple, and so very difficult. How much emotion can they express? That's the key." On another occasion he advised me that melody is less significant a factor than harmony. Enough said. Here then is vision without much reference to sound: Mr. Umewaka appears in a female mask for "Takasago," which celebrates the matrimonial harmony of two pine trees; he wears a purple kimono with golden chrysanthemums inset in triply nested hexagons; he stamps while the drummers wail like wolves.* The way his sleeves can suddenly swivel out and backward lies beyond words; but that is because Noh itself, as I keep repeating, lies beyond reality. Be that as it may, I'll do my best. Perhaps I won't completely fail; we need not all be botanists to describe a jungle's foliage. So please allow me to bring you into the almost unconsciously integrated, techno-coral-reef ambiance of twenty-first-century Japan, which allows one to walk out of a hotel lobby and immediately find oneself upon a transparent covered bridge which leads directly to a train station attended by tiny, perfect restaurants and book-stores; one changes trains, exits into the swarm of the hub station, buys another ticket on another line, rides one stop, passes through the turn-stile, ascends a flight of steps, passes down a corridor of many restaurants, takes another flight of steps to another hotel lobby, and the third flight of steps brings one right to Osaka's spacious Festival Hall where well-dressed Noh-goers now fan themselves in the anteroom behind sparkling glass doors, waiting for the metal grating to rise, which when it does will reveal first four pairs of shiny high heels, then four pairs of slender ankles, pretty legs, and in good time four burgundy miniskirts, four pairs of hands clasped across four uniformed abdomens, four smiles; these ladies accept our tickets and the crowd pours into the bright red velvet seats which resemble rows of lipstick-stained teeth. Before us lies a modernist Noh stage like a squarish, squat-handled axe upon a blackness which is organ-piped with silvery-golden floral decorations created by a leading

---

*The Noh expert Jeff Clark adds here: "Their *hos* and *yas* indicate where they are in the score, but the main function seems to be to intensify emotion and atmosphere."

*ikebana* designer. Mr. Umewaka, who likes the unrehearsed spontaneity of present-day Noh now that the ancient troupes have relaxed their strictures against exogamy ("this way it is more interesting," he says), and who calls Mishima's modernist Noh plays the best of their kind,* who has tried to create "new Noh," and is now considering collaborating in a Noh drama about the Minamata mercury spill, has given me to understand that the staging here at Osaka is a little too much. The third play of the evening will be "Yuya," about a Heike lord's concubine who longs for permission to visit her dying mother. At first the lord refuses. Desiring so greatly to kiss her mask, he commands her to accompany him to the cherry blossom viewing; he suffers, perhaps, from a presentiment of the Heike's oncoming doom, which is ours; but in the end, she writes a poem likening her mother to a cherry-blossom, and wins his consent to depart. In a traditional Noh performance, the pallidly beautiful doll-mask of Yuya's face and her orange brocade would suffice; she's sexual and silent, receptively, untouchably divine, statue and girl; and when the news of her mother's illness arrives, she kneels before her lord, imparting to us a feeling somehow sweet and cloudy, like the sake of the Edo period; and her mask bows exactly enough for its fixed lips to part in smiling grief; her face shines rapt over the letter of tidings which she sings in her deep man's voice. This is Noh: a doll-mask face weeping invisible tears, half covering itself with a brawny old hand in order to telegraph its weeping. All these elements remain present, but the *ikebana* modernist has added cherry blossoms and bamboo trellises; the lighting changes; the sky glows blue; it's all quite gorgeous, although it may not be Noh; it demonstrates why Noh is not in fact opera. One aficionado, a stewardess who's attended fifty of Mr. Umewaka's performances thus far, contemptuously refers to the cherry blossoms as "noisy" (*urusai*), and this is before Yuya's dance, when from above a myriad of shockingly literal blossoms come drifting down. My interpreter, Takako, who is so contemporary in every respect that she often finds Noh to be quite boring, later said to me, "If there had been one or two flowers, all right, that might have been nice; that would

---

*"He knew Mishima personally," inserts Jeff Clark, "but not closely, as he was only 23 when Mishima committed suicide, but he has referred to him as Mishima-sensei, sensei meaning . . . 'teacher.'"

have made the point. But didn't you think that this was too much?" In fact I was enough of a barbarian to enjoy the flower-rain; I'm my parents' son; they were thrilled to see a performance of "Aida" with live elephants. Hardly Mr. Umewaka's cup of tea!* And he will not perform in this version of "Yuya"; in fact; he will not stay to watch it.

But here he is in "Okina." "The mask is most important *always*." The drama begins. Slowly, silently, out creeps a kimono'd figure bearing a red-tied mask-box; then at Noh's customary wide intervals come two more apparitions, and the rainbow curtain, the womb's lip, trembles shut behind them. "Okina," which means "old man," predates most of the other Noh plays in its original form of three ritualistic dances. In fact, it cannot be called a play at all. Only in "Okina" will Mr. Umewaka mask himself onstage. Other masks are works of art, living tools. The Okina mask is something more. It now lies waiting in the red-tied box.

The foremost figure slowly kneels, bearing the precious box, which is itself, if I understand correctly, a Shinto shrine, and by now a file of celebrants waits onstage behind Mr. Umewaka, who approaches naked-faced, kneels, bows, his hand touching that endlessly lustrous stage; and he makes many graceful motions with his sleeve. Presently the mask-bearer also kneels down before him and takes the box. Mr. Umewaka gazes serenely into space. He begins to sing. The box is slid forward and, after some ceremony, opened. On the upper tray, the pallid, ancient mask gazes up into spaces we cannot see. (On the lower tray lies Black Jo, which is equally sacred.) The chorus sings in considerably higher-pitched voices than I usually hear, faster and faster, the flute livelier; the rigid figures seem more than ever to be enacting a ceremony, rather than a drama; the chant runs very fast and full now; and the man who had been kneeling in front of Mr. Umewaka now comes forward, sings, wings his sleeves almost viciously, and stamps. Still the dead mask gazes upward. Mr. Umewaka takes it in his hands and presses it to his face while a helper kneels behind him to assist with the tying; then they all chant

---

*In a brief essay entitled "On the Forty-Fifth Anniversary of My Stage Career," he lovingly recalls his "indoctrination" at the hands of his grandfather: "For example, in the cherry blossom-viewing scene of *Kurama Tengu*, which was my first stage performance, he painted the glories of spring in vivid imagery, telling me, 'Look how beautifully the cherry trees are blooming, my boy,' and thus drew me into the scene with his eloquence."

and the flute thrills and the dancer stamps, because Mr. Umewaka is literally becoming divine.

"Does the ceremonial aspect of 'Okina' feel special to you?" I'd asked him, and he said, "This is an extremely special thing since I'm becoming the god. At least formally, that's what it means," and he laughed a little awkwardly, as people do when they find themselves compelled to speak of sacred things to outsiders who probably will never understand.

Another great Noh actor, the late Mr. Kanze Hideo, said to me: "It's like praying to the god, wishing for a good harvest.* So first you have a box containing the mask. You bring it to the stage and first Okina bows

MR. UMEWAKA.

to the god and sits down. The box is brought to you and you take out the mask. From there, it starts. From the beginning, you say words of prayer without the mask, and then a child or young actor dances, wishing for a good harvest, and when he's doing that you put on the mask and then the god comes into you and then Okina dances."

In the old days, an "Okina" performer had to abstain from sex and meat for twenty-one days prior to the rite; his food was prepared over a separate fire, and by a man. "Today we do this just for one day," Mr. Umewaka said. "Even meeting a woman is prohibited, but practically speaking, well, I'm staying at a hotel, and I don't know who cooks my food, and there are women in the lobby, so what can I do?" — I asked what his religious beliefs might be, and how they relate to Noh, and he said, "I don't have any particular creed, frankly speaking. I don't think I

---

*One recent head of the Kongo School (he died in 1951) reported that in a certain village where he performed this role, people said, "If Okina does not come, the rice will not grow."

believe in God, but I worship my ancestors." But now (although he has assured me that he never tries to enter the role, that he always remains the individual Umewaka Rokuro) he is God indeed — Okina. He kneels, ancient and strange; he is the old man of the wild places; and he upraises his kimono-sleeves, opens his fan, and begins to dance, his mask, which in photographs I'd thought almost comic, now knowing and terrible. His kimono bears an almost Celtic pattern of circles. It is, of course, Heian period costume. He sings. His voice is not as deep as a Wagnerian Wotan's, more sensitive, less dark, not quite reedy, like a night breeze blowing through a mountain gorge. The eerie hooting of the drummer could be an owl's voice. Okina sweeps his fan outward in a distant, inhuman way; he advances silently, in slowly sliding steps. Then he stops to gaze down, down through the stage while the drummers sing; they're his night birds. To achieve his effect, he requires neither falling cherry blossoms nor the blacknesses of curving cherry tree branches which framed him that night at Yasukuni Shrine: He flies across the abstraction of the naked stage. Sometimes the golden fan almost hides his mask-eyes; then he whirls it aside. In due time he will remove this mask with equal ceremoniousness, coiling its fastening-string in a diagonal caress. Then he will again be Mr. Umewaka, who is gracious and smiling and old.

Once I wanted to know how he defined beauty and how he created it. He said to me: "This is very personal. I think, well, sometimes you just look at this drinking glass and you feel beauty, and sometimes you don't like the glass at all. When I think about Noh, it seems that Noh itself can be considered beauty. The masks, the costumes, those are beautiful, but Noh itself is the beauty. All the time I try to orient my mental state toward that. I see beautiful things and feel beauty and I try to do that as much as I can . . ." I have heard him say that in his kindly old man's voice, and now I hear that strange other voice issuing from behind the mask of the ancient frozen god with his upspread fan . . .

2:

# Schematics

*Roles, Rules, Props*

This book cannot pretend to give anyone a working knowledge of Noh. Only a Japanese speaker who has studied Zeami and the Heian source literatures, learned how to listen to Noh music and what to look for in Noh costumes, masks and dances could hope to gain that, and then only after attending the plays for many years. Zeami insisted that "in making a Noh," the playwright "must use elegant and easily understood phrases from song and poetry." Indeed, so easily understood must those phrases have been that one lord complained about the shogun's attentions to the child performer Zeami: "*Sarugaku*,"* the old name for Noh, or for the concatenation of jugglery, puppet-shows, etcetera, that Noh grew out of, "is the occupation of beggars, and such favor

---

*"Monkey music." So called because the monkeys on Mount Hiei spied on the deity Kuni no Tokotachi no Mikoto, who performed Noh dances for his own entertainment. The monkeys imitated; humans saw the monkeys and learned from them.

for a *sarugaku* player indicates disorder in the nation." But century buries century, and the performances refine themselves into an ever nobler inaccessibility, slowing down (some now require at least double the time on stage that they did when Zeami was alive), evolving spoken parts into songs, clinging to conventions and morals now gone past bygone;* as for me, I look on like an ape in a cage.

Be that as it may, Noh has enlarged my capabilities of discrimination and touched my feelings in spite of my inability to construe many of its symbols, not to mention its very words. The shocking beauty of Yuya, the way the dead boy Umewaka† can sing me to the verge of tears, the hellish malice projected by Princess Rokujo's spirit, had I witnessed their equivalents in my own life I would have treasured only the first, whereas the astonishing refinement of their stylization in Noh makes them all equally precious to me. (Noh expresses a combination of verisimilitude and elegant movements; Zeami says that a master must be equally proficient in each.)

Great art projects a sense of inexhaustibility. In literature, particularly in poetry, this may be accomplished through *ambiguity*: Beneath each and every meaning that I can descry lie others, so that rereading holds out the prospect of new subtleties, inversions, secret codes and ineffabilities. To be sure, the patterns on a *surihaku* Noh under-kimono may end in monochrome wherever they cannot be seen. But from within my ape's cage, it seems that the greatest Noh plays offer me still more inexhaustibility than any concatenation of words in my own language, even those of Shakespeare. "King Lear" is so literally profound that the deepest sounding will

---

*Another Westerner expresses this phenomenon with different feelings: "Originally it was considerably more natural than it is now. The years have widened the gulf between it and its origin, and have intensified its artificiality and its museum-like mustiness." In the consistently jaundiced account of Eric C. Rath, who emphasizes how over time authority became centralized in the Noh Schools, thereby rigidifying the medium and disempowering variant voices, this slowing down and ritualization of Noh occurred in large part at the end of the nineteenth century, as an expression of elitism, and ultimately of militarism, "a timeless image of imperial rule with an idealized and ordered vision of a disciplined public." Rath asserts that these alterations in Noh were, in effect, lies in the cloak of history.

†In "Sumidagawa," discussed below, p. 362.

never plumb it. "Izutsu" is doubly deep to me because I can never hope to know but approximations of the words; then triply deep thanks to Chinese and Japanese allusions only a few of which I recognize. In an adjacent cage, two of my fellow apes forlornly report that translating Narihira, to whose verses Noh is indebted, produces a "feeling one has the words right and everything else wrong" due to the poet's "aural, syntactical perfection." But precisely because great art is great, it achieves its infinitude not by relying on mere incomprehensibility or difficulty, but rather through fidelity to its appropriate grammar. In the case of Noh, of course, that grammar involves indirection, understatement, allusion to a substantial corpus — and a degree of obfuscation. Around the beginning of the thirteenth century, the priest Shun'e advises his disciple Chomei that

> when one gazes upon the autumn hills half-concealed by a curtain of mist, what one sees is veiled yet profoundly beautiful; such a shadowy scene, which permits free exercise of the imagination in picturing how lovely the whole panoply of scarlet leaves must be, is far better than to see them spread with dazzling clarity before our eyes.

I read these words without any sense of alienness, perhaps because as a child I sometimes read the Bible, sensing even then, as Auerbach expresses it, that the sublimity of Genesis and kindred Scriptures "is not contained in a magnificent display of rolling periods nor in the splendor of abundant figures of speech but in the impressive brevity which is in such contrast to the immense content and which for that very reason has a note of obscurity which fills the listener with a shuddering awe."

In short, the magic of understatement — beautiful mystery — allures us everyhere. When I glimpse a beautiful garden behind a wall, I experience the tantalizing category of appreciation called *miekakure*. When I longingly remember some metonymic attribute of a place where I can no longer be, that is *wabi*, the loveliness of loneliness.* When I fall in

---

*From a certain train journey in Japan I recollect sleepwalled valleys; reddish-brown foliage mixes with the green vertical streamers of fog; and there comes a cool silent rain under whose blows the gunmetal river twitches as if trout-stirred. My window occludes the shoulders of rust-leaved mountains. For an instant, the fog offers me a single leafless branch.

love, I am allured, abandoned and enriched by fantasies of entities which dwell beyond me and hence are greater than I. When my heart hurts me in longing for the woman I love, it is because there will always remain more of her than I can know, possess, or surrender to. In short, I see her through a changing fog. And when a Noh mask haunts me from the stage, the mists of austerity and stylization render that female presence likewise awesomely remote while still less attainable.

It is past time to formally introduce the tools which Noh employs in the service of those veiled gorgeousnesses of infinitude. If you are familiar with Noh, this chapter and the next (like all the others) may conveniently be skipped. Otherwise, please be reminded once again that these oversimplifications are an ape's utterances. For example, nearly all of the following sentences ought to end with "with the exception of 'Okina.'"

## ROLES

The *waki* or witness appears first on stage. He is, like all of us who live, a traveller in an unknown land, far from the capital. (Dante: *In the middle of the journey of our life I lost my way.*) Sometimes he is an imperial messenger, sometimes a monk. In "Sumidagawa" he is a ferryman who has crossed the river any number of times; this does not make him any less vulnerable to unexpected irruptions. The *waki* of "Kinuta," which play received mention in the previous chapter, is none other than the husband of the woman who dies from neglect. He worries about her and wishes to return to her, but worldly compulsion (a lawsuit, and then there is an intimation of a liaison with the younger housemaid) keeps him at the capital until she dies of grief. What next? He decides to invoke her ghost, "to call her to the curved bow's tip, / poor soul, so that we two may speak." And here she comes, feebly creeping onstage as far as the first pine. The unknown is upon us, bearing witness to itself in poetry sung and danced. And the witness to whom witness is borne, our representative, is the *waki*. Another gloss on his function is "watcher on the side." He frames the tale with contexts and introductions; he narrates. Then, like the implied first-person voice that introduces *Madame Bovary*, or the somewhat plodding gentleman at the beginning of *Wuthering Heights*, he watches from the side. His costume and demeanor accordingly aim for a subdued impression. He wears no mask.

Zeami for his part remarks that "a *waki* fulfills his function insofar as he follows what is good and what is bad alike," even a bad *shite*. In other words, while he might express, for instance, compassion, he does not judge. And when he is a priest, what has been called his determined immutability may achieve the power to liberate another character from the miseries of attachment.

On occasion, he figures in tropes beyond Noh. Kawabata's passive yet sensitive protagonists have sometimes been compared to *waki*s. Discussing *The Narrow Road to the Deep North*, a scholar concludes that Basho must have been "just as interested in meeting the ghosts of men who had lived there long ago as in meeting his contemporaries." Accordingly, our scholar likens him to a *waki*, who is "in many cases an itinerant monk who invokes the ghost of a past local resident wherever he goes."

The *waki* is sometimes accompanied by attendants, the *wakizure*. In the immortal words of Royall Tyler, "these generally have little to say."

Sometimes Noh employs a *koken*, a child actor, often as an object rather than a subject of the action. Spectators might also see a *kyogen*, who unlike the actor of a comic *kyogen* play relates some aspect of the story that has not been elucidated more explicitly. His recitation may, however, be the merest recapitulation, in which case the *shite* is probably busy changing mask and gown.

The *shite* is "hero" or "heroine" of Noh, but I have never been able to "identify" with a *shite* the way I can read myself into the soul of a book's protagonist. This must not be merely a matter of cultural distance; when I reread *The Tale of Genji* I get absorbed into the psyche of the Shining Prince, and at times, into that of Lady Murasaki herself. But the *shite* sings to me from the unknown land behind the rainbow curtain.

*Shite* means simply "actor." His role sometimes gets subdivided into two: *maeshite* and *nochijite*, meaning respectively the *shite* of the first part and of the second part. He may have *tsure*, companions analogous to *wakizure*, but these are generally more active and ornately turned out than the latter. They may wear masks when playing female roles. Occasionally they even eclipse the *shite*. In "Semimaru," for instance, the eponymous

STAGE BRIDGE AND RAINBOW CURTAIN.

*tsure* appears just as prominently and more constantly than the *shite*, his sister Sakagami. Had I been told that Semimaru were the *shite*, I would certainly not have known better.

It is, of course, the *shite* who epitomizes masked and costumed gorgeousness. Although I have seen him in a chorus, it is certainly in his *shite* role that I think of Mr. Umewaka.

In "Kinuta" the *maeshite* is the pining wife of the first act, and Zeami specifies that she be represented with a *fukai* mask, which pertains to a middle-aged woman; the *nochijite* is her bitter spirit, who may appear to us through the vehicle of either a *deigan* or a *yase-onna* mask, both of which are associated with "vengeful female ghosts." Other *shites* include the once-beautiful hag Komachi in "Seki-dera Komachi," the distraught mother in "Sumidagawa," the abandoned sweetheart Pining Wind in the eponymous "Matsukaze," and the old man (*maeshite*) who turns out to be the Dragon God (*nochijite*) in "Kasuga ryujin" (which gets discussed in the next chapter).

The *shite*'s situation, with its resulting dramatic and metaphysical possibilities, brings to mind a great critic's comment about the souls in the *Inferno*:

> From the fact that earthly life has ceased so that it cannot change or grow, whereas the passions and inclinations which animated it still persist without ever being released in action, there results as it were a tremendous concentration. We behold an intensified image of the essence of their being . . .

And this goes far to explain the melancholy of so many Noh plays. The desperately impoverished reed cutter in "Ashikari," whose wife gets rich and returns to bring him lovingly to the capital, is an exceptionally fortunate *shite*, and it is all the stranger that Zeami wrote this play. "Shunkan," once attributed to Zeami and now tentatively to Motomasa or Zenchiku, better fits the mold: On a place called Devil Island, three exiled Genji factionalists await, with very little hope, their pardon and recall, "the only wine a valley stream, and flowing with it streams of tears." In the end, two men will be rescued, and Shunkan will be left alone to die a hideous death.* " 'Wait a while, oh! wait a while,' say the far voices growing dimmer"; they promise to plead in the capital for his return, but never will. Indeed, many plays (like many geisha songs) are about waiting; and the weary pounding of the fulling block, which we have already discussed in regard to "Kinuta," appears also in "Torioi-bune," when the wife, who like the heroine of "Kinuta" waits many years for her husband's return from the capital, specifies one item of her misery as "the dull thud of the fulling block, in the chill of night."

Are we not all dead in something, confined within something, seeking restlessly to escape into peace? The *shite* of "Izutsu" is known as "the woman who waits for her lover." He is long dead, as is she. She recites a poem she once wrote comparing herself to a cherry blossom, which despite its reputation for transience, hence fickleness, spends the year awaiting the one who is destined to pluck it. But who and what is she? This con-

---

*In *The Tale of the Heike* he starves himself out of regret at not being able to reward the loyalty of a retainer who has visited him. This alternate ending is scarcely happier. When I think of Shunkan, I remember Hokusai's simple, vivid sketch: Long and skinny, his rags resembling leaves or scales, he has become a part of his tiny rock-island. Crosslegged, he leans back with closed eyes, waiting for eternity to finish.

stant ghost gazes into the well, and sees her reflected image altering into that of her beloved, "the man from long ago." This, of course, comprises no escape, but a mere vicious circle.

When I watch this species of Noh plays, I often wonder to what extent the ghosts comprehend that they are dead. (As a woman's specter in "Nishikigi" tells the *waki*: "We who dwell in dark delusions leave to you who are alive the question of reality.") This question leads me to the more fundamental issue of whether I can ever comprehend my own evanescence. I remember the final poem of *Tales of Ise,* whose dying narrator, the Genji-like courtier Narihira, expressed incredulity that he must actually die *today.*

## NARRATIVES

Zeami directs that most plays be written in five sections: one beginning, three middle parts and an end. In the first section, the *waki* comes onstage. In the second, the *shite* appears. In the third, the *shite* and the *waki* engage in dialogue. In the fourth, there is a musical interval. This is, in effect, the climax. Finally comes a resolution of some sort, and here in particular the *shite* dances.

Zeami summarized the above with *jo-ha-kyu.* These three terms, taken from ancient court music, refer to a smooth preface, a break, and then a fast climax.

A more fundamental aspect of Noh narratives has already been implied in the foregoing discussion of the *shite*: with the exception of a very few happy-ending tales such as "Ashikari" or "Hanjo,"* the most impressive plays tend to be cautionary tales about attachment. Yes, there is a mother-child reunion in the beautiful "Miidera"; lines from "Takasago" may inspire a pair of traditionalist newlyweds; but many of the plays of harmony and success strike me as dully propagandistic, as when a goddess rewards some Emperor's virtue with elixir. My book will avoid them insofar as it can.

When the *waki* first appears, he generally introduces us to a sad situa-

---

*Mishima wrote a typically gloomy modernization of this last.

tion of some sort: a wandering monk's musing over a memorial tablet for two long dead fisher-sisters whose courtly lover left them for the capital commences "Matsukaze," while "Semimaru" begins with its eponymous blind prince being led by the *waki*, an imperial messenger, into the wilderness to be left alone by the Emperor's command. The *shite*s of these two plays are respectively Matsukaze herself, ghost of one of the abandoned sisters, and Princess Sakagami, the sister of Semimaru. Both of these women are mad. At one point in her despair, Matsukaze mistakes a pine tree for the courtier who abandoned her and her sister. Sakagami, while she can converse rationally with her brother, mostly raves the rest of the time. When she parts from him at the end of the play, he and she both weep. Thanks to the *waki*, who is a priest, Matsukaze (possibly) finds peace. Sakagami does not. But the cause of their misery is the same: a parting from someone loved who, thanks to the temporary nature of human existence, can never be kept.

This theme is hardly unique to Noh plays. In the fourteenth-century *Taiheiki*, for instance, Nagoya Tokiari the governor of Totomi finds himself on the losing side of a civil war, and in danger of capture. He and his comrades slit their bellies open and then roast themselves "at the bottom of a war fire." As for the wives and children, they are sent to drown themselves in the sea. "May it not be that the spirits of the dead remained there, thinking wrong thoughts of attachment to husbands and wives?" For afterward the husbands' ghosts are seen attempting to reunite with the ghosts of their wives, who rise up out of the water, but fires separate them; the female ghosts sink back down, and the male ghosts swim away crying.

The transience of life and the consequent advisability of relinquishing attachments have figured in Japanese literature for centuries.


PROPS


With the exception of a few play-specific props, such as the temple bell of "Dojoji" or the bird-scaring boat of "Torioi-bune," the stage remains always bare, but thanks to the imagination of Noh it elaborates itself whenever needed into a landscape as remote and fantastic as Hiroshige's multiphallic mountains and elaborately vaginal gorges, which, surrounded by mist and trees, each comprise another world, perhaps the "real" floating world — floating on mist; and all of these tall, rectangular worlds have been mounted on scrolls which elongate them much further than in their original proportions; world upon world hangs framed upon the walls of the Ukiyo-e museum in Tokyo: a planetary system of the imagination without a sun. (These places, of course, are peopled. I remember the outlines of his women, simple, crisp and sweeping, stylized into life by the genius of his printmaking. Their "individuality" is gestural. They could be Noh actors.)

As I have said, the greatest Noh narratives have to do with separation and desire. Whenever the desire gets eased, the means is oblivion, visited upon a grateful ghost through the prayers of a priest. In the closing lines of "Kanehira," the ghost of the warrior for whom the *waki* has come to pray cannot help but exult over his glorious suicide. Sometimes, as in "Aoi-no-Ue," the ghost is initially not just ungrateful, but demonically menacing. But even that monster is finally overcome and attains Buddahood "free of delusion." In Noh we never meet with any of the passionate epiphanies that can fulfill a life; for desire, of whatever kind, is precisely the problem.

And so the stage *should* be bare. This is the *waki*'s world, and therefore mine. Mostly I can be no more than a framer and witness of quotidian hills and beautiful masks. I watch at the side, or I sit in my numbered seat in the Noh theater, transiently moved by the transient attachments of others.

This is likewise the *shite*'s world and therefore mine. Forgetting the impossibility it must lead to, I kiss the mask, whose loveliness distracts me from perceiving the essential bareness of the situation upon which my attachment has been projected.

The chorus can express a single character's consciousness, and Mr. Umewaka and his fellow *shite*s can subdivide into different entities at any time. And so the stage is everyone's world and no one's. It is bare because life passes across it only for an hour or two, then withdraws behind the rainbow bridge.

(By the way, what is bareness? Often, as at the Choraku-ji Temple and the Shoren-in Shrine, the garden itself becomes a performance framed by

*SHITE*, CHORUS AND MUSICIANS.

the stage-rectangle of a shrine's or residence's open wall; one sits upon a blank tatami mat, which is itself framed by time-polished boards around the room's edges, and there might be a sliding partition of white screens behind or to the side, while in front it is open; a gnarled tree extends itself around a convoluted stone-rimmed artificial pond; a stone bridge vanishes into a bush or not, depending on how one moves one's head; branches blow; birds croak, and shadow-patterns alter in two-dimensional dramas upon the swelling sea of foliage. Is this a world, or nothing, or a stage, or all of these?)

On the back of the stage is painted a great pine; the bridge to the rainbow curtain passes three smaller pines which are not painted but quite material. These will be discussed later, since every book needs a chapter about pine trees.

I have read that the stage is in twenty pieces, that the best wood for it comes from Owari, and that in the hollow space beneath it are set ten large earthen jars for acoustical purposes. "The roof should not be tiled, but should be like the roof of the shinto temples in Ise."

The stage is isolated from us by white sand or gravel — another reference to Shinto.


## MUSIC

In spite of Mr. Umewaka's dictum that *the mask is most important always*, Thomas Blenham Hare believes that "the music and dance of noh have always been the central concern of most noh actors." How can one not love an art form which provokes such disagreement even as to what is central?

I recently learned that water pails, swords, hats, fans and other such props have "always" been supplied based on the type of music. No one has yet explained to me how this determination is made.

The musicians are called the *hayashi*. Either two or three drummers may be present; there is always one flutist. The drums themselves are quite beautiful with their ornamented bands, tri-leaved patterns, and other variable features which are as invisible to the public as an opera diva's underwear. The *otsuzumi*, or larger hourglass drum (also called the okawa), is held against the hip. Its sound is the most conspicuous; one commentator describes it as a "sharp, urgent click." The *kotsuzumi*, or smaller hourglass drum, is played against the shoulder. The same commentator characterizes its sound as "a muffled, funereal boom." I have seen one with golden floral and leaf lacquer patterns on its black skin. Another "extra large" drum called the *taiko* is sometimes also used. All of the drummers can cry out. The flute (either a *nokan* or a *fue*) may be played improvisationally or by rule, depending on circumstances. The second category warrior play "Atsumori" begins with a single, shocking flute-note. The flute often also sounds at the end of many Noh plays. I am told that this instrument's narrow bamboo throat "upsets the normal acoustical properties . . . and is responsible for its 'other-worldly' sound quality."

The drums and flute may collectively be called *yonbyoshi*. The percussion may be likened unto rocks in the flute's stream.

The progression of the music is again: *jo, ha, kyu* — that is, introduction (slow), development (medium) and climax (rapid). As we know, the narrative follows the same progression. So, at least ideally, does an entire program sequence of Noh plays.

The first three sections of a Noh play are either spoken or else, in Hare's words, "rhythmically unobtrusive." Then, in keeping with *jo-ha-kyu*, the *shite* begins to sing in the fourth section, and dance in the fifth. It is here that Noh music is most impressive.

I have already compared Noh to a musical jam session. A Noh expert amplifies: "Improvisation in Noh is probably closer to that of Sviatoslav Richter, who said he never knew what he was going to play until he sat down and did it, than to Bill Evans." He grants that it lacks key signatures and tempo markings. "But a good listener will notice if the drums are off a beat or even a partial beat, or if the musicians are taking a dance piece too fast or slow." Noh possesses greater latitude in tempo and rhythm than, say, Western chamber ensembles, "so that the actors and musicians are in a constant state of artistic tension in order to stay in synch. The hip drum player is watching the actor, the shoulder drum player is listening to him, and they are carrying on a musical conversation, so to speak, with the flute eavesdropping. The *shite* has to be listening to the *hayashi* without losing a sense of his own inner rhythm. The stick drum tends to dominate the *hayashi* when it comes in, but the flute may

OKAWA DRUMMER.

also do so during the dance pieces. Each player has to keep on his toes, keeping up with the rhythm as it shifts . . . When [Umewaka] Rokuro is the chorus leader (who sits in the middle of the back row) it's worth going just to hear them. He always keeps the beat slightly off the metronome, so to speak, giving it that Noh cutting edge."

The strangely addictive, not-quite-monotones of the men's singing can be described in words only indirectly. They sing with slightly bowed heads, very grave and doleful, their voice-beauty not unlike that of certain Native American chants, and then the flute shimmers on.

*Kotoba* is chanted speech; *yowa-gin* or *wagin* is the melodic mode employed to convey elegance and refined emotion; *suyo-gin* or *gogin* is the forceful mode, expressing bravery, rapidity and the like. It may exasperate or comfort the reader who cannot attend a Noh performance to learn that "pitch in noh is relative. Individual actor-singers sing at their own preferred and/or comfortable pitch."

At the beginning of the twentieth century, Mr. Umewaka Minoru told Fenollosa that "the importance of the music is in its intervals . . . It is just like the dropping of rain from the eaves."

As for Zeami, he considered the very existence of the chorus to be "contrary to the principles of our art.*

I read that during the Edo period, skill in Noh singing was widespread among the samurai class. To me, and to many of my Japanese friends, it is one more of this floating world's unknowns.

Because my subject is the feminine, while Noh music, and certainly the singing that shapes and dominates it, has, for me at least, an extremely masculine character, this book mostly ignores Zeami's watchword that "a truly fine play involves gesture based on chanting."

## DANCES

Edwin Denby once remarked that "intelligent dancing — which might as well be called correct dancing — has a certain dryness that appeals more to an experienced dance lover than to an inexperienced one." He was not writing about Noh at all, but he might as well have been. Please remember Zeami's prescription that "all the exercises must be severely and strictly done. There must be no self-assertion." And Noh is indeed, for the most part, very dry (at least in comparison to, say, the Tokyo subway in my epoch, when it is impossible to turn one's gaze anywhere except to the floor without seeing some message; and on the floor one reads the tale of many different shoes, the feet within some of them fidgeting) — its related drynesses of dance movements, music, stage props

---

*Noh music probably entered its present incarnation around the beginning of the sixteenth century.

and scenery comprising a frame for the spectacular costumes and masks, not to mention the occasional almost shocking increases in dance tempo, the sudden shrillings of the flute and raised chorus-voices.

Another manifestation of Noh's severity is the extent to which the movements have been preordained. As a Kabuki actor once told me: "Noh is for the warrior. Kabuki is for the general public. Noh has many restrictions. For instance, you always have to start with a certain foot forward for a given role." Such specificities have characterized Noh for centuries. In one of Zeami's secret treatises we find this admonition for performing "Matsukaze": The *shite* must not approach the *waki* when reciting, "please pray for remains," or else the play will fall flat. Rather, he must remain where he is, then approach the *waki*, then withdraw. — In 1900, Umewaka Minoru mentioned to Fenollosa the existence of a "roll" for dancers with "minute diagrams showing where to stand, how far to go forward, the turns in a circle," etcetera. "There are drawings of figures naked for old men, women, girls, boys, ghosts, and all kinds of characters sitting and standing; they show the proper relation of limbs and body." Such diagrams are still used.

The teacher of a renowned twentieth-century geisha informed her: "All I am able to do is teach you the form. The dance you dance on stage is yours alone." Hers alone? Yes, but she too would have agreed with Zeami, who underscored his prohibition of self-assertion thus: "There is no room here for my own thinking." How then can the dance be the dancer's?

I once asked the Noh actor Mr. Mikata Shizuka: "What do you your-self bring to Noh from your own mind, heart and training? What is your signature style?"

"This will be judged by the viewers," he replied. "What I value most is what I would like to express to the viewers, not to show my individual-ity. When I am doing this, I am not expressing myself."

"Suppose it were possible to build a robot to move the mask, would that be effective?"

"No. It has no mind."*

---

*Meanwhile, one Noh critic asserts that "it is . . . possible for an actor to deliver a line perfectly without understanding it."

"Where does your consciousness go when you perform?"

"It depends. The state where you think absolutely nothing, I think it's hard to grasp. But the intention is to show. If it's a Komachi play, I don't think that I try to be like Komachi.* If you want to show something, it comes to you internally, then somehow shrinks."

I told him about feeling in my hands and fingers when I am caught up in my writing; it is an exhilarating feeling during which my fingers do not belong to me, but to something else which is writing. What is it? I do not know. At its best, it is not an assertion of myself.

"I feel exactly the same," said Mr. Mikata.

"How else do you feel when you perform?"

"Depending on the role, sometimes excited. First, one thing: When you put on your mask, your view is restricted. It's like you are standing in the dark."

"What effect does that have?"

"Like a binding. Because of the restriction, your mind comes back to you."

He became "half-eyed" when he played Yoroboshi. "That's how I can see. That means, I cannot see anything in particular. But somehow, you see the air."

I think the reason that he can see the air is that he possesses the true flower. I have felt it in his performances. It must be this that makes the dance his alone — and, of course, the flower does not belong to him, but he to the flower.

Noh dance (and some Kabuki as well) is associated most prominently with the style called *mai*, which is characterized by turning movements and stately slowness, with the knees bent a trifle and the soles of the *tabi*-stockinged feet always on the floor. Sometimes the actor stamps, this mannerism being a relic of ancient religious ceremonials. Zeami divides the dance into three modes: warrior, old person and woman. There is also the mode of god or demon. Mr. Kanze Hideo told me: "There is not much difference between god and human movements. It depends on how human the god is." I inquired about the case of Okina, and he said that there "it is different, because everything in the play is a form of prayer."

---

*The sad life of Ono no Komachi figures in chapters 26 and 28.

What are Noh players doing when they dance? It has been said that "their movements become dreamlike glosses on the ideas carried by the words" — which cannot be entirely true, because sometimes, as with Yuya's dance, there is no idea to convey, nothing except elegant mystery itself. But certainly, as Mr. Mikata said, "the intention is to show." And so, slowly, without assertion of self, great actors offer their life-force to a role just as a Catholic priest offers up a chalice to be filled with enigma. "All the exercises must be severely and strictly done," in the way that in "Semimaru" the green-robed imperial messenger turns his back on us and slowly, slowly leaves the blind Prince alone forever, gliding across the bridge toward the rainbow curtain, followed by the attendants with the palanquin frame. Semimaru kneels and slowly raises his sleeves to his face as if drinking loneliness from them.

## COSTUMES

"She was instantly recognized as a geisha of the very first class when she went out in a white-collared kimono decorated with a family crest." Thus wrote Kafu Nagai in one of his best novels (1918). Noh kimonos expect their own instant recognition — sometimes. People with middling knowledge, such as myself, may be aware that the presence of red in a brocade robe indicates youth (the more red, the younger), and that the rank of a female character can be inferred from the color of the under-kimono's neckband. Purple, plum, greyish-green, etcetera, represent middle-aged women. True cognoscenti will recognize, say, a gold-backgrounded *oryu* kimono and know this character as a monster from a Chinese tale. A *shirojusu*-backgrounded *tuyushiba*, which depicts dew and grass, would surely have been chosen to allude to evanescence. A *kurojusu*-backgrounded *ayasugi matsuba*, which stylizes pine needles, alludes to immortality or fidelity.

The way a costume is worn also imparts recognition. For instance, the madwoman *shite*s of "Semimaru" and "Hanjo" let their right sleeves fall off their shoulders.

A costume might portray dewy grass, or seven wise men, or butterflies, or grasses and flowers and insect cages; but often we idlers and passers-by of this floating world can see the stage only from a distance, the fantastic figure against the backdrop of painted bamboos, and then the patterns it wears are beautiful beyond specific knowledge. If we are lucky enough to sit closer, we may realize that the darkhaired pallid mask and the water-green of the kimono are "brought out" even more by the glimpse of red garment beneath.

Most of Japan's ancient* Noh costumes were burned up in the American air raids on Tokyo near the end of the Second World War; some of the best surviving examples may be seen at the Mitsui Memorial Museum. What can they mean to me? A black-dragon-wave-backgrounded "sword and mountain" or "flower holder" kimono, how much expressive discretion might its wearer possess? Perhaps the former might appear on the actor who portrays the jealous serpent-woman of "Dojoji," although a diamond-fish-scale design would be more à propos. (Being associated with snake-scales, triangle patterns often express demonic female roles.) What about the Karahana pattern with the brown background called "Komochiyama?" My translator, Ms. Yasuda Nobuko, gives the Japanese characters, then sadly reports: "Could not read nor find translation."

Some of the costumes frequently used for female roles are the small-sleeved *kara-ori*; the ones incorporating red portray young women. (Among those which do not I see one with a checkerboard of subdued rusts and lavenders embroidered black, pink, red and white wheel-patterns, ivylike foliage of various other colors, and pale arcs concatenated into schematizations of rolling hills.) Then there are the small-sleeved, foil-stenciled under-kimonos called *surihaku* (I remember seeing one in a museum in Kanazawa that was night-blue with silver flowers and grasses), and satin *nuihaku*, which again are small-sleeved, with *surihaku* and embroidery — but then again, *nuihaku* may be employed for noble young male roles. There are rules, but actors and schools may vary them. Moreover, the widths of the garments, and the shapes of the sleeves, have remained stable for a relatively short time — merely since the middle of the Edo period.

A frequent effect of Noh costumes is to balance the austerity of the

---

*This must be the only place in the book when I use "ancient" in so extremely relative a sense. The most gorgeous costumes tend to date no earlier than the Edo period, when fabric-dyeing was perfected.

stage, the chanting and the slow movements with spectacular elegance. If Zeami, many of whose performances were maskless, could see, would he approve? The colors worn by the principal actors are as shockingly beautiful as would be the plumage of tropical birds against a white wall. The necessary hideousness of the extremest monster-masks thus receives its neutralizing compensation; and the face of a lovely woman dances to life in the gorgeous body of a robe. The mask is the face; the costume is the body. Moreover, theses costumes are layered, like Noh meaning itself; I can remember seeing Mr. Umewaka in at least three, his under-layers showing through like accented allusions at wrist and neck and ankle. I wish I had the talent to describe the motions of his immensely wide sleeves.

## FANS

The flash of gold around leaves of green, purple and red on a *toujumon-kami-ougi* fan, you can be sure that it means something. Black slats are associated with women, naked bamboo, with men, gold, with old men. Spiral patterns are associated with strength. Abstractions tend to express demoniacal madwomen; the same goes for combinations of red and gold.

## SCHOOLS

At the time of writing, five schools or styles of Noh exist. The Kanze School, from which the Umewaka School once did or did not temporarily break away, depending on who tells the tale, is dominant. The other four schools are Hosho, Kongo, Komparu* (which is said to own the oldest Noh mask of all), and Kita, this last being a newcomer from the Edo period. An expert writes me: "Kanze has the reputation of being on the flashy side, though not as flashy as Kita . . . Certainly the dancing style of Kanze is livelier than Hosho, while the latter is renowned for the beauty of its chanting." These have to do especially with *shite* acting. Hosho, which is rightly or wrongly said to be less elitist than some of the

---

*Also transliterated "Konparu."

other schools, frequently employs *zo-onna* masks for *shite* roles and *ko-omote* for *tsures*. The Kanze School prefers *ko-omote*s for *shite*s. Schools for *waki*, musicians and *kyogen* actors exercise their own influence. Most of my experience as a Noh spectator has been with the Kanze School.*

In case you wonder how it happens that an actor follows a particular school, the answer, for once, is simple.

"Why are you a member of the Kanze School?" I once asked Mr. Mikata Shizuka.

Patiently he replied: "Because my father is a Kanze."


## EQUALIZATIONS, NEUTRALIZATIONS

As mentioned in the section on costumes, Noh seeks to balance or even neutralize the image color of a given play, to harmonize positive and negative. For instance, brighter Noh pieces should be performed at night, when the ambiance of the theater is always gloomy. "As a rule," notes the first-rank translator Royall Tyler, "the more intense the emotion, the more regular the metre."

This principle, so alien to my temperament, is fundamental to Noh. Later on in this book, I hope to tease out some of the implications for feminine beauty itself.

---

*"Our school is the most refined," Mr. Umewaka once said to me, "so maybe it doesn't have as many attributes as the others. We employ more subtle, more delicate expressions." (The Noh expert Jeff Clark remarks that this "comment expresses the connection of refinement with simplicity. The greater the artist, the less he needs in his bag of tricks.") Dr. Yokoyama Taro distinguishes the Umewaka School thus: "Umewaka belongs to Kanze-Ryu, the largest of Noh schools. Kanze's players have a reputation of enacting embellished stages, though not as much as the flashy Kita-Ryu people. In comparison, the schools Komparu and Kongo are both of them more restrained, preferring delicacy in their expressions. Within the Kanze School, the Umewaka Family and Tessen-kai (or Tetsunojo Family) have contrasted themselves with [the] Kanze Family (the head house) by introducing the minute vocal nuances originated in Hosho Ryu (another of the main five schools . . .), thereby taking the direction of more aesthetic delicacy. [The] Umewaka Family and Tessen-Kai are . . . stylistically close together, but while the latter has a comparatively democratic, rivalry-free system, Umewaka sticks to the 'Iemoto' (head family) tradition . . ."

3:

# Malignance and Charm

*A Catalogue of Female Masks*

N oh was supposedly born out of sacred Shinto chants and dances, which gradually became masked. Masked court dances also seem to have been already on the scene.* Their sacred character has not entirely faded away even now, as we heard from Mr. Umewaka's remarks about "Okina." Some masks were thought to have fallen from heaven or appeared miraculously in the sea; they might be credited for a good rice crop. I try never to forget this aspect of, say, the *zo onna* mask which has just come to life in a Noh performance; it is more than a beautiful object. The same is true of the face of the woman I love.

---

*The evolution of masks may have proceeded as follows: Greek tragedy masks carried on the Silk Road as trade goods helped inspire the huge Chinese *gigaku* masks, which arrived in Japan in the seventh century. These soon gave way to smaller *bugaku* masks for court dances; next came the still smaller *gyodo* masks for Buddhist processions. Finally, smallest of all, Noh masks arrived, beginning in the tenth century with Okina's wooden face.

Zeami himself says little about masks, and in the appended "Saru-gaku dangi," prepared by Motoyoshi, we learn mainly which mask carvers of that epoch had the best reputations, and why it is that masks should not have too high a forehead (a hat or crown will go out of alignment). "Sarugaki" can mean either "monkey" or "god," depending on the pronunciation; while "dangi" means "music" or "speech." In keeping with that name, Noh in its early days most often encompassed gods, devils and the like. Accordingly, those sorts of masks were most in evidence. But by the late sixteenth century, mask makers were no longer creating new categories of masks, but copying old ones, in part because, as one period treatise explained, "masks that are too new tend to glisten and give a bad impression."

I have not seen many early illustrations of masks. Even in the Edo period, when *ukiyo-e* frequently depicted Kabuki actors, Noh actors rarely got featured, because in the words of one expert: "Noh was considered the property of the government, so the samurai would not have ventured to own such a print." All the same, it was probably at the beginning of the Edo time that Noh, and Noh masks, got codified. There are now sixty main types, which can be elaborated into about four hundred and fifty exemplars. More manageable is to consider the five fundamental divisions: Okina, demons, old men, men and women. Of course it is the final category that is of greatest interest in this book.

It is common for Japanese art to imply that each social gradation is its own world, that women, for instance, may be subdivided into hyperspecific sub-types, so that geishas and prostitutes are readily distinguishable, and indeed employ different tools.* In about 1793 there was a vogue for teahouse beauties, and I don't mean just any teahouses, but *mizuchayas*, which is to say the teahouses next to temples or shrines. Utamaro depicted these fetching *mizuchaya-bijin* in several woodcuts. Here, for instance, is a large multicolored print of Ochie of Koiseya reading a comic book. Although her image might be stylized, the props she bears comprise a coded placement in this typology. For instance, how old is Miss Ochie?

---

*The charming Japanese tendency to subcategorize is further seen in Utamaro's listing of the three best types of vulva: *takobobo, todatebobo* and *kinchakubobo* (octopus, which sucks; trapdoor, which grips; purse, which is tight).

If we know that the *oomarumage* hairstyle is for old women in their late twenties, if we are capable of being informed by the shaved eyebrows and *shimadakuzushi* hairstyle of another Utamaro beauty that she is a still more elderly woman — very likely in her thirties — if we can turn to Ochie and determine that she is still in her fullest teenaged flower, then we are advantaged like that Melville reader who knows his Bible. As for Noh, since it possesses so deep and wide a visual vocabulary, quite a number of feminine epitomizations lie available to it as masks.

Reader, have you ever wondered which mask might be tip-top for expressing a woman from long ago who drowned herself when the Emperor ceased loving her? It is a certain atypical *kohime*, carved by the great Tatsuemon. One carver believes it to be "the origin of female masks." In old times, many *ko-omotes*, rather than being simply "adorable," retained a trifle of what the carver refers to as "chilling godliness." As you see, *kohime*s could be even chillier. This one possesses smaller eyes than a *ko-omote*. It lacks "the soft look of the dimples near the lips as in the *ko-omote*. Both upper and lower lips are thick" like a *fukai*'s, "giving a deep look of a woman . . . It has an image of a Buddha statue. This is the finest among the masterpieces, from a period before they began attempting to express softness with techniques in female masks . . . Eyes, nose, forehead shows the nobleness of a mature woman . . . the hair and double-chin are closer to a *ko-omote*'s." Indeed, the face is wider than that of many suffering masks, so that not only the eyes but also the mouth appears smaller. The double chin widens as it descends. The underside of the nose is relatively flat between the nostrils. The expression is almost troubled, the smile apparent only from the side, the corneas entirely dark except for some horizontal streaks of white to delineate the sides of the pupil-holes.

But why this *kohime* in particular? Would understanding require education in artistic verities, or in mere artistic conventions? — How many mask-choices an actor truly has to express a given role is debatable. In 1765, Kanze Motoakira published canonical versions of various Noh plays. Indeed, he went far to establish the modern canon itself, eliminating hundreds of plays from the repertoire. Furthermore, Motoakira strictly specified which masks and costumes could be used in each play. His rules continue in force, at least for the Kanze School. One scholar bitterly writes that "Motoakira's legacy today is the rigid world of noh in which a narrow canon of several hundred plays is enacted according to strict rules interpreted" by "the family head." For whichever reason, the Noh actors I interviewed for this book, who all belonged either to the Kanze School or to its very near relative, the Umewaka School, never mentioned Motoakira's name. They simply told me which masks they considered appropriate for a given role. I will now relay some of their remarks to you.

There are four basic types of female masks, or dozens, depending on how one counts. I will list sixteen, some of which are variously presented as subcategories of others. In contradistinction to this variability, the uniformity which convention has imposed upon these objects creates in them the same sort of spectacular coherence which shines in different stanzas of a great poem. Each female mask must be seven *sun* (13.03 centimeters) high. A male mask is shorter, since it lacks the stylized hair. Seen together, the masks haunt and ravish me.

The famous *ko-omote*, "small mask," is for the youngest girls who are no longer children — which is to say (as Mr. Umewaka has already explained) girls of about thirteen to seventeen.* Since Noh dramas take place in an era when people married young, it is quite common for lovely wives, concubines, etcetera, to be portrayed with the *ko-omote*. In "Hanjo," the *shite*, Lady Han, is one of several girls kept at an inn for the purpose of entertaining "travelling gentlemen"; she wears a *ko-omote*. When I asked him which mask he would choose to play another kept woman, Yuya, Mr. Mikata replied that out of his collection of fifty, the only possibilities would be his seven or eight *ko-omote*, "plus *waka-onna*, but we have not so many. I don't prefer those." For the role in "Michimori" of the wife whose Heike warrior husband must bid her farewell to join a last doomed battle against the Genji, Mr. Mikata chose an Edo-period *ko-omote*.

How does this mask differ from others? The renowned carver Nakamura Mitsue replied simply: "It has its specified shape that is commonly understood by the people in this world. There is a sample of the shape. There is a pattern paper to make it. Mask carvers use that." And she showed me an unpainted *ko-omote* that she had made. Since this book

---

*Other sources say simply that the *ko-omote* represents a girl of fifteen, the *waka-onna* and *magu-jiro* a woman of about twenty-five.

happens to be written in words, and since if anyone in this rushing, float-ing world is an expert on distinguishing one Noh mask from another, it must be she, I tried again, and Ms. Nakamura finally said: "I'm no good at expressing in words because I express in shapes, but I will try. The younger, the more plump. The lower cheek is rounder; that's my image." She cradled her *ko-omote* as if it were a baby, and it smiled guilelessly up at her. "Since it's more chubby, the end of the mouth goes deeper," she said.

— For me a *ko-omote* recalls the face of the plump-cheeked, snow-skinned girl in a certain Genji Picture-Scroll, her eyebrows high and considerably thicker than her demure slit of a mouth, her hair stylized much like a Noh mask woman's: on each side, a solid black zone from the crisp white parting down temple and cheek between two widening arcs, paralleled by long single strands which pass across eyebrow, eye, cheek, chin, neck.

It would be too easy if the masks of a given category could be inter-changed; and in the Kanze family's fabulous mask collection we find a "hard" *ko-omote* from the sixteenth century; this mask finds application, as in the play "Mina," in the portrayal of young women who turn into goddesses.

Then comes the equally famous *waka-onna*, which means sim-ply "young girl." Acccording to Mr. Umewaka, it is used to represent seventeen- to twenty-five-year-olds. "Look at her from the side," advised the mask maker Otsuka Ryoji of one of his creations, "and her mouth seems to smile wider." Ms. Nakamura remarked: "The difference between the *ko-omote* and the *waka-onna* is very slight.* The *waka-onna*'s eyes are a little higher."

"So would that make the forehead smaller?" I asked. "After all, both masks are about the same size."

"Oh, the difference is so slight," she repeated. "You can change this line or that line. But the cheekbones are a little higher."

These subtleties reminded me of a certain plastic surgeon's self-asser-tion: "In what I do, beauty is about millimeters."

I asked the great actor Mr. Kanze Hideo whether it was really true that only the Kanze School uses the *waka-onna* mask, and he replied:

---

*Even slighter is the difference between a *waka-onna* and a *fushikizo*. In this book the latter will be discussed only briefly, in regard to the great play "Matsukaze."

"That may be the tendency. But the *waka-onna* itself did not exist in the time of Zeami. In the Tokugawa era, about four hundred years ago, it was created, and Kanze had good *waka-onna* masks."

Mr. Mikata for his part remarked of this mask: "In the first and middle portions of the Edo period, it was very suitable for the Kanze School, but it simply looks pretty, graceful. Strictnesss or power I believe is hard to express with the *waka-onna*. Of course there are good *waka-onna* masks."

Having passed her years in praying and grieving for her mother and son, who drowned themselves rather than be captured by the Genji, the former Heike-era Empress of "Ohara Goko" must surely be careworn, and yet as the play opens we find her sitting in her hut, wearing a *waka-onna*. The mask can also used in the plays "Yokihi" and "Matsukaze," which will be discussed in chapters of their own. The *shite* of "Izutsu" wears it, as does "Eguchi's" courtesan-Buddha.

Slightly less well known is the *magojiro*, whose name combines denotations of "grandchild" and "second son." "This has a legend," said Ms. Nakamura. "It is named after a man who made this mask remembering his late wife. Compared with others, this one's proportions are closer to those of a real human. In a *ko-omote*, the eye-nose distance is shorter than in a *magojiro*, whose face is slimmer and slightly longer. But the truth is that the two masks are about the same size." Apparently the cheeks are also more taut than a *ko-omote*'s, and the lower eyelids more curved. This mask is frequently used to play Yuya or Hanjo. The Kongo School employs it almost exclusively.

The famous *zo-onna* (Zoami's woman) was named after its creator Zoami, about whom Zeami said: "Both his acting and his singing should probably be classed at the rank of the tranquil flower." Often the *ko-omote* seems "warm" and the *zo-onna* a trifle "cooler." "From the standpoint of age," said Ms. Nakamura, "this mask does not differ from the *waka-onna*. But the expression is different. The shape of the mouth is different. The *waka-onna* is smiling; the *zo-onna* is not. Actors often employ it for goddess roles." We see it worn by the *shite* of "Seiobo"; he is portraying a heavenly maiden who has come to reward an Emperor for his virtue. It may also be used in "Hagoromo" and other plays; the Kongo School employs it often. One actor remarks of it: "The delicate red on the cheeks of this

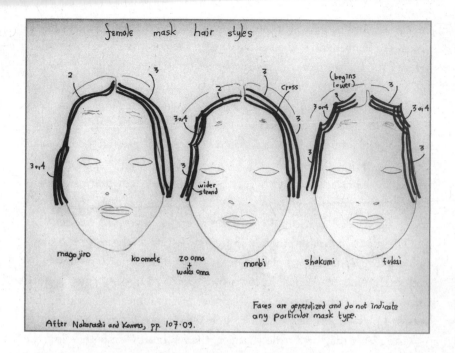

female mask hair styles

2     3     3    Cross    (begins lower)    3

2     3 or 4     3 or 4

3 or 4     3 or 4     3     3

3 or 4     3     3

wider strand

mago jiro     ko omote     zo onna + waka onna     monbi     shakumi     fukai

Faces are generalized and do not indicate any particular mask type.

After Nakanishi and Komma, pp. 107-09.

mask, the beautiful red color of the lips, are so beautiful that when I take a good look at it, it feels as if I am observing the first sunrise of the year on New Year's day."

These various young woman masks can most easily be distinguished from one another by the number (and sometimes the crossing-point) of strands which parallel the border of the hair's solid inky darkness in its journey from the part down the curves of temple and cheek.

As I've said, the masks become leaner with the years they bear. The *waka-onna* has a slightly longer nose and a narrower chin than the *ko-omote*; the corners of the lips turn upward a little less. These changes grow more pronounced in the *fukai* and *shakumi*, which are both associated with middle-aged women. Mr. Umewaka says that the *fukai* is for women in their thirties to early forties (and there are two subtypes of these, deep and shallow). Its gaze is sharp. In "Obasute," when the ghost of the deserted crone first appears in the guise of a living old woman, she wears a *fukai*. Representing "Kinuta"'s *maeshite* by means of *fukai* is elegantly appropriate, since the wife has just recently lost her desirability. In "Miidera" the middle-aged mother of a child kidnapped by slave traders can be represented by either the *fukai* or the *shakumi*, depending on which of the five Noh schools is putting on the performance. The *shakumi* sometimes has thinner, more slanting eyebrows than the *fukai*. (By the by, an American makeup artist informs us that "eyebrows convey different emotions depending on how they are drawn.") The *shakumi*'s eyes are also a trifle narrower and perhaps lower. "Basically they are the same," said Ms. Nakamura. " They are *slightly* different. The actor chooses what he likes."

"Is the difference so subtle that even you could not tell in a performance?" I inquired.

"It depends. Sometimes I clearly know and sometimes I wonder."

The *masukami* mask bulges and furrows on its forehead, in the shape of a curving, four-taloned claw. There is a wrinkle beneath its lower lip, and its chin has sharpened, its lower face narrowed into a sort of rounded arrowhead. But the cheeks are still smooth. It is sometimes used in that very sad play of blindness, madness and separation, "Semimaru."

The *manbi* may be a trifle younger; the forehead is smoother, but the underlip is accompanied by much the same crease, and wider, shallow creases swerve outward from the corners of the mouth across the woman's slightly flaccid flesh to above her chin.

The mask maker Hori Yasuemon describes *manbi*s rather more appealingly: "How can charm be expressed? That is what makes carving interesting. It is quite difficult to carve extreme charm after carving a noble piece such as a *zo-onna*. How can we express a sex appeal different than those of *ko-omote* and *waka-onna*? Some twists are needed, such as the way her eyes and mouth are carved, the shape of the nose, double-chin, making a small dimple near the mouth, lifting the lip high, making the face slightly clear-cut, and the parts larger." The *manbi*, he says, has wider eyes than the *ko-omote*. "The name is derived from the phrase *stronger than a hundred coquetries* . . . Adding some seduction with sex appeal to a *ko-omote*, the brush stroke sends a clear message. Perfect for the beautiful woman that a demon has turned into in 'Momijigari.' The Katayama Kurouemon family has another *manbi* mask carved by Omi, which has goggling eyes and mysterious sex appeal . . ." The *manbi* about which he writes "is young and beautiful, and is used for roles such as Hanjo, who is crazed in love."

In any event, the *manbi* has suffered more than her younger counterparts. Still older women are represented by the *rojo*, "old woman," and the *uba*, which means not only an old woman but also a wet nurse. In "Obasute," when the ghost of the deserted crone finally comes on stage undisguised as a living woman, she replaces her *fukai* with an *uba*. (Hokusai's final — and incomplete — series of colored woodblocks was entitled "Pictures of One Hundred Poems by One Hundred Poets, Explained by the *Uba*," and an editor believes that the artist's "style is the same as hers — not a style of ignorance, but of innocence.") *Uba* and *rojo* are both used, among other purposes, to portray the poet Ono no Komachi. The latter, so I read, can "reveal inner elegance. Only an occasional crease lines the clear skin." The first exemplar was carved in the fifteenth century.

In an old woman's mask, the lips turn downward, and sometimes the face becomes spectacularly hideous, as in the mask which Mr. Umewaka employs to represent Komachi, who turned away all her suitors and found herself alone,* it wears a downcurved, self-disgusted grimace and eye-slits which curve upward like Kagekiyo's (although they are slightly wider than his, since Komachi can see). Mr. Umewaka remarked about this mask: "In the end, her miserable appearance is a very sad final stage of her life. We just symbolize her as a beggar. She had the loneliness of someone who maintained her own thinking. There is another interpretation: It was actually not Komachi, who'd been famous for her beauty, but some spirit who took over this old woman who then thought of herself as Komachi. I follow the first interpretation in my performances."

Then, of course, come the ghosts of angry or unsatisfied women.

The *deigan* is a living woman crazed with jealousy. Ms. Nakamura showed me one of her unpainted blanks, a mask of a woman concentrating on something, staring up at me from the table, the mouth downturned. To my naive gaze, there was hardly even a suggestion of sullenness in her yet. Although the name means "mud eyes," a finished *deigan*, she said, would have the whites of her eyes painted gold. The jealous ghost

---

*This story enthralled Mishima Yukio, one of whose reasons for cutting his belly open was that his body was losing its youthful perfection. In his own version of the Noh, as we shall see, the old woman is a kind of vampire who murders youth with an illusion of her beauty.

of Lady Rokujo often appears in a *deigan* mask at the beginning of "Aoi-no-Ue." The abandoned wife of "Kinuta" can also incorporate herself in a *deigan*.

The *ko-omote*s, *waka-onna*s and *zo-onna*s look *through* me. A seventeenth-century *deigan* by Genkyu Mitsunaga looks *at* me, but seems not to see me. Her face is as smoothly beautiful as that of the other three masks, but her mouth, instead of ending in sad smile-points, forms a long rectangle, and the teeth are paler against its opened darkness. On each temple, two strands of hair curl out of place. The pupil-holes tilt slightly upward and outward. If the whites of the eyes have been gilded, it was with an understated touch. Who knows what she is thinking? As I stare at her I begin at last to sense that something is not right with her; some sorrow hurts her. But I would still be foolish enough to trust myself to her, since she seems to trust herself. This mask is a gem of subtlety.

In contradistinction to the *deigan* is the extremely varied category of *hashihime*, "bridge princess." In Ms. Nakamura's words, "the *deigan* has some grudge inside the mind, while the *hashihime* has not kept the grudge inside concealed but is showing it."

She showed me her masks of this type; they had protruding cheek-bones, gold-plated copper rings about the eyes. Often many Medusa-strands twisted down their foreheads; and they seemed to be lost between anguish and the subsequent stage of demonhood, malignant joy; for their mouths narrowed in the center and widened at the corners, while the downward gaze of those black and golden eyes expressed great pain. Some of them were snarling, some had smaller, demurer mouths, all downturned. Their attachments had so far enslaved them that they seemed less feminine than their *deigan* sisters and predecessors; they were humans becoming monsters. "The reason why there are so many types of *hashihime*," she smilingly said, "is because the mask makers are male, so for them probably each one has a personal experience with a jealous female."

In this group is the *ryo-no-onna*, and also the *hannya*, which one source singles out as "particularly famous as a mask embodying a woman's hatred and sorrow." Pound and Fenollosa opine that *hannya* comprise not one type, but a full group of masks. "The hannia in Awoi no Uye [another transliteration of 'Aoi-no-Ue'] is lofty in feeling; that of Dojoji* is base . . . The Adachigahara hannia is the lowest in feeling." These masks resemble horned, grinning skulls with the flesh still on them, darkness glaring around the round holes in their golden eyes, the teeth huge and variously discolored, with greyish-black hair flowing thinly around the horns. Their malignance is spectacular, their hatred terrible. They tend to express grief when tilted down, and fury when raised.

What the *hannya* proclaims the *ryo-no-onna* understates. The Kanze School considers it especially appropriate to represent the ghost of Unai-otome, who, harassed by two suitors, diplomatically drowned herself.

The *yase-onna*, "skinny woman," is in a different group from the above. As already mentioned, sometimes the ghost of Kinuta wears this particular wooden face: hollow-cheeked and bony-cheeked, with sunken eyes and a narrow almost rectangular gape — all in all, a softer feminine version of the abandoned exile Shunkan. One commentator remarks on its "calm, almost rectangular pupil openings." It is used to portray vindictive female spirits "when the intention is to empathize their pathos." The ancient carver Himi is said to have used the frozen corpse of a starved woman as his model for the *yase-onna*. Asked to differentiate between a *rojo* and a *yase-onna*, Kanze Hisao replied: "The bones are the same. However, the *yase-onna* must have a beauty which shows that a beautiful woman became thin because of love."

Such is my resume of female Noh masks.† Needless to say, any other

---

*This jealous woman-snake is customarily represented by either a *ja* or *hannya* mask. She may also incarnate herself in the *omi-onna* mask, as in the first act of "Dojoji."

†As for male masks, in the interest of gender equality I condescend to give them a footnote. Boys' masks are the *doji* and the *kashiki*, "a young male role that has both secular and religious aspects." *Chujo* and *imawaka* are for young noblemen and warriors. *Chujo* means "deputy," and is fairly frequently seen — for instance in "Michimori." *Heita* represents a warrior of middle age. An old man is shown by the *akobujo*, a category which may or may not include the *san-ko-jo*, which once again appeared in Mr. Mikata's production of "Michimori." The *ayakashi, yase otoko* and *kawazu* represent angry male ghosts. There are also masks specific to, and named for, the roles of Kagekiyo, Semimaru, Shojo, Shunkan, Yorimasa, Yoroboshi. (When I asked how many of his fifty masks would be available to choose from for "Kagekiyo," Mr. Mikata accordingly replied: "Basically two, one with a beard, and one without. But that was not a good question.") The Okina mask has already been introduced. *Hakushikijo* and *kokushikijo* are for gods, *tobide* and *beshimi* for demons.

book will categorize them differently. I have bypassed the *higaki-no-onna*, which the Kanze School occasionally employs to play the fabled Ono no Komachi; and doubtless I have committed many other errors.

"Do you have any general advice for people going to a Noh play for appreciating the beauty of a female mask?" I asked Ms. Nakamura.

"If you have an opportunity to look close up, the combination of the actor's ability and the mask makes a change in the expression of the mask."

"When a mask maker fails, what is the most common failure?"

"Too much engraving. Sometimes, that you can fix by painting something over it, but when it's complete, sometimes I just don't like the expression."

In short, the trick was understatement.

In both Noh and Kabuki the changing of one mask for another provides critical information (for instance, a *shite* who first appears as an old woman returns as the young girl-ghost whom the old woman always was). In Kabuki one additionally sees the changing of wigs. Kabuki is more prop-rich in every way: Gorgeous groups of man-women arranged by color, ladies all in a row, sing to the shamisen up and down; while the warrior struts and stamps like a whitefaced devil.

Kabuki is the way that I so often write; Noh is how I would write if I were more "spiritual," more understated or perhaps just older.

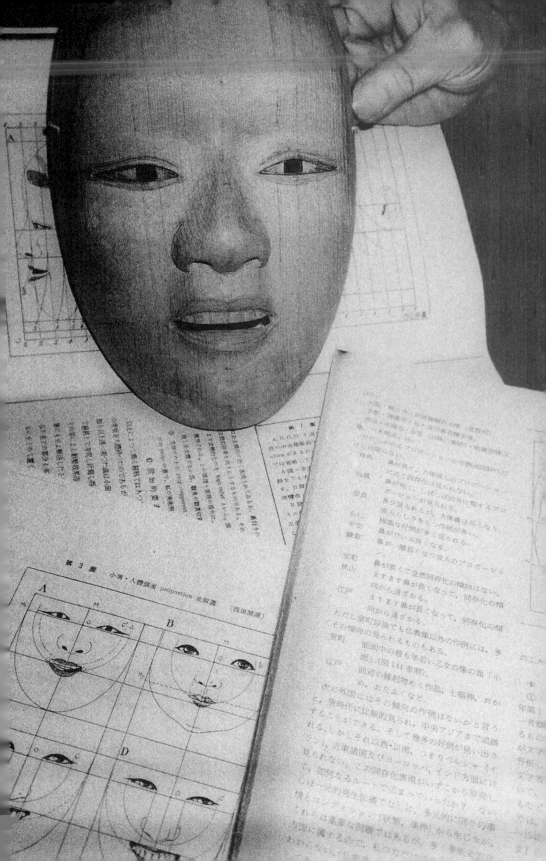

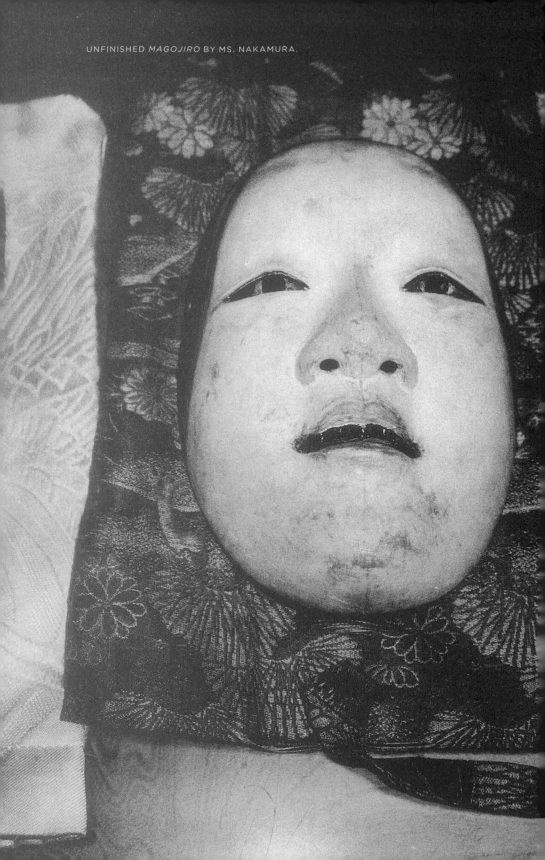

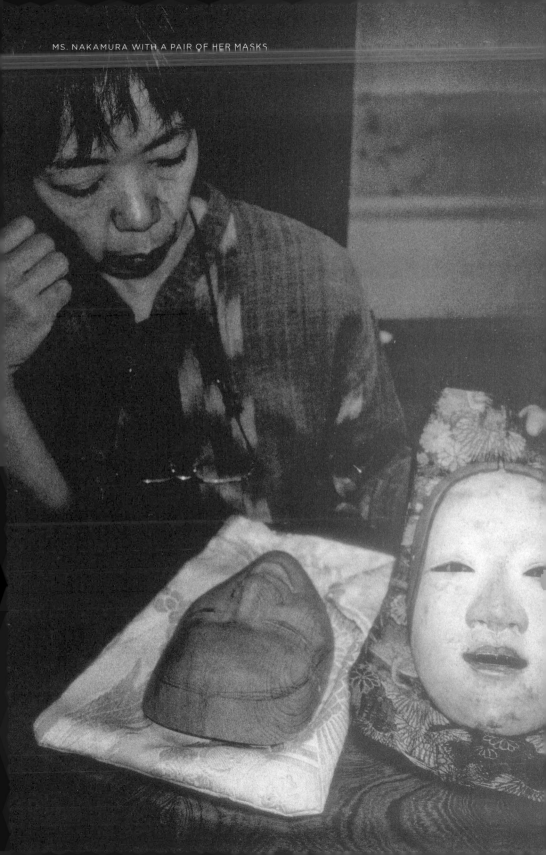

MR. UMEWAKA'S APPRENTICE WITH A *KO-OMOTE* MASK.

DETAIL OF *KO-OMOTE* ON PAGE 80.

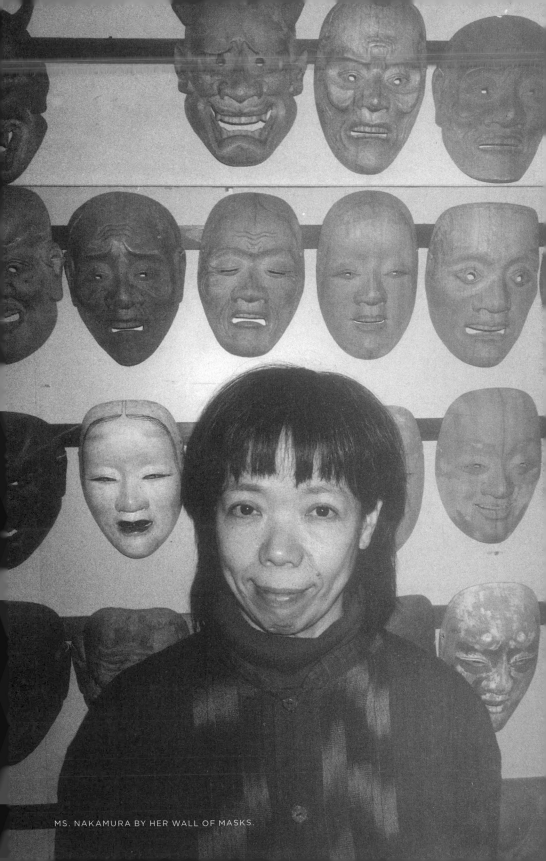

MS. NAKAMURA BY HER WALL OF MASKS.

# A Branch of Flowers

*Steps to Ineffability*

Zeami is not only one of the greatest artists of all time, but a brilliant and inspiring adviser to anyone who either makes art or appreciates it. Given the arcane character of Noh drama, which takes so much study merely to watch with understanding, given further that his treatises were secret documents, for the benefit of his eldest male descendants only, I find Zeami's relevance to my own obsessions remarkable. But, after all, he sought to further one of the most profound of all artistic aims: namely, the creation of beauty.

Because the beauty he describes consists of epiphanies and ineffable accomplishments, it seems to me more universal than it probably was; and there is no doubt, as I continually remind myself, that because so much of Zeami lies beyond me (for instance, his musical theories, right down to their very technical melodic terminology), I am mis-applying him. No matter. The jungles in Rousseau's paintings (none made from life) have been attacked as misunderstandings not only of jungles, but of basic painting technique; all the same, Rousseau's paintings are beautiful. Accordingly, I insist on appropriating Zeami for myself, and I invite you to do likewise; because he indicates, insofar as a human can, the *infinite heights* of beauty. The possibilities he raises within me magnify my freedom and my ambition, now and for the rest of my life.

In the treatise "Fushikaden" ("Teachings on Style and the Flower"), he writes that a successful play of the first rank is based on an authentic source, reveals something unusual in aesthetic qualities, achieves an appropriate climax, and shows grace. To me the first requirement is inconsequential, and I will ignore it in what follows. As for the third requirement, appropriate climax, here it suffices to repeat that Zeami builds his plays out of parts which escalate the movement, song and dramatic action right up to the proper point.* The important points here are that no aspect of artistic presentation should be ignored, and that each level of organization considered has its scaled counterparts on all the other levels.

The second matter, unusualness, is at the heart of what Zeami calls "the flower" — namely, the beauty of a Noh performance. This flower will under certain conditions be "false"; for example, an actor might through his youthful voice and appearance make a handsome impression, and complacently believe himself to be a master. (In my own epoch, the cinema's leading ladies usually are, and the heroines of erotic centerfolds almost always are, young, or at least young-looking. Here one Japanese expression for prostitution, *selling spring*, is à propos.) The false flower must fade, of course, and the performer who, as an American would say, "banks on it," will presently find his credit dwindling. Meanwhile, one of the many astonishing achievements of Noh is when a dumpy old man becomes a lovely young girl, all the while showing his swollen feet in the white *tabi* socks and working his Adam's apple as he sings in his old man's bass. No matter what his body is, the young girl *lives* in him! He possesses the true flower.

Zeami writes that each flower has its season, so that any flower is of itself ephemeral, like a Noh performance itself; therefore, when an actor

---

*The very sequence of plays performed on a given day ought to conform to this scheme. Thus the plays may be considered acts of an ephemeral meta-play. This conception dates at least back to the Heian period, when tankas of Japanese court poetry were sometimes organized into great narratives whose elements had been composed by many poets in diverse centuries.

possesses "the flower," he owns in fact the ability *to flower* in the appropriate way. He "possesses all the flowers." "Flower, charm and novelty: all three of these partake of the same essence. There is no flower that remains and whose petals do not scatter." For just that reason, when a new flower comes into bloom, it will seem novel. And novelty is indeed the thing. A Noh actor who sets out to portray only demon roles will not possess the flower, because his demons will merely be demons; whereas an actor who can play not only demons but also women, old men and warriors will manage to impart some characteristic of one or more of these other roles to the demon role, so that his demon will unexpectedly, yet convincingly resemble "a flower blooming in the rocks." To take a still stranger case, an actor who has over time achieved greatness by systematically excluding all impurities of technique wins the freedom to color his representation with novelty by introducing this or that impure element — a strategy which would only make the performance of a lesser actor all the more deficient.

These considerations lead me to wonder whether all beauty is somehow surprising. This is a question to which I do not have the answer. It is certainly true that when an alluring lady sweeps in, be she a woman or a man in a mask, I feel a sense of unfamiliarity; and part of my joy in gazing at the loveliness of a woman I know well is trying to determine what makes her so beautiful; I wish to solve a mystery, and so my gaze cannot be satisfied. In any event, there is no single final form for beauty; if there were, it would not be novel. Hence Zeami reminds us that "the flower does not exist as a separate entity."

It follows that "a flower blooms by maintaining secrecy." This is why the mirror room where the Noh actor dons costume, wig and mask is out of sight of the audience; and surely this explains why so many self-transformers, especially cross-dressers and old women, hate to be seen at their makeup. And due to this secrecy, even the principle that novelty is essential must be kept hidden. The point is to make the audience experience *skilled unexpectedness*. If they anticipated novelty, they would undervalue it.

We now arrive at the fourth requirement: grace. This is the quality that "stage characters such as Ladies-in-Waiting, or women of pleasure, beautiful women, or handsome men, all show alike in their form, like the various flowers in the natural world." Grace is represented by the deportment, "dignified and mild appearance," "refined and elegant carriage" (which must move us without being ostentatious) and "beautiful way of speaking" of the nobility. — But what *is* grace exactly? Zeami does not say, because his effects exist beyond words. In the treatise "Shikado" ("The True Path to the Flower") he advises us that "roles requiring great taste and elegance come naturally from the style of women's roles," and he may well have grace in mind here; in any event, there are plausible if contradictory indications that for Zeami as for me, *the representation of femininity is the profoundest art.* In "Kakyo" ("A Mirror Held to the Flower") he speaks of the five skills of dancing, each of which is an extension of the preceding one into greater inexpressibility. The penultimate skill, "mutuality in self-conscious movement," which is already nearly indescribable, and then so only by extension from the three skills before it, is appropriate for male roles. The most arcane skill of all, "mutuality in movement beyond consciousness," "produces an art beyond any mere appearances" and is, I am happy to say, proper to female roles.

When performing a woman's role, the actor should "slightly bend the hips, hold his hands high, sustain the whole body in a graceful manner, feel a softness in his whole manner of being, and use his physique in a pliant manner." He must wear skirts long enough to hide his feet (as implied, this rule gets frequently disobeyed in Noh performances of my epoch). His body should be hidden below the neck. And Zeami will offer any number of such instructions to the man who wants to be perceived as female, as warriorlike, as old . . . But this does not get to the heart of grace. The following does, stunningly: Whether an actor plays woman, warrior, demon or old man, "it should seem as though each were holding a branch of flowers in his hand."*

The more I consider this statement, the more it thrills me. I am not at all sure that it must be true, but why not create something on the assumption that it is? The late A. R. Ammons once advised me in a poetry course that if one's effect feels a little off, it is time to push the off-ness as far as it will go, until it achieves strange beauty (in other words, Zeami's flower of novelty). — Zeami for his part asserts that off-ness has to do with being out of balance. Therefore, add the complement. If something is rough, add flowers to it. If it is weak, add strength. Even the beyond-conscious role of a beautiful woman will be out of balance

---

*Renoir: "For a battle piece to be good, it must look like a flower piece."

— strengthless, even vulgar — without its opposite. The woman is more effectively female when tinctured with maleness. For his own part, the warrior must bear his flower-branch. Of course it would be superficial, reductive, to suppose that the man's flower-branch must be the same as the woman's. All the same, this feminine emblem which brings the various male roles into balance must surely *remain* feminine for the female ones; therefore, even though a Noh heroine as much as any Noh hero contains her opposite already (through the appropriate strong characteristics of chant, posture and dance), that branch of flowers can only make her more herself,* in which case it would seem that *the female principle is fundamentally more in balance than the male.*

Set this aside for a moment, or for the rest of your life. I am not sure whether I believe it myself. But let us think more about this matter called balance, which can mean one or both of two things. An artist might impart opposite qualities to what he creates, either to make it neutral, or else to make it infinite. Photographers like to speak of a neutral surface for a print, meaning a scale of values whose color or value is not obtrusive.† A rich but somehow nondescript black which can be decomposed into various greys neither warm nor cold, and a white which is not too sunny or snowy, will best allow the image to offer itself without extraneous connotations. Of course I might break this rule, and often do: following the more-is-more principle of Ammons, I selenium tone subjects which to my feeling possess "warm" connotations, so that the shadow areas in that portrait of the Mexicali street prostitute singing narco-ballads on a hot night take on a blackish-crimson tinge; while such "cold" subject as the jet-black men in the Congolese prison-cage deserve

---

*A brilliant case in point is the character of Princess Rokujo in "Aoi-no-Ue." Envy of Prince Genji's other lovers, and in particular of his first wife, has transformed her into a hideous demon represented by a *hannya* mask. One observer speaks of the play's demand that the *shite* "temper the compelling sharpness of aggression with the elegance befitting Princess Rokujo . . . jealousy was transformed into an experience of beauty."

†However, when many pictures on the same paper stock, processed identically, are viewed together, the image color loses relevance. This is so even in the case of cyanotypes, whose blue seems peculiar or even (a favorite adjective in the literature) "objectionable" when seen alongside their platinum or silver gelatin cousins; a portfolio of a hundred cyanotypes, however, restores the composition itself to primacy.

to be toned with gold chloride until the white areas bleach down harshly and the shadows take on a bitter blueness. But could it be that this procedure is a shallow or even hysterical insistence on telling the viewer how to feel? Should I cold-tone the street girl and warm-tone the prison-cage, so that only the subject remains?

In daytime, says Zeami, perform subdued plays, and in nighttime do brisk bright ones. When an actor expresses anger, "he must not fail to retain a tender heart. Such is his only means to prevent his acting from developing roughness . . ." When he stamps his feet, he must suppress his upper body into near immobility; and *vice versa*. The treatises offer many more such examples of cancellation. Always the tendency is to reduce, understate, dampen vibrations, approach neutral buoyancy until beauty hovers in the water, massively still, profound beyond sight, so pure that it might be mistaken for nothingness. "If the motion is more restrained than the emotion behind it," he writes in "Kakyo," "the body will become the substance and the emotion its function, thus moving the audience." What would happen if the motion were insufficiently restrained, the silver gelatin of the photograph insufficiently neutral? Then our hothouse could raise only false flowers. This is why Zeami warns that a "surface brilliance" of visual spectacle may actually be inimical to a great performance, because the audience might then miss the subtle beauties of the acting. To avoid this, plays have slowed themselves down over the centuries; and, for the same reason, the sound of Noh ought to be "sober" even if that bores provincial audiences.

To artists who create in an unmediated rush of feeling (Céline, Rachmaninoff, Gauguin), this prescription will be deadly. Balance itself is hardly a prerequisite to beauty. But for the remainder of this book, I will either respect Zeami's rules or else react to them.

When I see a Noh play, I think of *strong, stately stillness*. Indeed, as Zeami remarks, a good actor may fascinate his audience when seemingly doing nothing — in other words, when he is between two actions or movements. This achievement is possible thanks to tension and concentration.* It is as if I could simultaneously increase both the warmth

---

*To accomplish it, the performer is more essential than the text; for Noh can sometimes succeed through a half-definable quality called *heart*. When this occurs, an actor is so outstanding that even a banal play will move the audience.

and the chilliness of my photographs, leaving each print to appear *almost* untoned. If so, my representation would be richer.

What then is the flower? What is grace? What is beauty? Many specific things can be said; for instance, body posture is as important as the specific characteristics of any role. Never mind. In another of his methodically enigmatic utterances, which always point beyond conceptualization, Zeami writes: Forget the details of a play in order to see the entirety. Then forget the play itself, and consider the actor. Next, forget the actor himself and observe his spirit. Finally, forget his spirit; and the essence of the Noh will be manifest.

And so the lovely woman approaches, sliding silently across the stage, the ancient mask of her face shining warmly like ivory. She is *not* a woman — not only because she is a man but also because she is inhuman: perfect grace and womanhood itself. Slowly, slowly she inclines her head, and her face alters expression an infinity of times, each expression feminine, tranquilly lovely, and alien to the faces of any of the living women I have ever known. Who is she, but the true flower herself? I cannot tire of her, perhaps because I cannot keep her. She gazes through me, into the spirit world; she sings in a deep old man's voice. How beautiful is she to me precisely? With his customary flair for subcategorization, Zeami offers nine levels of beauty. Lowest of all is *the way of crudeness and leadenness.* I can understand that; I can grasp all of the lowest three levels, and even the middle ones, but of the highest three levels, each of which is associated with its own flower, I can comprehend only the third, and my comprehension, like my admiration for this woman on the Noh stage who is still more transient than I but whose face may still hover above a stage centuries from now, is wordless. Never mind the highest level; I am too small to *see* its beauty, let alone describe it. Never mind the next highest. Let me express, with grateful thanks to Zeami, the beauty of this woman from the perspective of the third level, which she might already have gone beyond — a beauty beyond logic, as beauty must surely be: *"The art of the flower of tranquility.* Piling up snow in a silver bowl."

5:

# The Dragons of Kasuga

*Texts, Places, Histories, Masks*

Then out comes the masked actor, silent against this spring night's birdsong. His wife, the *tsure*, knows all too well that he was not abducted by the enemy but accomplished the glorious act of suicide. In short, he betrayed her. So she attempts to return to him the red-wrapped bundle on the white fan — a lock of hair he's bequeathed her. Her rejection embitters his ghost. And they fall to blaming one another, the salaryman beside me sleeping through it all, until the inevitable reconciliation allows the dead warrior to become a Buddha. Thus the plot of the eponymous "Kiyotsune." The wrinkle between the flutist's eyes as he blows, the chorus's chrysanthemum-in-diamond kimonos, the way the shoulder-drummer strikes the base of his instrument with his palm, may be less "important" than the plot, but one can experience them, as do I, without comprehending a word. Kiyotsune* turns

---

*Played by Kongo Hisanori, *circa* 2005.

around. He is so wide without depth, like a beetle, that his rotation is one with a fan's supernatural revolutions in a geisha's hand. From behind we see how the kneeling Noh actor slowly paddles himself about with his white-stockinged foot, but even that motion is eerily perfect.

What would it mean to truly "understand" Noh? Presumably that would entail mastering not only the interrelated texts, places and events in a play's epoch, but also the refinements and allusions of the centuries between that play's composition and today's performance.* Noh actors tell me that a mask grows more alive with age. The same must be true for a play. Does the thing itself "gain character," or is it our collective experience and appreciation that grow to "characterize" the thing? The answer depends on whether we objectify what we perceive or the lens perceiving it.

Once upon a time — in 1203, to be exact — the monk whom we now call the Venerable Myoe received visions of the god of Kasuga Shrine, a place whose present day white paper prayer-curlings on vermilion latticework, wet pavingstones, forests of stone lanterns and overarching trees may offer some equivalent of its thirteenth-century incarnation; but Kasuga must have diminished, relatively speaking; for the neighboring temple of Kofuku-ji, whose god adopted a dragon's form as one of his attributes, gradually devoured more and more of the legend for itself; and when the unknown author, who could have been Zeami's son-in-law Komparu Zenchiku, wrote the Noh drama "Kasuga ryujin," which translates as "The Kasuga Dragon-God," the Venerable Myoe's visions scarcely resembled their originals, which, by the way, had been facilitated by a female medium whose body emitted divine fragrance. The Dragon Girl's kimono-sleeves pass across the ocean; the Eight Great Dragon Kings bow their crowns to her. There is now a Dragon God Noh mask, a *kurohige*, employed in such plays as "Kasuga ryujin." "The face is long, the chin protrudes and the tongue is visible in the widely opened mouth. The

*Since this book has to do particularly with feminine beauty, my textual analysis of Noh need not attempt profundity to such an extent as would embarrass my mediocrity. All the same, just as to know the beauty of a woman is not only and sometimes not ever to know her nude, but yet to know her pretty clothes and charming artifices, her ways of speaking and of thought, the virtues of her heart, her tastes and whims, and not least her relatives, so when kissing the Noh mask it is all the more delicious to have a sense of its allusions and antecedents.

slanting eyebrows and moustache are delineated in black." Kofuku-ji had aggrandized itself through its dragons, invading Kasuga's story. And why not? After all, it was older and more prestigious than Kasuga. In its sap-lingdom, Kasuga Shrine's eight-hundred-year-old cedar might have wit-nessed different events than this; such are time's customary corruptions. "No doubt the Dragon God of the play . . . is continuous with the Kasuga deity proper . . ." grants the play's translator. "But although dragons are not absent from Kasuga lore, nothing in this lore suggests that the deity could actually star in a play in dragon form."

In this play, Kasuga recalls Kofuku-ji.

(How does it do so? Why, in its own indirectly Noh fashion, of course! It mentions the Venerable Gedatsu of Kasagi, a pre-eminent Kofuku-ji monk;* it refers to the Seven Great Temples of Nara, most of which figure in Noh plays and one of which, Kofuku-ji, is supposed to be supreme. We might also note that Zeami's Noh troupe were one of several affiliated with both Kasuga and Kofuku-ji.)

Behind Kasuga's sliding screens of paper and latticework, within rectangular tatami-matted rooms overhung by tassels, the chantings of monks tell their own stories, as does the sad back of the woman who prays motionless, slowly bows, then returns to her frozen kneeling. A greyrobed priest with a peaked cap seats himself on a mat with his back to us outside, and begins to chant; to my foreign ears his lilting male cadences resemble those of a Noh song although they are more rapid, less trained, less musical, and he is not reciting but reading. Kasuga is itself — indeed, so perfectly as to be one of merely two shrines which Zeami specifically mentions before remarking of Noh: "One must not permit this art to stray from its original refined elegance." The other shrine referred to is Hi-e. But Noh has joined in eternal marriage Kasuga not to Hi-e but to Kofuku-ji, where on a late spring night just after the fall of the cherry blossoms I sit watching a Takigi-Noh performance of "Kiyotsune." Although torchlight Noh plays now take place in more than two hundred sites in Japan, they say that it was here at Kofuku-ji that

---

*He stars briefly in another classic, *The Taiheiki*, which ascribes to his virtue the power to see his enemy, a twelve-headed sky giant borne by eight dragons. And so the mansion of Noh has opened unto us one more textual room.

the tradition began* eleven hundred and thirty years ago as I write —
nearly five centuries before Zeami. The Noh stage evolved from the paper
which used to be laid down upon the grass. If moisture passed through
fewer than three sheets, performance was permitted. Takigi-Noh events
originally lasted for seven days, and forty-nine Noh dramas were accomplished on one such occasion. Of course they were speedier then.

## KIYOTSUNE'S FACE

Very close by, the temple bell sounds tinnily. Another mask comes to life,
incarnated in a blue-grey pillbox hat, long hair and a blue-grey kimono.
Turning, it becomes an old ivory profile against the summery trees. The
black teeth, moustache and frozen fan are all beautiful. A bus passes
behind the temple wall; the foliage falls still; paper knots hang limp
from the ropes. And Kiyotsune is *dead*, his mask staring and gaping,
its expression somewhere between despairing and ecstatic. What *is* that
expression, exactly? I once asked Mr. Kanze Hideo the same question I
so often asked others, namely, why it was that the faces of woman-masks
differed from the faces of living women, and he replied: "Particularly
the female masks, if you make them with much expression of joy or sorrow, you can express only that one emotion in performance. So you must
express the joy or sorrow only in the gestures. Of course a living person
makes different expressions! With a mask, using the *same* expression you
can convey different emotions."

Mr. Kanze is dead now. He died but lately as I write. He was never
as warm to me as Mr. Umewaka; on the one occasion he allowed me to
interview him, he seemed guarded and harassed, so that I felt a trifle
ashamed. The mood of his performances was more gnarled than Mr.
Umewaka's, and when I watched him on stage, my aesthetic pleasure
partook of an awe whose colors balanced one another to near invisibility;
while in Mr. Umewaka's case, the experience, by no means inferior or

---

*Meanwhile, Fenollosa writes: "In the fifteenth century after Christ, the Japanese drama
arose out of religious rites practised in the festivals of the Shinto gods, chiefly the Shinto
god of the Kasuga temple at Nara."

less "subtle," was iridescent. One man's art budded as if from an ancient pine; the other's was greener, as if Keith Jarrett had replaced Tatyana Nikolayevna in playing Shostakovich's preludes and fugues on the piano. Now the ancient pine is dead. Someday Mr. Umewaka and I will also be dead, like Kiyotsune, whose mask will be reanimated by an actor whom Mr. Umewaka or Mr. Kanze might have taught. That unknown actor's Noh will remain Zeami's, and his, and theirs. And the expression of his mask will be nameless.

Kiyotsune swings his kimono sleeve around and it suddenly, naturally unfurls. It is shorter than a geisha's. The stage creaks, unfortunately. Somebody coughs. Then in sudden darts of the head the mask comes once more alive against the darkening foliage. The staff flashes out; the fan curls.

Regardless of its textual component, Noh is ultimately indescribable, like sexual ecstasy; what consoles me for my failure of language is the fact that so is everything else. Moreover, Noh *aspires* to indescribability. Beautiful mysteriousness, shot through with supernatural or sacred beyondness, possesses a name: *yugen*. Zeami informs us that this is the highest principle of his art. The actor must be simultaneously emotive and unostentatious. When he portrays a demon, his body may writhe fearsomely but his feet must glide gently. In all things he understates himself with the nuanced mildness of some bygone (and probably fictitious) noble of the Heian court. Such are *yugen*'s prerequisites, but expressing them correctly can take a lifetime, as can appreciating them. Of Noh's nine stages of excellence, the highest of the middle three is *the flower of truth.* "It is superior to the art of versatility and exactness," writes Zeami, "and is already a first step toward the acquisition of the flowers of the art." In short, even here we have gone beyond expressiveness! What comes next? The lowest of the three supreme stages is *the flower of stillness.*\* Zeami likens this, we now know, to the pure white light of snow piled in a silver bowl. What does this "mean"? What *can* it mean?† If I could rush this

---

\*In the previous chapter, I quoted another translator's phrase, "flower of tranquility," in order to remind myself of the folly of grasping for exact equivalents.

†One English-language compilation presumes that the bowl must be oxidized, since then its hue would bear "the mysterious beauty of stillness."

little book to the highest of the three stages, I certainly would, but what if the mask of *yugen* can never be kissed? What if *distance* will always remain essential? Doesn't snow melt in the mouth?

Whatever *yugen* may be, its very delicacy might partake of indestructibility. I admit that Takigi-Noh sharply distinguishes itself from indoor, electric-lit Noh; and in his classic essay "In Praise of Shadows," the great Tanizaki, devotee of aestheticism, eroticism and sadomasochism, insists that Japanese lacquerware was not meant to be viewed under Thomas Edison's glaring radiance, that Japanese rooms look plain only when darkness's pretty mysteries have been swept away like cobwebs, that the gilding of a priest's robes grows garish under any luminescence more powerful than candle light or firelight. "Whenever I attend the No," he pursues this topic, "I am impressed that on no other occasion is the beauty of the Japanese complexion set off to such advantage — the brownish skin with a flush of red that is so uniquely Japanese, the face like old ivory tinged with yellow." What about when the actor is masked? Well, his neck and hands can still be seen. At a performance of "Kotei," Kongo Iwao impersonated the tragic Lady Yang,* "and I shall never forget the beauty of his hands showing ever so slightly from beneath his sleeves." And Tanizaki elaborates for another page, finally warning what disastrous vulgarity would ensue should floodlights violate the Noh stage as had already occurred in Kabuki. "It is an essential condition of the No that the stage be left in the darkness in which it has stood since antiquity." Most of the Noh performances I have attended took place at a remove from this darkness. Was their beauty all vulgar, then? Is my understanding deficient, that I can't dismiss them? Or is my capacity, or this world itself, so debased that *yugen* needs but to exist in a half-dead state in order to successfully hover above and beyond me? Do they present my blindness with an aluminum bowl of white sand? Even should this be so, the beyondness of *yugen* survives.

The trees begin to move behind Kiyotsune, and I remember a passage from "Kasuga ryujin": When the Venerable Myoe first arrived at Kasuga, the trees and grasses bowed down before him.

---

*Who gets her own chapter below, p. 166.

A great many of Noh's plots derive from *The Tale of Genji, The Tale of the Heike* and *The Tales of Ise.* It's in Kasuga that the very first story-and-poem of *The Tales of Ise* occurs: A young man who goes hawking on his estate there gets enraptured by a pair of "very elegant sisters" whom he spies through a fence. He cuts off his purple sleeve, writes a verse expressing the turmoil of his heart, and has his attendant convey these tokens in. The extremely sad Noh play "Matsukaze" is said to have originated from this episode, since it's about two saltmaking sisters loved by a courtier in his exile, and left alone by his recall and death. But "Matsukaze" is likewise indebted to *The Tale of Genji,* for the courtier and Genji are both exiled to this same spot, the Suma seashore; and Genji's impression of the ocean waves calls for comparison with the courtier's poem. At the end of his exile, Genji's desires draw him into an affair with a lady from Akashi, whom he impregnates. Once his position in the capital has been restored, he sends for his mistress and daughter, but finds little time for them. Accordingly, the lady makes a sad reference to the wind in the pine trees, a phrase whose Japanese equivalent, and the title of this chapter concerning her, is *matsukaze.*

Indeed, *The Tale of Genji* offers several two-sister love triangles. In an album of illustrations from the Muromachi period,[*] we gaze down through clouds of pure gold into a tassel-hung room of green tatami mats on which sits Genji in his elegantly spread kimono of diamonds and quadruple dots, equidistant from Reikeiden and her younger sister Hanachirusato, whose long inky tresses sweep across their own more flamboyant clothes. Soon his enemies will get him expelled to Suma, and this double love will glimmer down into admitted ephemerality. The sisters will be left behind in the capital — a sort of reverse prefiguration of the situation of the Noh play "Matsukaze." Years after the death of Genji, another

---

[*]One commentator opines that "the nostalgia for the life of the Court" of the Heian period, when *Genji* was written, "was the real keynote of the renaissance in the Muromachi period. But because this past splendor could no longer be recaptured in the world of reality, the memory was transmuted into a longing for things eternal and imperishable, with profound metaphysical results in the world of ideas."

illustration from the album shows his supposed son Kaoru (actually the offspring of Genji's wife and his best friend's son), dressed in a red flower-patterned cloak and bluish kimono, peering through a bamboo gate and beneath a cloud of gold into a raised house whose blind has been partially raised for moon-viewing, so that Kaoru can spy out four longhaired beauties whose respective kimonos depict spiderwebs, hexagons, sanddollar-like octagons, and triangles whose internal parallel lines alternate at right angles; two of these girls presumably are maids, and the other two are Big Princess and Middle Princess — sisters, of course. Recapitulating *The Tales of Ise*, Kaoru writes an elegantly sorrowful verse and has a servant bring them in . . .

And so a visit to Kasuga takes us not only to Kofuku-ji (and thence to a nineteenth-century Hokusai woodblock drawing), but also to Suma, and, through Suma, to Kyoto and Uji — the places depicted in the two Muromachi illustrations. In "Hanago," the love-crazed prostitute Lady Han recites an old verse about Kasuga moor.

A millennium after Lady Murasaki completed her masterpiece, I saw geishas dance the Yukigeshiki Uji no Ukifune, which is to say the Snow Scene in Uji from the *Tale of Genji*. And this dance was an allusion to and partial resume of "Matzukase." Just as when the flute ascends in two hands from the hidden folds of the flutist's kimono, so Noh's references arise unpredictably out of texts.* An old man swirls his fan in the firelight, whose reflections crawl on his forehead. The fan passes from gold to silver depending on its angle. Sometimes the two sisters are Matsuzake and Murasame, sometimes Reikeiden and Hanachirusato, Big Princess and Middle Princess, or the unnamed pair who excite the anonymous protagonist of *The Tales of Ise*. Our spirits wander through firelight and embroidery.


## THE TORN SPIDERWEB

At one time this game was not just for aesthetes, but for all educated people (in other words, for aesthetes). In 1271, a proposal that the fourteen-

---

*Most Noh plays contain such a *honzetsu* or "seed." For instance, the sad love story "Izutsu" is based on three chapters from *The Tales of Ise*.

GEISHA FESTIVAL DANCE, PONTO-CHO, KYOTO.

year-old Lady Nijo become the Emperor's concubine gets couched in a metaphor from *The Tales of Ise*. She knows the reference. And in fact, this interesting, accomplished and ultimately very sad person quotes constantly in her memoir from *The Tale of Genji*. (In her time the sacred tree of Kasuga Shrine was brought to the capital, in order to overawe the mighty and thereby to influence policy. Fleeing an unhappy attachment, she refreshed herself with Kasuga's rainy air and moss-paths walled by stone lanterns, but her lover dreamed where she was, and got her.) Several centuries earlier, another Emperor amuses himself by testing his concubine on the twenty volumes of the *Kokin Shu* poems. Perhaps because her father desperately hires the chanting of sutras for her in one temple after the next, or else because she has an impressive memory, the lady, enduring the Emperor's resentful amazement, completes the ordeal without a single error.

In Heian times, this web of allusions must have been at least theoretically coherent and manageable. Arthur Waley believes it to have been sufficiently limited that an illiterate would have known much of its weft from popular songs. One measure of a society's degree of refinement and "culture" may well be the number of references its people share in common.

"In Zeami's day," I asked Mr. Umewaka, who was sitting before a white paper screen, "were all the conventions understood by the general public?"

"I think so," he said.

"And now?"

"Maybe it was easier then."

The difficulty of an undertaking need not increase its value. However, if, as Fenollosa claims and I believe, the alteration of language involves the sedimentation of layers of metaphor upon fundamental relationships ("a nerve, a wire, a roadway, and a clearing-house are only varying channels which communication forces for itself"), then to undertake an excavation beneath the calcified usages upon which any given generation thoughtlessly treads offers the hope of revelation. "The chief work of literary men in dealing with language, and of poets especially, lies in feeling back along the ancient lines of advance." Accordingly, as Noh grows and grows into a constellated super-text, our journeys from star to star grow likewise, from leaps into quests.

So the game goes on. In 1825, the woodcut artist Utagawa Kunimori I makes erotic parodies of both the Suma and the Matsukaze parts of *Genji*. Why not? Isn't frivolity a virtue when we play upon this floating world? In a subsequent century, the Nobel Prize winner and soon-to-be kidnapper-suicide Mishima Yukio recasts several Noh plays in contemporary settings. And as the new allusions swirl down, century by century, the old plays themselves begin to alter.

If Zeami could be resurrected, he might take issue not only with the increased length but also with other alterations of his plays. The scholar Hare, who knows infinitely more about such matters than I, finds it "safe" to say that "the *shite*'s parts are more reliable than the *waki*'s, and that passages in congruent song are more reliable than those in noncongruent song, which are in turn more reliable than spoken passages." (Regarding the instrumentation and the dance choreography less can be said.) About the *Genji*-based play "Aoi-no-Ue" a performance guide advises that the version "Zeami experienced must have been more visually explanatory and possibly centered on *yugen*, while the revisions focus more on Rokujo's jealousy." Moreover, once upon a time Rokujo's robe was green. Now it is black and grey.

Zeami advises that if a Noh play has to do with a place, "then you should take lines from well-known poems about the place, in Chinese or Japanese, and write them into concentrated points . . . In addition to this, you should work distinguished sayings and well-known expressions into the *shite*'s language." To me, of course, those sayings and expressions will never be well-known. But in some regards I am richer than Zeami and Lady Nijo. Amidst my treasures I possess, for instance, some reproductions of Hokusai, whom those two never saw. I also prize my foreignness, thanks to which Noh, not to mention Japan, can never be mastered by me. I am accordingly spared much recognition of *triteness*. The pretension that snowflakes can be cherry blossoms and *vice versa* begins to irritate me in its knowing repetitions across eras and dynasties.* Wouldn't I be better off if I avoided getting annoyed? Translating the eleventh-century *Pillow Book of Sei Shonagon*, Ivan Morris sets out to escape the "false exoticism that can arise from identifying the Emperor's residence, for example, as 'the Pure and Fresh Palace.'" I could not disagree more.

So I am ignorant. So I have lost much. No matter. Malraux writes: "All that remains of Aeschylus is his genius."

---

*Thus my barbarian's approach to the concept of *hon'i*, the decorum appropriate to the expression of a given subject — very relevant to Noh, obviously, or to a geisha's multi-step procedure for opening a sliding door. On the subject of cherry blossoms, poets had to "express impatience in waiting for their blooming, delight in their beauty, and distress in their falling." This goes far to explain why it is in Mr. Umewaka's words "very controversial" if a theater paints a young instead of an old pine tree on the mirror-board.

6:

# Sunshine at Midnight

*An Interview with Mr. Mikata Shizuka*

B ut in spite of these lovely textual landscapes, which are fully as rich as a Kyoto garden, it must be repeated: The text, beautiful although it often is, remains of limited importance in comparison to Noh's wordless lovelinesses. The mask is most important always — the *living* mask.

The day after he gave a spectacular performance of the warrior play "Michimori," I asked Mr. Mikata Shizuka the following question: "In the essay 'Kyui,' Zeami discusses the top three levels of Noh: flower of peerless charm, flower of profundity and flower of tranquility. Could you please explain in your own words how spectators and actors can perceive and distinguish these three levels and what they mean?"

"For the spectators to appreciate them," he said, "the actor must be in that stage already. Otherwise it does not look like that, because he has not achieved that level. Even a good audience who looks at a deficient actor cannot see it. The actor who is able to achieve that level, if he acts with the right timing and tension, and if the other actors' *ki* has been unified with the surrounding air including the audience, only then will there be peerless charm."

(Proust must have been referring to this same phenomenon when he described Madame Berma in the title role of *Phèdre*: "Certain transcendent realities emit all around them a sort of radiation to which the crowd is sensitive.")

"For a great actor, how often can this take place?" I asked Mr. Mikata.

"It is difficult," he said. "If he feels the intention, and wants to feel this way or that way, and everything goes well, of course, then he can achieve this state . . ."

All I took from this was: *It is difficult.*

"What do you think Zeami means when he speaks of snow in a silver bowl?"

"Because snow does not have any noise, the noise of no noise, and silver rather than gold is very like Noh. That indicates the tranquility."*

"In the second highest level, when there is no snow on Fuji because it is not just high but also deep, what does that mean?"

"I cannot imagine clearly," he said. "But one thing is that Fuji is higher than a cloud, and then it does not snow. It is just stable, just itself."

"And in the highest level, the sun on Silla?"

"You can imagine the temperature and the coldness of snow in a silver bowl. But you don't feel any sound there, no smell there, so you *cannot* imagine really. As a picture it looks pretty and it is easy to imagine, but peerless charm is an expression to try to express what each member of the audience has inside himself or herself. Tranquility, profundity

---

*Noh was influenced by Tendai Buddhism, some of which can be traced back to Ch'an in China. Among the treasures of Ch'an teachings we find *The Blue Cliff Record*, whose preface is dated 1128. I quote that book's Thirteenth Case in full: "A monk asked Pa Ling, 'What is the school of Kanadevi?' Pa Ling said: 'Piling up snow in a silver bowl.'" The pointer to the case reads in part: "When snow covers the white flowers, it's hard to distinguish the outlines. Its coldness is as cold as snow and ice; its fineness is as fine as rice powder. Its depths are hard for even a Buddha's eye to peer into . . ."

and peerless charm, these refer to some aura that the actor can naturally exude without doing anything. But the audience's ability to appreciate and receive is definitely necessary."

And still I did not know what the sun on Silla would entail. Still I could not define the beauty of women.

# 7:

# Perfect Faces

*Maiden, Mask, Geisha, Wife, Princess*

Someone once said that black hair is a *shunga* [erotic picture]. If our models were dressed, the aesthetic feeling would vary from age to age. However, the beauty of a fairskinned woman, and of a woman's black hair, are universal. Thus the two major elements of eternal feminine beauty. In particular, the black hair of naked women offers texture and volume, and also expresses the flowing affection and subtleties inside the woman.

MASAYUKI TOMITA, PAPER
CUTOUT ARTIST, 1988

Why do I want to kiss the *zo-onna*? Because she is a woman and I am a man.

Why do I believe in her? She is nothing but a wooden face; therefore, for me to believe in her, she must be a *perfect* face.

And what makes for a perfect face? Edo period prints of beautiful women and young boy-actors look much the same. At times (infrequently, to be sure) Noh actors employ a mask of one gender for a role of the other. Feminine beauty is not so easy to define.

All the same, Japanese art of any given period can express it explicitly and consistently, even to the point of stereotype.* To be sure, in the various traditions called Euro-American we also can meet with this or that artist who devotes himself to representing the type that he desires: Just as the twentieth-century Parisian sculptures of Maillol glorify women (and often *a* woman: Dina Vierny) sporting lushly slablike thighs, so in the beautiful-lady woodblocks (*bijin-ga*) of the early *ukiyo-e* master Kaigetsu one very frequently sees a woman standing in a particular way, using both hands to comb her hair. But what defines the face of a Kaigetsu beauty? Would she be equally appreciated by a tenth-century Heian courtier and a twenty-first-century corporation president?

Noh mask, *ukiyo-e* lady, geisha — these three points upon the arc will occupy much of this book's investigation. Divergent as they are, they all partake of a certain kind of radiance, which over the years has become as preciously familiar to me as the blue streetlight glowing up into my coffin-hotel in Shinagawa. What is it? In the Ukiyo-e Museum in Tokyo you can see, for instance, chrysanthemums and birds; the fishes are simultaneously representational and stylized, wide-eyed and aware, frozen in an upward or downward lunge through a blankness which sometimes shades into blue; a prawn rises up behind a pale pink bream which is swimming across a blue bonito in an aquarium whose borders are blue paper imprinted with white birds. Can we say any more of all this than that it is "Japanese"?

## "LIKE A JEWELED HAIRPIN"

Let us begin with the black teeth. A nineteenth-century American (one of Commodore Perry's men) appraised them without undue enthusiasm: "As their 'ruby' lips parted in smiling graciously, they displayed a row of

---

*The Heian aesthetic both derives and diverges from Chinese sources. Among the latter we find the eighth-century joy girl Chao Luan-Luan writing encomia of scarlet-nailed fingers as narrow as new-peeled onions; of teeth like white melon seeds and lips like pomegranate blossoms; of willow-leaf eyebrows, of cool, creamy soft breasts whose nipples resemble "the pegs of a jade inlaid harp." "Her poems were a common type," remarks the translator, "a sort of advertising copy in praise of the parts of a woman's body, written for courtesans and prostitutes." Hence she ought to be an authority on feminine beauty; her clients put their money where her mouth was. Among the items on her list, only the

black teeth, set in horribly corroded gums. The married women of Japan enjoy the exclusive privilege of dyeing their teeth . . ."*

Five and a half centuries earlier, a famous tale immortalized the eccentric young lady who in spite of her noble blood and upbringing admired snails, insects and other such creatures; moreover, she refused to blacken her teeth! People said, "Her eyebrows look like furry caterpillars, all right, but her bare teeth you would think have been skinned." The ugliness of black teeth or white ones, like that of the unbound Chinese lady's foot, or the uncircumcised Sudanese clitoris, definitely varies by time and place. I have been educated by my dentist to consider black teeth a sign of decay. One Filipina prostitute of my acquaintance, possessor of what could politely be referred to as a "midnight smile," found her business suffering on their account. I took her to get all her top teeth pulled (anesthetic unavailable, I am sad to say, but this did not deter the patient), after which plastic teeth were installed, and Virgie expressed satisfaction. On the same planet where she allures men with her new white smile, I open a book, and look in on court ladies blackening their teeth for the New Year's banquet of 1025.

Hence the blackened teeth of a Noh mask, which even nowadays may occasionally be emulated by a geisha in her last month of maikodom.

Tanizaki, in whom I see myself because he too embraces the no-longer-existent, offers a characteristic theory about the old practice: "Might it not have been an attempt to push everything except the face into the dark? In the past this was sufficient. For a woman who lived in the dark it was enough if she had a faint, white face — a full body was unnecessary."

A face alone, with even her teeth dulled down into darkness, is this not a mask?

But what, if anything, does a lovely mask "represent"?

"Like a jeweled hairpin, / a vision of her alone / pierces my sight more

---

willow-leaf eyebrows insist on being noticed in the Japanese *Manyoshu*'s court poetry. The white teeth of Chinese pulchritude certainly do not find their match in the *Manyoshu*. If I can visualize more attributes of the Chinese than the Japanese ideal, perhaps both Chinese and Japanese would have wanted it that way.

*For just this reason, in the pornographic *shunga* woodcuts of the period, the color of a woman's teeth provides a cue as to whether or not her depicted liaison is adulterous.

and more." Thus runs a poem in *The Tales of Ise*. I would have supposed that any vision sufficiently noteworthy to pierce my sight must require *specificity*. An Italian Renaissance poet might spell out the beauties of the cheek. But *The Tales of Ise*, which concern themselves mainly with romantic assignations, many of which bear voyeuristic overtones, say no more of the women (or men) involved than that they come from this or that social station, or are old or young. The sole physical description of any lady in the *Tales* is this: One or two boils erupt on an unnamed someone's body, so she declines to meet her lover. She shrinks from being imperfect before him, withdrawing into the darkness forever.

Some years on in this dreamy epoch, maybe sixty, perhaps two hundred, Lady Murasaki writes in her diary a line that epitomizes feminine beauty in the Heian period: "The moon was so bright that I was embarrassed to be seen and knew not where to hide."

For her, the beauty of a lady's face resides most of all in the hair, which in the Japanese case is darkness reified into a waterfall; much of the time Murasaki hides herself behind the ornate fan she bears for that particular purpose, so that her garments define her still more than her face; certain color combinations are elegant, others shockingly incorrect. In the picture scrolls and sometimes at Noh plays I feel almost exhausted by the detail of so many kimonos, their lovelinesses' intricacies beyond not merely my powers of recall but even my ability to see them entire; occasionally a garment may bear a simple, repetitive geometry, like the one which alternates triangles of beautifully tarnished gold with triangles of dark purple; but more often the effect is to understate any human face above it into a pale oval. This must have been the intention. Here is Murasaki's description of Lady Dainagon: "Her hair falls just about three inches past her heels and is so luxuriant and kept so beautifully trimmed there is hardly anyone to match her for elegance." Miya no Naishi: "The contrast between her pale skin and her black hair sets her apart from the rest."

What is blackness? Ms. Nakamura left white specks in the black hair of her Noh masks, remarking: "If we make it solid black it looks strange." — To me it was *all* strange.

In any case, the value set on black hair endures. In the *bijin-ga* woodcuts of the eighteenth and nineteenth centuries, we find depictions of courtesans whose black hair is studded with ornamental picks. Ichirakutei

Eisui's print of "The Courtesan Karakoto of the Chojiyu House" shows its subject's heavy bun of hair pierced with pale hairpins like wheelspokes, her hair shaved or at least lighter at the temples. Meanwhile, in the poems of the *Manyoshu*, or *Collection for a Myriad Ages*, whose contents go back to the eighth century and before, the stock epithet for a lovely maiden's hair is "as black as the bowels of a mud snail." One poem deserves to be quoted at greater length, since it spells out the attributes of loveliness:

> Her tresses black as a mud-snail's bowels,
> The way she wears those fluttering yu-ribbons,
> The way she wears her Yamato boxwood comb,
> That beauteous maid, — my love.

Aside from her hair, whose length and color resist uniqueness, our only vision of this girl consists of her accoutrements. She might as well be a mannequin — or a mask. Why not? *Yu* ribbons can stand in the girl just as well as a jeweled hairpin. The longer I have loved women, the more deeply and sincerely I love them. And as I study Noh's props and as I watch the women I love ageing, suffering that loss which some of them anxiously, bitterly, defiantly, despairingly or coolly fight with makeup, creams, wigs, the more I have learned to love the things associated with women, for instance a ribbon blowing in the hair. In the *Manyoshu* the lovely woman is often compared to a mirror; and the seashore of Osaka Port recalls to a lonely poet-husband's mind the mirror on a certain girl's comb-case.

Other poems in that famous collection are less understated. One poet informs us: "When I visited the abyss of Tamashima, I happened to meet some girls fishing. Their flowery faces and radiant forms were beyond compare. Their eye-brows were like tender willow leaves and their cheeks were like peach flowers." "On the Death of an Uneme from Tsu, Kibi Province" goes so far as to describe a girl's "soft white arm"; and the most concrete encomium of all, "Of the Maiden Tamana at Suee of Province of Kazusa," lets it be known that its heroine was "broad of breast," wasp-waisted and radiant-faced — an irresistible combination, apparently, for "charmed were all men." Lady Otomo of Sakanoe praises her absent daughter's "lovely eyebrows / Curving like the far-off waves," and "the young moon afar" reminds another poet of "the painted eyebrows / Of her whom only once I saw."

But I repeat: The jeweled hairpin is not merely metonymic for the woman; by the preference of the time, it hides her. Beauty wants to mask itself. And while Murasaki takes occasional note of the personal charms of her intimates — the delicate shape of Lady Saisho's forehead and the loveliness of her blush, the "translucent delicacy" of Her Majesty's complexion shortly after giving birth — the picture a reader obtains is never by my standards complete. "The shapes and faces" of court ladies "reflecting the moonlight in the garden with its white sand were most intriguing." This aesthetic feels not overdistant from the aphorism in Zeami's treatise *Sando*: "As long as the character is mysteriously beautiful, whatever is done should be interesting." Sometimes Murasaki's companions flirt a trifle with the men, or even make love with them, but they prefer to do so when they think they will not be recognized later. Call it understatement; call it discretion. A man taps on the door with a single finger, and the woman recognizes him; whether or not she lets him enter, she replies with a faint swish of her fan. As for her sisters, lurking gorgeously behind screens and fans, they are mysterious not only thanks to their various veils, but also on account of their close resemblance to each other. I call to mind the women depicted in the Tokugawa Museum's Genji Picture-Scroll, snow-faced against gold, beige, lavender and turquoise: One peeps out of the gap she has made in a sliding door, her white hand still on its edge so that she can close it upon anyone's approach; another half-hides her chin in the flow of her kimono; a third gazes downward. Their oval, high-eyebrowed faces have been understated into near sameness.* And

---

*The scrolls employ the so-called *hikime kagibana* technique of drawing faces. First and foremost, features are rendered obliquely rather than frontally. The outline of a female face is *urizane-gata* (winter melon shaped), plumpening from eyes to cheeks. The forehead is lofty, the long hair parted in front and layered on the shoulder. A few strands pass across the edge of an eye. Eyebrows are drawn straight and long in many lines, with the ends shaded off. Eyebrows and eyes are considerably separated and straight and slanted. "The nose is drawn only as a little '*ku*' (resembles a "<"), with no more detail than that. The mouth is a small red dot with a slight black ink line. This is accordingly called the (small mouth). The chin is also small. If the face is drawn from the side, we see only an eye brow and an edge of the eye." We are informed that the *hikime kagibana* face is calm, emotionless. "It seems to be understood that showing big emotions are ugly. Elegance

indeed, one passage of Murasaki's diary describes a formal function in the following approving terms: "Just as in a beautiful example of a Japanese scroll, you could hardly tell them apart. The only difference you could detect was between the older women and the younger ones," and that once again on account of the hair.

If we could have glimpsed Murasaki in her formal beauty, we would have seen someone with depilated eyebrows replaced by painted ones higher up, someone with black hair, black teeth and a white-powdered face. But she would not have been happy if we had glimpsed her, let alone *seen* her. In her *Tale of Genji*, the Shining Prince has relations with many a woman whom he cannot see. Invisibility becomes still more pronounced for *The Taiheiki*'s fourteenth-century heroines, and we saw it associated with Tanizaki's mother's epoch. Needless to say, the Japanese minted a term for this: *miekakure*, the tantalizing glimpse.

In this context, let us now revisit another term. Defining "the basic form of *yugen*" in his manuscript *Nikyoku santai ningyozu*, on a sheet alongside a drawing of a longhaired naked woman with her face bowed and her hand between her thighs, Zeami writes: "Make your sensibility the basis of your acting and reject any show of strength." Here is the mystery of the beautiful mask: It expresses itself without showing itself. It is the hairpin, not the face; the face, not the body; the voice behind the screen; the carved block of cypress-wood. Who was Lady Murasaki? I am acquainted with her a little; I've experienced her *yugen*, because I have read and loved *The Tale of Genji*. But if I try to imagine her, I see her only as she would have wanted me to: a calligraphic ink drawing.

Such is certainly not the case for the beautiful woman with the man inside her, dancing for all of us on the Noh stage. Once upon a time, perhaps, there was a girl after whose face a specific *ko-omote* had been modeled. — Why not suppose so? It is rumored that the sixteenth-century priest Himi Munetada carved a certain *ryo-no-onna* after the sunken face of a woman who had perished of cold and hunger.) Surely both of these ladies would have been ashamed to let us stare at likenesses of their naked faces. And yet we do, and those faces appear to live. Still they retain their secrecy — because they are masks.

and silence comprise the beauty of the *Tale of Genji*."

The following seventeenth-century description exposes the perfect face in greater specificity: "A courtesan shaves her eyebrows, paints heavily above her forehead and eyes without an ink stick, wears her hair in a great Shimada without inserting any wooden support," and shows the nape of her neck in its perfect nudity. (By the way, her buttocks, unlike a Brazilian beauty's, should be "flat as an opened fan.") All the same, each detail of the face is an imposition of a uniform style, the face thus overlaid with indications of its status and availability. Is this anything but another mask? Whenever I see a long line of Nakamura Mitsue's woman-masks, all seeming to half-smile if viewed at the same angle, always presenting the white parting of the black hair, I feel that I have met many sisters, whose black teeth (less age-glossed than those of Mr. Umewaka's much used masks) and protruding under-lips all allure me into reveries of kissing. But their nudity, delicious as it is, lacks most of the power of their embodiment upon the stage, when they will tilt in strange half-smiles, gazing through me from far away. As a certain lover used to whisper into my mouth: "What are you *doing* to me? Oh, what are you doing . . . ?" And then she would close her eyes. I always wondered why she asked that, why she darkened her gaze. Now I think I know.

The poet Kamo no Chomei, who died in 1216, used the following example in explicating "the style of mystery and depth": "A beautiful woman, . . . although she has cause for resentment, does not give vent to her feelings in words, but is only faintly discerned — at night, perhaps — to be in a profoundly distressed condition. The effect . . . is more painful and pathetic than if she had . . . made a point of wringing out her tear-drenched sleeves to one's face . . ." To me this statement recalls the quietly disturbing beauty of a *deigan* mask.

And not quite eight centuries later, on the morning after seeing one of his Takigi-Noh performances, I had the opportunity of interviewing Mr. Kanze in the lobby of his hotel in Kyoto; and asked him to elaborate on this very question:

"In the great novel *Dr. Zhivago* a character states: *It's a good thing when a man is different from your image of him. It shows he isn't a type. If he were, it would be the end of him as a man.* What is your reaction to this from the standpoint of Noh? Is your goal as an actor to express a specific humanity or personality in a role, or to express a type? If you play Yuya, for instance, do you seek to bring to life a specific woman, or a general type of feminine beauty, or something different still?"

"In a role, you have to discover something every time," Mr. Kanze replied. "If you are regarded as a stereotype, even before you perform they will know, so that is meaningless. Everything will fail unless the performer has a new discovery every time."

MR. KANZE HIDEO.

"When Yuya does her flower dance, is that an abstracted dance that expresses a general female role? After all, the choreography never varies— "

"It cannot be general when you perform a person. So you must as I said express new discoveries that the performer himself has seen *just now*."

"What is the difference between female beauty as represented in Noh and the female beauty of real women?"

"They are not different," he insisted. "When you perform, you discover the role's mind and the beauty and try to represent it. It's not that it's different. There's no general beauty in the world. Or you can say that general beauty is not living beauty. If you just collect together beautiful points, that cannot be a human being. The human being has defects as well as beautiful aspects. That is why *general beauty cannot exist.*"*

Could that help to explain the alluring reclusiveness of a Heian court beauty, the triumphant incompleteness of a mask? Could it be the reason that the true flower must perish?

---

*I have read, but do not believe, that "the transsexual's position consists of wanting to be All, all woman, more woman than all women, and representing them all." Transgender women each have their own look. In any event, it is interesting that both Catherine Millot, the psychoanalyst who wrote the quoted words, and Mr. Kanze insist that femininity's general representaion is impossible or fallacious. Based on how I experience prehistoric Venus figurines (see below, p. 260), I cautiously assert that a general beauty can indeed be expressed.

In 1901, when Fenollosa was studying Noh, a lady named Alice Mabel Bacon published a book entitled *Japanese Girls and Women*. The Empress had appeared in public with white teeth more than a quarter-century before. But many specifics of "general beauty" continued to be the same, so that our Occidental lady opined:

> The ideal feminine face must be long and narrow; the forehead high and narrow in the middle, but widening and lowering at the sides, conforming to the outline of the beloved Fuji . . . The hair should be straight and glossy black and absolutely smooth . . . The eyes should be long and narrow, slanting upward at the outer corners; and the eyebrows should be delicate lines, high above the eye itself. The distinctly aquiline nose should be low at the bridge . . . The mouth of an aristocratic Japanese lady must be small, and the lips full and red; the neck . . . should be long and slender . . . The complexion should be . . . a clear ivory-white, with little color in the cheeks.

"That reminds me of *The Tale of Genji*," said my Japanese interpreter when I read it to her more than a century later.

"Would you say that it is accurate?"

"At that time it was correct, but it is way different from what people nowadays think."

"And for you, what is the perfect female face?"

"Like some of the actresses," she said, "although they are not typically Japanese. The eyes are big.* The eyelid has two folds, unlike mine."

A fortyish first-generation Japanese-American immigrant laughed at Alice Mabel Bacon and said: "I totally disagree! That is *so* weird! By today's standard, it's not beautiful face at all. Nowadays, the hair should

---

*Small eyes remain emblematically Japanese outside Japan. (Many Vietnamese women also like them; sometimes they submit to operations to narrow their eyes.) In Nan Ning, China, a woman told me: "Chinese girl beauty is large eye. Japanese girl beauty is in narrow eye." Then she added: "Japanese *ochobo-guchi* woman is obey husband. Chinese woman, in old society they have something the same as Japanese woman, but now more independent."

not be black, but light brown. The eyes should be wide. And some girls have an operation to make the eyes a little bigger. The mouth should be big. I think a longer neck is good; Caucasians have that. I think triangle forehead is still okay. The eyelids should have two folds, like a Western face."

She then said: "My grandmother used to tell me that the beautiful face is long neck and small mouth and long black hair, hair shining blue in the sun . . ."

# Aya Kudo and the *Zo-onna*

*A Porn Model Compared with a Noh Goddess*

S canning into my computer an image of a certain *zo-onna* mask, then likewise capturing the face of the erotic model Aya Kudo, whose never quite nude form graces every page of the glossy hardcover tribute to her entitled *Koi me no rippu*, which is to say *Heavy Love Lipstick*; and rotating her scan nearly forty-five degrees to correct for the fact that in the double-page spread from which I wrested it, the divine Miss Aya was sprawled on her side in a bathing suit, red-lit, with her right hand out before her, palm down like a Sphinx's paw, while her left vanishes in her rich hair in order to better pillow her diagonally inclined head; next resizing the two scans until their eye-to-mouth distances were approximately the same, I became able to make certain comparisons. Never mind the difference between the ivory complexion of the *zo-onna* and Miss Aya's red-and-orange-flushed face; who knows what color the young woman's face *really* is?

Each of these fantasy ladies may be said to have what Tanizaki called "a slender, oval face of the classic melon-seed type, the kind of face you see in ukiyoe woodblock prints," although if they vary with respect to this characteristic, it may be that Aya Kudo possesses what may be nearer to "a face well-rounded in the modern style" (those words were written in 1686). The lips of Aya Kudo are shinier, glossier, wetter and fuller than those of the zo-onna. The width of each mouth is approximately the same. Interestingly, the height from the top of the upper lip to the bottom of the lower is also comparable, but the porn princess's lips appear considerably puffier and fleshier, in part because the zo-onna's upper lip narrows in the center by almost half; moreover, Aya Kudo's lips are parted just enough to show the tiniest glint of two upper teeth, whereas the zo-onna's lips are open and half-smiling in that meditatively melancholy Noh way, allowing us to see a crescent of pure black emptiness alongside the top of the lower lip, crowned by a curving strip of at least four or five bluish-black upper teeth. So the zo-onna's lips are narrower; she can open them to breathe, and, of course, to sing, without taking up more space in doing so than the nearly closed lips of Aya Kudo.

Meanwhile, the Noh mask's distance from lower lip to chin is nearly twice that of Miss Aya's face.

It is a strange exercise to gaze back and forth between the two visages. The zo-onna's features are so perfect that by comparison the short chin of Miss Aya seems almost deformed. And the woman was given the ultimate twenty-first-century accolade for her loveliness: we paid her! — But here I remember another juxtaposition I made, between a waka-onna mask and the bound model in JaponiSMe, whose name I do not know; I decided to match these faces against each other because both were turned slightly downward and to the side (although I admit that the S/M model reveals herself in three-quarter profile while we see the mask nearly head on). In this case the longer chin of the Noh mask makes her almost witchlike in comparison to the sweet young girl with the rope around her neck; the smile of the waka-onna is, as H. P. Lovecraft would say, eldritch, whereas the girl is simply human, lovely and sad, a demure sacrificial victim. The waka-onna's sharply upcurving smile partakes of craft, although as usual her eye-holes gaze at a point between us and her, so that one has no need to feel cautious around her; she cannot even see me; she is engaged with

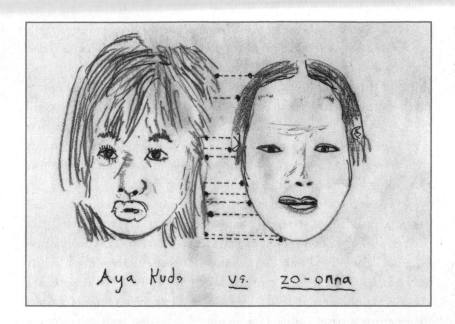

Aya Kudo    vs.    zo-onna

somebody on the other side of the Bridge of Dreams. — So how can I say
that a long chin is superior to a short chin? It is not that the *waka-onna*
is less beautiful than the bondage model. And when I turn back to Aya
Kudo and the *zo-onna*, I find myself similarly at sea. Whose chin is most
beautifully proportionate? Side by side, each undermines the other; alone,
each becomes perfect.

The eyes of Aya Kudo are wide, innocent, little-girlish and slightly
surprised. They gaze upon me candidly. Her parted lips add to the
impression of trusting youthfulness. She seems to be on the verge of offering herself to me. But she and I both know that we will never meet. Her
face, like the *zo-onna*'s, is but an image.

The *zo-onna*'s eyes are longer and much narrower than hers. The pupils,
which of course are really holes, are not centered as are Miss Aya's, but
drawn in slightly closer to the nose. So how can I imagine that the Noh
goddess sees me at all? Like her *waka-onna* sister, like the makeup artist
Yukiko who gazes into my face but not at me as she paints my eyebrows
on, she declines to reach me. She smiles, almost, or perhaps not; yes, with
perfect concentration she gazes at something between herself and me,
something in the black heaven she came from.

The Shinto-derived* crescent-shaped indentations between her eyelids and forehead are as nude as a young girl's vulva, for in approved Heian style she wears her painted black eyebrows (willow-leaves, no doubt) two-thirds of the way up to the parting of her hair, whose inky dullness is much more disciplined than Miss Aya's luxuriant bangs and those slithery locks which frame her head all around. Indeed, the *zo-onna*'s face, which unlike Miss Aya's narrows as it goes upward, is outlined by its three innermost hair-waves, two thin ones within one thick, then comes the darkness of the mask-edge, ready to meet the wig.

In comparison to her rival's, the porn princess's eyebrows almost resemble moustaches, so frankly hairy and corporeal do they seem. Poor Miss Aya belongs to my mortal race! ("Her eyebrows look like furry caterpillars, all right . . .") Please don't accuse me of demeaning her; her beauty is comforting, sweet and not in the least eerie. In her various poses she changes bathing suits and backdrops as rapidly as the cyclings of Tokyo's long narrow vertical brilliant neon signs in the rain, and the colors of the gel lights used to photograph her remind me of the glaring fires of car-eyes smeared on the black pavement, which is as shiny as new rubber boots. Perhaps I've even unknowingly seen her in one of Shinjuku's bright small busy restaurants whose windows are wallpapered with the gilded or jade-shelled windows of skycrapers, white shirts of pedestrians swimming by as the night becomes ever more excitingly foggy, reflections blending with real signs and windows to form mutually translucent facets of a single giant crystal. I rush through the Japanese night, devouring it. Shall I experience the *daburu sabisu*, the double service? Then, as it gets clammier outside and hotter inside with cooking and the perspiration of human beings, the windows of the restaurants mist up, reducing all external shapes and lights to delightful non-definition. And somewhere in that steamy life, Aya Kudo breathes.

As for the *zo-onna*, she sleeps inside of a wooden box, and her waking night is perfect blackness, with three pine trees to guide her way across the bridge from the rainbow curtain. Once upon a time, the idealized

---

*I am informed that "the crease lines between the eyebrows on statues of male Shinto gods and the dimples on the cheeks of young male and female Shinto statues appear to have been incorporated into Noh masks . . ."

Heian woman whom she was painted to invoke rushed through her own steamy life. "On the last night of the year," writes Lady Murasaki, "the ceremony of casting out devils was over very early, so I was resting in my room, blackening my teeth and putting on a light powder . . ." And on the last night before the next performance, the *zo-onna* awaits the ceremony of being inhabited by yet another man, a man whose true flower sweetly guides him, like the woman I love who sometimes sits astride me to better control her pleasure; he inhabits her in order to bring her back to life in the manner that he expresses life, so that we may watch and experience the joyousness of our own desire, which he and the *zo-onna* have understated into metaphysics.

The distance from nostrils to eyes is slightly greater in the young woman than in the *zo-onna*, but this difference is less conspicuous than the others.

I said that I began by making the eye-to-mouth distances of both female faces the same. If we resize the *zo-onna*'s head to make it the same size as Miss Aya's, we immediately discover that the face has moved upward on it. If we align the eyes with Miss Aya's we find that the mouth and nose are still higher than hers. In other words, the *zo-onna*'s face actually occupies a smaller proportion of her head than Miss Aya's. And this difference is most disconcerting of all.*

What then makes a perfect face? In this male investigation of femininity and beauty, the answer must be: *the face that is most perfectly female.* Psychological research indicates that people asked to choose their favorite out of a set of face photographs tend to choose that which looks young, symmetrical and composite. Moreover, compared to masculine faces, feminine ones are narrow and short. In women the following two distances are longer: From one eye's outer extremity to the other, and from eyes to eyebrows. (Now we know why women sometimes apply white eye pencil around the edges of each eye in order to "extend the whites.") Meanwhile, these three distances are shorter: Between the cheekbones, between mouth and eyes, and nose width. — But do such variables help

---

*One study of the effect of mask angle upon perceptions of its expressed emotion found that a certain *magojiro*'s mouth was much deeper than a human's. This helped to facilitate the illusion. In laser scans of the masks at three different inclinations, we seem to see the top of the upper lip as a frown, a neutral horizontal which resembles the stylization of stretched bird's wings, and a smile.

anyone but a mask carver or a casting director? — Moreover, even they fall subject to emendation, subcategorization. The mask maker Hori Yasuemon informs us: "Female masks, whether *ko omote*, *waka-onna*, *zo-onna*, *fukai*, or *yase-onna*, are said to require three variants — 'Yuki', 'Tsuki' and 'Hana'" — which is to say, Snow, Moon and Flower. "In general," Hori continues, "masks give a strong look when the eyes, nose and mouth are closer to the center, but with 'Hana' they are about four millimeters apart from the center, giving it a generous, gentle expression."

So what makes a woman look womanly? Just as in Tanizaki's reverie of his mother there was no female body, so in Taliban Afghanistan there was *no female face*, not in public, at least; and that cool, conscious purveyor of femininity's theatrical allurements, a prostitute, might flash her red-fingernailed white hands, or wear fancy socks. Femininity is an embellishing act as much as specific concatenation of bone and flesh. Like a Noh mask, a woman's face alters infinitely and eternally as it moves.

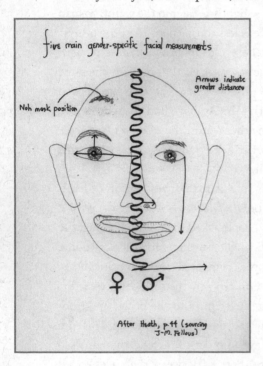

A Noh mask gazes through me with her hollow eyes, and she is so real that I believe in her and love her; accordingly, I want her to see me, but she cannot, not without an old man inside. It is he who makes her alive.

A woman sees me, and kisses me. I refuse to believe that because she is real she is not perfect.

## WITHIN THE MASK

Ms. Nakamura Mitsue was the one whose exhibition I'd seen in Yokohama. She had made the *zo-onna* mask under discussion here, and also the *waka-onna*. Mr. Umewaka spoke highly of her abilities. As for Mr. Mikata, of his fifty or sixty masks, the oldest of which derived from the late fifteen hundreds, he possessed seven made by her. "Her technique is good," he said, "although some things can be attacked. But some spirit will start dwelling in it as time goes by, since many actors wear it. Because of that, the colors may change and the mask's power will increase. That's why I appreciate the old masks."

I interviewed her over several years at her studio in Kyoto. Down-curved, her masks often appeared dreamy and distracted like the faces of the dead. When looked at from below, they smiled less. The smile narrowed; the upturned eye-corners turned down, the blankness between the black teeth widened; so the lips curled into a grimace and then as I lowered my gaze the lips went down, too. Very set and sad at the appropriate angle, these young mask-women; and the middle-aged *fukai* expressed still more perfectly the truism that all of us must die.

Once I asked: "When you're making the mask, at what point does it come alive?"

"It's hard to say, but from a certain point it starts to exist."

"How much individuality can you put into your masks?"

"There are cases when I make a mask and the mask starts to affect me somehow, so I start to follow that something from the mask, rather than doing something *to* the mask. In other cases I have a clear idea of what I am doing, and I simply obey that. Both approaches can be powerful."

"Do you feel that there is a real spirit to the mask, or is it simply a tool for the actor?"

"Both can be true. This thing that is just made with wood; I don't completely believe that there is a spirit in it; but there *is something*. And of course when it is worn on the stage and the actor is on the stage, the eyes start to be alive."

"It must have required a certain level of accomplishment on your part for that to occur."

"I studied for many years, trying to imitate the forms which had been maintained traditionally,* to deeply understand the traditional standard

---

*This is what I heard over and over, especially from Noh actors and geishas. First, in the years of apprenticeship, the expression of beauty consists of exercises done by rote; then it happens, as Zeami implies, beyond consciousness. Of all the inhabitants I met in this

of beauty. I have done that for many years, so it's not that long ago that I finally started making masks of my own."

"How long ago?"

Her elaboration of "not long ago" was in keeping with the manifold slowness of Noh: "I have been making masks for twenty-one years."

She thought that "a really talented person can learn to make a mask in five to ten years." It took her about a month to complete one mask. She had tried to use power tools, but they were too noisy. Sometimes she experienced wrist pain from working too hard with her chisels, and back pain from bending over too long.

"Is is difficult for you to say goodbye to the mask?"

"If it's going to be used on the stage, I'll be happy," said Ms. Nakamura. "Last year, somebody from Ireland just passed by and bought a lot, and I felt a little sad."

"Are there any stories about somebody who fell in love with a mask?"

"I can't think of any story like that, but I wish that someday someone will fall in love with one of mine."

"Since you are now so familiar with the standard of beauty for the Noh mask, can you tell me what proportion determines the perfect female face?"

"It's very hard to say. Of course I cannot indicate any numbers. The standard varies. When I'm making something, that is the most beautiful for me, but when I start making something else, then it's the most beautiful."

"Why is there a different standard of beauty of the *ukiyo-e* face than for Noh faces?"

"Probably, depending on the time, the standard of beauty changes. Noh masks originated six hundred years ago. Even before that, a standard of beauty existed which the masks reflected. *Ukiyo-e*, on the other hand, is from the Edo period. The standard of beauty in the Edo period, I think it is different . . ."

---

subculture, Mr. Umewaka was the only one who articulated for me in detail what conscious choices he made. When I watch a woman making up her face, her self-description resembles that of the geishas. She rarely says: "I chose today to apply foundation in this way *because* . . ."

I had brought with me a book of Utamaro reproductions, so I pulled it out and we leafed through it together. The mask maker said: "Here the face is long, an oval face, and the eyebrows are rather clear. That is totally different from a Noh mask."

And she instantly began to sketch:

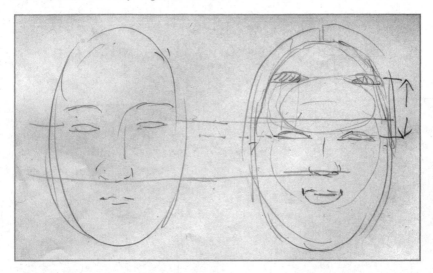

"The balance of the items on the Utamaro face, it's just like a normal, ordinary person's," she said. "Whereas on a Noh mask, the eyes are somewhat lower, and the mouth and nose; this is like a child. And the eyebrows are here" — Ms. Nakamura pointed upward. "So this balance is totally different. And the reason, my guess is, these eyebrows have some *meaning.* Why they are so lifted and why the forehead is so large must be that probably in Heian period, their beauty was between eyes and eyebrows."

"How often do you see a Japanese woman whose face is proportioned like a Noh mask?"

She giggled. "Whenever I'm in a train I always look at the other faces, but I never see such a face! But a person who has a nice forehead, I notice that and think it is like a Noh mask."

"So if it is not lifelike, why is it so beautiful?"

"Probably it's not because of that proportion of that balance, but something appealing inside, something that is attractive."

"And what would that something be?"

"That's what I'm always wondering, actually," she said.

# 9:

# Her Golden Lips Slightly Parted

*An Image of Kannon*

Astanding robed figure of gold shows her round-cheeked face through the oval window of her ornate golden headdress. Her face, proportionately much wider than any Noh mask, is a golden cube with rounded corners, with long tresses of a darker, perhaps tarnished color. The blackish pupils are alert in her gold eyes. Tarnish or dirt has given her a slight moustache. She upraises one hand and extends the other, seated cross-legged in a spill of concentrically pleated metal skirts above her various lamps, her eyes looking straight at me. First her brilliant golden eyebrow-crescents in that slightly verdigrised face snatch my gaze; then I see more golden sweeps of under-lids, very geometric and distinct, more so than the golden places where light is caught upon her cheeks and chin. She is very far beyond and above me in the temple's darkness. When I raise my binoculars to her, I find that her face is of stunning beauty. Her golden lips are slightly parted, shining.

On page after page of a fashion magazine, the movie star Kate Bosworth, twenty-five years old, parts her dark pink lips, showing me a sliver of white upper teeth framed by darkness, her lower lip ornamented in each photograph with a segmented stripe of gloss-glow. Her skin is a flawless blend of pinks; I suppose it has been powdered and airbrushed. Her mascara'd gaze beseeches me with the appearance of melancholy or erotic intimacy. Her mouth pretends to say: "Kiss me." This professional signifier appears on many women in pornographic magazines and in the long slow sequences of romantic films. For some reason, I rarely see it on the faces of strangers in the street.

That knowing, almost half-smiling face of Kannon, which first seems merely watchfully aware of me, then does perhaps offer me lurking gentleness or even pity, metallic pity, what does it project and what does it contain? Kannon is what? How *feminine* is she? How human is she? Among the thirteen best-loved mandala deities of Esoteric Buddhism we find Amida and his attendant, a certain Kannon, more obscurely known as Avalokiteshvara. Sometimes she is male, often not. Never mind that or even her ancientness in that twice-bygone capital of Nara; how could I kiss those lips of hers? Grown man that I am, I remain small enough to be born from them . . .

A *waka-onna*, *zo-onna* or *ko-omote* possesses this same inhuman beauty. So does a geisha; so does a maiko; likewise the woman I love. The grace they shower upon me surpasses even my capacity to desire.

# Crossing the Abyss

## *The Three Beings of Three Women*

B ut where to start? Who is *any* woman? In the Tokyo National Museum, a certain cosmetic box depicting a scene from the Noh play "Kikujido" is squarish, with golden flowers on a speckled gold-and-black background — a heavenly zone rendered still more lucent and distant by the lacquer. What is kept inside I will never know.* And as I revise this chapter in an airport I look up and see across of me a middle-aged woman with stringy hair, her glasses halfway down her nose as she reads a book beside her husband; who is she? I will never know that, either. A slender, elegant old lady sits down with her legs pressed together and her feet precisely aligned; she begins to operate some flat silver electronic device.

---

*In her early eleventh-century list of things that are near though distant, Sei Shonagon included "relations between a man and a woman."

"Who is a woman?" I inquired of an American woman whom I had never before met — that way the "who" that I "knew" her to be might be less likely to occlude the "who" that she "really was" (thirty-eight, a wedding and portrait photographer, well-muscled, tall, Aryan) — whether she would answer questions about her female self. She was kind, and said that she would. Just as a geisha's shamisen has three strings, so a person has three beings. I thought to ask Hilary Nichols about each of them.

I began by asking: *What is your soul?* and she replied by subdividing the entity of which I was thinking into two parts:

"I think our spirit is our life-force. It's the god-force rather than the beautiful mystery which is life. And the soul is our persona. I think my energy is eternal and will continue and will carry some essence or knowledge. It sort of reforms and becomes a new life. I kind of feel a connection which is not really of this lifetime, something I have no choice in. I feel that we're working out whatever issues we came into this world with, and if we don't work it out in this lifetime, it will continue in the next." (This point of view is not so far from a Noh play's: Characters who fail to release their loves, griefs, angers and suchlike attachments remain on stage as masked ghosts.)

"My twin sister and I have all the same DNA and upbringing and friends," Hilary continued, "but we just came into this world with different souls. I feel my soul is my essence which allows me to I feel that I'm very at ease. I think that my soul is an old soul, poetic. I have a grace that's come through lifetimes, of acceptance. My sister's a little more anxious."

"Could you have been a man in a past life?"

"Absolutely."

"So for you the soul is not gendered."

"The soul is not gendered, because it's undefinable life-force which is the great mystery. It's in the decision of these molecules to maintain shape, to maintain the agreement *to be*, to retain the life-force. In some source I feel that we can't really separate that energy from life. I love that there's a great mystery and I don't want to figure it out."

(Recall Zeami: "As long as the character is mysteriously beautiful, whatever is done should be interesting.")

"Now for the second question," I said. *"Who are you as a person?"*

"I am a social butterfly, very outgoing. Friendship is really one of my highest priorities. I am easygoing and fun-loving, but I am also fiercely loyal and definitely community-minded. My lasting philosophy is that I like everyone until they've proven themselves otherwise. My sister's the opposite. I have an optimistic outlook."

"To what extent does gender influence your personality?"

"I think gender is in the chemical makeup of girl *versus* boy. I am happy to be a girl and take that on. My nephew is such a little ball-throwing kind of boy, and my niece is such a little girlie-girl, and I love that. But I feel like at my age I was almost unfairly influenced by being a girl. I really admire women who are so kickass at gender roles. I allowed myself to get off easy because I was a girl. I didn't have to apply smarts to get by, because I was just acceptable and sociable and cute. I do really value the ten percent that's genderless, but I am ninety percent girl. I am not a natural athlete, although I've rock climbed and skied. I would enjoy an opportunity to be a boy and since I live in San Francisco, I don't think I'd have to change my persona all that much. The boy I love is a very sensitive man. I could date girls. That's always fun! I think I could be a boy and still be me. I do play kind of a mother role in my community. I don't know if that would have to be regendered. I guess I could be a Papa. I think that element of nurturing is natural for me.

"I feel at a disadvantage as a woman, because society encourages me to be a giver instead of a receiver. My Mom was definitely a fifties woman.* But then again, my older sister who's ten years older than I, is a breadwinner and her husband is a stay-at-home man. So I can't really say it's strictly society or strictly family. And I am single and have always taken care of myself. And I wouldn't expect anyone to do that for me. I'm not saying

---

*Obviously the content of femininity varies over time and space. For instance, a certain young boy in Berlin feels drawn not only to wearing women's clothes, but also to dusting. His great-uncle lovingly remarks that he should have been a girl in 1900; then he would have been "a pearl of a servant." How many women do I know who actually enjoy dusting? The boy, who becomes Charlotte, describes herself throughout her life as a *Hausfrau.*

I would turn it down necessarily but I want to feel that I can stand on my own two feet regardless. As far as the boy I love is concerned, I think that I have to prove my independence every day, and yet I really love interdependence and I want him and me to be there for each other. If I had gotten married younger, I would not have that feeling. But as a single woman I don't want to be considered that desperate, shopping for a man. I think it's more the way I appear to other women that concerns me."

One quality which marked Hilary as an early-twenty-first-century American woman was her gender-anger. When I asked her to compare male and female behavior, her descriptions of the former were invariably critical. It was not that she herself was angry; in fact she was a very sweet person. I asked her if she could think of any positive aspects of the male gender, and she replied: "We all have brothers. We all have fathers who are family members. I do think that testosterone does inform the violence in this world, but I don't have an animosity toward the men in this world. The nurturing of men has been unfair in that they seek solace in violence and power instead of in art and soul."

She paused and added: "But I trust the men in my world to be humans just like me — not to say that men don't frustrate me."

This assertion of support for the qualities of my sex seemed to me lukewarm, at least in comparison to the support I would have expressed for femininity; and I liked her and wanted there to be symmetry between us, so a few moments later I rephrased the question and asked it again, as well as I could without actually leading or forcing her.

"Well," said Hilary, "there's a fearlessness, a natural inclination to be more active and athletic, also more of an encouragement to be self-sufficient and self-reliant."

But in her next breath the anger came out again, in however a mild and covert a form, when she said: "And I do think there's kind of a birthright to being a male, that you inherit the world, but that's societal, and I don't think that's true of all males, just of white males."

She then went on in a more conciliatory fashion: "I think there's nothing more admirable or enviable than being like a rock star, just having that confidence of thinking you can be a surfer, skier, ladykiller, just have it all. But I do think there are women like that, too, who have it all, just not as many. But I think there are great advantages to being a woman. I traveled alone for ten months and I did take advantage; it was easier for people to offer generosity or comfort to me. People weren't scared of me, so they'd take me in. And they did take me in, all across the world. On the dating front, I think that men are definitely more conflicted around the concept of pairing up, because they definitely do feel a prowess around the more the merrier, and they feel encouraged to seek that power and see it as a weakness to choose loyalty over quantity. I think that men have more of an intrinsic fear about coupling than I do. Maybe it's a fear of intimacy that they mask by being out on the town. I pinpoint it perhaps to separation from Mother. I'm thinking of a certain male friend who epitomizes the idea of a loner getting laid. I think that men can kind of separate the sexual urge from the emotional, and women can't."

Another of Hilary's American qualitites: She believed that relationships can and should be *negotiated.* — "I think that basically men and women have to agree," she said. "You have to be comfortable with the fact that you're mutually fulfilled, or nearly. You just have to come to the relationship with an agreement about money, sex, and alcohol or drugs."

She had been in one three-year relationship which she described as follows:

"We didn't have a very good sex life but we had an okay love life. The less sex we had, the less we needed. We were very affectionate and cuddly and sweet. But we had different hours."

"To what extent do you think that desire differences in a relationship are the simple result of the fact that any two people are different, and to what extent do you see them as deriving from some sort of difference or even incompatibility between man and woman?"

"I thought that living with these lesbian girls was going to be, what a joy not to deal with *that*! — but they had the exact same fits and jealousies, so a lot of it is just specific to two unique people! But I do think that part of the joy in a male-female relationship is crossing the abyss."

That abyss, and *the other* on its far side, as haunting as a pagoda's shape in the night, how can I hope to describe them? Crossing changes the crosser unforeseeably, as we read even in the ancient epic of Gilgamesh, when the beasts of the desert reject the wild man as soon as he has taken the harlot in his arms and murmured love to her; "now you have become like a god." Later on, when this tamed hero lies in agony on his deathbed, we learn that it was not the sexual act in and of itself which altered him, for in the desert mountains he had had a wife. The cause must therefore be the harlot's beauty and grace.

"I think that men are often pretty comfortable with a double standard," she went on. "They can have a wandering eye but can feel insulted if their woman is found attractive by another man. I also just feel sorry for them. There is a societal influence that they have to know their power to be accepted, that they have to prove themselves professionally, and it really is depressing for a man to feel that he doesn't have anything to show for himself, whereas a woman can simply *be*."

Now came my final question: *"Who or what are you as a female body?"*

Hilary had said that she felt at a disadvantage because society encouraged her to be a giver instead of a receiver. But from an anatomical point of view, she *was* a receiver. I've often wondered to what extent the penetration of a woman, with its associated rhythm, force and duration, which in so many positions she can control only indirectly, through communication with the man, affects the way she thinks and feels. Obviously the woman can ride the man and control almost the entire experience of copulation in that way, but the fact remains that a flaccid penis is a greater barrier to intercourse than a dry vagina, which must be one reason why rape is more often committed by men against women than the reverse. Mouths, tongues, hands, buttocks and other pleasure-accessories possessed by both sexes can certainly take on their own primacy in an act of lovemaking; all the same, the core of the heterosexual coupling experience is the interaction of the complementary genitalia.

Hilary said: "I think that women can be okay with that controlling part, just by doing more of the moving, but women have always *had* to be okay with that, and when you're not in synch with it, it can be very offputting. I've said that women are taught to be acquiescent, and I do think that there is gender role-playing in bed. Just mentally there is a kind of an external persona that you invest in. My best relationships have been pretty well matched and equal. I think I've been pretty much the initiator. I do think that having a certain amount of sexual persona, letting those elements of self to come out, adds to the enthusiasm, even if they're stereotyped and even if people wouldn't want to necessarily talk about them out of bed."

"To what extent do you think that the fact that your body gets penetrated defines you personally?"

"I definitely think that it has a huge impact. Being a receiver, taking someone into a very sacred place and in the most intimate position, you do feel that there has to be trust. You do feel that you've given so much that you expect gratitude."

I said to Hilary that there often seemed to be miscommunication between the sexes over this matter of gratitude. Some men I know have expressed bitterness to me that after a sexual act in which both they and the women concerned achieve orgasm, the women seem to feel that the men should feel indebted to them.

"I do feel that women give so much to let a man inside," said Hilary. "I do grant that women can be less giving than they should be; they can be passive. And they could be more grateful themselves. I can be. But I do feel, the first time especially, that it's so sacred."

"And when would you say that the man's gratitude becomes less of an issue for the woman?"

"I imagine that the comfort level determines it. The women need to create the rhythm so it won't be as if they're vulnerable to the man's dominance."

"Since your female body affects who you are, can you imagine yourself as a ninety-year-old woman and tell me how your femininity will express itself then?"

"I do think that a very big sense of self for me is recognizing my attraction. And I live in a very social scene, so it's all about exchanging attractiveness and being recognized. I know that that goes away. So what will go away? I definitely want to make a contribution and feel that I am appreciated by what I can offer: to support people emotionally and every other way. I'm not really involved in volunteer efforts these days, but I would like to seek that out and give some kindness. That would be a critical part of still feeling useful. One thing comforts me: I think there are different ways when we are in touch with our sensuality, and not just through sexuality itself. I'm not a painter but I do feel that a visual art is some kind of way to do it. Even driving here today, it's such a wonderful feeling; the soft wind on my hand was just kind of silky. I wanted to be taking pictures of the light and sunflowers on Highway 80. It was almost a sexual feeling."

And, speaking of visual art, Hilary showed me some of her portraits; I especially remember the gaze of the young mother Tirza, calmly loving and knowing Hilary's gaze as she lies naked in the bed, breasts and drawn up knees, long dark hair; I am made happy by that calm smile, while the baby (whose name is Lakesh) gazes through us into heaven. There is something here, the woman gazing at another woman, at femininity itself, which lies eternally beyond me, which I can love and long for while knowing that I will never live it; this may be what Hilary means by the attraction of crossing the abyss.


## GENDERLESSNESS, DILIGENCE, PERIODS

I next asked a bespectacled, middle-aged Japanese professional woman the same questions that I had asked Hilary Nichols. Sachiko (an alias) had never been athletic. She did not consider herself graceful or pretty. Year after year she said to me: "When I look into the mirror nowadays, I feel so disappointed." ("I think American woman is more confident about the body," commented a Japanese-American lady when she heard.)

*"What is your soul?"* I began.

"I'd like to think that it is gender-neutral, but I am not objectively sure."

*"Who are you as a person?"*

Her reply was typically, self-deprecatingly Japanese, at least for her generation: "I think I'm rather diligent, sometimes selfish. In a way, I'm lazy. I was brought up to be diligent, so it's part of myself, but if I don't have any deadline, then I won't work very hard. Fundamentally I'm not diligent."

So far, this, too, sounded quite gender-neutral.

"Probably I'm not one of the average women," she continued. "I'm more concerned about discrimination against women. Other women are not concerned about that, but my femininity is partly reflected in that."

In other words, she perceived her femininity ideologically; she interpreted her womanliness on a class basis.

When I asked the third question, *"Who or what are you as a female body?"*, her answer was very different from Hilary's:

"Periods," she answered at once. "I always hated them. Giving birth, that experience was good, because thanks to it, I became able to think about other children. When I was young, I did not like little kids. I thought they were noisy and so on. Only after I had my own baby I could be nicer, kinder, to them."

"What about erotic experiences?"

"I have no complaint. At least I can feel good many more different ways than a man can when he ejaculates. The way I feel about sex, it depends on the character of the man."

I asked her about the effects of living in a more penetrable body than a man, and the utilitarianism of her response exceeded Hilary's: "Actually, one of my friends used to tell me just that, that after all, men are superior, because when you make love, men are on top. When I was with X, I felt that way. When I am with Y, I never feel that way. When I am with Y, I feel equal to the man."

She said nothing about grace, or attractiveness. Her femininity seemed to be a mix of ideology and biology. This person, who possesses her own discreet silver-haired elegance, described herself as if her female sexual characteristics were accidental.

Of course, some of this must be ascribed to Japanese modesty and understatement. She frequently expressed her gender through the Japanese housewife's conditioned reflex of tidying and cleaning, which had grown so deep-seated that she was scarcely aware of it. And here it is worth inserting that the Japanese-American woman whom I have quoted ("American woman is more confident about the body") perceived personality as a much more mutable quantity than did Sachiko or I. In fact, the Japanese-American woman said: "Gender personality is different. There is a social expectation for man and for woman. So when they are growing up they acquire some personality" — for instance, the conditioned reflex of the Japanese housewife. She decidedly believed that personality could alter over time. All the same, she was willing to categorize: "General female personality is emotional and easy to get hurt. General male personality is more rational because in the cases they encounter, emotion is not involved. When they decide something, they can be more rational. When women decide something, they try to be rational but cannot."

Sachiko was perhaps more rational than I, but no less inclined to be hurt, which sometimes occurred as silently as when the rainbow curtain ascends to admit the *shite* onto the bridge to our world.

Could I say I understood her? What would it require to know her? How many allusions, antecedents, texts would it take? If she came with me to Kasuga Shrine, which gold clouds and spiderwebs would lead me to whatever lay behind her mask as she stood smiling politely at me on that mossy path of stone lanterns where Lady Nijo once walked? To whom and what does a person refer? — To her parents, of course, and her lovers and children, but then? To the idea of the Emperor, as in Mishima's case? — Certainly not in her case. (But before atomic persuasion brought about the Japanese surrender, Sachiko's mother had believed that the Emperor did not urinate. He was a god.) To the physical necessities of breasts, periods and menopause? To Heian reverberations? Sachiko was quite good at naming and placing ancient poems. What is a woman to me? What can she be, but *other*?


### THE BYZANTINE

Marina Vulicévic was a reporter in Beograd. She had huge dark eyes. We met several times. She and I both felt at ease being open with one another, and when I asked her those three questions she was generous enough to describe her three beings to me.

*"Who are you as a soul?"*

"I agree with Plato: Our soul comes from the unknown place, the clean place. Maybe before, you are in a very nice huge place and then God comes out and shows Himself. And then that soul reaches for the future or for a certain person. I believe in eternal life, because it would be stupid if this were the only life. In my feeling, the soul lacks all gender, all it needs is to love and be loved, and to swallow love — but not just love made of sex, which is material. — And there is something inside the soul which neeeds to go out . . . Maybe I have an equal quantity of female and male inside of me.

"I think about my soul only in relation to someone else," the Serbian woman continued. "When you feel very lonely and sad, people can always hurt you. And yet there is something I need to believe is eternal. Now that my parents are dead, I need to be with them sometimes. I would give my life just to be with them for a few minutes. There is one moment in the day when you feel so free and clean and fresh that you can forgive even your own killer. This happens maybe when you hear a certain kind of music, or when you are alone in church. Before, I went every Sunday. Now I go only when there is a holiday. When I feel especially alone I go to the icons and feel comforted. I have one from Jerusalem: Saint Marija.

"I am a Byzantine. I love, and I suffer for it. You are a Western type. You love just for your own satisfaction. We are something of sad persons, because of our own Byzantine tradition. We are very emotional, very sensitive."

*"Who are you as a person?"*

"I'm still a little girl inside, afraid she will be left alone, rejected. One time I was travelling with my parents, and there was only one seat in the train compartment, so they left me with perfect strangers. All through the voyage I was afraid that they would leave me. Sometimes I feel like that; I feel that I'm going to be alone. At home I still have my toys and my brother's toys, his little automobiles, and I still keep them. I sometimes feel that it's better that my brother and me should stay kids, without problem. The other part of me wants to have a husband and a child, but I'm also afraid. I want something but I'm afraid of wanting something."

*"Who are you as a female body?"*

"When I was with my boyfriend G., he told me he felt like a real man with me, and in my body, my female body, when he would say *animal female*, you are *a real female*, I would feel very female. He bought me some pantyhose and wanted me to wear them. I didn't mind it; it felt nice. I liked to please him in different ways. Sometimes he wanted me to bathe him. I liked to prepare a meal for him. It felt nice to be to him as a body.

"Most of the time I feel good about my body. When I was a little girl I went for ballet lessons. I like that feeling of working out, of calm, of drifting away, a nice feeling after the pain. Sometimes in life I feel a need to make something of a problem, and when I solve it I feel the same as after taking off tight shoes. I feel relaxed and in ecstasy."

"Why do you wear tight shoes?"

"I hate wearing them, because if you stand a lot, they start to hurt you. But the only nice thing is that sometimes I wear those high heeled shoes; I feel I should have them because I want to be noticed. What I especially liked when I was with G., he had special white slippers for me and I wore those with his white socks. I also wore his T-shirt to sleep."

So who was Marina? And if I had seen her step into her tight shoes, would I have felt as I did when watching Mr. Umewaka gazing at his masked face in the mirror room of Yasukuni Shrine? Who was *he* as a soul, and who was I? If I could discern Marina's soul in isolation, would I know her to be a woman, or would I conclude, as she, Hilary and Sachiko all had, that the soul is ungendered? Did Mr. Umewaka's soul alter when he put on a *waka-onna* mask? Whenever I considered my soul, I imagined something shy, clean, young, pertaining to a small boy. I had accordingly expected the three women to have girl-souls, especially since I believed the abyss to be exactly as Hilary had formulated it. Its existence used to exasperate me. Now I found that the possibility of its nonexistence unsettled me.

# What Is Grace?

*A List and a Possible Hermeneutic*

How to cross the abyss, if it does exist? Can we even describe what we see, much less what to look for? Just as one can be moved by the grace of "Kiyotsune" without necessarily possessing a substantial conscious understanding of Noh's gestural and thematic vocabulary, so one can be conquered by a woman's face and form, yet fail to articulate just what makes her beautiful.

Artists try to do so nonetheless. Here is one of Kawabata's many expositions of qualities, from *Beauty and Sadness*: "Some Japanese women have fair skin glowing with femininity, perhaps even finer and more lustrous than the faintly pink glowing skin of young girls in the West. And the nipples of some Japanese girls are an incomparably delicate shade of pink." In *Snow Country* the word most frequently employed in praise of the heroine, a hot springs geisha named Komako, is "clean." "The high, thin nose was a little lonely . . . but the bud of her lips opened and closed smoothly, like a beautiful little circle of leeches . . . With her skin like white porcelain coated over a faint pink, and her throat still girlish . . . the impression she gave was above all one of cleanliness, not quite one of real beauty." And yet of course she *is* beautiful. Enervated though he is, the protagonist remains obsessed with her. "The smooth lips seemed to reflect back a dancing light . . . Her eyes, moist and shining, made her look like a very young girl," and her skin reminds him of "the newness of a freshly peeled onion or perhaps a lily bulb . . . More than anything, it was clean." "In the moonlight the fine geishalike skin took on the luster of a sea shell." Finally and most relevantly to our concerns, we read that in starlight "Komako's face floated up like an old mask. It was strange that even in the mask there should be the scent of the woman."

This dancing light, the clean skin, etcetera, what precisely makes them alluring? Inspection may promise to elucidate this, but closer inspection may keep that promise only in the way that Mr. Umewaka's Edo-era Noh kimonos resolve into real golden scales and soft multicolored threads, all the while giving off a smell of dead men's sweat. Where is the scent of the woman here?

American fashion magazines from my own time present beauty in some of the same ways as does Kawabata. Most revealing are the advertisements, which concretize the beautiful in order to sell it. Very often they claim to improve a woman's skin, making it soft, smooth, elastic, moist, taut, "wide awake," young and luminous. They do so in pseudo-medical or magically chemical ways, hydrating, nourishing, mineralizing, concealing within their measured statistical language of benefit (within the first six weeks, seventy percent of our customers report lightening of the dark pouches beneath their eyes) some hope that beauty can be saved from the ageing which brings it such terror. Indeed, much of the discourse of these magazines has to do with fear of imperfection. (We know what the *waki* priest would say about *that*.) Perfection, at least as seen in the skin cream and lingerie ads, equals a long sweep of unblemished skin. Not long after A.D. 1169, Chrétien de Troyes made his lovelorn hero report that "from the hollow / Of her throat to the top of her bodice / I spy a trifle of uncovered / Breast, more white than snow." Thus the beautiful Sordamour. And in a twenty-first-century perfume advertisement I see the face of Britney Spears, in whom everything is paled down, slightly frosted, so that her blonde hair resembles white gold;* her pale coral lips freeze in a faint and steady smile; and her complexion's superficial monochromatism of pinkish-white is actually, like the old ivory of a Noh mask in torchlight, a family of tints and shades whose subtle variations almost escape the gaze; and so it is with her skin — quite a lot of skin; we see most of her, down to the ring in her belly button. The Noh mask gleams a trifle more glossily, the model's, a bit more moistly. Much of American fashion is the constant presentation of moist pinkness. A face's shining smoothness becomes naked or nude, one of a piece with the exposed thighs, throat, hairless armpits, all of which appear nearly the same color upon a given model's body.

And so one might get the impression from these magazines that the preeminently feminine attribute, aside from primary and secondary sexual characteristics, is the skin. But while that might have been so even for Kawabata, we remember that for Lady Murasaki and the *Manyoshu*, the essence was long black hair. (Meanwhile, Yeats wrote in his poem to Anne Gregory that only God could love her for herself and not for her yellow hair.) And until now I have failed to mention the collarbone, which is "arguably one of the most feminine parts of the body." Another magazine informs me that "high cheekbones are considered desirable and indicative of high levels of estrogen necessary for procreation." The thirteenth-century Sufi poet Saadi epitomizes female charm by means of "talons dyed with the blood of lovers, fingertips colored red. Such beauty of face and form would distract the lover from unlawful acts . . ." And in his *Baiae*, the Renaissance poet Giovanni Giovano Pontano (who is hardly the only such exponent) singles out from all feminine charms breasts, eyes, hair and mouth — to be specific, the shining breasts of Hermione, which stirred the aged poet into youthful craziness; the dazzling breasts of Lucilla; the eyes of Deianira, and above all of Focilla; the flowing locks of Focilla, the aromatic hair of Theonilla; the honeyed lips of Constantia, Focilla's aggressive mouth, Neera's and Batilla's delicious breath. Of all these manifestations (and, by the way, Pontano neglects the collarbone),

_____

*For her part, Sordamour sewed one of her hairs beside a golden thread in the white silk shirt she gave to her sweetheart, because (says the poet) she wished to know whether a man might see any difference between the two.

only the breasts are particularly female in their natural state. Significant differences in shape and proportion obviously do exist in women's bodies: the belly curves more and is relatively longer, the back arches, the buttocks protrude; the legs are less knobby; the waist is absolutely narrower and the hips absolutely broader, which combination creates the so-called "feminine A-line," the feet shorter and narrower. But Pontano dwells on none of these things. Nor does Kawabata. What then can be said about the female attributes of greatest allure to their celebrants? These must partake of some artificial aspect, presumably the aspect of performance. Eyes are shadowed with makeup; hair is grown long, lips rouged, etcetera. Femininity thus becomes not only a noun but a verb. This verb may be grace.

Another way of making the same point is that gender partakes both of anatomy and accomplishment. One feminist scholar of Meiji- and post-Meiji-era Japanese theater describes that time as the replacement by the former, literally embodied by actresses, of the onnagatas, the female impersonators of Kabuki. Accomplishment replaced anatomy. — It must be the case that between those two quantities lies a *feeling*: the sensation of such feminine accoutrements as earrings, which swing and tingle with delicious weight against the neck; smooth and even silky undergarments; necklaces and bracelets, geishas' precious hairpieces, etcetera. Then there are femininity's tools, for instance cosmetics and hairbrushes. (For the ancient Greeks, we are told, a mirror's "mere outline, next to that of a distaff, suffices to conjure up a specifically female environment." In Niger, a young man of the Wodabe nomads employs yellow skin powder, black kohl for his eyelids and lips, and a white stripe on his nose. If he is pretty enough, a woman will want him; he will have become a distant version of her. In either case, and in many others, the instrumentality of such items cannot be overlooked. As we read in the *Gotagovinda* of Jayadeva: "She is sumptuously arrayed in ornaments for the war of love.") These objects, some of which keep a woman constant company against her very skin, may soothingly reinforce her sense of her female self.* Moreover, a woman puts on a pearl necklace, the recent gift of a sweetheart, and feels, perhaps, more beautiful, confident, loved and worthy of love. And because they are accessories rather than body parts, an onnagata or a Noh actor may well obtain benefits from them equivalent to what they offer someone born with breasts and a vulva. An old lady named Sharon Morgan, who once upon a time was anatomically male, remembered that the sight of her mother getting tightly laced into her corset by a neighbor lady inspired the thought: "That's for me!" After the thought came experiments, and eventually a transgender operation. In other words, it seems to have been the props that commenced her female performance, which became an identity.

But who am I to say that it must have happened in this way? Another young boy experienced an inexplicable "well-being" when he dressed up in his sister's clothes; when he tried to stop, he felt physically ill. As his body matured, he found himself more hairless and his nipples more "extensive" than other young men. Many years later he too underwent the operation.

Farther along that continuum, a case study in Krafft-Ebing's *Psychopathia Sexualis* (1886) quotes a patient who experiences "the penis as clitoris, the urethra as urethra and vaginal orifice, which always feels a little wet, even when it is actually dry . . . in short, I always feel the vulva." This is no performance, but a state of being. For a biological man, the result is agony pure and simple.

----

*The transsexual Jennifer Finney Boylan states that her boyhood certainty of being in the wrong body "had nothing to do with a desire to be *feminine*, but it had everything to do with being *female*." When I first began writing this book, I attempted to distinguish between these two terms, but found that each means so many different things to different people that insisting that one was this and the other was that came to seem like an insult.

What is feminine? Who are you? I cannot even promise that my understanding of who *I* am will never change. If I tell you, "a woman is *this*," I may through luck, thoughtfulness and experience approach describing something that many women in this epoch are; but then what? I might believe that Mr. Umewaka's bouts of womanhood do or do not resemble Sharon Morgan's experience, or the porn model Aya Kudo's, but to delineate the lives of others in *any* insistent way is to produce offensive absurdities comparable to the following (Janice Raymond, 1979): "All transsexuals rape women's bodies by reducing the real female form to an artifact, appropriating this body for themselves. However, the transsexually constructed lesbian feminist violates women's sexuality and spirit as well." — Gender varies over time and place. There *is* no all.

(What is a woman? She is a Noh mask with rectangular eye openings. Male masks' eye-holes are a trifle curved, and demon-masks' utterly round. *Now* the question is settled!)

As I write this book, biological research suggests that male brains are more prone to systematize, female ones to empathize. "They are not mystical processes," writes a scientist, "but are grounded in our neurophysiology." But then how should an onnagata's accomplishment be characterized? — As a mix of empathy (projection) and rehearsed procedure, it would seem. — Meanwhile the performances of Noh actors and geishas, as we have already begun to see, are more procedural, more memorized, less projected. And some women are far less empathetic than others. Who am I to rule out any construction of self? Please raise your sake cup in honor of mystical processes.

Saadi again: "A pretty face and dresses of brocade, sandals, aloes, colors, perfumes and passing fancies; these are all the ornaments of a woman." Thus femininity: appearance, attributes and performance all together. Hence femininity's metonym (if you don't care for the black bowels of the mud snail): A painted fan, which is beautiful in and of itself, which belongs to a dancer, and expresses deliberate grace in motion.

The woman who had once been the little boy dressing furtively in his sister's clothes (she was nearing the end of her thirties now) asked herself what features or proportions made a face feminine, and could not answer. All she could say was that gender, for a transsexual at least, must be the longing of the mind to be embodied and thereby recognized.

How can the mind succeed in that? Yes, there is an operation; there are pills and props (and a psychoanalyst rather meanspiritedly reminds us that "the transsexual does not exist without the surgeon and the endocrinologist"); there is identity itself;* the rest is performance — and for all humans who project an image of "who they are" (in other words, of who they truly want to be — someone slightly more perfect, attractive, etcetera), performance is a quotidian fact. Hence the anxious preoccupation of these American women's magazines with covering the dark circles beneath the eyes, lifting sunken pouches to make skin "flawless," hiding freckles, shaving armpits, preventing the audience from seeing past the mask of performance. If one's figure is imperfect, wear an embellished collar to direct attention upward to the face. Employ the lipstick slightly past the border of the lower lip to make it appear fuller; in Tokyo, the makeup artist Yukiko does this when she is feminizing her cross-dressing clients. High heels will help either sex project the buttocks in female protrusions. In California, a femininity coach advises her "new girls" to smile and hide their large mannish hands behind their backs when they walk. A helpful T-girl suggests that novices go out in public "with a man, preferably one whom you do not tower over, because his presence validates you as a woman." — Back to the magazines for biological women: A high-waisted skirt flatters the hips. Cream on the lashes will make them

---

*To which this book gives short shrift. The most plausible parsing that I have found of gender identity appears in an essay by the trans woman Julia Serano, who delineates (a) one's "subconscious sex," in other words one's desire to be, for instance, female; (b) one's "conscious sex" (being male-bodied and raised as a boy, she initially identified as male); (c) the gender to which one is attracted; and (d) the gender which other people tend to project upon a person. I feel ambivalent about the final quantity's passive construction. The femininity of a great Noh actor is a triumph of active projection; and I would like to believe that every one of us can at least hope to control how he or she is seen. But it is certainly and sometimes sadly true that who we think we are may be irrelevant in the eyes of others. Some performances fail; others simply come to an end. I imagine a Jew who passes brilliantly as an Aryan, until a document reveals him to the Gestapo. Clearly a performance may be dangerous, exhausting or demeaning to the performer. In any event, *Kissing the Mask* deals less with any of Serano's four categories than a "full treatment" would call for. My focus, being less moral than aesthetic, is limited to the strategies and effects of great performances. Serano for her part remarks: "When I eventually did transition" from male to female, "I chose not to put on a performance — I simply acted, spoke and dresed the way I always had . . ."

shine. Use an eyebrow stencil because "anything around the eye that can make it look brighter and make you look more awake is amazing!" Play up the eyes or the mouth but not both. And of course beauty emulates celebrity. "You have to treat your hair like it's a baby . . . It looks super strong but it's not. It's an illusion." Perhaps this is merely a gentler form of the rigorously disciplined imitation through which apprentice geishas and Noh actors learn from their teachers how grace ought to be stylized. In the advertisements, beauty is invited to buy things through which to express and improve itself. After all, costume comprises a significant aspect of performance. And so a blonde actress in a strapless pearly gown gazes out at us with the calm of a goddess. Her breasts are supported and mostly covered, but the gown offers us some décolletage. The fabric falls away from her in crisply elegant folds. Don't tell me that this moment, this configuration, is not a performance.

Here I disagree with Zeami (or perhaps misunderstand him), when he says that if a woman "connives" to beautify herself "and expends effort to manifest Grace, her actions will be quite ineffective," since "an actual woman living in the world has no thought of imitating a woman."

Each of us is an audience of her own performance. "Beautiful nails are a constant reminder of the feminine you," advises *Miss Vera's Cross-Dress for Success.* For Miss Vera, femininity is its own reward, and the main person to be reminded by the nails is their wearer.* Identity's performance partakes as much of inwardness as a marble Aphrodite's pupil-less gaze.

But the male gaze deserves its own moment of consideration. Most of the observations and opinions you are reading in these pages were made through just that lens. A Noh play takes place for its spectators, and the performance of femininity, while it does of course to a considerable degree exist in and for itself, like the stirring of a man's penis when he lies beside a woman to whom he is attracted, seeks its appreciators. (Kanze Hisao: "It is highly detrimental to a mask to be treated like a piece of antique art, to be shut up in a box or shown only in a glass case. It is only on the stage that it continues to maintain its vitality.") Why else would a

---

*As Lichtenberg wrote in his notebooks, *ca.* 1798: "Even the gentlest, most modest and best of girls are always better, gentler and more modest if their mirrors have told them that they are looking more beautiful than ever."

woman put on lipstick before going out into a public composed mostly of strangers? Women sometimes tell me that they dress not for men but for other women, but when I consider the gender composition of the human race, I wonder if this might be merely half true. Whether or not somebody pays any attention to me as we stand in rush hour in a subway car, it remains my inclination and privilege to appreciate *her*. There are men whose appreciations are limited to recognitions of breasts, buttocks, thighs; and in a strip club the point less often tends to be the revelation of some individual beauty than the display of that general quality, nudity of the female body in a state as near as may be legal to nubility. Proust, whose characterization of love is frequently pathetic, introduces the subject with the cynical assertion that when one is young one mistakes for the bounteous grace of a specific sweetheart simple erotic satisfaction, the objects of our desire being "the interchangeable instruments of a pleasure that is always the same." But the accusation, so often leveled at men in my time and place, of objectification, could be applied to all of us, and therefore seems no more inherently "bad" than the function of the anal sphincter. The gaze can praise grace in the way that this book hopes to do, by memorializing it. I am getting old now, and the women of my age who were beautiful in their first flower are ageing, too. Mr. Kanze is gone; Mr. Umewaka has performed for sixty years. I cannot give grace as they have, but I can reflect and perhaps preserve a trifle of it.

A man on the street who shouts menacingly admiring obscenities at women, a theater-goer, an uxorious fellow who buys a pair of dress shoes for his wife, an ancient Egyptian poet who likens his sweetheart's breasts to mandrakes and her hair to a willow-snare in which his hands have been caught are all four, like it or not, relatives — my relatives. Just as the golden hairpicks of bygone Japanese courtesans may to my eyes resemble the haloes of Byzantine saints, so any number of specifically feminine expressions may be misperceived by their audience. I readily admit that before I began this book, I had no idea of the difference between mascara and blush. Thus for most of my life my appreciation of women's made-up faces was as ignorant as my pleasure in Noh plays: I could be gratified by an effect without being able to say what had caused it, or even if what I saw was "natural." What is grace? We men may not know. Sometimes our gazes' desire to be temporarily completed by the Other becomes as frantic as the sharp flakes twisting down between the platforms of Niigata station, changeably pitting the silver trains as if with corrosion. The ice cream machine stands empty beside the cigarette machine; the conductor walks the platform, peering into every window. A family in hooded parkas wanders along the edge of the train in bewilderment. In an office which resembles a phone booth there is a window through which another conductor can be seen standing at attention. A young woman enters my traincar, brushing snow from her rich brown hair. I see her; she is beautiful; I feel happy.

In Kanazawa I hear the rain on the square grey paving-stones, and within many walls of shingle and latticework, some glowing yellow, some glowing blue, many dark, there is a quiet teahouse whose ochaya-san sits beside me, Fukutaro-san smiles sweetly over her shamisen, tuning it while the geisha Masami-san bows on the tatami, her head toward me, and I wait until Masami-san has commenced to very slowly flip her sleeve in time to the thrilling of Fukutaro's lovely voice. I am striving to *see*; this dance, which connotes the New Year and is called "Fresh Water," is for me and no matter how many times she performs it will never be repeated. Whatever I miss comprises my failure to *her*. And Masami is kneeling, her hands clasped together on the floor. Slowly she opens the fan, lifting it to her lips; I suppose it must be in that moment a sake cup. Her snowy face is paler still by contrast with the shining black wig. Her expression is much more mobile than an Inoue School geisha's.

I hear the sharp snap of her fan. Fukutaro is staring down at her music, singing, the fan has frozen over the geisha's head; Masami bows, and it is over. I loved what I saw, but already I have begun to forget. If I last out many more winters and summers upon this floating world, and if I remain at least as prosperous as a sake merchant, then perhaps, if I come to Masami over and over, I will someday succeed in adoring her with the gaze her grace deserves.

In a certain bar in Los Angeles a beautiful woman stands on the chessboard-tiled floor just outside the entrance to the women's room (about which my companion, who was born with a vagina, remarks with smiling innocence: "I wonder why the toilet seat is always up?"). The beautiful woman shines through her smooth collarbone and pale white thighs. Her smooth new breasts fill her black top to the best measure of abundance. Her tartan skirt charmingly infantilizes her chubby knees. Her beauty is a shock. Smilingly she offers her lips to be kissed. I feel happy to remember her here.

Zeami's notion that the spectators arrive at a performance in a given mood based on external conditions — for instance, the degree of heat and darkness — surely applies to the preexisting factors of male desire; and a woman who seeks to best exploit her audience might as well know what those are. A cherry blossom seems "appropriate to a highly cultivated audience." Beauty with provenance, he writes, such as a shrine associated with a specific poem, makes a greater impression than beauty without. Provenance depends on the audience's lives, the man's proclivities; and the cunning performer knows these. How could this chapter's attempt to generalize about grace fail to be an objectification? And what are props for, but to assist in objectification? Sharon Morgan employed her corsets to help herself and perhaps others believe that she could be categorized in a certain way (as female). But she remained Sharon Morgan, not some anonymous upholder of womanliness. And so it seems to me that the male gaze, which benefits so much from feminine grace, can increase its own pleasure, and nourish each bearer of grace with its respect, first by recognizing category, as does Pontano when he draws our attention to particular body parts of the women whom his poems adore — and the rare Noh spectator who can distinguish a *zo-onna* mask from a *ko-omote* acts likewise — then by paying homage to uniqueness.

Memorializing the poet Kanoko Okamoto, the great woodblock artist Munakata took up his chisel and "express[ed] his joy at being able to openly take up female verses, thanks to the arrival of the age of 'freedom of expression.' He commented that he created this piece by purposely using a 'U-shaped gouge,' perhaps in order to express the roundness and softness of the female's body."

What is a woman *to me*? The answer must be: A projection. Who is projecting, and for what reason, I cannot necessarily know from the performance itself. Mr. Umewaka and Mr. Mikata do not when playing their feminine roles feel themselves to be women; they strive, as I so often in my wonderment repeat, to be *nothing*; yet when they enact women I see them as women. Meanwhile the psyche within a male body which mechanically performs itself as such may see *itself* as female. One eloquently canny researcher of such matters concludes that femininity may be defined as "the possession of *either* a vagina that nature made *or* a vagina that *should have been there all along, i.e.*; the *legitimate* possession." The presence or absence of this emblem remains conjectural to any stranger; yet its enactment, and the stranger's response to it, will confirm the performer, or not. The performance of gender is received by an audience whose members then react. Were the audience unnecessary, the mask would remain safe and unmarred in her dark box.

"Let the glow of Radha's breasts endure!" begs a twelfth-century Indian poem. Alas, a young woman's beauty resembles a single performance of a Noh play. It would be unkind and untrue to equate that with the "false flower" of the young Noh actor who portrays her. Basho, the great haiku poet, writes that "the old-lady cherry / is blossoming, a remembrance / of years ago." I certainly believe that the beauty of the true flower, surpassing mere remembrance, can remain in an ancient woman. In fact, it can bloom all the more, nourished by what it has already been. I think of Mr. Kanze playing Komachi near the end of his life; in a play in which almost nothing happens; in which the weary old lady scarcely moves; in which the priests sadly ask themselves: "Is this Komachi that once was a bright flower?"* Played by Mr. Kanze, she still is. When I remember that performance now, I am moved almost to tears.

In the Noh play "Aoi-no-Ue," a witch or medium summons Lady Rokujo's spirit. First we see a noblewoman in a *deigan* mask. Her face is lovely and almost unlined, but she bares her teeth just a trifle; she broods; perhaps she has begun to be predatory. When the witch fails to break her hold on her rival, Lady Aoi, who is now perilously ill thanks to the emanations of Rokujo's jealousy, the court sends for an ascetic. This man impels the spirit back. We now see the noblewoman muffled in her cloak. For a considerable time she bows before her summoner, writhing beneath her robe in anguish. Then, as his magicking becomes more imperious, she begins to raise her head; and we discover her in a sickening *hannya*

---

*In his twentieth-century version of this same play, Mishima has Komachi say, no doubt with nasty irony: "I suppose a fool like you thinks every beautiful woman gets ugly as soon as she grows old . . . That's a great mistake. A beautiful woman is always a beautiful woman. If I look ugly now, all it means is that I am an ugly beauty."

mask, her head now an angry grinning skull's, horned and shining-eyed, with enough flesh left on her — a nose, for instance — to render her all the fouler: a decomposing corpse which cannot find peace, nor even crave it, such is her desperate malice against Aoi, who (represented by a kimono) lies on the front left of the stage, perilously pregnant with Genji's child. And now Aoi's *hannya* dance begins, a pantomime of battle against the ascetic, who of course will win out ("never again will I come as an angry ghost"). But first, defying his Lesser Spell of Fudo and much of the Middle Spell, Rokujo dances her dance of hideous menace. And in so doing, she follows Zeami's prescription, holding her invisible branch of flowers. What I see behind her horribleness and hatefulness is firstly her *anguish* — I pity her — and secondly her grace, her feminine loveliness.

Well, then, what is grace? How does it differ from beauty itself, or from *yugen*? Can the lovely impression projected by a certain woman hold its own over time, or even increase, like the alluring pathos of Matsukaze? The Komachi embodied by Mr. Kanze is a bright flower, yes, but she is not as lovely as she was. Her accomplishment, her *noh*, has increased, but in her anatomy she has obviously decayed. Still she holds us. Well, what would or should this positive outcome entail? If desire is the essential problem of the Noh situation, then what does that say about this book's celebration of desire?

Might there be not merely ambiguity but *hypocrisy* in Noh's representation of feminine beauty? On the one hand, most of the plays under discussion address the suffering of delusional attachment to this world, and in particular to Eros and Agape. On the other hand, just as Milton's Satan overshadows the other characters in that great poem, so the beauty of the masked Noh figure is such as to invoke our yearning, sometimes to such an extent as to overshadow the warning, or even be augmented by it. When the ghostly "woman of the wooden well" who is the *shite* of "Izutsu" wraps her long dead lover's cloak around her and seeks to reflect him in her dance, the chorus sings: "Blossoming sleeves, flakes of whirling snow." And here the true flower of her supernatural beauty is likewise in full blossom, almost without pathos. At the play's end, to be sure, she will sing: "Pine winds tear plantain-leaf-frail dream, too, breaks awake; the dream breaks to dawn." And she dissolves back into death beyond the rainbow curtain. But in the dance of blossoming sleeves, her dream was not yet broken. What then is Noh-grace when dissected from pathos? Is the result approximately what I feel in gazing at a living woman? Perhaps it is the same as the dance in "Yuya," which is elegantly gorgeous without being sad.

We know from "Kinuta" and other plays, even other prose, that the sound of a woman fulling cloth on a board is considered dreary, mournful, signifying the agony of delusional attachment. But Basho writes a haiku about how clearly the blows ring, travelling all the way up to the Big Dipper. This clarity possesses, among other qualities, beauty. The sometimes agonizing allure of the feminine might as well be contemplated as akin to those rising sounds. Blossoming sleeves must molder like the flesh within them; snow must melt; all the same, in the moment they triumph. Back and forth this book must go, from snow to water, all the while baffled or inspired by the slowness of a perfect Noh mask whose silent wooden alteration of expressions saves us from admitting the inevitable.

Beauty is grace. Grace is pose and poise, as in an ancient Greek bronze of a running girl whose smooth dark legs remain in balance; the bare feet remain flexed, the toes outthrust, the arms upflung in power and joy — but grace is *life*, hence inconstancy, which can inflict constant and perhaps even eternal attachment. A wise Sanskrit poet advises his heroine not to leave her flaring hips idle, but rush to the darkened forest where her lover-god waits. Her hips must die, but not yet. And the god desires her. Grace may be, as for a Noh actor who strives to feel nothing, projection alone; it can also be a woman's living feelings. "A flower shows its beauty as it blooms and its novelty as its petals scatter." This aphorism of Zeami's must be true; otherwise why would modes and fashions change? And so the heroine goes to the dark forest and unties her belt. Whether she gives herself or refrains, a hundred years later the outcome will be the same.

In that ochaya in Kanazawa the geisha Masami was sitting before the gilded wall where her dances happened, and when I asked how many dances she had memorized, she replied: "Even if you know many dances, it depends on the season. If a dance is long, we may perform only a part of it. Right now the atmosphere of New Year is still present."

Until yesterday, the fifteenth of January, her hair ornament had been a tortoise shell with rice-stalks (*inaho*) and a white crane, which for geishas was actually supposed to be an eyeless white pigeon. If a geisha's wish came true within the fifteen days, she painted an eye on her pigeon. Two eyes meant that two wishes got granted, for instance fortune in love. Geishas would observe each other's pigeons and make jocular or envious comments. Now her ornament had become a rat, to mark the beginning of the Year of the Rat.

"Each season is different," added the shamisen player Fukutaro. "If you come here in the summer, there will be no paper on the latticework wall . . . ."

What then is grace? Does its transience sufficiently explain it? Should we construe it as extrahuman? Royall Tyler writes about the play "Matsukaze" that the two sisters "are not actually people . . . they are the purified essences of human longing." And how could they be otherwise? If, as Malraux opines, great artists are "conditioned" not by the world itself but by other art, then the sisters *must* be projected entities, like Hollywood actresses glimpsed through their limousine windows.

In this vein, a certain mid-twentieth-century Kabuki booklet makes remarkable claims about that art's onnagata: "The art of female impersonation has refined feminine beauty to the extent that it exceeds the beauty of real women in many ways . . . a man will always have basically stronger, sharper lines than a woman, but in Kabuki, a level of sensuality . . . has been achieved that is not found in real life . . . a strength of purpose is required, along with a soft gentleness that makes it quite impossible for a woman to perform satisfactorily."

This notion rests on the stale presupposition that women are capable only of softness, whereas a man can be both soft and strong, harmonizing and neutralizing those opposing characteristics much as would a Noh actor who is following Zeami's prescriptions. Not incidentally, Zeami advises his female impersonators to reject any show of strength in their depictions — but this might be because their male strength will shine through regardless. An actor ought to "abandon any detailed stress on his physical movements (since, if the feminine spirit infuses his mind, a relaxation of physical strength will surely come about of itself)." — And what if his female projection relaxes too much? In 1912, the feminist novelist Tamura Toshiko made an exactly opposite claim to the Kabuki booklet, namely, that an onnagata may be able to express feminine weakness, but not feminine strength.

I once asked a Kyoto geisha whether there was anything in dance that women can do that men cannot.

"Women must look softer," she replied. "A woman gives birth. That a woman can do better than a man. But if she wants to do anything else, a man can probably do it better."

"Can a woman open a door or serve a drink more gracefully than a man?"

"Instructors of tea ceremonies, who are usually men, can do it better than we can."

My own opinion is that telling other people what they are incapable of expressing is always absurd. We have already met the Noh actress Yamamura Yoko, whose career is a rejection of the Kabuki booklet's logic. Originally she had begun taking lessons in the craft in her then home island of Kyushu because it was "nice for my parents." She followed Mr. Umewaka to Tokyo and studied with him for twenty years. In the Umewaka School (in Tokyo, at least), six or ten percent of the qualified players were female. The Kita School still prohibited women. No school allowed a woman to perform "Okina."

"The first women performers imitated very hard," she said. "Fortunately, in my generation we don't try to imitate men. We try to perform in a different way, exploiting the differences in sensitivity, strength and body figure."

Even she believed that women were insufficiently adept at Noh to perform alone, especially for *waki* and *kyogen* roles. "At this point, we rely on male masters," she said.

(With his customary openmindedness, Mr. Umewaka said about the few Noh actresses: "I tell them, don't imitate; *make Noh*. Create your own female Noh." He then added: "However, for me there is no female role or instructor.")

"Why is it so difficult for women to perform the *waki* role?" I asked Ms. Yamamura.

"Because the mask is not used, and because the *waki* is a travelling priest," she replied.

"Do you prefer playing female or male roles?"

"It depends. Boys' roles such as Atsumori are easy for women. Hardest of all is playing an old demon."

"How do you play a woman?"

Her reply was not too far removed from the thinking of an onnagata:

"As it stands, men put on a costume and a mask to become a woman. But if a woman is to play a woman's role, the woman must first be a man and learn that. The costumes are made to express femininity. If a woman uses the same technique to play a female role but lacks male strength, then it will be a weak Noh. So you need a man's strength."*

Once again, it would paradoxically seem that this species of feminine elegance requires a portion of masculinity. One transsexual speaks of the insecurity which once led him to "hyperfeminise" himself, "to adopt the artificial stereotypes attributed to women." In time he realized that he could act "naturally," making use of all the advantages of his previous male experience. Here we might remind ourselves that Zeami was at one time the Shogun's pretty boy. The grace of the Noh actor dwells near the grace of the transvestite prostitute Ms. Tosaka. All the same, who am I to say that a woman's grace contains no tincture of maleness?

But how strange to utterly privilege performance over anatomy! A scholar of ballet notes that when the ballerina performs a certain move such as an arabesque, "she's calling attention to a shapely ankle, an arched instep . . . and the round hip and ribcage. You can't mistake it if you're alive yourself." Ono no Komachi might have possessed these things when she was young. She could not have kept them all in old age. And how could an onnagata achieve that particular sort of ribcage? The obvious answer is that he avoids the issue by covering himself. He becomes a woman by becoming a female specter. He keeps his male parts shapeless.

A commitedly literalist female impersonator can indeed weigh down his lower body with pelvic prostheses so that his hips will swing like a woman's. He can wear false breasts, or take estrogen. He can angle his forearms away from his torso to simulate the human female's greater

---

*She added: "In Noh the male actor does not sound like a female, unlike in Kabuki. When we play a woman, we use our natural voice. In my opinion, we use our own body as a resonator. Try to make the best sound according to your own body. In other words, don't imitate the male voice."

elbow angle. Because the male voice shares about half an octave of overlap with its female counterpart, a transvestite can train his voice to sound both natural and feminine, in part by pitching it between falsetto and the point where it breaks into its natural bass or tenor. All these props and performances make use of concretions, handicaps, efforts and distortions of nature. But while a man may broaden his hips, it is not so easy to narrow his shoulders; and even if he could, if we imagine a great Noh actor in the full bloom of his true flower, and a young woman possessed of a gorgeous face and body, and if we further imagine the two of them to be naked side by side, how could we guarantee that the judgment of Paris would come out as art would wish it to be?*

"Do you try to become the character?" I asked Ms. Yamamura.

She said what almost all of them did: "I try to stay in my ordinary state, calm. When I'm taking lessons I think a lot. But when I put on the mask I try not to think."

In the climax of "Izutsu," the *shite* gazes down into the well, into which she used to look with her lover Narihira, and instead of her own ghostly reflection, or nothing, she sees *his* image.† To me this seems to be less about androgyny or ambisexuality than about crossing the abyss, identifying completely with the beloved other.

So why is it that the overwhelming beauty of a woman's face and carriage can so dominate the world that the latter becomes a bare and polished Noh stage?

Before attempting to answer, I must remind myself of Zeami's caution: "A flower blooms by maintaining secrecy." A scholarly book about courtesans concludes them to be "fundamentally elusive fantasies of the imagination." This leads to the question: What would be gained and what lost by seeing a great actress or geisha naked? It also makes me worry that trying to dissect the flower of feminine grace will destroy

---

*Here it is worth quoting the very convincing-sounding woman of the digital video disk called "Finding Your Female Voice." "After you've hit puberty . . ." she says sadly, "that's when your vocal cords thicken, and it's irreversible."

†In this play's source, the *Tales of Ise*, there is an episode (Dan XXIII, p. 64) in which two children of the opposite sex grow up together, marry, have troubles and get reconciled, all after having played together at the well.

its effect, which approximates what Zeami called *mutuality in movement beyond consciousness*. All the same, I will now take out my scalpel.

Just as the geisha's dance is hers alone, and the fiftieth actor to use a Noh mask makes it his own just as much as did the first, so feminine elegance is unique to the woman or her impersonator. Zeami again: "The life and spirit of Noh is nothing without the player's forming of his own style . . . The real *shite* is the one who studies various kinds of other styles after achieving a unique style of his own."

"When a Noh actor takes on the role of a beautiful woman," I once asked Mr. Mikata, "how is it that the illusion is so perfect? The actor sings in a male voice; we can see his adam's apple, and yet he becomes a beautiful woman.* To me this is even more magical than when an actor becomes a Kagekiyo or Atsumori. How is this accomplished?"

He replied: "I think it's because what's expressed is neutral: not man, not woman. That's what we pursue. Since we are men, when we play a man, it's just as what we usually do, but when we play a woman, if you move like a woman or sound like a woman, well, that is what an observer can easily see, but in fact we don't really want to express a woman as such. Woman's mind, what she feels, her pure mind or jealousy, that's what we want to express through a woman's figure. This figure should not stand out, even though when we play the role of woman or elderly man we do slightly change the voices and the moves."

Here we find ourselves returned to the genderless soul independently posited by Hilary Nichols, Marina and Sachiko. An eighteenth-century Japanese scholar of classical literature writes that "the true heart is not masculine, firm or resolute; such attitudes are mere decoration. When one delves to the bottom of the heart, even the most resolute person is no different from a woman or a child."

At any rate, the detachment within that masculine-feminine balance must to some extent require that grace be a set of conventions; indeed, part of what gives Noh its impressive effect is its very *rigidity*.

By no means can this be a universal characteristic of feminine grace.

---

*This "yet" betrays my parochialism, for Aphrodite statuettes frequently identify themselves by means of their rolls of neck-flesh, which are accordingly known as "Venus rings."

Sappho, whose girls of her desire are all soft, tender, supple, violetlike, informs us that "I love refinement," just as a Noh connoisseur does, "and beauty and light are for me the same as desire for the sun."* Grace is, among other things, the voluminous S-shape of a standing courtesan in a narrow vertical *ukiyo-e* print, her hairpiece as many-spoked as a mushroom cap is gilled, utterly in balance in spite of all, and not rigid. But even that softest, tenderest and most violetlike expression of Noh, Yuya's flower dance, could never be called supple; and in her stately glide across the stage bridge, any *shite* at all, no matter how girlish her mask and garments, reminds me of one of the prehistoric grave-figurines of southern central Europe: thick-legged, her ankles ending in rounded stumps, her thighs as wide as her hips, rendering her middle a sort of apron comprised of her stony or bony substance; this region is generally incised with the disproportionately large female triangle described by one scholar as a "supernatural vulva." Her arms, considerably shorter and more slender than her legs, which they recapitulate with their own rounded stumps. Her head and neck are a single rounded vertebral cone. Archaeologists have named her the Stiff White Lady. And stiff she is indeed. In her utter rigidity she reminds me of a geisha's black wig — but she is the color of death: bone-pale. Some of her exemplars are in fact nothing more and less than bones carved with a few stylized female markings. "The symbol closest to death is a bare bone." I am categorically informed that she, like her sister avatars of the Great Goddess, "has nothing to do with sexuality." That is one opinion. As for me, I find her beautiful, graceful, erotic. Like a Noh heroine, she has been stripped down, understated until she paradoxically *towers* before me: In the plate I now study she is not much larger than my finger, which makes no difference because, being a goddess, she has won the victory over ever so many things, including scale.

The Stiff White Lady's daughters, the Cycladic marble figurines from 3000–2500 B.C., are a trifle more human, but still coldly, beautifully alien, with their noses jutting from otherwise featureless face-disks and their arms folded beneath their breasts. These items likewise seem to have been fashioned to lie in graves. Their smoothly abstracted geometries are

---

*An essay on Greek hetairai calls them "'superfeminine' . . . supersoft, structurally most opposed to the masculine of hard Ares/Mars."

their grace; their narrowness is their elegance. Their female triangles are their real faces. What are they, but perfect bones of femininity?

Their granddaughter, a marble statue of Tyche, Greek goddess of fortune, gazes through me with pupil-less eyes. Young and cold, smooth and whitish-yellow, with her arms broken off and her nipples erect beneath the folds of the robe, small-lipped, plump-cheeked like a *ko-omote*, veiled, crowned with a miniature city's towered walls, what is she but perfect grace?

A man in a seventeenth-century *ko-omote*, a man who is now a woman, approaches us. Her cheeks are shadowed faintly black; the corners of her mouth turn upward in an ingenuous smile; the middle of her upper teeth have been blackened. She stares through us with the contentment of a young girl who is still tasting the sweet that she has been sucking on. Even when she gazes downward, she expresses no sadness. Her true face, his face, is as absent as the features of the Stiff White Lady (who may on occasion have a nose). Or are these their faces? How can a woman express perfect grace without supplenesss, without facial muscles, without eyes? And yet she does. I remember with affection how a certain straight pine tree in Nara tapered upward with surprising symmetry, each branch short, slightly upcurving like a fern-fingertip. A Noh goddess and a Stiff White Lady both partake of pine-grace. They also, it would seem, have been made specifically for their roles, and perhaps it is this specificity which distinguishes them from flesh.* Hisao Kanze once wrote that Noh woman-masks pass "beyond all specific human expression." What then is grace, if it leaves the human behind? Perhaps it is simply that it, like great poetry, brings us as close as possible to, and then points toward, what ultimately cannot be expressed. By the *shite*'s pillar of the stage, the Noh mask of a young girl orbits my floating world, laurel of the moon; I cannot go to the moon but I can watch it rise through ever so many of my blue-black nights. And this Noh girl of the *ko-omote* employs a man's

---

*At the beginning of the fourteenth century, Lady Nijo expresses the idea that specific beauty will be fitted for a specific use: "But she was without question a beautiful woman — her face delicate, her nose finely molded, her eyes vivid . . . She was a well-developed girl with a fair complexion and had the advantage of being both tall and plump; had she been a member of the court, in fact, she would have been perfect in the principal female role at a formal ceremony of state, carrying the sword, with her hair done up formally."

*tabi*-socked feet to glide inhumanly across my life, like the moon, which is Elder Sister to Stiff White Ladies.

And so, in contradistinction to Sappho's yielding lightness, I cite Fenollosa's belief that "the beauty of the Noh lies in the concentration. All elements — costume, motion, verse, and music — unite to produce a single clarified impression." And a Sardinian lady made of bone — she is perhaps six thousand years old — overpowers me through her horizontal eye-slits; she will not kiss me because she lacks a mouth; folding her bone arms across her breast, she displays her wide and simple vulva to me, standing upon her rounded stumps; she is femininity; she is grace; I would be comforted to sleep with her in my grave.

For women, goddesses and figurines, grace must be, again and again, *performance*. And the famous Kabuki actor Bando Tamasaburo once said: "All performance is essentially erotic. To *really capture the attention of the audience* — to fully ensnare the yearnings of each member of that audience — a performance must be based in eroticism."

And we remember that Hilary Nichols told us: "I do think that a very big sense of self for me is recognizing my attraction. And I live in a very social scene, so it's all about exchanging attractiveness and being recognized." Surely this must be somewhat akin to concentrating on all elements of one's female self-expression and creating a coherent, refined expression of that attractiveness. This process may require lies and absurdities. In a fashion magazine I find an ad for a skin cream whose magical ingredient is "savage cacao, delivering the antioxidant power of 204 pounds of blueberries." If a woman buys it literally and metaphorically, perhaps she will perform with greater joy and confidence.

In this context I also want to quote Mr. Kanze Hideo, who in contradistinction to Mr. Umewaka, Mr. Mikata and Ms. Yamamura told me that in playing a role he did not simply remain himself: "First you have to be that role yourself, but you need another self to supervise the person, to control yourself. You need two gazes. Zeami wrote about that: sight from a distance. You have to look at yourself from behind or from the top." — Here was a man old and surprisingly small, with pouches under his eyes; I had seen him as a beautiful woman; he was an expert; he possessed the flower. He was saying essentially what Hilary had said.

The *mai* dance characteristic of Noh entails, as we have said, rotating movements, stiffness, with the back straight, the knees bent just a little, the feet flat on the stage and the arms a trifle away from the body. This helps harmonize the actor with the mask, which expresses the hardness of its wood but can certainly swivel upon the turning neck. Maintaining the required stance calls for a measure of physical endurance, and it may be for this reason that so many authorities have disbelieved in women's capacity to achieve the *mai* effect. Its grace is certainly tinged with eeriness, and part of the eeriness is that it can be so feminine when that is not the way most women comport themselves.* In fact it is unnatural. Bando Tamasaburo once remarked on the fact that women's clothes are more uncomfortable than men's, which furthers the end because "when they are slightly uncomfortable, women are more erotic." Most of my Euro-American women friends bristle at this; their vision of an erotic female is of a woman in freely flowing clothes, or a woman nude. Thus the eros of Matisse. What about the eros of Bando? Bare legs on a cold day, sandal straps abrading bare feet, tight-laced corsets, tiny and half-helpless high heeled steps, knees pressed carefully together when sitting, pierced ears, these and various Western signals of femininity do bear out the great onnagata's assertion, and likewise of course the fifty-odd pounds of kimonos and hairpieces borne by a maiko in her formal glory, not to mention the wooden pillow she sleeps on in order to keep her hair well styled.

In any event, when playing a woman, the Noh actor keeps his feet slightly closer together than otherwise, and his glide is comprised of shorter steps. A feminist describes the old European minuet as expressing both sexes' body movements "mincingly and decoratively, contrary to the latter delegation of this stylistic pattern to female." — I quote again the transvestite bargirl Miss Tosaka: "When I'm a woman, I try to keep my knees together. I take very short steps. When I sit down, I keep my legs together." — And I remind myself that Mr. Umewaka commented that this was Kabuki style. It can also be geisha style. All the same, it bears comparison to Noh's feminine mode, which is known as *nyotai*.

---

*For instance, one renowned seventeenth-century habitué of pleasure quarters describes several sorts of walking-steps engaged in by courtesans: the "floating walk" entailed kicking; the "soft-footed walk" might be accompanied by a swaying of the hips, and "on reaching the house of assignation, she trips in nimbly." None of these styles correspond to *mai*.

Every performance must come to an end. Every fashion alters, even for the Stiff White Ladies, as when, for instance, Spedos Style A yields to Style B: "round modeling now gives way to flattish relief and a preference for clean incisions to mark transitions and details."* *Aware*, that classical Japanese perception of this world's autumnal transience, is sometimes associated with feminine sensibility, and both the woman who allures me and I myself keep conscious or unconscious hold of the fact that the petals of the true flower must fall. This feminine quality that we share, if it is indeed feminine, what does this make us? Does a woman's grace inspire me to merge sexually and spiritually with its possessor, or to maintain my separateness from her so that I can better see her and drink her in?

A drawing instructor of my acquaintance, who has employed nude models for many years now, said that in his opinion womanly grace is the result of someone's being at ease in her body, attractive to the gaze, and willing to offer her beauty to the eyes of others. (The American fashion magazines agree; they often say that grace equals confidence.) One of his models was now ageing and had become self-conscious about posing with younger women; all the same, he saw no reason why she might not retain her grace in old age if she continued to exercise it.

Mystery (which surely includes understatement), concentration, gender harmony, self-awareness and distance from self, consciousness of transience — this very short list of qualities appears to be a trifle mechanical, like a template for a mask as opposed to the animated mask itself, with the actor inside it. In part this animation achieves its success by giving off the shock of reality itself, of a person whose power of attraction over us is so great precisely because we could never have imagined her; she is alive, unique, unforeseeable. But much of the effect does come about mechanistically; a honeybee leads her hive-sisters to the richest flowers by means of a dance, and the graceful woman carries herself in obedience to (or in some rare cases in reaction to, but even then in reference to) her time's rules of carriage, beauty and the like. "Movement metaphors distinguish male from female," writes a feminist scholar of dance, who has compiled

---

*The carnally inclined reader will be glad of the following reassurance: "Almost without fail, the deep, wedge-shaped cleft dividing the legs is perforated between the calves . . ."

a very interesting table of "stereotypical nonverbal gender behavior": For instance, in comparison to men women make smaller gestures (in part because shorter limbs, more constricting clothes and custom constrain them), but they smile more; their movements are more "emotional, expressive" and horizontal, their gazes more submissive and averted.

But then, the experience and interpretation of loveliness is always, as an aesthetician has said, a work in progress, "completed only when beauty has nothing more to offer"; which is why our list could not be complete without killing several of its own quantities, such as mystery — not to mention grace itself. And so I return to Zeami, hoping for help in seeking to uncover with words what lies beyond words.

Once again I remember his prescription from "Kakyo": Forget the details of a play in order to perceive it whole. Then forget the play itself, focusing on the actor. Next, forget the actor and study his spirit. Finally, forget his spirit; and what remains will be Noh itself.

Accordingly, I propose to forget face, body and clothes in order to take in the entire impression that the woman makes. Next, forget her impression and consider its maker: *her*. Now forget her, and perhaps you may find a way to see her soul. At the last, forget even that, and then you will know her grace.

# Rainbow Skirts

*The Loveliness of Lady Yang*

Once upon a time in China, near the center of the eighth century, the Tang Dynasty Emperor Xuan-zon became enthralled by a certain Lady Yang Yu-han, also known as Yang Kuei-fei, who was at that time his son's wife; no matter; Lady Yang rapidly became the Prized Consort. "Tresses like a cloud, face like a flower" is how the poet Bo Ju-yi describes her in his "Song of Lasting Pain." In the twelfth century, another Chinese author invokes the ideal singing girl: "As lovely as jade, with rosy lips, white teeth, and a complexion like ice." Perhaps that is how Lady Yang was. When she craved dragon's-eye fruits, the Emperor established a chain of post horses in order to rush them to her fresh. Soon her relatives had become noble and rich; how could that have gone otherwise? It is equally, since consequently, no surprise that after her uncle's rebellion-guilt had been rightly or wrongly established, angry officers and courtiers demanded Lady Yang's execution. "His Majesty knew that it could not be avoided," writes the ninth-century author

Chen Hong, "and yet he could not bear to see her die, so he turned his sleeve to cover his face as the envoys dragged her off." What kind of love was this? Why could he not have abdicated, or died with her? Perhaps he thought it his duty to remain above ground, or possibly he did not adore her as much as the legends say; but very likely the choice did not occur to him. And so Lady Yang was strangled.

This story, which in many versions concludes with a sadly supernatural reunion by proxy between the two lovers, took place not far from the city of Xian, whose narrow high-walled streets remind me of Peshawar's with their old stone and brick and signlessness. The many-notched old wall bears many arches; the old streets are quieter and dirtier than those of many other Chinese cities. Elderly people sit in chairs on the sidewalk; men stand sweaty and stripped to the waist; it is late afternoon in an air-conditioned restaurant into which man are carrying cases of beer. The waitresses are laughing, lazing and flirting. One sleeps, with her dark head tucked down on the table between her crimson-clad shoulders; and in this extremely modern-looking place of new tables and polished granite tiles, everybody engages in what a Westerner would call "doing nothing," because Xian dreams and dreams, her pillow being the dust of the past. Whomever I asked about Lady Yang knew her and presented an opinion without surprise or excitement. The long past of China felt far more present here than the most recent previous war ever had in my own country. After all, Lady Yang's story was taught in primary school.

A quarter-hour away by car from the long white trenches where the famous Terra Cotta Warriors stand, some of them headless, many attended by horses of the same colorlessness as they (for centuries have licked away the vivid glaze), the Royal Baths still remain, and here, in the twelve-sided Crabapple Pool, Lady Yang used to bathe while the Emperor watched. Far down within the lacquered red railings lies that dry cavity where, according to the mural one sees at her tomb, her pale and chubby nakedness drowsed within a gold-rimmed border; now there is no gold, and a tour guide gripping a yellow flag speaks into her microphone, causing tourists to gaze dully down into the emptiness. Once upon a time there was a Lady Yang; she was a pawn, a corrupting influence or both; now she is a flock of poems.

By taxi, at least by a certain taxi with a red and silver talisman hanging from the mirror and a Chairman Mao song on the cassette player, it takes an hour to reach the town of Ma Mei Zhen, where anyone can direct the traveller to Ma We Po; and here Lady Yang is buried. The flickering of a flashlight discovers the pale white figurines of representative grave-goods, but none of them come from the tomb itself, which is a beehive-shaped mound now covered with bricks because people kept coming here to steal the earth which enclosed her, on account of its beauty-working properties. By the tomb stands the name-marker, a black tongue engraved with gold. A marble statue depicts her as uncharacteristically slender, with mushroom-gill hair and her trademark tree-peony in it. The smell of stone in the rain, then the mound, then the town far away, blue-green with fields, noisy with engines and horns whose sounds rise up like incense, all this comprises another of China's multitudinous islands of tranquil ancientness.

The taxi waited. Soon we returned, passing white-clad minions in the greenery beneath the wall, where people exercised like armies every morning; then came the train station with its two giant characters for Xian, and a flag in between. The driver said: "Anyhow, Lady Yang had body odor. The history says this. But the Emperor liked it."

What other enticements had she possessed? Bo Ju-yi writes that her "helplessness so charming" when attendants escorted her out of the bath allured the Emperor to her for the first time. (Bando Tamasaburo again: "When they are slightly uncomfortable, women are more erotic.")

Bo Ju-yi further envisions her flowered hairpins, jade hairpick, marble-white face, "and the fragile arch of her lovely brows." Chen Hong calls her hair "glossy and well arranged"; and she was neither slender nor plump. The great poet Du Fu laments the loss to us of her shining eyes and sparkling teeth. In the seventeenth-century supernatural tales of Pu Songling, a semblance of the goddess Chang E performs "Rainbow Skirts"; and a beautiful ghost, whose name just happens to be Yang, presents breasts "as virginal and soft to the touch as freshly peeled lotus kernels," a simile used by Emperor Xuanzong himself in his praise of the breasts of Yang Guifei.

But probably it was the Dance of Rainbow Skirts that made the Emperor pliable to her every caprice. I have never seen it performed, and the only description I know comes again from Bo Ju-yi's "Song of Lasting

Pain": It was slow and stately, apparently.* There was already a renowned melody entitled "Coats of Feathers, Rainbow Skirts"; this was what Lady Yang danced to. Her performance probably involved arm movements, and in Komparu Zenchiku's Noh play "Yokihi," Lady Yang refers to the dance of Rainbow Skirts as follows: "A young girl's fluttering sleeves well express her heart." In the play "Hagoromo" an angel performs the same, and we read: "The sky-robe flutters; it yields to the wind."

Because the Emperor's love for her disordered the realm and she can therefore be construed as sinister, I imagine Rainbow Skirts to resemble the serpentine dance of the demon-woman in the play "Dojoji"; by means of it she hypnotizes the temple servants, next vanishing into the bell she would destroy. But why not envision it as the writhings of seductive pseudo-helplessness?

The Noh actress Yamamura Yoko said to me, presumably in reference to "Dojoji": "When I play a woman who becomes a serpent, I want to express the sadness rather than the scariness." — And it is true that my vision of Rainbow Skirts must express pathos, given the doom of Lady Yang.

This would certainly be the Noh vision; for in Noh a man provisionally becomes a woman who temporarily controls a man. The Emperor kisses the mask. So he wounds his son's happiness; she sickens the empire; she dies; he pines; it ends, and the actor takes off his mask.

We have said that the Japanese concept of *aware* refers to the beauty and harmony beyond direct expression which shines uniquely from various entities in their own occasion — for instance, cherry blossoms about to fall. "Gradually," one commentator informs us, "*aware* came to be tinged with sadness." In due course, the tranquil Heian splendors of Kyoto were razed by violence, the Empire shattered into myriad competing dictatorships, and *aware* "darkened to its modern meeting of 'wretched,' which represents perhaps the final evolution in its long history." On another page this scholar remarks: "The court lady who in the past had brooded over a lover's neglect was now likely to suffer more immediate grief on learning he had been killed in battle. In some diaries, women described their emotions on seeing their lover's head on a pike being paraded through

---

*She is said to have also possessed a fast dance in her repertoire: "When Yang Kui-fei did the Whirl, she addled the ruler's heart."

the streets."* And how did the Emperor feel while the one he loved was kicking and choking in the noose?

Lady Yang must have moved the Japanese nearly as much as the Chinese, for we find her haunting the very first page of the *Tale of Genji*. She appears two more times in close succession: Genji's dead mother gets likened to her. Indeed, as early as the tenth century we find a tanka about the Emperor's desperate attachment to Lady Yang: At dawn, it runs, his jeweled dais tries to remain dark out of compassion for him whose passion has not been slaked by the night's pleasures.

And in the early fourteenth century, Lady Nijo watches the dance of Rainbow Skirts at a shrine, which "summoned forth my own nostalgic memories." She sees a dancer wearing a fancy crown and hairpins, and imagines her to be Lady Yang's image. A few decades later, a chronicler of a medieval Japanese war harks back to Tang Dynasty China: "While the emperor listened to the song of 'Rainbow Skirts,' the war drums of Yü-Yang came shaking the earth." *The Tale of the Heike* makes a byword of the famous couple's sorrow. In 1931, Tanizaki alludes to Lady Yang in his "Blind Man's Tale." In short, it is no wonder that Komparu composed a Noh play about her.

In "Yokihi," which follows the narrative of Bo Ju-yi's poem fairly closely, the spirit of Yang Kuei-fei, whose name has now been Japonicized per the title, dwells behind jeweled blinds in the Residence of Great Purity on the Island of Everlasting Youth. To visit her, the Emperor's sorcerer must fly through the void, as all of us have to do in order to reach whomever we desire. The sorcerer begins the play with these words: "I seek a way to a world unknown." (Hilary Nichols: "I do think that part of the joy in a male-female relationship is crossing the abyss.") So off he goes, into the darkness of stars, the flutesong an evil wind of destiny, all the voices of the chorus like rocks in a river or wind in a twilight pine grove. Why not say that it is for him as for Kawabata's protagonist riding the train into the snow country, finding the fields ever thicker and whiter, the houses ever purer, the ponds shining with ice, the horizon vanishing in white mist? Here he will presently encounter a heroine of incomprehensible beauty. Dark birds fly across white ricefields. Where is he going, but into the

---

*For further discussion, see the "Sadism and Expediency" chapter of my *Rising Up and Rising Down*.

brightness of the wet snow beneath the dark sky, from which snow speeds down? On the grounds of many a Japanese temple stand tombs as close-packed as teeth, their rounded tops white with snow. A stone Buddha sits with snow in his lap, the snowy wind stirring the trees with the sound of rain. He goes into the snow, into the cracked and frozen urns. He goes into the peach-colored snowy twilight. Silver-forested hills of pines gather around the train. He passes between a man's lips and a woman's in the instant that they kiss. For him the rainbow curtain is raised.

When he arrives at the island, he discovers Yokihi's ghost in the act — how could it be otherwise? — of grieving over her transient attachment. The mask she had kissed (or was it merely a crown?) abandoned her, as every mask must do. Had she sought to be her father-in-law's wife? Did she then become guilty of abusing her exalted position? It hardly matters now. She gasped and struggled, like a child in a tantrum; then the play was done. Her desire should have died likewise. But instead, transform-ing her into a vampire who feeds hopelessly upon herself, it condemns her to consciousness upon the Island of Everlasting Youth.*

Yokihi's face is most often a *waka-onna*. Occasionally she embodies herself in a *zo-onna* or *ko-omote*. Although the latter customarily portrays a young girl who has not yet suffered greatly, the *tsuki*, the moon-style *ko-omote*, can project the inhumanness which is so characteristic of entities on the far side of the abyss. A mask-maker informs us that "the fundamental aspect of 'Tsuki' is that the nose is tilted to the left. From the audience, the left side of the mask is the best view. The right half has a rather peaceful expression, in order to show relief from hate and sadness, and enlighten-

---

*It was not, as might have been the case in some Occidental legend, her violent death itself that transformed her into the equivalent of a ghost; it was her unwillingness to die. But most actors are losers in the Noh cosmos and its derivatives. In the fourteenth-century war tale *The Taiheiki* there are numerous instances of warriors who are too cowardly to cut their bellies open and die for their lords, because they cannot overcome their attach-ment to this transient world. Of course, we know from Mr. Umewaka's explication of "Kagekiyo" (above, p. 20) that such warriors will be condemned to hell. (*The Taiheiki* itself puts the dilemma in terms only one of which is eternal: "Those of the Heike who cherished honor and died quickly — they became wretched asuras, doomed to suffer for many ages. How regrettable it was! And those who subjected themselves to humiliation by remaining alive — they fell into destitution at once, and were mocked at by all men. How pitiful it was!")

ment when she receives prayers from a monk while departing the stage on the *hashigakari*," the pine tree bridge. Yokihi, of course, obtains no enlightenment. Presumably she will show us her left side. The perfect-complected face of this mask is almost a squash-yellow, the double chin softer than in many *ko-omote*, the smile strangely wider, the upper eyelids darkly overlined, the lower ones shadowed; overall, the face expresses *hard newness*. When it swims upward, the peculiar smile begins to yield to a wide darkness beneath the black-grey crystals of the upper teeth.

The mask-maker continues with a quotation: "*The ko omote's cold brilliance which even reflects the shade of the accessories, touches one's soul*. – Baba Akiko. If this is about a program in which a crown is worn on top of the mask, this poem must be for 'Hagoromo' or 'Yokihi.'"

The Noh mask in the box (in Yokihi's case, usually a *waka-onna*) desires nothing. I, a spectator in the theater, willingly trick myself in order to drink more beauty from what I see. Then the play ends, and I go out into the excitement of the crowds, the hurrying crowds of this world, in whose manic exaltation Baudelaire was caught up two centuries before me. Unlike the mask of Yokihi, I am still alive; so I seek out other masks to kiss, refusing to believe that crossing the abyss will cost my lovers and me any suffering. Soon I will creep across the stage in my stockinged feet with an old man's movements, my face almost a skull; by then many of the other personages I now see on Tokyo's streets will have already glided along the gangway with slow and spaced deliberation; in due time I will meet them behind the rainbow curtain. But if I am lucky I will no longer know them and they will have forgotten me, unlike Yokihi the damned, who informs the sorcerer: "Your visit only multiplies the pain."* Her complaint is misplaced; for she loves her agony's cause: the Emperor. To him she would send that familiar token, a jeweled hairpin. (In Chen Hong's version it is actually the golden hairpin that the Emperor gave her when he first slept with her.) But then she takes back her gift, I presume to use it while she now performs her alluring dance of Rainbow Skirts.

---

*When Mr. Umewaka performed this role in a certain Takigi-Noh, he is said to have remained very still on the bridge for a long interval, with his arm folded and his gaze downward. One observer "experienced the beautiful illusion of watching feelings that could no longer be kept pent up inside welling forth as tears."

Here is Yokihi the beautiful, her bass soliloquies rhythmic, rising and descending in pitch, sonorous, guarded and respected by pause, not quite song; she inches through eternity upon her old man's feet. In most performances she wears a gold kimono and a phoenix headdress from which angular treaures sharply hang. Her red lips remain eternally parted in what is both more and less than a smile; her black teeth sparkle like evening ice. The points of her long, narrow eyes reach her temples. Her eyebrows are high clouds of black fog upon her moon-colored forehead. Her painted black hair merges with the darkness of her tortured Paradise. Through the holes in her wooden face, an actor is gazing beyond all of us.

Has he entirely crossed the abyss? Is he Yokihi, or is he, for instance, Mr. Umewaka? And who is Yokihi to me? Can my aesthetic enjoyment of the play be reduced to male sadism in the face of female agony? — In her late middle age, a certain nineteenth-century Japanese lady advised other members of her gender that "human feelings are rooted in the genitals and spread from there throughout our bodies. When men and women make love, they battle for superiority by rubbing their genitals together." Admirable consistency to this world-view drew her to conclude that no matter how feminine an onnagata (and presumably a Noh actor) might appear, "since he has a man's body, in his heart he harbors abusive feelings toward women. As he performs he thus in fact takes pleasure in what should be a pitiable scene . . . that is why he performs in ways that appeal to the men in his audience. Women, on the other hand, take no pleasure in a villain's capturing a beautiful young woman and doing with her what he wishes."

Would love exist, if what she wrote were true? If the abyss could be transcended, why must Yokihi and the Emperor remain alone in the end? Who is a woman? If I understood, why would my visit to her multiply the pain?

The sorcerer presently departs, and the play ends when the chorus chants: "Oh, this futile parting! In the Tower of Eternal Life she falls, weeping, to remain for all time." Bo Ju-yi's ending was typically more ornate, and may well be echoed in the Noh play "Miidera": "Heaven endures, and the Earth; but someday they'll be gone; yet this pain of ours will go on and never ever end."

# 13:

# Jewels in the Darkness

*The Dances of Kofumi-san and Konomi-san*

In Kyoto there is a temple that I love called the Shoren-in. The eerie energies of the place's camphor trees figure lovingly in Kawabata's novel *The Old Capital*. Pagoda'd pavilions upon the sphagnum moss mark the resident priesthoods of abdicated Emperors. Closing my eyes to various wars and accidents, I agree to call the garden eight or nine hundred years old.* Like any other stage, it can represent whichever time may be indicated. And I, *waki* of my own life, not to mention the lives of plants and rocks, exist here only to specify for you what I have been told I see. ("While this garden is not considered one of the major examples of

---

*The information sheet assures me that "although some of the present buildings were rebuilt in 1893 after a fire, they kept their original foundations," and that "the position of the stones" in the garden "were reconstructed by archaeological method about 30 years ago."

landscape art," says my guidebook, "its admirable details and fine plant material reward the visitor.") Between the toes of an immense tree, I sit and watch the hours of my life blissfully idle themselves away. Gazing down from the bamboo grove at the stone lantern and the perfect asymmetries of the rock-bordered turquoise pond below it, I find no false alignments. A narrow porch runs around each edifice so that one can walk around it, gazing out at this changing world. Sometimes I do just that, or I might drink in the shadows of a wooden fence upon an ancient wooden gate. One October afternoon, with the tiny mosquitoes silently biting me and the leaves of the camphor trees as still as the tapering gable roofs, the reddish wood, yellowish wood and blackish wood in the gable lattices began to announce themselves almost with sounds. Beneath the trees, the immense bell seemed to vibrate beneath its gable roof. But then and always the favorite drink of my eye remained beyond the yellow wall: the many narrow turquoise-jade risings of the bamboo grove.

In the grove itself, particularly on cloudy summer days, bamboo and sky comprised a single jewel. Here might have been the best place to lose myself. But then, being a *waki* who lacked the power to release from attachment anyone, including himself, my desire wandered back to the carp pond and the camphor trees.

It was a smallish place, the Shoren-in; and so this circling completed itself easily. There was much to see, and all of it infinite, but the infinities were not glaringly daunting, like the night crowds of Shinjuku; they were almost as sparse as the cosmos of a Noh stage.

Wherever I am, I remain inside my body looking out; all the same, it is obviously possible, as at any other Japanese temple or shrine, to gaze into rectangular wooden darknesses with coppery or golden glitters of statues within. Thus gazing in, the horizon becomes silhouetted waves of roof-tile, with silhouetted leafy branches cutting very occasionally into the pale sky above it, and below the sky, a wall of dark wood studded with darker metal fittings, and in that wall a rectangular opening illuminated by three lamps just bright enough to reveal a bamboo railing within and then the dull gold glint of treasures in the darkness behind it.

And in Gion, whenever my eyes are granted the thrill of a maiko standing in a half-open lattice-windowed doorway, with darkness behind her, she is still more splendid than those temple treasures; she is a jewel in the darkness!

Another maiko bows to us and darts across the street into a private teahouse, the dark knot of hair at the back of her darker than the darkness, the strange pastel look of her like neon subdued into elegance.

## SPECULATIONS ON AN UNWRITTEN TREATISE

What is a woman? What is this woman? Can her soul possibly be ungendered? Could there be any unfeminine element to her grace? What makes her perfect?

Every act and gesture of hers that she allows me to see is, like its Noh counterpart, a performance. If I am the *waki* who witnesses her from the side, she is certainly the *shite* who blooms with ghostly glory. Mystery, yes, she possesses that. With his usual subtlety, Zeami defines fascination as a sensation which occurs before the consciousness of that sensation. So what sensation does a geisha first excite in me? Not lust, not quite excitement; almost awe, but not exactly . . . That is her mystery. Even the Noh mask-maker Ms. Nakamura, whose studio lay the merest quarter-hour's walk from Gion, was thrilled to accompany me to a geisha teahouse; for a glimpse is one thing; but to really look upon a Kyoto geisha, perceiving any of her jewel-facets — for instance, the painted eyebrows and black-outlined eyes, the vulvalike patch of unwhitened skin on the back of the neck — as more than vague but thrilling light, one must pay extremely, or be invited by a client who does. Anatomy, performance, mental and emotional expression, embodiment, like a Noh actor, of old rote movements, these have something to do with whom or what she personifies, but they cannot explain it. Were some wise old female Zeami of the Inoue School of dance to compose a treatise on the secret teachings of geisha arts, I wonder what she would say? Concentration and self-awareness, how could a geisha of the true flower fail to master those? As Lady Yang's ghost remarks in "Yokihi," "a young girl's fluttering sleeves well express what is in her heart." She must *know* what she expresses. And regarding awareness of transience, that remains inescapable, both to her who performs and to me who pays — to be specific, a thousand dollars and more per hour. Moreover, her profession is associated with Gion Shrine, whose bell at the very beginning of *The Tale of the Heike* rings out this world's evanescence.

## THE PRICE OF THEIR FAVORS

Speaking of compensation, geishas are not prostitutes, although over the centuries they have certainly comprised much of the foliage in the "flower and willow world." The courtesans were the flowers and the geishas the willows. As the metaphor implied, those two types of loveliness unfolded their leaves together in the meadow of delights. In the Yoshiwara, the red light district of old Edo, geishas performed alongside women of the other vocation. One of Utamaro's woodblock prints shows the geishas Oiyo and Takeji preparing to dance around a lantern in an annual Yoshiwara event which was held in company with young prostitutes and their apprentices. And here is Chobunsai Eishi's eighteenth-century painting of geishas in Yoshiwara, clutching their trains, gazing sideways up or down; black hair and subdued geisha colors.

In 1686, Ihara Saikaku assures us: "Even highly reputed maiko have the price of their favors set at one silver coin." In the "Sleeve Scroll" of Torii Kiyonaga (1785) we find, among other erotic scenes, a geisha, identifiable as such by her black *haori*, with her mouth on her hand, grimacing and almost gnawing her finger while the man on her back slides his imperial-size penis into her anus; indeed, it is already almost all the way in and her eyes are closed, but every hair remains in place, as does her golden headgear. In Keisai Eisen's woodblock album of about 1825, a client has just opened his geisha's thighs and is about to roll her down onto the floor. From 1827 we see a woodcut by Utagawa Kunisada, showing two red-clothed geishas peering down into a bathhouse orgy, some of whose participants may be other geishas.

Writings on this subject sometimes insist on one or the other point of view: Either geishas are artists of a rarefied sort (and authors with this point of view love to berate Occidentals for their salacious suppositions on this score), or else they exemplify "a world where love is bought and sold like merchandise," in which case they appear as victims or perpetrators.

In fact, the duties and reputations of geishas differ quite specifically. Instead of graceful white-faced goddesses, the early-twentieth-century novelist's Kafu Nagai's geisha characters are grasping, pathetic, jealous individuals of extremely variable appearances, talents and morals. Nor are their accoutrements uniform. Were I to describe a geisha to someone who had never seen one, I would probably, following the Peabody Museum, mention the black kimono, accentuating that eerie white of geisha skin, the wig with the hair ornaments, and the crisscrossing-in-front obi; all the same, I remember a certain mid-twentieth-century photograph of a geisha in a straw hat: stripes of shadow painting woodgrain on her upper face to match the stripes of her kimono; a character-studded sash traverses her breast as she beats a drum. I never saw her like in Kyoto.

Likewise vary their styles of dance. Once I saw geishas at the Gion Kobu Kaburenjo; they were performing the Miyako Odori or Cherry-Blossom Dance. Their movements were much less strict and angular than those of the Inoue School, two of whose practitioners will be described in this chapter. The Kanazawa geisha Masami-san danced with decidedly un-Inouean ease-enthusiasm.

Still another distinction between geishas is place of work, which offers clues analogous to those revealed in old times by a Japanese woman's clothes — for instance, she might be a whore if her kimono is tied in front. A geisha in one of the hot springs might not receive great respect. In Kawabata's *Snow Country*, the situation of many such women shows itself in a couple of lines of dialogue. The protagonist asks the heroine, Komako, who is herself a geisha, to summon him a geisha. She expresses bewilderment, at which point he says: "You know what I mean." Although Komako insists that "no one forces a geisha to do what she doesn't want to," a geisha, who presumably has been apprised of his requirements, does in due course present herself. Shall we suppose that she wants to?*

---

*One especially strident person takes Kawabata to task for *Snow Country*. She objects to his staying in an expensive room (evidently this confirms his status as an implement of

On the other side of the divide, the Heian capital retains its glamor. Kyoto's geishas are high ranking, and those in Gion remain preeminent. We learn from Saikaku that seventeenth-century Kyoto ladies possessed an especially fetching way of speaking, "handed down from ancient times in the Imperial Palace," and in my day the enunciation of geishas in Gion, at least — I lack the funds to widen my Kyoto investigations — remains distinctive.

In his final novel, Kawabata opines that "only the balconies along Kiyomachi and Ponto-cho were reminiscent of the old summer evenings by the river"; and by "old" he means deriving from a bygone century. Strangely, Gion figures seldom in his descriptions of Kyoto, although he does describe a photograph of two Gion geishas playing rock-paper-scissors in about 1880.

But what is actually the difference between a high-ranking geisha and a courtesan who dances? Doubtless the former have had to struggle continuously to maintain their distinctiveness. From a pleasure quarter of Edo in 1850 comes this dispatch from the arms race in rival fashions:

THE GEISHA MASAMI-SAN.

. . . the dress of the geisha now far exceeds that of noble ladies. But the common prostitute oversteps all bounds in modeling herself on the geisha. When the common prostitute adorns her hair with pins of glimmering tortoise-shell, the geisha must also insert a long tortoise-shell pin into the bun of her coiffure.

---

patriarchal objectification), to his creating a character based on a real geisha without telling her (he did change "Komako's" name), and — here my blood boils — to his "aestheticization" of the geisha's place in the political-social structure, thereby serving to "block the possibility of criticism."

And so many geishas accumulate debts. Sometimes they find it necessary to pawn their clothes.*

One 1913 essay about whether or not onnagatas should be replaced with actresses sees in geishas a "superficial purity which was their only weapon" against prostitutes. In literature they sometimes lack any purity at all; indeed, they can appear as interchangeable, rather commonplace companions whose association with carnality is the rule. A scholar from my own time positions geishas between prostitutes and artists — and between prostitutes and mistresses.


## "THE FACE IS NOT ALLOWED TO EXPRESS ANYTHING"


In the establishment of the ochaya Imamura-san, to whom I was introduced through the good offices of my friend Mr. Kou (employing a geisha in Gion works as follows: you will not learn what you owe until a week or a month later, and for the first time the invoice will be sent to your introducer, who stands responsible should you default), I now await Kofumi-san with her kind smile and her stiff black wig curling upward from her white face. And this year, which marks my second occasion, she will bring her maiko, Konomi-san, who wears a flower ornament in her hair.

Kofumi-san belongs to the Noh-related Inoue School. Noh's influence may be seen in other sorts of geisha dances. For instance, in a certain Utamaro print of an *odoriko*, a young geisha who specializes in dancing, we see the "Shakkyo" of Noh altered into a Kabuki dance. It is, we are told,

---

*And how could it be otherwise? Kofumi-san, whom you will meet later in the above sentence, told me which hair accessory store she patronized. When I peeped in there, I saw translucent golden combs of pure tortoise shell, which to my ignorant gaze resembled plastic; and there were hairpicks of mother-of-pearl; for some of these one could pay three hundred and forty thousand or even seven hundred thousand yen. And it is proper for geishas to change these ornaments each month! No wonder that their nineteenth-century predecessors sometimes pawned their clothes to keep up. Speaking of clothes, geishas also require new kimonos quite often — every month in the case of a maiko. They can be two million yen each, or occasionally even seven. Obis and wigs, which also must be changed every month, cost as much as kimonos.

a dance performed with a lion headdress decorated with tree peony à la Lady Yang. The caption continues, in my translator's raw English which I have no heart to alter: "One of the good pieces in the series with a nice balance of the headgear and lowered hair, adorable hands and expression." But Inoue dance is said to remain particularly close to Noh. Danyu-san the musician, who on that night would accompany each of the two geishas on the shamisen, explained to me: "The Inoue school is very unique. The legs and feet should not move too much. The face is not allowed to express anything." This explains why the geishas of Gion exemplify, in some ways even more than Noh actors themselves, Noh masks livingly embodied. For the blurry understatement which the man's inspired craft veils about his Adam's apple, substitute the woman's and her slender throat. In the Getty Villa in Malibu there stands a certain cult statue, Demeter, Hera or most likely Aphrodite, who reaches out to us with her broken marble fingers. The top of her head was robbed from her in

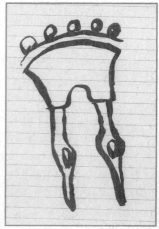

GEISHA HAIR ORNAMENT.

a clean slant so that her face resembles a mask, a *zo-onna* perhaps, for it is, while equally smooth, less girlishly plump-cheeked than a *ko-omote*. Aphrodite stands, clothed in garments of limestone whose pink, blue and red paint remains only in hints and stains. A breeze is blowing her robe tight across her breasts and thighs as she prepares to step forward. In no way inconvenienced by her incompleteness, the goddess is alive! But how peculiar she is! A head upon a neck, a mask within a box, a masked actor, yes, I've seen those, but a hollow mask upon a neck, this proof that beauty is indeed, as the cliché runs, skin-deep, affects me like something between a paradox and a mystery. As for the geisha, she exists as a stylized body in heavenly robes. Her face has been painted until much of its fleshly individuality has been masked by the unearthly whiteness of the goddess. Here in short is another *zo-onna*. "The Inoue style is noted for its ability to express great emotion in spare, delicate gestures," wrote one of its practitioners, a twentieth-century geisha. And Mr. Kanze told me: "Originally, there was a family who served the Emperor. The maiden from that family who was serving the Emperor, she created a dance which is similar to Noh. In the second generation a woman married a Noh actor, and her daughter got married with my great grandfather's brother. A cousin of my great grandfather came to Kyoto and taught this Noh school dance. His name was Katayama." — I wish I could tell you more about this famous branch of geisha dancing, which is said to be the most prestigious; unfortunately, its head, Inoue the Sixth, required me to submit my questions in writing and in advance, then declined to have anything to do with me.*

About Kofumi-san herself I can say that she must be in the neighborhood of sixty (Konomi-san has been a maiko for two years and is now seventeen), and that she is at the top of her profession. Mr. Mikata paid her this compliment: "Kofumi-san is a very good dancer. Her mind and technique are very well trained. My teacher used to perform at the Gion school, and he teaches Noh dance there. When I was still learning from him, sometimes I was a substitute teacher, so I saw her then. Zeami emphasizes that you need to practice a lot, and she does know a lot about that; she is really trained. That's how much she has practiced — even more than enough!"

When I asked her to describe her experience of dancing, Kofumi-san replied: "I feel just natural. I know how to do it artificially, but I just can't."

(And here I recall Mr. Mikata responding to a question of mine about his previous day's performance of "Michimori": "There's a rule about the boat. Within the range of the rule I can do as I like.")

"Is it really the case that there is a defined sequence of movements for a geisha to open a door?"

"When you enter a tearoom, you open the door a little bit and then another little bit."

---

*The reason might have been that my method of comparing various representations of femininity causes some people to bristle. Mr. Mikata was not atypical here. When I asked him how Noh and Inoue dance might be similar and different, he replied: "Because that dance originated from Noh, it has an essence of Noh movements, which have been altered and refined. If you superficially compare Noh and Inoue dance, yes, there are similarities. But Noh has more than six hundred years, and Inoue is later. I don't think that there is any meaning in comparing the two."

In fact, so I have read, the way she opened a door, and bowed, and many other such acts, derived from the fourteenth-century samurai code known as the Ogasawara style.*

One transgender workbook defines "passing" for a member of one's desired sex as "getting as many signals as possible lined up" — for instance, the "presenting" angle of the buttocks caused by high heels, the protrusions of womanly breasts. As with any performance worth accomplishing, the standard can be high. The rules of "passing" as a high-ranking geisha are more rigorous still.

What one noticed first about her as about her colleagues was the white, white skin, part of whose makeup was bush warbler droppings. In that classic twentieth-century short story "Portrait of an Old Geisha," Okamoto Kanoko describes a thickly painted cheek as being "radiant as enamel." As for Kofumi-san, her cheeks had hollowed slightly with age, so that the creases between the corners of her mouth and the wings of her nose could be seen as blue snow-shadows. The perimeters of her eyes did not appear young. All this was true especially in three-quarter profile. When she stood side by side with her maiko Konomi-san, her face showed at better advantage, widening and flattening like the legs of a Noh actor in his kimono. She seemed less at rest than Konomi-san, more conscious, more taut. A lock of her wig descended the center of her forehead, perhaps two-fifths of the way to her flattish painted eyebrows, so that her face expressed a heart shape.

Japanese women tend to mute the colors they wear as they age; and Kofumi-san's attire was far more understated than her maiko's. She wore a single reddish-gold hairpiece inset with sparkling hexagons. Her kimono was purplish-black with its obi making a red-overlined white square in the front, the braid whitely striping around her waist without any clasp. Around the knees and on the train went other clusters of much narrower horizontal stripes which ended variably. Some clusters were red and some

---

*In Kanazawa, the geisha Masami-san said: "This is very basic. In the tea ceremony, opening a door is quite involved. Our procedure is less formalized. In the tea ceremony there must be a certain number of steps. But we go to rooms of different dimensions, and we must calculate such that we do not step on the seam between two tatami mats. Of course all tatami mats are the same size."

were white. She had turned the whitish underside of the purplish-black outward to hold the edge with her hand, so that I could see the pale green leaf pattern on it.

As for Konomi-san, she knew fewer than ten dances as of yet. Here is Kawabata's description of a prospective maiko: "The girl, about fourteen or fifteen, had beautiful white skin. Over her light summer kimono she wore a narrow red obi. She was shy . . . Her black hair glistened, the color of some mysterious water creature . . . As she walked away, her gait took on the look of a middle school student." (The proprietress coaxes an old client: "Won't you come with us? If only to see the young girls?") Konomi-san was no longer a young girl as categorized by connoisseurs of the Edo period; but by the standards of my time she was almost still a girl; her beauty, which was breathtaking, had not quite completed its flowering into womanliness. She had smaller eyes than the other woman, and her painted eyebrows partook to a greater extent of the classic willow leaf shape. The lowermost edges of her hair (for maikos wear no wig) resembled a thick upturned U, sloping diagonally away from her ears; while Kofumi-san's wig ended flatly. Her face resembled a perfect white egg, and her mouth was a crimson heart. The restful shadows around her eyes were of palest ultramarine; they served to accentuate the purity of her snowy cheeks. Her hairpiece was a bouquet of white and yellow chrysanthemums which might have been porcelain or stiff paper, a circlet of green grapes whose composition was glass or emerald but most probably jade, and a miniature shelf of crystal honeycomb from which hung long crystal fringe; this was almost surely a tortoise shell comb. Had I been able to see the crystal honeycomb more closely, I believe I would have found it to be a double row of glowing rings or beads. In my ignorance I cannot tell you why it was appropriate for that particular month.

She wore a night-blue *hikizuri* patterned with white and pale green leaves, flowers and huts. There were also widely S-curving stripes which might have been stylized ripples. Her right shoulder remained undecorated, an indication that she was a senior maiko, nearing the time when she must take on the more sober appearance of a geiko. Just beneath her breasts ran the wide red band of her obi-*age*, or silken obi support, whose pattern — eye-flowers within round-cornered broken diamonds — were all gold. (Kofumi-san's lacked any pattern.) Beneath this was a band of equal width, the obi itself,* made of orange, white and green triangles. These repeated below, much more widely — doubtless it was another fold of the same fabric, formed into a pubic-like triangle by the clasped sleeves of night-blue she held before her — and across it ran a red belt, the braid or obi-*jime*, which contained stitched or knotted or studded stripes of white, dark green, yellow or green. The clasp (*pocchiri*) was a glittering rectangle of pale crystalline whitish-green, bordered all around by white beads, perhaps pearls, and inset with a round ruby stone at each corner and an ovoid green stone at the center. For some reason she was not wearing the *eri*, or scarlet collar of the maiko; but just above her white-stockinged feet peeped a red robe with white chrysanthemums. (A Kyoto geisha informs us that red symbolizes female pubescence, "and we carefully show a trace at the collar and hem." Thus the aesthetic known as *iki*.) There were also very dark, perhaps black, glimpses of what must have been the underside of the night-blue outer kimono; here I could see one elaborate and lonely plant, probably a chrysanthemum in profile, crowned by one yellow and two white flowers; spear-shaped leaves, either green or white, rose up off its pale blue stalk in diagonals, and a white root snaked to the border of the red robe.

Although she had not yet reached the legal drinking age, of course nobody was stupid enough to enforce the law in her case — one mark of Japanese superiority over my own nation of one-size-fits-all Puritans. Tonight she was going to perform a dance whose name meant literally "Fan to You," the implication being of a male lover bestowing a fan upon a lady, and indeed, Konomi-san's two fans would be crossed in significa-tion of the union of man and woman.

Kofumi-san seemed quite happy with her. "She takes care of me," she said lovingly. It would have been inappropriate for me to ask, but I supposed that when the girl commenced her formal maikodom, the

---

*Masami-san said that an obi expresses nothing in particular and is "just decoration"; hence a geisha can wear whichever obi she likes. For all I know, the severer requirements of Kyoto may assert otherwise.

two women must have "married" in the *san-san-kudo* ceremony binding a maiko to her "elder sister."

Mr. Kanze merely laughed and said, "I don't think so" when I asked him whether the face of a geisha with traditional hairstyle and makeup reminded him of any particular Noh mask; and when I asked Ms. Nakamura if a geisha face more greatly resembled a Noh mask or an *ukiyo-e* print, she replied: "I have never seen any geisha face that resembles a Noh mask. Thinking about *ukiyo-e* may be closer."

Of course there is no one *ukiyo-e* face any more than there is a single female style of Noh mask. Utamaro's girls are more plumpfaced than many others, with slightly wider eyes. The faces of Eishi's beauties tend to be elongated. But it remains possible to speak of types. A generalized *ukiyo-e* face would incorporate a small rosebud mouth, narrow slanting eyes and flattened crescent eyebrows at human height. And so I pursued: "What would a geisha mask look like?"

"Maybe in the middle, between the two."*

For many people, a geisha face would be Konomi-san's, not Kofumi-san's. It would be the face of a maiko. That is why a twentieth-century geisha of Gion remarks:

A maiko in full costume approximates the Japanese ideal of feminine beauty.

She has the classic looks of a Heian princess, as though she might have stepped out of an eleventh-century scroll painting. Her face is a perfect oval. Her skin is white and flawless, her hair black like a raven's wing. Her brows are half moons, her mouth a delicate rosebud. Her neck is long and sensuous, her figure gently rounded.

I listened to the women giggling together and the sounds of the shamisen being tuned. Then the "Fan to You" dance commenced.†

---

*"What would happen if you tried to make a mask with *ukiyo-e* proportions?" I inquired, and she said: "I think it's possible, but probably it's harder to wear. It's easier if the eyes are lower."

†The words of this song and of "Black Hair" are translated in the endnotes.

The maiko's pale face, her slender pliant slowness, accentuated that freshness she had, that sweet immaturity so dear to Kawabata, which even now as I write, two years after the fact, must be gone, just as her crimson half-smile subsided once she began to dance. I hope that she is a full-fledged geiko now, like Kofumi-san. (It is said that only fifty or sixty maikos remain in all Kyoto.) Her gold and red fans were flashing. The sad slow pizzicato of the shamisen, which might not have sounded sad at all when the song was new, functioned like the chants of a Noh chorus to fill the performance with ritual and rhythm, adding volumes of that hushed slowness, so that her movements approached both carefulness and living perfection. I had time only to note down this or that instant, such as when she pivoted, and I saw the way she grasped the gold fan behind her back, the darkness of her hair-knot when seen from behind the feeling of *never again*; and by now she had turned back round again, her face severe as she gazed down, crossing her arms, folding her knees, almost stamping her feet, the fans swirling, all the colors of her kimono imparting themselves in patterns that altered water-like, so that there was so much controlled multitudinous beauty that it was impossible to perceive it all at once; therefore it was infinite.

Her gaze was so far away. Sometimes her face was ivory in the electric light, and I remembered the hues of Noh masks in summer torchlight. The two fans touched. She whirled; she stood; she knelt. Danyu-san stared straight ahead, singing.

## BLACK HAIR

The next dance was Kofumi-san's, and the name of it was "Black Hair," which may for all I know be the "Dark Hair" mentioned twice in Tanizaki's *Makioka Sisters* and sung by the geisha Komako in *Snow Country*. The hero of the latter novel wonders whether it might have been the first song she learned, and it might well have been; for one night after a Noh performance I visited a Gion bar owned by a retired geisha in her sixties; she showed us an album of photos of herself from the days when she was young and beautiful; she had started at fifteen. She said that *everyone* learned the Black Hair song; it went with a certain style of hair; she didn't know why.

When I asked Kofumi-san to explain it to me, she said: "This is the story of waiting for a lover or an ex-lover, and she cannot forget and the snow falls and she is remembering the past."

"How old is it?"

"Maybe more than one hundred years."

"Beautiful black hair is supposed to be a girl's best feature, as important as her life," Kofumi-san also said; and I thought: How could it be otherwise? Didn't Lady Murasaki say the same? Near the end of the eleventh century, Izumi Shikibu composed a poem of ostensible indifference regarding the disarray of her black hair while she was lying either alone or with a lover, the verse does not say which; meanwhile, she expressed longing recollections of an unnamed someone who had caressed and combed it. And from the *ukiyo-e* prints I remembered Utamaro's ladies, with their vast inky rolls of hair bristling with precious hairpins.[*]

The sad white face of Kofumi-san, which was not supposed to express anything in the course of a dance but which I think did — but what? What is a woman? — showed me how lovely age can be; and Kofumi-san, whose own self, whatever that meant, must live so far away beneath

THE LYRICS OF "BLACK HAIR."

---

[*]In her geisha autobiography, a sorrowful woman tells how "I hacked off at the roots the waist-length hair that'd been so dear to me for so many years, and offered it up to who-knows-which-god at a small shrine . . ."

her black wig, froze; then she stamped; she was still and she was still and then she stamped. For me, at least, part of grace is *space*, each expression of femininity's performance being bordered by such understatement or blankness as the kneeling immobility between actions in Noh. (In another Utamaro woodcut, a woman reads a letter with parted little lips, slender-wristed, her skin the same color as the scroll she reads from; a caption hangs on the page behind her, everything flat, blankness given its due.) And so she was still and then she stamped.

Her hand brushed her face almost as would a Noh actor's when he symbolizes tears. She raised one hand, touched both hands together, then slowly seated herself, drawing herself in as the singer's voice slowed and descended, the shamisen slowing and enriching its mournfulness while the geisha gazed with black eyesocket-awareness into the heart of everything. One hand poured time into the other, and the edges of her pale aged hands swept the air. (In the first century B.C., Philodemos the Epicurean sings the explicit charms of Charito, who is in her sixties. "Lovers, if you flee not from hot desire, enjoy Charito / forgetting her decades' multitudes.") She stamped once, grasped her long sleeve with the other hand, crossed her wrists again and again, gazing along her crossed sleeves.

Even at that time, when I happened to be involved in a love attachment in whose transience I could not at all believe, the beautiful mournfulness of Kofumi-san's art was almost unbearable. When I remember that dance now, bereft of my attachment, I am moved in a particularly painful way. But when she was actually dancing, what I felt was simply, as I do at a great Noh performance, recognition of the moment. Although they certainly cause the future and fulfill the past, moments remain themselves, perishing as they flower; and because in order to live we perceive so many of our moments as identical or nearly so, this comprehension with the heart, which is to say this being aware of *aware*, is rare, and for all I know may be rarer for Kofumi-san while she dances for me than to me while I watch her. Like Noh's slowness and the brevity of a Heian tanka, the gestures of this great geisha articulate my present instant into art, into beautiful meaning. Once upon a time, the secret moans of the woman I loved did the same, but only for me (or so I hoped). And what Kofumi-san now did was only for me, and only for my interpreter, and only for whomever else might have been there (at that time only the ochaya-san was present, and then only between dances). Her fingertip-gestures were as delicately open as the ferntips before the base of an ovoid rock rising from the moss in a temple garden.

## "HIS CARRIAGE NATURALLY BECOMES IN ELEGANT TASTE"

So what is a woman? How is this geisha's superb womanliness constructed? Much of it comes into being in her dressing room — for instance, when she dons her wig, whose crisp edges remind me of the way a perfectly manicured pine offers distinct ovoid lobes of needles to the eye. But what artifice or fluency occurs when while dancing she raises one sleeve to her mouth? Looking into her red-underlined,* black-overlined eyes, I asked her: "When you're dancing, do you try to think of anything or not?"

"I wish to think nothing, but it's rather hard. Nothingness would be the best."

"Do you feel?"

"I strive to feel nothing."

Mr. Mikata had remarked to me that "Inoue the Fourth says that she does not think anything. Their sons, they're professional, too. Her second son used to ask her why she could do what she did, and then she said, well, you just practice, practice and still practice, and there's nothing that you need to think."

Could this be all there is? If grace is indeed a performance, how can it be accomplished without thought? No beautiful woman has yet explained to me in detail how she expresses her beauty; probably the grace of the body lives in the body and therefore beyond words. I used to think that

---

*The purpose of the red is to increase the perceived depth of the eyes and lightness of the iris.

Zeami's instructions on these matters tended to beg the question. "If the *shite* dances and acts with elegant speeches his carriage naturally becomes in elegant taste." How did Zeami arrive at his determination of what was elegant? Who decided what and how to practice, practice and still practice? Or did this elegance, like a folktale, derive from the collective consciousness? For that matter, might not it be that dance also exists beyond words? (Danyu-san for her part said: "Because songs have words, I have to think.") I never became sufficiently experienced to perceive much of geisha dance's expressions. And the geishas gave me less guidance than had Mr. Umewaka. Perhaps they followed Zeami's spirit, and kept secrets. ("Secrecy is the essential art of geisha," says a Tokyo member of the profession; and a frequenter of geisha houses in Kyoto remarks that he has seen geisha making themselves up but prefers not to because "I don't want to know their tricks; I don't want to know their sad stories.") Perhaps there was nothing that I needed to think.

But I frequently felt myself to be on the verge of learning quite specific matters. For instance, Konomi-san had said that her most significant challenge was this: "To turn the fans. Turning the fans you must do many other things at the same time."* (Here again I remember Zeami's dictum that whether an actor plays woman, warrior, demon or old man, "it should seem as though each were holding a branch of flowers in his hand." The geisha's branch of flowers is of course her fan.) And so I supposed that these many other things that she did could be itemized and categorized. After all, it had helped me to learn that an actor's finger slid down the cheek of a Noh mask from the corner of the eye signifies tears. Just as in *mai* dance the Noh actor glides his fan up and down before his heart to represent joy, so the way that Konomi-san turns her two fans presumably means something. But the maiko did not seem inclined or perhaps able to tell me which other things she needed to accomplish when turning the fans; and when I asked Kofumi-san what I should do to prepare myself in advance to appreciate geisha dances, and how I could learn their vocabulary, she replied: "It's a personal feeling. Isn't it better that you *don't* get anything in advance? It's all up to the viewer."

---

*The mask carver Nakamura-san thought the fan movements in this geisha dance similar to Noh, "but something about the movement is different."

A translator of the thirteenth-century German *Nibelungenlied* remarks of its unknown author that "he did not reduce his characters to a mechanism, however refined . . . He has greater insight into human nature than he puts explicitly into words, and to find it we must read between the lines, adding nothing of our own. His characters' actions are mostly so incisive that although we cannot always show their continuity we sense it and accept it." When I read between the lines of, say, Kawabata, I sometimes feel confident to identify a specific motive or event which has not been spelled out; at other times I sense no more than a continuity not even of plot but simply of style or atmosphere. At such points I grow haunted, and do in fact add something of my own. What is the meaning of a certain silence between the old man and his daughter-in-law in *The Sound of the Mountain*? Does Komako in *Snow Country* truly believe her own assertions regarding the futility of her attachment? As Kofumi-san said, "it's all up to the viewer." And when feminine movement engages me, perhaps it does so only through continuity. What does a geisha dancer bring to my gaze? What does my perception add? What, indeed, constitutes understatement in a woman I desire? In part, it comes from the fact that she wears clothes. When I see her, I want to undress her. There is more to her than she allows my eyes to know. This restraint upon my gaze cannot be the thing of value in and of itself. After all, the erotic woodcuts of Utamaro, which depict genitalia in frank and sometimes even exaggerated detail, are far superior to most of Japan's contemporary photographic pornography, which blacks out, white-encircles or else pixellates the clitoris, pubic hair, etcetera. In other words, if it is to enhance the aesthetic effect, the restraint must itself be beautiful, like Shun'e's thirteeenth-century example of a curtain of mist which teases us with incomplete glimpses of the scarlet leaves of autumn. The titillations of keyhole voyeurism's glowing jewel-like little image swimming in perfect darkness, and then again the spectator's peculiar ease of vision — vision led or misled — when watching a Noh play, may both achieve a comparable impression, the first most likely unintentionally on the part of what is perceived, the second thanks to art. Dress, stockings, earrings, lingerie, all these make barriers, to be sure, but, like the robe and mask of a Noh actor, they ought to be beautiful in and of themselves. One American fashion star praises the erotic allure of her black high heels' red soles. And in the case of a geisha dance, the greater elaboration of dress, completed with fan motions, and left still more unknowable to me than Noh's arcana, makes for any number of beautiful mysteries. Just as when for the first time a man glimpses the skin below a woman's neck he can envision her nakedness more plausibly but certainly not exactly (and, as I have mentioned, the W-shape of the unpainted skin on the *back* of a geisha's neck — adjoining fangs — is said to represent the vulva), so when I see the edge of a geisha's under-kimono I begin to imagine not her naked body necessarily, but the layers and layers of unknown colors, dances, thoughts, all the way down to the woman herself, whom I can never hope to know. One observer opines that a Noh mask is in fact more expressive than a geisha's white-painted face, which nonetheless he calls "electrifying," I suppose because it is simultaneously pristine and alien and because it understates. What might the geisha be expressing otherwise? There's another mystery.

These enigmas may in fact have no solution; they may be meaningless. In "Black Hair," which stillness or fan sequence of Kofumi-san's specifically represents remembering the past? This might be asking the wrong question. Shostakovich insisted that the dissection of his great compositions into program music was spurious, as may be the case with "Black Hair." Then again, it may not. Perhaps not even Kofumi-san knows the answer, which might have died with the original choreographer — or was never born.

Here the divergence from Noh felt most significant to me. When I asked Mr. Mikata how one learned and progressed as a Noh actor, he said: "Well, first you try to do your utmost, just try to shout loud, and move a lot, and these are the very basics so that you can get the sense. After that, if you work hard, then, you need some spiritual training. The body-sense and the mind-sense are also needed." As for Mr. Umewaka, when he was a child his grandfather taught him to visualize the loveliness of imaginary cherry blossoms. The geishas never mentioned either visions or spiritual training, and their silence on that subject was appropriate, for their dances did not simultaneously express and distance themselves from attachment; they created it.

Some geisha performances resemble Noh less than they do *kyogen*. It is not uncommon for geisha singers to make fun of Noh; the Inoue School

aside, many do not want to be too serious. The music may sound Noh-like; the flute is similar and the three kinds of drum, which may or may not appear, are all the same.

Kofumi-san did tell me this: "What my elders used to say was: You have to spend all your life carefully. If you live every day carefully, then you will flourish in your dance. They kept saying that. If you're on stage, it's as if you're completely naked. A perfect artist needs the grace and dignity to exist in that situation. This advice will become even more important to me as I grow older. When you're young, people will look at you no matter what."

This of course was equivalent to what Zeami had written about the true and false flower.

I have already proposed, following the spirit of Zeami, to progressively forget a woman's appearance, identity and soul in order to perceive her grace; what Zeami means by the last two categories is obviously quite different from what you or I would; otherwise how could such deep seeing be possible for a spectator as opposed to a lover? When I myself experience this sort of forgetting at, say, a symphony, I may be closer than I imagine to the people who fall happily asleep at Noh plays; but the way it feels is as if I have been taken beyond my path in an autumn forest, the brass instruments creating a ground of red, brown and yellow leaves, the flutes breezes, the piano something icy; I no longer know that I am listening to a specific composition, or that I am sitting in the dress circle, gazing down at the orchestra; I have forgotten the composition, the composer and my life; this must be the cliché called "reverie." There were moments when I entered into a similar state when Kofumi-san danced for me. When I study the photographs of her I made, I see ever more distinctly the lovely decrepitudes of her cheek; I grow familiar with the texture of her painted lips; but when she danced her face became, as she wanted it to be, a mask; she herself became a performance of gorgeous movements. I never lost my sense of the transience of Konomi-san's dance;

while Kofumi-san, I suppose because she is the more experienced artist, can lead my perception into a place which is fuller than time, not a forest, exactly, but a realm of stillnesses and angular motions. What is her identity and what is her soul? How could I dare to say I ever knew them? But although I may be incapable of perceiving as Zeami might wish me to, I can say that this place or space, founded as it is upon Kofumi-san's continued dancing, takes me *away* somewhere. Is what I feel then her grace? I cannot say. And (so I suspect) neither can she. — If only I had thought to ask about *her* three beings! — Zeami: "Genuine Perfect Fluency in fact has no connection with the actor's conscious artistic intentions or with any outward manifestation of those intentions," since he now transcends his training.

Thanks to Mr. Umewaka I have been privileged to see Yuya's dancing, which is as pure as the leaf-breath of the Shoren-in, breath I have longed to breathe, and while there was a natural residuum of erotic desire in my longing, it was also peace that I longed for; the more I breathed, the more I craved to keep inhaling the purity of those afternoons beneath the camphor trees. Thanks to Kofumi-san I have lost myself in stillness, swirling, ruthlessly stylized flashing movement; and the sadness of her "Black Hair" dance, like the pathos of attachment in a Noh play, achieves neutral tranquility, in much the same way as the green segmented cylinder-towers of the Shoren-in's bamboo grove grow grey as one falls into their shadow, silver-grey, not lead-grey; greyness becomes simply one more precious pigment in their light.

## JEWELS IN THE LIGHT

At the end of the eighteenth century, Chobunsai Eishi's grand courtesans come palefaced, serene as moons, escorted by their pairs of little girl attendants. Sometimes one can see them boating on the Sumida River. In Chokosai Eisho's Kansei era woodcut "Two Beauties Holding a Lantern," the white faces are especially delicate against the pale greyish wash of grass and faintly yellowed sky, each lower lip full as in a Noh mask, the black hair spiked with ornaments. And in the early twenty-first century I glimpse geishas; their hair was black and their faces were powdered ever so white, because a millenium before the Heian Emperor wished to watch court beauties from behind his screen; they were jewels in the darkness.

In that Gion bar owned by the retired geisha there was an unspeakably beautiful maiko whose client was an old gentleman; he was drinking little cups of whiskey and she was drinking tea. What can I say of her except that she was beautiful, so beautiful that I cannot remember more than the light her face cast upon me? When she left, she knelt and bowed to us with heartbreaking grace.

GION SHRINE.

I lacked the funds to hire Kofumi-san again that year, so I went out, and rapidly reached the grounds of Yasaka Shrine, or Gion Shrine as it is also known. By day I sometimes saw distant reflections of gold things in the latticed windows; but the day had ended long ago. Once upon a time, a certain eight-headed snake, symbol of all evil, was defeated by the shrine's god, the younger brother of the lovely Amaterasu; that had happened almost as long ago as today's sunset. Around the beginning of the fourteenth century, Lady Nijo (who also visited the Shoren-in) made a one-thousand-day retreat here. Gion Festival, now twelve hundred years old, is centered around this shrine. Here the geishas still come to pray, so it is said. Although I have rarely seen anyone in geisha dress pass through these grounds, I am but a foreigner who perceives little; and it may be that some of the women who come here in early afternoon are geishas wearing the attire of this world.

It was a midnight of crickets, glowing white and orange lamps with red crests on them, and lightless stone lanterns. My desire for attachment did not circle round and round as at the Shoren-in, because this place was less a world behind walls than a compound of trees, or of wide flagstoned alleys with lamps and trees on either side. The main building with its lanterns and golden-tipped vermilion roof-beams was not the center of anything. Passing between islands of wooden darkness surrounded by glowing lamps, I felt lost. The tops of the wide steps glowed in the greenish lights. And just as the white, white face of a geisha can shine out of darkness like the moon itself, the ancient laurel moon of Prince Yuhara, so the labyrinthine void of Yasaka Shrine rose out of my expectations' darkness; but it shone around me rather than at me. I remembered the maikos of Gion and Ponto-cho, whom I was occasionally lucky enough to glimpse as they flitted out of a gleaming black taxicab and into the teahouse where they had been called upon to dance; at those times they showed themselves to no more purpose than the moon did. In the few seconds allotted to me to gaze upon them, I was thrilled and fulfilled; afterward the memory became one of my treasures. And something of this came to me from the orange light which shone through the shrine's latticework.

14:

# "She Cannot Do Anything Else"

## Compulsions, Costs, Achievements

Her own training, Kofumi-san remarked twice, had been quite different from Konomi-san's. "The people around me were good people but very strict."

"It must have been very painful at times," I said.

"The dancing was, yes. When you start learning to dance, you're disciplined for how to bow, how to remove your footwear and everything, it's true. I would just look at the senior maiko and copy her."

As for the musician Danyu-san, she had begun when she was six. She looked young but might have been close to fifty. I asked whether she would have chosen her career of her own accord, and she said simply: "They make it so that the child realizes she cannot do anything else." — And who is a woman? Perhaps her identity is founded on the realization that she can be no one else.

*What* is a woman? A twentieth-century American classical ballet dancer remarks upon how in nineteenth-century Vienna "a gentleman

would place a handkerchief between his hand and his partner's when he embraced her to dance, so that he wouldn't touch her even with his gloved hand. Spiritually and aesthetically, a woman was untouchable, unobtainable, the dream for which he longed" — at which point the feminist critic who has just cited this reminds us to consider that period's "gynecological ignorance" and the resulting suffering of women, in order for us to better "appreciate women's enjoyment of this illusion." What Kofumi-san suffered during her apprenticeship, and the choices Danyu-san never had, not to mention the sorrows of all those women who for centuries were sold into geishadom, their mercantile value fading year by year like the dyes of those woodblock prints of teahouse girls, overtower my imagination. I hope not to insult any of them with the false sympathy which derives from imagining myself in their situations, being all the while half-blinded by my own particular fantasies of self-actualization. Nor would I care to dismiss their "enjoyment," such as it may be, of whichever femininities they must perform.

A modern-day Tokyo geisha informs us that most of her colleagues began very young and poor, and that they needed to find patrons "as early as eleven." The translator of a rural geisha's memoir of heartbreak, exploitation and abuse opines: "The romanticization of geisha life as dedicated principally to the pursuit of traditional arts ignores the poverty that drove many parents to indenture their daughters to geisha houses. Such romanticization also erases certain geisha from the collective memory and overlooks the bottom line of the whole geisha business," which is, "of course, sex for money."

Kofumi-san would, I suspect, be less than pleased if I dared to refer to her bottom line in any terms, let alone these. Of course she must survive; I hope that she profits. I have been privileged to witness her accomplishment of excellence. The relationship between us was formal, asexual, mercantile, aesthetic — much as when I bought a ticket to one of Mr. Umewaka's performances. I proudly *do* romanticize my experiences of both of their performances. That is the greatest compliment I can pay them.

Once upon a time there lived a Noh actor named Takabayashi Ginji. In 1956 he was disbarred from the Kita School for the offense of "impertinence." He seems to have offended his teacher's son. He wrote: "I was a defendant who did not know his crime." And once upon a time there was a Noh actor, or a geisha — come to think of it, there were thousands — who attempted the dance of feminine grace, and received "discipline," shouts, beatings, punishments. They had not yet learned to imitate beauty with sufficient exactitude to make it their own. They could not glide while bearing an imaginary branch of flowers.

This book is about representations of feminine beauty. I hope that I never lose sight of the price that so many transvestites, transsexuals, Noh actors, onnagatas, prostitutes, courtesans, geishas, elegant women, women longing to be elegant, women who believe that they exist for men while men do not exist for them,* women keeping themselves "decent" or hoping against hope to look five years younger, lonely widows, ancient ladies who weep when they look in the mirror, desperate high school girls, careful executive women, and so many other expressers of femininity must pay. (Here again, and still without comment, I cite the onnagata Bando Tamasaburo: "When they are slightly uncomfortable, women are more erotic.") To the extent that beauty and grace succeeds as performance, I fail to see behind the mask. What is a woman? Doubtless she may also be, among other things, someone who suffers. All the same, she must also be, at least sometimes, someone who actually does enjoy the illusion she projects, the power she commands.

My dear friend Shannon has sometimes expressed bitterness that she is not a man. She says that men are freer, more powerful. I once remarked that surely an attractive woman, for instance Shannon, can be envied for her ability to turn heads. She replied: "I'll tell you how it actually is. You go downstairs in your high heels and you worry about tripping. You worry that your lipstick is smearing, and you need to find a restroom to check yourself in the mirror and there's no restroom. You constantly repair yourself, and you have no time to be in the moment. When you're young you don't understand what little power you have, which means that you don't have it; and once you start getting older you spend your time worrying."

---

*Tadano Makuzu, 1818: "Women exist for the sake of men; men do not exist for the sake of women . . . Even if she is the more intelligent, how can a woman who thinks that she is lacking something" — i.e.; a penis — "triumph over a man who always thinks of himself as having a surplus?"

Disagreeing with her, Zeami wrote in 1428: "The actor will be able to discern clearly his strong and weak points and lessen his bad, thus becoming a peerless master in his particular art." He "no longer needs to think out his performance, but can perform without artifice."

But lessening one's bad points requires continuing discipline, no question about it. Mishima Yukio, whose sexuality was ambiguous, spent the final years before his suicide "cultivating my orchard," which is to say his body, "for all I was worth. For my purpose, I used sun and steel." In short, he became a bodybuilder. Meanwhile, the glamor queen Molly Sims keeps a spoon in the fridge and touches it to each of her eyes for five minutes straight. She refrains from eating soy sauce at night in order not to look "puffy" in the morning; for the same reason, she sleeps with the heat low. As for the onnagata Shozo Sato, he makes it his habit for a full three hours before any Kabuki performance to abstain from drinking, in order to avoid ruining his face with perspiration.

Those who eschew or fall short of such professional constancy may fight more temporary campaigns against ugliness. As I write this, I wonder how many dedicated soldiers are presently engaged in the "Goodbye Cellulite, Hello Bikini Challenge," which is "a four-week program designed to get you bikini-ready in four important areas"? Fortunately for them, a manufacturer of skin cream stands ready to furnish munitions for their arsenals.

Self-loathing complements discipline. "We've all been there — that feeling of not wanting anyone to look too closely at your face." Thus runs an advertisement in *Allure* magazine. *New Beauty* wants us to know that some women are humiliated by "the appearance of their genitalia or enlarged labia," not to mention vaginal looseness during intercourse. "Feel Feminine Again," *New Beauty* invites us; and why not? "Vaginal rejuvenation" requires merely pain and money! Another procedure explicated in this same publication is called "balancing your ethnic features." A self-dissatisfied woman can, for example, buy a rhinoplasty to overcome the frequent hump and sagging tip of the Mediterranean nose, or increase the prominence of the tip and bridge of the flat Asian nose, or narrow the nostrils and correct the "under-projected tip" of the African-American nose. Cost as of 2008: Up to fourteen thousand dollars. Breaking the nose "is not necessary in every case."

Several women I know rip out their pubic hairs in globs of hot wax. "The child realizes she cannot do anything else." Some subject themselves to breast augmentation operations, despite the twenty-four percent reoperation rate (for breast reconstruction, that figure is nearly forty-one percent). A friend of mine got breast reductions. Now she feels self-conscious about her two grinning red scars. There is a proven market for the buttocks lift, whose mildest form involves slicing into the small of the back, then pulling up the buttocks "like a pair of pants," as one doctor describes it. The injection of botulism toxin into the face is almost commonplace among my middleaged female executive friends; the effects last only about four months. For women to whom the danger is a secondary consideration (or, more likely, unknown to them), Brazilian hair-straightening treatments will anoint them with the carcinogen formaldehyde.

Sometimes one part of the body gets transplanted to another. A commercial photographer who proposed to employ the "liquefy" option to digitally edit a picture of me explained that at my age (I was then forty-five) the flesh of the face has begun to ooze down the sides of the skull, so that one develops both hollows under the eyes and sagging jowls. Needless to say, surgeons offer a solution: fat grafting from the lower cheeks to around the eyes. Pulchritude's technicians can also graft skin from the soles of a male-to-female transsexual's feet to the walls of her new vagina, whose attempt to heal shut must then be excruciatingly frustrated three times a day through the insertion of a vaginal dilator; I think I would prefer laser lipolysis, which "literally melts away fat in trouble spots like your abdomen." Meanwhile, how many ten-year-old girls are weeping at this moment while their mothers grip their faces and pop their blackheads?

"It's no fun being a geisha," complains the heroine of a Nagai Kafu story, to which her on-again-off-again lover replies: "It's no fun being anything else either."


## A WISH FOR CHARLOTTE VON MAHLSDORF

"They make it so that the child realizes she cannot do anything else." "It's no fun being anything else either." The efforts made to accomplish femininity may derive from exploitation, false consciousness, or what the actress may consider, or come to consider, as her very nature. "Ultimately, ours is a journey of anguish," writes the transsexual woman Aleisha Brevard. A girl playing with makeup or an apprentice of Mr. Umewaka sets out, one hopes, on rather more pleasant excursions.

When I first met Mr. Mikata, within that temple in Kyoto, in a room of tatami mats and whose sliding partition showed a hint of shining floor beyond, he was giving a lessson to an older lady who knelt chanting from a text. He sang with his pale hands clasped in his lap, stern and a trifle severe, as a Noh teacher probably is expected to be. Or could he simply have been serious about the craft and his own duty to those who came to him? He was darkhaired, much younger than Mr. Umewaka, less naturally sunny. It seemed to me that he was singing from the bottom of his throat, frowning, closing his eyes, holding the syllables and lifting them upward like the corners of pagodas. His voice resonant, projecting, powerful. Nodding in time with the singing of his pupil, listening with closed eyes and downcast head to that timid old lady, he steered the lesson to its end. She bowed and thanked him.

I complimented his beautiful voice, and he dismissively said that he had a sore throat, thanks to the dry air.

Next came a lesson to a young man. I tried to interpret the golden flash of Mr. Mikata's fan, which moved first in a circular motion parallel to the ground, then up, then down, every aspect of its journey very careful and exact. It rotated, then the foot stamped; he was singing all the while. I found it surprising to see the expressiveness of his face with the mask off, even his eyebrows moving dramatically as he sang, although perhaps this was to emphasize some point for his pupil.

It all seemed arduous, and to me tedious, like observing the practice of any musical instrument, but not unpleasant to the participants. Perhaps it even gratified them sometimes. As my best friend Ben remarks, "I can't say I'm against it."

Self-effacing repetitions of a dance, of a hammer-stroke or a particular calligraphic twist, not to mention the dilations of a transsexual's neovagina by means of graduated plastic stents, may eventually bring the practitioner to a state of perfect accomplishment. This notion is called *muga*, selflessness. The strict discipline required to become an Inoue School geisha dancer (in contradistinction to the intoxication of a Greek maenad who throws back her marble head in ecstasy) evidently produces a similar result. Might the accomplishment of femininity, or its performance, sometimes be characterized by a state of being in which the woman realizes that she cannot (and hopefully would not) do anything else?

Such being entails continual becoming. Once upon a time there lived a young woman named Agnes, who did whatever she had to do to keep her boyfriend from discovering that she had a penis. When she finally told him, it still remained essential to conceal the fact that she had been raised as a boy. Eventually she succeeded in gaining permission from the Gender Identity Clinic to have the operation. What then? "A review of Agnes's passing occasions and management devices may be used to argue how practiced and effective Agnes was in dissembling," a researcher concludes; he also writes: "It would be incorrect of Agnes to say that she has passed. The active mode is needed; she is passing. Inadequate though this phrasing is, it summarizes Agnes's troubles."

In her apprenticeship, the famous Gion geisha Iwasaki Mineko was sometimes punished without cause — but of course with reason. One need not approve of this procedure to comprehend its possible effectiveness for inducing *muga*. She writes, much as Zeami did: "I believed that self-discipline was the key to beauty."

What is a woman? Here comes a maiko. "More of a painted doll than a woman, her oval face is painted lustrous white," writes one observer, bringing back to my mind any young-lady Noh mask with its depths of pure white oyster shell and hide glue before coloring. "At the nape of the neck, which Japanese men find especially provocative, is a lick of naked, unpainted flesh." — But to me, she *is* a woman, a painted woman, not a painted doll. Her face and neck entice and sometimes awe me. Perhaps they provoke me. But her self remains fundamentally whatever it is, with or without her self-discipline; I believe that neither she nor I could be anyone else. To be sure, she could perform her geisha femininity more or less expertly, perfecting her imitations and then inhabiting them. In more than one of his treatises, Zeami quotes the proverb that "the truth and what looks like it are two different things." This is why a beginner's exactest imitation of any gesture made by a possessor of the true flower will not achieve that flowerhood.

But what is a woman? Unlike Hilary Nichols and "Sachiko," the renowned Berlin transvestite Charlotte von Mahlsdorf believed herself to be a woman *in her soul*; her male sexual organs "meant nothing" to her. The compulsion to be a woman was so great that she dressed up, curled her hair, picked up her purse and went out with her similarly minded friend Christine — in the Third Reich, after curfew. Later, when the Russians arrived, she risked rape by continuing to appear in public as a female. Christine was in fact raped. Charlotte lived into old age, and was honored by her government — indeed, honored *as a woman*. I wish the same for Aleisha Brevard, for Konomi and Kofumi, for all achievers of femininity, in all degrees of pride, longing, suffering.

15:

# Suzuka's Dressing Room

*A Geisha Gets Ready*

Early on a cold evening in Kanazawa, in a small square tatami room on the first floor of the ochaya, the young geisha Suzuka kneels before the mirror and seats herself neatly on her crossed heels, which of course are snow-white in their *tabi*. Her long hair hangs straight down her back. She is a very pretty girl, but not yet a jewel in the darkness.

Rapidly wiping the white foundation onto her face, she begins to pale. Now the second layer has already touched her left cheek. Its whiteness stands out against the first layer as much as that did against her natural skin. It has been reformulated, she answers me; it no longer contains lead, and (how sad!) may not have bush warbler droppings, either. To me it seems to be paste, not powder. In many light, expert dabs, rubs and pats of the little cloth, she makes her face snowier, whiter, then white on white. Her untouched ears take on a peculiar conspicuousness; they will be hidden beneath the wig.

She has agreed with her ochaya-san (who soon will be sitting cross-legged over a low table with my interpreter one sliding door away, first serving her tea, then accepting from her careful hands an envelope filled with the appropriate number of clean ten-thousand-yen notes) to show me how she prepares for the night; hence supposedly I can ask her whatever I like; she always replies, but her mind is quite properly focused more on her face than on me. To be honest, I cannot tell whether she is curt, absent, indifferent, hurried or simply shy in this slightly intimate situation. I kneel on the tatami floor well behind her; twice I request the interpreter to remind her that I will leave whenever she wishes. Most likely I am less an embarrassment than a moderately lucrative annoyance.* I ask her what defines a beautiful woman, and, tilting her face toward the mirror, she calmly says that a beautiful person must face the issues and make her best effort. Watching her resembles standing in reddish darkness above my developer tray, which I gently, ceaselessly rock while the lovely silver image begins to bloom forth from the snow white photographic paper; except that in Suzuka's case it happens in reverse: her face is perfecting itself into something new, but this newness is ever lighter, more featureless and masklike. Now she is whitening her neck, which seems to lengthen into a swan's. She pats the cloth upon her eyebrows; they fade; her lips whiten. What is she, this shining feminine being with white lips? I ask her how she feels when she looks into the mirror, and without much interest she replies: "It makes me feel that the atmosphere of my face is different."

Her lips are snowy! I never could have imagined the resulting eerie gorgeousness.

The little round hand mirror and the squarish wall mirror give me three images of her, two from the front and one from her back. Carefully speeding round and round her eyes with a little brush dipped in red, she continues her construction of extrahuman femininity. The water-based red

---

*This encounter with a geisha was the only one whose mercantile character, or impersonality, was palpable. I sometimes wonder whether I should feel sorry, or guilty, whether I was in fact intrusive. Having myself occasionally "felt violated" by certain journalists or other outside observers, I strive to behave on such occasions with a resigned professionalism. Perhaps that is how it was for her. I hope that I behaved with respect, and that she was simply in a rush. Indeed, five minutes after she had finished the ochaya-san summoned her urgently to depart for her first appointment of the evening.

paste will stay on all night. The white foundation will need touching up, just as does the foundation which the Tokyo makeup artist Yukiko applies to her clients (male cross-dressers); like Yukiko, Suzuka uses the special paper from Kyoto to remove oil from the skin when those touchups occur.

Now Suzuka brushes a layer of black over the red. Each woman finds her own style, she says.

More slowly now the brush goes round and round. When she tilts her chin forward, her white face in the hand mirror shockingly resembles a Noh mask. This mirror she holds approximately at mouth level, looking down, brushing around her lashes. Her eyes are now more contrasty, the lids very black, standing out. Three long locks taper down the back of her neck.

Now she is brushing on her eyebrows, in broad arcs whose outer side continues down around the eye nearly twice as far as where they started. Rapidly, like a tongue stimulating a lover's body near the point of climax, she goes over and over it. And suddenly the geisha face is there.

I step out for a moment. The ochaya-san helps her on with her kimono.*

Brushing the whiteness down her throat, which seems to lengthen like a swan's, kneeling at the mirror as if at an altar, she now gives the sponge to the ochaya-san, who has been coming in and out of the room. The older woman pulls down the back collar of the kimono to brush semicircles of whiteness on the back of Suzuka's neck. There will be no three legs of paint; those are for maikos, who exist only in Kyoto.

The ochaya-san, who made her debut at fifteen, used to be excellent at both dancing and drums; in those days one had to be accomplished at two things. She knew how to dance much younger than that, she says. I compliment her on how well she has trained Suzuka-san, and she says that the girl learned quickly; she herself had been very slow and stupid, she politely adds; I reply with my own stab at politeness that I will never believe the latter.

The obi-tier already sits in the next room watching television. He is a cheerful, burly man in late middle age who no longer possesses all his teeth. His main profession is the manufacture of shoji screens, but he has fallen into this other work because, he reasons modestly, he happens to

---

*She could remove it by herself. I asked how many kimonos she had, and she said that she had never counted them; since they did not go out of style she sometimes used her grandmother's.

live nearby. I tell him that he must be very skilled, and he laughs and said that nothing is required except for physical strength.

At the summons, he comes into Suzuka's dressing room and yanks her obi tight. Together, he and the ochaya-san wind it round and round the girl until it seems to cut into her waist. Her hips protrude at first, but they commence stiffening her like the rings of bamboo in a paper lantern, the green kimono flowing out from her hips like a bell. The zoologist Desmond Morris believes that the ideal waist-to-hip ratios of men and women (nine to ten in the former, seven to ten in the latter) defy cultural differences; the protrusion of the breasts above renders female waist indentation still more of a gender signal.* The obi-tying most definitely contradicts this. (Morris does admit: "The tightly laced young woman is forced to adopt a stiffly erect, vertical posture of a kind that gives her an air of graceful aloofness." And Kenneth Clark praises the Capitoline Aphrodite, who half crouches with one hand under her breasts and the other almost shielding her crotch, as an exemplar of "compactness and stability. At no point is there a plane or an outline where the eye may wander undirected." Thus, excepting her hairpicks, the form of a geisha.)

Now the ochaya-san stands behind her, tying the second strip of obi under the breast so as to pull in those wide, wide sleeves near the armpits; that way only the outer portions hang down like wings. From the rear, Suzuka-san looks ever more like a stylized angel.

Next comes the red sash, the man pulling it extremely tight across the back of the waist. Sudddenly the girl has become a confection of wraps and knots, the red sash going round and round, stiffening her further, thickening her from buttock to armpit.

Then the brocade strip goes on, the girl turning round and round as the other two spool her in. I see golden arcs and white flowers, golden fronds of grass, the man pulling tight, tight, with all his strength, the ochaya-san raising verticals, then tucking in, the young woman growing ever stiffer and straighter, so that a rectangle of brocade hangs down her back, almost reaching itself in its previous fold.

The ochaya-san takes a slender white cord and laces Suzuka in more, firmly pushing and rapping her hips and back.

---

*Average female hip width is supposedly three centimeters greater than for the male.

Suzuka-san is tying a scarlet cord over her front. The obi-tier has departed. The ochaya-san goes out to make tea. Now it is time for the wig.

The wig box is an irregular hexagon whose three back sides meet at right angles. It is dark-colored and reaches to the girl's waist.

The wig weighs a kilogram, Suzuka says. The wigmaker in Tokyo has told her that each head is different. When their careers begin, the geishas all visit him to have their measurements taken. Sometimes she must send it back to the wigmaker to have it redone. All this must be inconvenient, but at least, unlike Konomi-san and her sister maikos in Kyoto, Suzuka can remove her wig at the end of a night, so that she need not sleep on a wooden pillow.

Opening the box, and thereby exposing this concretion on the long white neck of its stand, she begins to spice it up with hairpicks from one of many drawers. She sticks in a long gold one bearing a gilded plum flower, emblem of this season (it is acceptable to symbolize a time a trifle too early, but never too late). Next she sinks a crescent-comb into the hair. The comb is red "because I'm young." (You may recall that red is also a sign of youth in Noh kimonos.) At last comes the black barrette, much heavier than barrettes I normally see.

She crowns herself with the wig in one easy motion, then ties it on with a narrow green ribbon which goes round the back of the neck; her forefingers smooth the wig down around her ears. Now she is a true geisha right down to the heart shape in her forehead. Continuing to deploy the magnifying mirror, she touches up her mouth with a brush, carefully going over and over her red lips, making the upper lip into another heart, filling out the lower, then gently patting everything.*

There is time for me to take a photograph or two. The obi-tier seizes this chance to rush in with his own camera, gleefully snapping away. Then Suzuka goes to her taxi.

---

*How long did it all take? The other geisha at this ochaya (for there were only two) had danced for me a night or two before. You have met her, her name was Masami-san. She was older than Suzuka, more experienced. She told me that she took ten or fifteen minutes to accomplish all her making-up; but someone still had to help with her kimono. All included, the procedure took an hour and a half. Suzuka might have taken a trifle longer, but perhaps that was the result of my presence and questions.

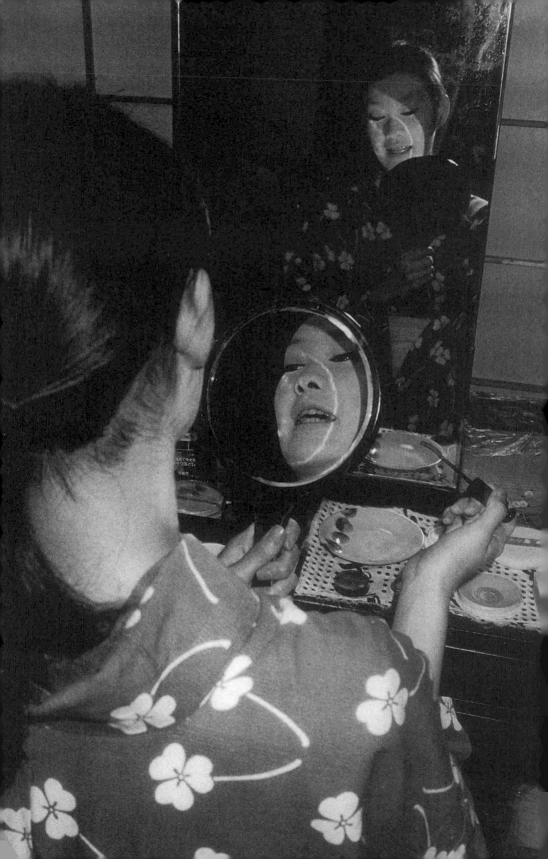

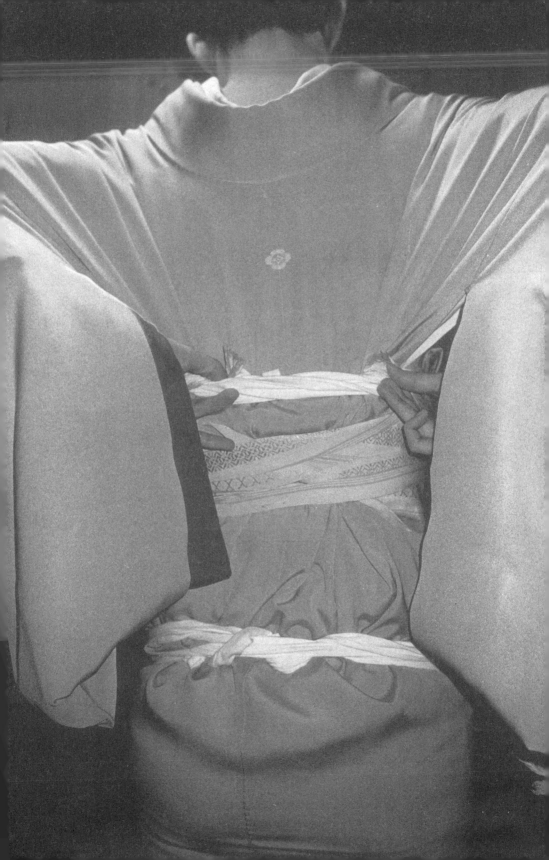

16:

# "They Just Want to Look in the Mirror"

*Yukiko Makes Me Over*

Yukiko's salon is unmarked, naturally, and there is a discreet second-floor entrance. The street is quiet, at least for Tokyo; her clients must feel safe. The room is by my standards small-ish — about the size of the chamber where Suzuka-san's colleague geisha Kasami-san danced for me. While Yukiko makes tea, I go into the tiny lavatory to change into my new black dress.

Laying out three disks of foundation, Yukiko, who is thirtyish and very pretty, with long brown hair, shows me the corresponding pictures in the Japanese fashion magazines: One foundation looks best photo-graphed and printed onto glossy paper; one is more appropriate to going out on the street; and the third is intermediate. I choose the second.

Gandhi advises us to do what we do without expecting results; and I entertain decidedly minuscule hopes of achieving maiko-esque beauty, especially since although I carefully shaved in my hotel less than two hours before, Yukiko sweetly, reproachfully inquires whether I have shaved.

She begins with a cream-type astringent: Clarins's Lotion Tonique.* The base cream will be Diorskin 001 *base de teint*, which contains a hint of pearl, making it a trifle shiny. The purpose is to even the skin. One adds less of it in summer, more "where it needs it more." Yukiko begins with the Diorskin by dabbing with her forefinger a spot on my forehead, an upper and lower spot on each cheek, and a spot between my mouth and my chin. On the forehead she works the stuff horizontally, elsewhere vertically. Then she addresses the zone beneath each eye, proceeding in descending arcs from the center of the underlid out to the cheek, her touch so firm that my flesh moves. Next she rubs it on the eyelids. All the while, I must keep my eyes open.

Now it is time for the number three cream foundation. Formerly, she says, Japanese women used to lighten their faces with foundation, but at the moment they prefer to slightly darken them, making them appear smaller. Firmly patting with the sponge (she always employs a new sponge for every step), smoothing around my eyes, she instructs me to look up while staying still. After two hours my skin oil will reappear, she says. She mentions a special paper from Kyoto which can absorb it (an easy procedure: simply pat and adjust); all the same, I am reminded how limited and ephemeral this is; and for a moment I nearly begin to comprehend the sacrificial hours paid by women at their mirrors and in beauty parlors and department stores and manicure-pedicure studios. Suzuka's nightly effort is, as we have seen, significant — not to mention the long preparations of Mr. Umewaka in the mirror room before his Noh performances. And all of it must be done over again next time.

"You see," says Yukiko, lightly touching my chin, "even now it is starting to show. Since your beard is not black it should be okay for a couple of hours." As a result of such transience, her customers generally do no more than remain here with her, for about three hours. After a chat and tea, they return home to their families.

Next comes the concealer, in order to render the contour of my

---

*It is not my normal practice to include brand names in my books. However, since the makeup procedures of geishas and onnagatas are described in some detail, I thought to achieve a comparable level of specificity. Moreover, since my interpreter rarely deployed makeup herself, it is possible that some unguental functions have been misunderstood in this chapter; if so, the brand names may reveal whichever errors I have made.

new age spot more vague. It is a stick cream, Anti-Cervier, Yves Saint-Laurent product number 41911-1. Yukiko also applies it to my wrinkles, and especially to the wedge of skin below and outside of each eye, using two fingers, always going up, not down, since we don't want to show the sagging of my face.

In general, runs her diagnosis, my poor male flesh is afflicted with many red spots; her goal is to render it a uniform color. She works for quite awhile on the creases between the two wings of my nose and on the corners of my mouth. With special care she rubs concealer over the age-downturned corners of my lips.

"How old can a man become and still resemble a woman?"

"After age sixty it is quite difficult."

Following the concealer comes the powdery foundation (a white substance, Anna Sui Face Powder 700), rubbed in, first on the wrinkles around my eyes. First touching me with her brush, then rubbing with a finger, always upward, in firm strokes that move flesh, beneath each eye she creates a downpointed right triangle whose inner side parallels my nose. Yukiko can render this undercoat (the equivalent of gesso on an oil painting) either glossy for a "cute" look or else more natural so that the client appears "classical." Suspecting that cuteness lies beyond my power, I have elected for the classical look.

I ask Yukiko how I could best approximate all this at home, and she advises me to buy a magnifying mirror.

Now for an eyeshadow, which she smears gently in, selecting here and there from many different looks in the palettes, where it resembles vanilla, chocolate and strawberry ice cream. "When you get older it gets darker under the eye, particularly for Japanese," she informs me tactfully. "Then the eyeshadow will not appear nice." This amelioration likewise lasts for about two hours. Using a special brush, she makes seven round trips across each eyelid "like a windshield wiper." Where the brush first touches, there it will be thickest; those round trips smooth it out. Then she proceeds upward, afterward rubbing up and down with her finger in order to blur the contours.

She warns me to avoid allowing any eyeshadow to fall on my cheek, since it cannot easily be removed.

Again, the goal seems to be making the facial skin more uniform, disguising lines and color changes. If so, then the white mask-face of the geisha, or the literal mask-face of the Noh beauty, are simply farther along the continuum.

Now with her soft brush Yukiko mixes two kinds of purple Japanese powder. Then she bends over me, commencing beneath the center of each eye, following the cheekbone "to make it natural." Her applications consist of circles proceeding down and away from the eye, then up back toward it. She continues until my skin appears just a trifle lighter in color than my cheeks.

Here come the many square pats of lipstick in Yukiko's mirrored palette. She mixes a crimson and a pink. Obediently, I keep my mouth closed. With a brush she paints my lower lip larger. She seals her work with transparent gloss.

A slanted-tipped brush is good for the eyebrows. She opens the eyebrow palette.

First she brushes on powder-outlines, since mistakes can be removed without trouble; then she fills in with the eyebrow pencil. Carefully she graduates the edges. It is difficult not to make crooked eyebrows, but I must report that Yukiko has risen to the occasion.

She selects a wig. Then she invites me to study myself in the mirror; and it seems that a woman is looking back at me — not a beautiful woman, perhaps; but still, here is someone who came into the world just now and will exist more briefly than I, a woman who has feelings (my feelings); she wants to look her best. What is grace? I assuredly lack it. But I have become pleasing alien to myself; I am *other* just as distinctly as misted purple-grey mountains stand out from blindingly snowy ricefields.

What changed my appearance the most? — The wig and the lipstick, I would say; much of the other procedures simply diverted attention from the age of my skin. In this connection it is interesting to insert another claim by the zoologist Desmond Morris: Long hair and a hairless (or pale and uniform) face increase contrast, thereby making the woman more visible to potential mates. Puffed-out lips (and my made-up mouth does express the illusion of more voluminous lips) are more juvenile, hence indicative, I suppose, of fresher ova. — But then I wonder to what extent convention plays a part. Why wouldn't Cro-Magnon men

have let their hair grow as long as their women did? Besides, the Noh museum in Kanazawa displays a certain *atsuita*, a thick cloth robe mostly for male roles, which offers its audience a base of turtle-shell octagons, with embroidered patterns pertaining to each of the four seasons within cloud- or fan-shaped borders; it is beautiful, but why should it be male? — And so once again I feel myself to be, as I so often do when I try to comprehend the nuances of Noh, an ape in a cage. — In Yukiko's studio, an ape in a wig stares back at me with sad blue eyes.

I pull the wig off as carefully as I can (for some other client will surely require it), and hand it to Yukiko, remembering that Sei Shonagon's eleventh-century list of things that have lost their power includes a woman who has removed her wig in order to comb remnants of natural hair.

Now Yukiko makes me up another way, with her hands rubbing in the cold, pleasant-smelling cleanser (harder to apply; maybe it is this that makes my skin feel so tight later), rubbing its coldness in with her hands, going over me with cotton, putting on a liquid foundation, chatting and patting — how nice to be taken care of! — my face paling in the mirror; my eyes seem to glitter more.

Only about ten percent of her customers dare to go out. They often wear femme-executive or businesswoman outfits when they come to her; a few play with lingerie, but never here; some keep secret apartments furnished with their woman things, so that their families will never know. They tend to order clothes on the Internet, a circumstance which requires them to buy repeatedly before discovering a garment which actually fits; but anonymity remains infinitely more important to them than cost or convenience.

"Why do they do it?"

"Stress," she replies. "And they have the pleasure of hiding something secret."

Her clients ("twenty or thirty") tend to be doctors, attorneys, etcetera, since she is so expensive — seven hundred dollars for three hours.

"Many of them are narcissistic," she adds, perhaps with a touch of contempt, "so they just want to look into the mirror."

"Do you think most men would do this if they could?"

She smiled. "Well, I believe that few men would like to do it. But some of those goodlooking young male singers who are handsome in an effeminate way, maybe they would like to be like them."

"Would you date a cross-dresser?"

"Never."

As she works on me, I fall into a drowse, enjoying the caress of the black brush, the sound of rain outside, Yukiko standing over me. I gaze up at her chin and lips, her brown hair, her tinted eyelids. Her eyes are far away, for she is gazing not at me, but at my face, which is now halfway feminized. She is painting my eyebrows on. I open myself to her soft fingers on my temple, the silver gleam of the brush, and her fingers on my eyebrows.

"What is the most serious obstacle faced by a man who wants to pass for a woman?"

"Coarse skin."

Now that she has finished, it is time for the excitement of the new wig (style B02, color T/430; made in Korea), of wondering what it is going to make me look like. "This one is more becoming," she says. The hair, reddish like the first wig, is longer, "more simple," with short bangs. "Because it shows the eyebrows it looks more feminine," she concludes, sliding it on.

Who am I? My reddish-gold hair spills down to my breasts, so soft and golden in its highlights, matching my new eyebrows. I have pearly-pale skin — no, actually, I seem to be a rather hard-skinned woman; the creases in my face show more and more; soon my stubble will overpower the concealer; at least I possess a bright glowing smile. (Thank goodness I recently got my teeth cleaned.)

But who *is* this lady? Her eyes seem somehow a darker blue than mine. Is she fake? Her soft red-purple lips smile back at me. I toss my head, and her hair changes to gold.*

For an instant, and with joy, I believe in her, all the while experiencing *aware*, the knowledge that this impossibility cannot be sustained. (The Vimalakirti Sutra, seventh century: "This body is like a flame born of longing and desire . . . This body is impure, crammed with defilement and evil . . . This body is like the abandoned well on the hillside, old age pressing in on it. This body has no fixity, but is destined for certain death.") This session at Yukiko's has strangely resembled a Noh performance, and lasted approximately the same length of time.

The best mask of my self (never mind my soul) may well be a *chujo*; my forehead will soon begin to wrinkle in a pattern like roots, and I often bear the sparse moustache, gaping mouth and blackened teeth of the loyal bewildered lieutenant; perhaps I belong to the Komparu School. What the artist inscribed on the back of my face I will never know, being unable to see myself objectively the way a professional Noh actor would. Most of the time I am a sturdy man who wears the same clothes often, preferring garments of lifelong reliability; I shave carelessly and shrug off my latest wrinkles, because anyhow I never possessed even a *waki*'s hope of being beautiful, nor felt the loss.

What is grace? — In the mirror room, Mr. Umewaka gazes at the lovely woman he will soon become; he sits white-wrapped like a man in an American barber shop, with the wig of long blue-black hair already crowning him, and in the mirror the woman of frozen-faced perfection, one of his several other selves, gazes back at him calmly and untouchably.

---

*Morris claims that blonde hair indicates the juvenile stage for many Caucasians; hence it is desirable for many women.

# "I Sit with My Legs Closed"

*Glimpses of Onnagatas*

And on another cold Tokyo night at the Kabuki-za, where people can sit above the red and white lanterns, drinking beer and eating roasted eel as they watch the performance, the long stage curtain's repeated vertical triads of green, black and orange rush away; we see the legs and feet of someone rushing within it, so that the long wide world of spectacle reveals itself: strings of white over a slanting roof, a blue stripe beneath, then bright red and yellow lattices, a man with a white, white face and triangular shoulders with small square devices on them, not unlike those of a Noh chorister's robes. Through the red lattice we glimpse flashes of white hands playing the shamisen. Many geishas kneel within.

Across the stage bridge comes a white-faced onnagata. The bell sounds. The geishas sing. Thus begins "Sukeroku Yukari no Edo Zakura," starring Nakamura Fukusuke as the first-ranking geisha Agemaki, and Ichikawa Danjuro as the warrior Sukeroku.

Instead of recounting the plot (only a portion of which was performed), let me tell you about the lovely strangeness of the feminine imitations, the *opulence* — for instance, of that geisha in high thick shining clogs; she is crowned with a spike-studded golden crescent, and her voice is wavering, breaking and almost whining, with falsetto cadences.

On the bridge, a whitefaced geisha in green stands beneath a tall parasol, her black katsura in golden spider-ribbon, a giant golden jewel on her speckled turquoise breast. As a little child sings in falsetto: *"Eeeee!"*, she undertakes slow fantastic steps in her clogs, which resemble towers.

Kabuki femininity expresses itself through the lovely wooden clopping as the lavender-clad courtesans run, not to mention the way an onnagata crosses her wrists, raises her hands, unfolds a scroll-letter from a lover, her voice resembling a pouting child's, the low, majestic wiggle of the exaggerated buttocks of a lady with a rather squeaky, raspy voice. As for the breasts, those are created with a padded apron tied around under the waist.

A courtesan takes off her green mantle and shows red and gold long sleeves. She is very high-waisted (her waist comes almost up to her armpits, in fact). Long strings of jade beads spill down her front and make fringe between her widely spread legs. She resembles a queen in a deck of playing cards. Her lavender-hued attendants rush to kneel at her back to adjust her. Her square hips sway like panniers. Her female voice is rising and falling, often ending in a descending wail.

The feet mince up and down when a Kabuki lady passes through a doorway, her full buttocks swaying. How important is this person or that? Inspect her buttocks. Those of a great lady are stacked, sparkling half-doughnuts. Lesser goddesses wear less padded skirts.

Their kimono sleeves have been specially elongated in order to miniaturize their male hands, the hems lowered to partially conceal their feet. Sometimes they feel the need to wax the corners of the eyes and the eyebrows. (An older Kabuki actor may pull up his eyes by wrapping silken gauze around his forehead.) Their made-up faces are cruder but much more mobile than Noh masks. Their meowing voices sound weird, yet feminine. Exposing the backs of their necks much as geishas do, they accomplish, for instance, the semiformal female walk: slide the sole of one foot forward, then slide the other ahead almost on a parallel line; walk with the legs always together (for practice, the apprentice ties his knees together with silken thread, which must not break even when kneeling or standing).

A princess thrusts her shoulders back and keeps her body out; she has a low center of gravity. The next category, more feminine, weaves her face, shoulders, torso and buttocks in figure eights as she goes. A courtesan holds up her kimono with the left hand, an aristo-cratic lady, with the right. A "simple woman from next door" moves more rapidly.

The onnagata Mr. Ichikawa Shunen had been an actor for twenty years, and before that a student for two. He had an active fan club. When I met him, he was out of cos-tume, but his face was so lovely and deli-cate, his hair so long and caressable on his neck, his lips so smoothly pink (by the way, he wore a little padlock around his throat), that I told him that I could see he would be a beautiful woman. He thanked me.

"Is there a difference between a man playing a woman and a woman being a woman?"

"Yes, I think it's different. The strange aspect of being an onnagata is that we do not seek to be closest to the real woman.* Our training is otherwise. That's what we call the onnagata skill. We have four hundred years of history. This skill is something we learn. My teacher said that onnagatas don't have to be beautiful creatures from the beginning. How-ever physically male a person might be, he can be a woman."

"To what extent is femininity a matter of movement?"

"It's close to the Noh feeling. The voice is a man's, but you can see that compared to Noh, Kabuki is more visually real. We are closer to real

---

*So one customarily hears about this particular manifestation of femininity. For instance, Mishima writes that "an onnagata is the child born of the illicit union between dream and reality." Furthermore, an onnagata must not strive to act like a woman or he will fail in his effect; he must simply live as a woman when he is not on stage. Mishima says again: The onnagata cannot achieve anything "by a mere slavish imitation of real women."

KABUKI THEATER FACADE.

MR. ICHIKAWA SHUNEN.

women than Noh actors are. We learn that for *this* role you move *this* way. The angle of the neck, the hand movements, how one walks, depend on one's age and rank as they would have been expressed in the Edo period. The Snake Princess's movements will be different from a geisha's."

When I asked which roles he preferred, he said: "Rather than prin-cesses, I like geiko-sans. I like a look that is witty and sophisticated and even flippant. Simply put, I like to be a bad girl. There are many such roles in Kabuki — sophisticated delinquents."

His makeup began with the stick of "oil" (which might in fact have been some sort of oily wax) that a sumo wrestler uses for his hair. There are many consistencies, and the onnagata chooses the one most appropri-ate to his role. A different sort of oil hides the eyebrows. Then comes a brown cream foundation, followed by *oshiroi* paste thinned with water and applied with a hake brush. Sponge and pat. Next comes the pure white powder in two layers, "then pink gradation, depending on the per-son." Some people use a stick of red oil first, then pink, making a kind of foundation. The red oil is also used as lipstick.*

---

*The only vendor of Kabuki makeup in that district, he said, was a certain kimono acces-sory shop in the Ginza. When I went there to buy what they recommended, a Kabuki actor who happened to be a customer right then gave me the following directions:

The red applied to eyes (around the outer corners and the undersides) is called *mehari*. "Each onnagata uses his own way," he said. "What I'm explaining is very basic. An onnagata does not use black around the eyes. Pink *oshiroi* may be applied after the white for some people."

"This is the base," he said. "Pink gradation is between the upper eye and the eyebrow, and also on the outer cheeks. Then the eyebrows are painted with oil mixed with charcoal." Again, different onnagatas did it differently. "I use red dissolved in water without oil, but water when I mix the paint for my eyebrows."

Regarding the eyebrows, those are supposed to have the same classical "bamboo-willow" shape that we have already encountered in the ancient poems of the *Manyoshu*.*

He said that there were "many variations" for the mouth, but that it was lipsticked very small; one shrank it down to two-thirds of its previous size.

It took him only a quarter-hour to make himself up, but of course he had been doing it for twenty years.

His wig was a custom-made solid copper plate, made and fitted, like Suzuka-san's, by a wigmaker. "You apply it like a metal helmet," he said. Over this went human hair upon a base of white silk and black cloth, the white to match the onnagata's face and the black to border the hair, which by the way required a beautician to attach.

Customarily onnagatas worked twenty-five days a month, then redid their hair.

"Do men and women have different souls?"

"As a Kabuki actor, I don't feel that my soul needs to play a woman's soul," he replied, perhaps a trifle offended. "Because the soul is the most important thing we show."

---

1. Apply cleansing cream; do not wipe off.
2. Apply half a fingertip's worth of oil, the hard kind in summer, soft in winter.
3. Mix powder with water in a dish to make paste. Apply with a hake brush, which should be washed afterward.
4. Sponge away any extra water from the face.
5. Apply face powder with a puff.
6. Use separate brushes to apply the red and black.

*See above, p. 110.

I told him how different the person who looked at me from the mirror had seemed when Yukiko had made me up, and I asked how it was for him. "When you start doing this, it's strange to become the role itself," he agreed mildly. "That goes away." I asked him at what point he actually became the role, when you put on the makeup or costume, or immediately before going on stage. "In my case," he said, "it's when I see myself in the mirror just after I make up. What I am feeling is not soul but *appearance*. But he" — he indicated the man who sat beside him — "is also an onnagata, and he feels differently. Immediately before I enter the stage, that is when I really switch."

"Is it exhilarating, or just work?"

"Exhilarating. For example, if you have a high fever but cannot cancel the performance, then you do it, however sick you are. During such times I can be standing in front of an audience and physically my voice is not as good as usual, but mentally I totally forget that I am sick."

My question had had to do with becoming female; his answer, it seemed, with performance in and of itself. He was, after all, a professional; and the essential difference between him and Yukiko's clients who "just want to look into the mirror" was that after looking in the mirror he showed himself to others. Grace, as we keep seeing, is performance; and Zeami advises that instead of merely looking ahead of himself at the audience, a Noh master must "grasp the logic of the fact that the eyes cannot see themselves," which means to "make still another effort in order to grasp his own internalized outer image . . . Once he obtains this, the actor and the spectator can share the same image." The novice crossdresser sees himself (one hopes) as he would like to be. The onnagata or Noh actor sees himself as he has made himself, remembers this after leaving the mirror, and deploys his grace accordingly.

Even I, the most gullible ape in the entire cage, sometimes suffer fits of skepticism about the profundity of Zeami's secrets. How does the Noh actor's envisioning of his internalized outer image differ from the way that a faded street prostitute on entering a bar will often gaze into the nearest mirror, so that without frightening anybody with her weird old hard-sell eyes she can discover who is staring at her shape? — Perhaps the answer is simply that if she and her audience do share the same image of her, it is not necessarily the image she would want to project.

"Born in an ordinary family," Mr. Ichikawa had loved Kabuki ever since he was three years old. — I wonder if what first seduced him was the brilliant two-dimensionality of it all, especially the trees and walls, with checkered-robed samurai and geishas in their spectacularly crested kimonos somehow resembling animated playing cards? Was it the falling trapdoors, rushing curtains and folding walls? Was it all the murders and suicides happily observed by old ladies in the audience who sat sucking on molasses candies? Or did he already yearn to become as graceful as a marble-faced onnagata? — When he was five he saw his first live performance. Since he was an indifferent student, his parents would not permit him to train for Kabuki until had he proved himself by being accepted into a prestigious high school. He passed the entrance examination, quit school after a month, and immediately took the entrance examination to study Kabuki. He was then fifteen years old.

"Since beauty is performance, what do you do to stay beautiful?"

"My everyday life affects my performance, not the other way around. Because I am physically a man, I normally wear pants. It's natural to sit *this* way, with my legs apart, or to hold a glass *this* way, but by doing that in everyday life I could harm my life on stage without knowing it. So to the extent I can, I sit with my legs closed. I try not to hold my fingers apart, in order to make my hands more womanly. Kabuki actors in the past used to wear women's costume in everyday life. They were so lovely. Clothes have changed, of course. If I wore Western women's clothes during the daytime, that would not affect my stance. But I always try to restrain myself."

The book he had written for Japanese women advised them to wear kimonos so that they could be more feminine afterward, merely by remembering how they had been restrained. "By wearing kimonos, many movements you cannot make; your posture will be upright, and you will not be able to open your legs or recline or raise your arm very high." — And I remembered the way that Japanese women so often sit in a kneeling-like fashion, with their feet tucked beneath their buttocks, while Japanese men may cross their legs, with each foot beneath the opposite thigh.

Tightening the obi thrusts out breasts and hips, and thereby enhances the performance of nubile femininity. Fetishistic tight-lacers are said to enjoy any or all of the following sensations: bodily support, muscle surrender, transmission of the sense of touch over a wider area ("any movement in the hips passes at once to their breast and vice versa"), pleasurable numbness, erotic heat. I have never presumed to ask a geisha, onnagata or Noh actor about such sensations; but one kimono-wearing Japanese woman whom I knew well enough to discuss such things with smiled, blushed a trifle, and allowed that perhaps she was not entirely unfamiliar with the joys of constriction.

Gesturing fluidly with the sides of his smooth small hands, parting his pale lips as he spoke, sipping from a straw, Mr. Ichikawa said: "For Japanese women, beauty is in the kimono."

He agreed with Yukiko that one must be very careful about one's skin . . .

BASIC KABUKI MAKEUP FOR AN ONNAGATA.

18:

# "There's No Ugly Lady Face"

*Katy Transforms*

Katy considered herself a gay man, and performed femininity primarily for purposes of attracting men; all the same, she preferred to be addressed and described with female pronouns. She worked in a restaurant in Los Angeles, wearing male clothes and her male birthname.

I met her in a certain bar not too far from Sunset Boulevard where the beautiful late night girls were laughing and kissing each other's cheeks. I remember their long hair and smooth skin and smell of powder. Katy was the least shy and most patient of them. That night she wore silver bracelets and long silver earrings with her long long eyebrows.

After a couple of hours a blonde came in. — "Look!" said Katy. "She's so beautiful. Looks just like a woman."

Did Katy resemble a woman? Yes and no. She performed femininity with the rocklike gentleness of an ancient Kannon statue.

"Why do you wear a dress?"

"For me, there are some men who would like to see me that way. For some men it's their fantasy, to be with a woman but also with a man. Some *travesti* cannot be beautiful like woman, and because they know the woman looks better, they hate the woman. I have one friend who likes the dress, but hate the woman. I have another friend who wear the dress and never go out, just wear the dress. Some men tell me, why do you do this? But I like it. People wanna wear a dress, then wear a dress. I talking, looking like a woman, everyone tell me."

She believed that the souls of man and woman were the same. And here she interjected: "Some people tell me God doesn't hear me, because I'm gay. But I pray, and I think God hears me."

The next night was Halloween, so I went over to her apartment.

She was sitting at the illuminated triple mirror in her black and red dressing gown, deploying stick foundation on her tired male face. She had hoped to sell me some of her clothes, but they didn't fit me.

"Why are some women more beautiful than others?"

"Because when you put some makeup on, it's a different face. And how you like it, it's a different face. There's no ugly lady face, only ugly makeup."

Then she bowed over the mirror again.

First came foundation, then powder, then blush, then more white pancake to fill in the cracks of her man's face.

Her housemate Jennifer wore smooth young skin, soft cleavage, a bared navel, a smooth face, young tight hair and perhaps a faint moustache as she sat on the sofa in bra and jeans and sandals, her toenails painted a dark red. I believe she had recently begun to take hormones.

And Katy, who once upon a time had been a cowboy in Guatemala, sat squat and wide in her dark black bathrobe with the red cuffs.

I was there with my G-girl,* and Katy and Jennifer tried to figure me out. On the one hand, I was interested in T-girls† and makeup, so perhaps this G-girl might simply be my close friend from whom I was learning how to act feminine. On the other hand . . .

And I was trying to figure *them* out. This is what I saw:

Katy applied Duo eyelash glue over her natural eyebrows, since they were very black. That way she could paint foundation or other cosmet-

---

*Genetic girl. A woman who was born with a vagina.

†Transgender girls.

ics over them, and build her T-girl eyebrows in liberty. And now indeed the eyebrows grew long and dark on the Kabuki-like face, although the brown pockmarks still remained on the sides of that male nose.

"The most time is the eye," she said.

Elongating the eyebrows still more so that they curved down over her nose, she proudly remarked that this makeup would endure for twelve hours. Sometimes she drank too much and fell asleep with her paint on. When she woke up it was still there. It helped that she did not sweat much.

She applied a big brush around her chin and neck, contouring brown so that these male features seemed to recede. Then came the mascara, whose progress she earnestly controlled through the mirror, her mouth open, like a small girl who is surprised by what she has been told. (What did she see? The photographer Hans Bellmer writes of incidents of "congruence" when the universe seems to become "a double of the super ego." If I were Katy, I would rather have it become a double of my id.) After that it came time for the cheek blush, brushing *up and up.*

The makeup box was as big as a picnic cooler, the tripartite mirror's bulbs shining like church candles, and there was a treasury of white, silver and gold high heels heaped like jawbones on the grubby carpet as the two transvestites sat adjusting their hair.

As Nakamura Mitsue said to me about the Noh masks she carved: "When I feel some existence there I feel happy." I remembered watching a block of wood getting first cut into faces like a diamond, then its faces smoothed away in the correct planes; that was where the art came in.

In the sixth century it was written that dharmas (objects of perceptions) "are never created or annihilated by themselves, but come into being because they are created by illusion and imagination and exist without real existence." — If so, all the better, perhaps. Katy and Jennifer wished to go out into the world as women. If their femininity were created by illusion, then which "reality" could presume to annihilate it?

# The Phallus of Tiresias

*What Is a Woman?*

And so what is a woman? The long history of Noh has been described as the alteration of an "entertainment enacted by a loosely defined occupation into a classical art performed by a closed profession dominated by a select elite." Meanwhile, in various cultures at varying times, the tale of femininity expresses the exact reverse: The select elite, biological females, makes room for the loosely defined occupations of those who call themselves female.

And once again I wonder about the possible genderlessness of the soul, whose most appropriate reification might then be that ancient Hungarian figurine whose shape was of an erection with testicles but whose glans was a woman's face and whose long neck bore hard-nippled little breasts almost halfway down; the scrotum was a woman's buttocks. — I want to reject this androgynous conception and until now always did, having been socialized into a conception of maleness which in part defined itself as the antipode to that exotic, desirable thing called femininity. — To be sure, what I want makes small difference. Herewith, my prejudices. They will seem absurd far sooner than I can suppose, and it embarrasses me a trifle to lay them out even now. But reticence is cowardice, and irony would be fatal to any discussion of beauty; so all that remains to me is sincerity:

I resist the idea that the soul is genderless; I want my soul to be masculine and a woman's to be feminine. It may be that I do not love myself; accordingly, to the extent that a woman might partake of my nature I would find her less perfect. — And why would I want her to be perfect? (Well, why do I watch Noh plays?) Shortly before his suicide in 1942, Stefan Zweig, born in Vienna before the end of the nineteenth century, looks back upon the sartorial expressions of gender in what he calls *the world of yesterday* — the hats, beards and stiff collars of the men, the corsets, bell-skirts and towering hair of the women — with astonishment, disgust and pity, the latter especially for the women, whom prudery confined in ignorance, timidity, unhealthiness and, worst of all, "pitiful" dependency. But he continues: "By this unnatural differentiation in external habits the inner tension between the poles, the erotic, was necessarily strengthened." And so it might be equally likely that selfishness, not self-loathing, impels my obedience to the notion of a gender abyss. Or am I simply a thoroughly conditioned product of my own world of yesterday?

In any event, I desire a feminine grace to remain uncontaminated by masculinity. And I refuse to relinquish the beauty and nobility of attachment. I would rather be an anguished ghost.

It may well be, in spite of my own Zeami-esque prescription at the end of "What Is Grace?", that a woman's grace actually prevents me from seeing who she is. But the grace of the women I already know derives from their voice and their scents, the way they sleep beside me, the way that in quarrels they hurt me and are hurt by me.

The Buddhist subtexts of Noh assert that because desire can never be satisfied, I should discipline myself into renouncing desire. A sense of freedom may well steal upon me when I die, and all my love will fade gratefully away with the rest of my consciousness. But the suffering that feminine grace inflicts on me by the very virtue of my impossible craving to drink it in, why is that bad or wrong? And when the flower, be it false or true, scatters its petals in the dirt, should I turn away from it on that account? Like so many *shites*, I would rather defy time.

In about 1793 we find the renowned Yoshiwara geisha Tomimoto Toyohina (she is a *natori*, meaning that she is sufficiently skilled to have received a name), posing between the teashop beauty Naniwaya Kita and a certain rice cake store proprietor's eldest daughter, Takashima Chobei,* who happened to be one of the two most popular beauties of the time. I admit that since then their funeral-smoke has blackened the leaves of trees now long dead, but Utamaro made a woodblock print of them, and it remains ours to dream over. I pore over the image, and experience joy, so why not keep this book safe from as many pyres as I can?

What is a woman, if not an *ukiyo-e* courtesan or teahouse beauty performing femininity by means of a face in repose, a cheek which refuses to widen like a *ko-omote*'s, tiny pale vermilion lips parted in both directions, every aspect of her stylized through understatement? Does she in fact require the overstated narrowing from waist to legs of a Chalandrian type Cycladic figurine — flat, with nipples and arms in relief, and the pubic hair-dots pecked out?

In Kyoto at a certain Takigi-Noh performance graced by a very slow, mellow, sad style of singing, different from anything I had heard up to then, I saw a stately firelit woman slowly rotating by supernatural power. She was so lovely, half dreaming. Black-and-green tree-darknesses and forests of bamboo drumbeats kept rising around her, her eyeslits of female darkness sometimes drooping as if with sadness while she gazed down through me. Presently the flute blew, and she slowly outstretched her golden sleeve, then locked the fingers of both hands together, slowly, slowly, so that each flame had time to alter its shape an infinity of times. Her kimono was patterned with might have been boulders and gem-crystals (how can I say for sure? She was far away from me, up high on the stage on that summer's night). How did she accomplish her womanliness? Was it the way that her sleeves spread, her fan opened like fingers, the flames strained toward her alien glossy face, and her vermilion skirts hung down? Half a decade later I remain happily haunted by that tranquilly changing face, the fan pointing up at the smoke which passed through the trees, the sleeves sweeping apart decisively yet slowly, the white face often in the midst of a dark space between foliage even as fire

---

*Or possibly Hisa.

played sunnily on the kimono — and again I need to tell you that that mask seemed so far away in this night that it could almost be a rocket ship — why not? It had a crew, the wide-eyed, kneeling chorus; and Ground Control handlers such as the man who crept deftly in to hand up a prop or straighten a robe; all the while, the mask continued to sing. Who *was* this woman? *What* was she? How could I tell you?

From the standpoint of the other who sees her, is a woman simply someone who looks or acts in a certain way? If so, her defining expressions may indeed, as an unsympathetic French psychoanalyst insists, uphold "sexual stereotypes, with a view to maintaining women in the conventional, subordinate role from which they were on the point of freeing themselves. Transsexuals' image of women is wholly conformist . . ." After all, how far the onnagata or the transgender woman can go toward "passing" depends substantially, as we have seen, on femininity's performance aspect, and to be recognized as feminine that performance must express ritualism or at least familiarity: Touch one's hair, face and jewelry often. (In the *manga* comics, and in the coffee shops of my own country, ones so often sees the hands of heroines fluttering inward together against their breasts and throats.) When walking, especially in high heels, place one's weight on the back foot, keeping the front foot free to tap down, then click lightly forward in one's high heels, swinging arms from the elbows and brushing the thighs together. Roll back hips and shoulders. Navigate stairs at a constant diagonal, and sit the same way, on the edge of the chair, with the knees together, and the feet behind them. "Bright colors on the eye look feminine," says a makeup artist (who this season recommends peacock blue and tangerine). But the aspect of body makeup remains. That blonde in the black metallic miniskirt I see in the fashion magazine, how many men who wanted to be her double actually could? And how many women? After all, Keisei sends us the following monitory pearl in *A Companion in Solitude* (*ca.* 1222): "A woman's nature is such that whether of high rank or low birth, she pins her hopes on all sorts of things, but in the end is unable to realize her expectations."

The following description of what can only be called failed femininity comes from an American novel published in 1934. Can a born member of a given gender express that gender deficiently? Can a person who was born with a vagina and considers herself female be somehow less female than other vagina-bearers? The omniscient narrator thinks so:

> Watching her, Cynthia ached with sympathy. Amelia was so tall and gaunt and flat-chested. She was not really a woman at all. She did not have a woman's body, with a woman's breasts and full shoulders, a woman's firm round arms and legs. The lines of her mouth were tight, as a man's sometimes is. Except for this there was nothing masculine about her — nothing strong, nothing alive. This was neither a woman's body nor a man's, but something in between and less than either — something gray which women become when desire dies out in them, for lack of cherishing, when no child takes shape within them.

Well, in my time Amelia could have donned breast forms, makeup, a mask! Why not select one's heart's desire from the varying plumpnesses of girl-masks' white cheeks? Even round arms would have come to her, had she only stopped being anorexic. What about her tight mouth? — Use concealer over the lip line you were born with if you wish to reshape it. Then apply lip pencil and lip brush; blot and repeat the lip brush. — But then she might not have been Amelia. Who was she and who should she have been? Was anything wrong with her aside from loneliness? When Danyu-san said of her career, "they make it so that the child realizes she cannot do anything else," did that touch upon some wider and perhaps even inescapable assertion about gender which condemned her to some sort of deficiency? Do gender roles, like capitalism, require there to be winners and losers? Very likely, Katy's performance of womanhood would have been as depressing to Sei Shonagon as seeing in the third or fourth month the red plum-blossom dress appropriate to the eleventh or twelfth month; and in 2009 in California I found myself sharing my usual bus stop with a ghetto prostitute on her way home from the weekly visit to her parole officer; she hated the police, who were "packing heat and offing people," but across the street three police officers stood like a helpful audience around a young man with a shaved head for whom the prostitute had no sympathy because "he's a faggot! Just look at how he moves them arms! Oh, it makes me *sick*! I wanna see them hit 'im in the face."

In a novel by the novelist Heinrich Böll, whose Nobel Prize was in my opinion otherwise deserved, one encounters the rather Lamarckian assertion that one's sexual behavior actually alters one's *appearance*, so that a heterosexual male can be literally unmanned by a homosexual act whether or not it happened of his own volition, and another man can recognize his gender-corruption on extremely short acquaintance.

> Now all at once he realized what the repulsive aura was which emanated
> from this man who at one time, when his eyes were still clear, must have
> been handsome, fair and slender with well-bred hands. So that's it, thought
> Andreas. "Yes," said the blond fellow very quietly, "that's it . . ."

A sergeant major had "seduced" him more or less at gunpoint. Now he bears the mark of Cain. He can never *pass* again.

Moreover, we are not infrequently instructed that somebody's attempt to pass as a member of the opposite sex comprises a general social or religious pollution, a contagion. "No doubt you have heard," writes Cicero to Atticus in 61 B.C., "that when the sacrifice was taking place in Caesar's house, a man in woman's clothes got in"; and that after the Vestal Virgins had performed the sacrifice afresh, the matter was mentioned in no less august a place than the Roman Senate. The Vestals and the priests decided that a sacrilege had been committed, and the matter had to go to trial. As that prostitute said to me: "Oh, it makes me *sick*!"

What would the young man have needed to do to make her pity his arrest? Simply refrain from moving his arms like that. Or instead he could have *passed*.

(The noses of *tsuki* style Noh masks are canted slightly leftward. If a right-leaning *yuki* mask were employed by a brash actor whose colleagues would have used the *tsuki* for that part, would he fail to *pass*? Would the audience ever know? If they did, what would they say?)

From the year 1232, we meet the understated anguish of a young woman whose soul has been inhabited (and constructed) by a male poet aged seventy. Knowing full well that any rendezvous is but separation, she gives herself to the man, "unconscious of approaching dawn." But after all, this empathy with the feminine which the translators marvel at is no more than the expression of what any lover male or female might experience. Should we then say that Teika passed?

Vanesa Lorena Ledesma, born Miguel Angel Ledesma, aged forty-seven at death (by police torture, evidently), lies with her head slumped down. Her face is gaunt. Her eyelids are dark. Her lips are full. Her cheeks are drawn in. She appears to be a poor woman in late middle age. A white cloth, perhaps the shroud, frames her black, black hair.

Mattilda, also known as Matt Bernstein Sycamore, wrote: "If we eliminate the pressure to pass, what delicious and devastating opportunities for transformation might we create?" Perhaps there might come into being a world in which Amelia's "in between" was no longer considered a deficit, like some Kabuki drama involving a retainer arrayed in armor, riding a prancing black horse which has four human legs. I look at a collection of mid-twentieth-century snapshots taken in and around a house in upstate New York whose hostess entertained many guests over the years, guests in dresses, some of them more womanly-looking than others; on occasion they might sit at the kitchen table smoking the odd cigarette, or show off their legs and red shoes; they might smile sweetly with their white gloves on, with their handbags in their lap, or they could squint their mascara'd eyes when they blew out birthday candles. Often their jawlines were square and their brows projected; sometimes (and this would not have surprised Yukiko) their skins were coarse. But they looked happy. It did not seem to matter that some could not have passed.

After all, even a Noh actor does not seek to pass, only to perform feminine grace. That seems difficult enough. — How did Mr. Kanze do it? — Edwin Denby on Nijinsky's dance poses: "One might say that the grace of them is not derived from avoiding strain, as a layman might think, but from the heightened intelligibility of the plastic relationships."

Regarding these relationships, Zeami (who believes that almost nobody expresses them all at the highest level) offers for our consideration three basic elements: *bone*, or inborn strength (which is to say heart; breathing technique); *flesh*, or the effect of chant and dance (sound; melodic interest; this will make an actor's art seem inexhaustible even when frequently seen, and so I think of a beautiful woman, or a lovely Noh mask, whom one loves to look at); finally, *skin*, "a manner of ease and beauty in performance" as a result of appropriate flesh and bone (sight; beauty of a voice).

Meanwhile, in an ancient Egyptian tale, King Snefru commands: "Let there be brought to me twenty women, the most beautiful in form, with firm breasts, with hair well braided, not yet having opened up to give birth." Their task will be to row naked for his entertainment. This list of beautiful attributes is brief; were it not for the nakedness part, any number of onnagatas could appear to satisfy it to some degree. If they could, and if any number of geishas could dance "Black Hair" without a flaw, what would we say? One famous geisha's instructor informed her: "All I am able to do is teach you the form. The dance you dance on stage is yours alone."

Yes, some forms of grace can be taught. For instance, "a fan must be carried," one handbook explains. "It should be of gold or silver with bones of black lacquer or ivory." And any gender-actress can paint her toenails to coordinate with her lipstick; this look I happen to prefer to the appearance of geishas' *tabi* socks, but of course it would be harder to dance barefoot. Then what? Kanze Kiyokazu's father used to say of a certain seventeenth-century *waka-onna*: "This is a higher-level mask with strength, but it is rather difficult to use. Depending on where you see it from, it can appear as if it is slightly smiling, or as it is commonly called 'lonely young woman,'* it can easily be made to show a sad look, with changing expressions." How many toenail-painters can do that? And the way a model's long nude leg, which one often sees frozen in motion, matches her collarbone, can depilation and estrogen reliably duplicate *that*? In the ferry terminal at Niigata, a young woman in a yellow kimono with copper-red bangs and plump lips painted to match wears a yellow paper chrysanthemum in the side of her hair, probably for her twenti-eth-year ceremony. How much of her success derives from *bone* or *skin* or *flesh*, how much from the false flower which I accept as true? — Another model wears a long black spangly gown that outlines hip, buttock and breast while introducing nudity from below the collarbone upward and then in tiny peekaboo triangles between the breasts; the yellow dress whose creases radiate crisply down and out from the bust bares nearly the same area. How much does the gown help her pull it off? — In the Genji Picture-Scrolls, beautiful women are not much more than their clothes. Unfortunately, I read that "many, if not most women are the wrong shape for most women's clothes." — Well, then, by all means remove clothes

---

*You may recall that *waka-onna* means "young woman."

from consideration! The oval-faced *kore* from the Acropolis with braided marble hair, how much of her could be copied into a male representation with no gender-sniffer the wiser?

The American magazines inform me that the ideal woman is X-shaped; wide bust and hips, narrow waist; one can wear clothes to approach that impression — or a corset to enforce it. Puffed-up hair and satin blue ballet slippers, how analogous are such props to a *ko-omote* mask and wig? The model's expression in today's magazines (who knows about tomorrow's?) is neutral, not unlike a Noh actor's, the eyes wide open, but in concentration, lips parted or not, but rarely smiling. Turning the page, I find the actress Katie Holmes with a rather schoolgirlish look, serious yet saucy, in a short skirt, and hair in thick dark waves down to her chin. In her linen designer dress she could almost be a girl out of a photo from the 1940s. Her eyes are underlined, her brows painted down the sides of the nose to a point level with the lowest part of her upper eyelid. How much of the allure is her makeup and dress, how much is diet and discipline, how much the young, lovely female body she was given? The French psychoanalyst just quoted is sure that "sexual difference, which owes much to symbolic dualisms, belongs to the register of the *real*. It constitutes an insuperable barrier . . ." But perhaps all it takes to overcome this barrier and resemble Katie Holmes is the latest trick: eyeshadow like bruise, "a smoldering smoky eye."

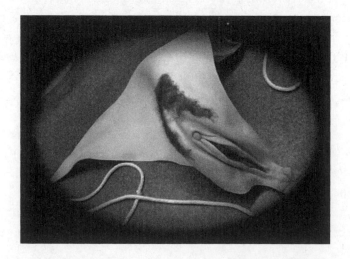

# II

# WHITE ARMS

20:

# A Curtain of Mist

*Understatement and Concealment*

You use nice color," the mask carver Mr. Otsuka had said, "and then on top of it you put something else to make it look more subdued, so it doesn't look too shallow. After fifty or a hundred years, if you've used something unsubtle, it's really going to show; it'll start looking worse and worse." Thus again the ancient aesthetic of Chun'e with his "autumn hills half-concealed by a curtain of mist" — not to mention the secret teachings of Zeami, which are in and of themselves, so some have said, no more important than the fact that they are secret. — What if I simply can't understand them? I remember Mr. Umewaka telling me that he prohibited his apprentices from perusing those treatises during their first years of study, since "unless you master Noh to some extent, you interpret the instructions incorrectly." Moreover, I confess that whenever I decline to track the numbers and paths of telltale hair-strands, a *waka-onna*, *fushikizo* and *manbi* seen all together can scarcely be distinguished from each other; perhaps their mouth-darknesses vary a trifle, but it could also be the angle at which I view each one. And on a certain afternoon of shining black rivers in Snow Country, when the train rushed me through a blizzard, I lost track of the various watercourses, and occasionally even wondered what I was seeing — an experience also offered by the dreamy, blurry translucency of Renoir nudes, in which everything reveals itself only through a very thin membrane, the light puddling and gently oozing, the pastel flesh modeled, not reticulated as a gum bichromate print would be, but simply melded, blurred. — Why shouldn't it be? Don't makeup artists so often blend powder eyeshadow with blush? — In this spirit, Zeami alludes to snow in a silver bowl.

And in self-defense, the reliably sour Eric C. Rath refers to the unfathomableness of "Okina" and of those secret manuscripts as "empowering interpreters with expertise while facilitating the disenfranchisement of those who could not claim to possess such intimate knowledge." — I accordingly wonder: Is disenfranchisement necessarily a bad thing? The wall which disenfranchises me from a full view of the garden behind it, the lingerie (or ballroom gown) which prohibits much, but by no means all, of my gaze's access to the woman who performs femininity within it, these two cases produce respectively, as we know, the beauty of *miekakure* and likewise of *iki*: allure softened and hidden, like the metonymic gestures of a multiply wrapped dancing geisha. The fact that I will never fully understand "Okina" makes it all the more haunting to me. — "Okina is not a pine tree spirit," replied a Noh expert to my first attempt at definition. "Just what Okina represents is as much a theological problem as a literary one. Some people claim he is the Sun, and there are Buddhist connections as well. I'd stay away from this one if I were you."

The proverb goes that it is better to love than to be loved; perhaps I am lucky to be an ape in a cage.

The withholding of a thing invests it with desirability; to the extent that it grows (or remains) opaque to the gaze, resistant to the will, it draws us toward itself. In his unfinished essay on the poetry of Chinese ideograms, Fenollosa asserts that "poetry is finer than prose because it gives us more concrete truth in the same compass of words," and again, "poetic thought works by suggestion, crowding maximum meaning into the single phrase pregnant, charged, and luminous from within." In part (one hopes), this luminosity is accomplished through brilliant selections and arrangements of words, multiple under-kimonos, makeup; but the metonymic compulsion placed upon that single phrase, the representation of Genji's dying wife by means of a folded robe on the Noh stage, or that hint of red on the sole of the woman's high heels, requiring it to do duty for a dozen other phrases any of which could have served equally or nearly as well, catalyzes the impregnation and the charging of the thing. Hence the tale of the tea-master Sen no Rikyu, who at around the turn of the seventeenth century built a garden on a hill overlooking the waves; within the garden hedges utterly shut out the world, but at the entrance, above the stone water-basin where guests bent to purify themselves, a hole had been bored through the hedge; there and only there one could spy the sea.

In around 1794 we see one of Utamaro's *yuujo* fanning herself. Her hair is tied back with the string called *motoyui*, and she wears a red slip, white underwear and a thin black summer garment. Her ankle entices us through the black dress.

Do such procedures best teach me to appreciate ankles and ocean views? Mr. Mikata once said to me (and I wish I understood him completely; the enigmatic quality of the word "capacity" surely derives from my interpreter's choice of words): "The right capacity is where you can see with your eyes and then you can hear with your voice. If you need light to see, then you cannot really appreciate the depth of Noh." — His sentiment felt strange to me, since under such conditions I could not possibly distinguish a *ko-omote* from a *waka-onna*, but by that very token it increased the understatement, bringing the Noh farther beyond perception and discrimination, so that it might as well have been infinite. Could it be that if I subjected myself stringently and sincerely to such conditions, I would learn to recognize those two masks at a glance? Would it improve my aesthetic sense? Or would I merely accomplish my own Rathian disenfranchisement? Is it the Emperor's new clothes?

But as this book so frequently and perhaps wearisomely repeats, understatement need not accomplish itself only through reduction; stylization will also serve its turn, as in, for instance, the simplified visages of the ladies and their courtiers in the Genji Picture-Scrolls, or Utamaro's round-cheeked white geisha faces standing out from yellowish mica grounds, their stiff black hair-waves bristling with golden hairpicks, some of which sport floral decorations; the red lips and black eyes are always tiny in the plump white features; they preen themselves or bow snowily over love-letters; their expressions are nearly identical, like the lines used to compose them: the nose is two curves, each eye a pointed-cornered ellipse, the mouth two simple droplet-shapes joined on the pointed side.

Again, please consider the way that Matisse's drawings of women offer a combination of spontaneity and economy, a right breast, for instance, being represented by an arc akin to a backward L, with the nipple a tick inscribed in a tight little circle; the woman's face is often no more than a wide U, closed at the top by a few squiggles of hair, and within, the brows and nose generally receive one line apiece, the mouth two or three, like each eye. A woman stands nude, clasping her wrists in a curvy arch above her head. Her contours twist smoothly and simply down. These few lines are so carefree, yet so convincing in their placement, that the woman, sleek and rounded, has been caught forever in an instant of her moving grace. Another woman wears a necklace, her bowed head almost classically Greek; Matisse has not troubled to connect her left shoulder to her neck, and it makes no difference. A woman's face is half-smiling at me, her lips full, her eyes squinting sleepily and sensually; counting the earring, hair-ribbon, necklace and all, this drawing cannot comprise more than twenty-five lines. And here a wide-hipped woman sprawls on her side, her uppermost thigh an inviting white blankness, with a pretty little pubic squiggle for a decoration; it reminds me of her sister's hair-ribbon. What is grace? A naked woman plays beside a bowl of goldfish. A woman on her knees arches her back and stretches, with her face not more than a single line; her genitals, made of line-twirls and a few cross-hatches, are the least blank part of this drawing, which is not saying much; for Matisse's women, like atoms, consist primarily of empty space. Another woman touches herself above the right breast, staring at me seriously and perhaps a trifle sadly. Who can rival her complexion, which is smooth white paper? I close the book, and all these women seem to hover before me on my bed's white sheets, in a single understated assemblage of black line. I glimpse them as I would the ocean through that hedge-hole in Sen no Rikyu's garden.

But what if I could teach myself to see and understand more than I have ever done so far? Might I not want to roll back Chun'e's curtain of mist in order to admire every last scarlet leaf? Why not strive to perceive the thing unwithheld, the naked thing? (Matisse's nudes are not naked; they conceal their pores.) Again, if the goal is to embrace the ineffable, would not a greater goal be to render it effable? If this is impossible, is it because there is a divine principle which cannot be bound or limited by human expression, or simply because nobody has yet figured out how to do it? Must my perceptions remain ever slightly faded, like the colors of Edo silk?

For some reason, most women on Earth wear clothes in my presence. Am I disenfranchised, then? (Sade insisted that true social freedom would occur only when all of us had complete access to each other's bodies at all times. And an Egyptian papyrus advises: "The waste of a woman is in not knowing her carnally.")

Understatement is as smooth as an onnagata's skin when it is seen from a distance. Would I persevere in my appreciation if I saw his face up close?

An enthusiastic scholar of corsetry advises us:

The 'fetish-object' in the history of courtly love is a surrogate, and decreases in value as the loved one is present or appears more attainable. Similarly, the true tight-lacing fetishist does not wish to possess (or masturbate with) the corset itself, but to apply it possessively upon the beloved, so that it, his desire and her body become one . . . The fetish-object serves both as a symbol of union and a symbolic obstacle.

"You want a relationship without boundaries," a sweetheart once complained, and I proudly assented. I resist the notion that either the fetish-object or the utterly accessible lover must decline in value. I *wish* to believe that if the beautiful object of my desire revealed itself or herself to me unstintingly, perpetually, any resulting failure of my appreciation would result from my own imperfections of love, concentration, etcetera. But in the British Museum there is a Babylonian clay plaque from *circa* 1800 B.C., catalogued as the Queen of the Night; and this roundfaced, necklaced, highbreasted, nude goddess, whose pupilless eyes offer me the hollow darknesses of mask-holes and whose taloned feet rest upon a pair of reclining lions, raises both her hands to me, holding ringed scepters; she wears a headdress shaped like pairs of bull's horns and her wings flare out to her thighs; and she is all pale clay on clay, so that I am drawn into a realm almost as flat, despite its three-dimensionality, as it is erotic. Her lions goggle at me, and so do the two owls who bookmark them. I would not hesitate to call her pure, ethereal. But the Museum has digitally reconstructed her as she must have been when she was painted; and striking as those hues certainly are, they define and thereby limit her; what stylized her before I now experience as crudity, or, more precisely, the shallow color which Mr. Otsuka warned against.

Or again, understated clothing and breast forms sometimes protect the male bodies of transgender women from being recognized.* Is this treachery or something else?

A transgender woman writes: "The one thing that women share is that we are all *perceived* as women and treated accordingly . . . the most important differences between women and men in our society are the different meanings that we place onto one another's bodies." — Since a Noh woman is more likely than not to be a man, what gender does that make her? The brilliant black zebra-stripes of a Kabuki geisha's kimono, the delicious clatter of her clogs upon the wooden stage, they titillate my belief — in what? And since I who watch the performance and am allured, knowing all the while that between her legs she has what I have, does that mean simply, as I used to believe, that the mask, costume, acting and choreography achieve — as of course they do — such artistic perfection that their beauty itself allures me? What is her story or any other to me at all?

In Mr. Otsuka's studio, orange-cinnabar pigment gets softened with oyster shell into a flesh-blush on a Noh mask for "Dojoji." Is that understatement or actuality?

Actuality reifies itself within those Upper Paleolithic and Neolithic figurines which archaeologists jocularly call "Venuses": faceless, grossly breasted and buttocked, incised with what deserves to be called by that frank Anglo-Saxon word, a *cunt*; what is hidden here, what understated?

---

*As Kenneth Clark wrote on the subject of Titian's "Danaë": "The extruding animal breast has been brought into conformity with human expectations."

— Only the individuality of any woman. — My intimacy with my own body, and with the bodies of women I have loved, allows me to feel an instant comprehension of these stylized miniatures, which must in part be spurious, since their context is conjectural, their fecundity idealized, sometimes beyond the final extremes of human femininity; all the same, there is no longer any wall between me and the garden; the cunt is *here*. The slit between Venus's thighs is as bright as the lips upon a geisha's white-painted face. *Miekakure* and *iki* are in the eye of the beholder; I could for instance project my longings upon the Venuses' haunting facelessness; but there is a sharp distinction, nearly an opposition, between a Venus and Yuya. It is the same distinction that one can make between Proust and Kawabata, David and Rothko, laws and mores, exposition and suggestion.

The American fashion magazines of my time create their own partial Venuses. Their approach is to employ something vibrant, often gaudy, *new*, more often than not unsubdued, hence, so Mr. Otsuka would say, "shallow." — Is it or isn't it? Is a Venus-slit vulgar or revelatory? — Only you can say. In any event, here is *Allure* magazine: "In punchy shades of purple, green and blue, eyeliner shifts out of neutral and into high gear." The reason that *Allure*'s projection of femininity remains not entirely Venusian is that, after all the glaring lipstick and dramatic eyeshadow, the skin itself remains; and what woman does not wish to conceal her pores, lines and blemishes beneath a curtain of mist? Yukiko spent most of her effort with me attempting to achieve precisely this objective on my face. —Chun'e's autumn hills would still look pretty without the mist; my face would not. Keats's famous assertion that truth equals beauty is valid only some of the time. — The onnagata conceals his hands, the Noh actor masks himself, the geisha whitens her face, for much the same reason. Sometimes the wall conceals a garden's blightedness — another reason that disenfranchisement may be cause for gratitude.

But when I start down this path, I remember with pain the man who declined to see unpainted geishas because "I don't want to know their tricks; I don't want to know their sad stories."* Understatement is evil when it facilitates our dismissal of the suffering of those who are beauti-

---

*Tadano Makuzu, 1818: "It is usually said that a woman should keep everything in her heart, say little, and be modest."

ful. To take pleasure in the bound feet of a Chinese concubine might have been permissible; why make her feel that her years of agony had been in vain? But to take pleasure without respecting that agony, never!

On the Noh stage, Matsukaze and her sister-ghost Murasame mime dipping sea-brine, gracefully. "Although they are peasants," a scholar writes, "they embody the refinement of a centuries-old courtly aesthetic . . ." And so our gaze is pleased. How would it be if they truly had to dip brine all their lives and afterward?

Mist lies on the autumn hills. That can mean so many things.

# In the Forest

*An Apology*

And because understatement is so enigmatic a quantity (understating even itself), I propose to seek it in ever widening hunting-swathes, beginning in ancient Scandinavia.

# Sun-Bright Like Swords

*The Beauty of Valkyries*

The genius of the sagas and Eddas lies almost entirely in their action. Feminine beauty is represented not, as in English poetry, through comparison and description, nor, as in Noh, through a controlled neutrality of stylized demeanor; in both of those cases, Beauty dances before us as a reified Subject; whereas in Norse poetry and prose, Beauty reveals herself through her effects on her objects. My Anglo-American heritage happens to be expository, and from this point of view, both Japanese and Norse wordcraft is understated, all the more so to me since I can evaluate them only through the smoked glass of translation. This befits my situation. An astronomer dares to gaze upon the sun only through a filter of almost leaden opacity. And in *The Saga of the Volsungs* we find this sentence: "They saw a large band of shield-maidens," meaning Valkyries; "it was like looking into a fire." Great beauty can be unbearable to look upon.

Begin with the most fundamental and alien of all Norse literary arti-facts, the *Elder Edda*. This group of poems stands richer by far in descriptions of men, battles, weather and ships than of women. Consider the Lay of Volund, whose eponymous hero marries a Valkyrie; it is on her restlessness that the action turns. Who is she? Well, we are informed that she comes of "fair southron maids." What constitutes her hold on him? After all, "for the white-armed woman he waited long." We learn nothing else about her appearance, but this whiteness of her arms gets mentioned twice. Her beauty is less directly manifested by means of the loveliness of the seven hundred ornaments he forges in hopes of winning her home; these in turn express their own irresistibility through the misfortunes they cause: Volund will be kidnapped and maimed for their sake.

Taking all the Elder Eddas together, the lovely Norsewoman,[*] and presumably her various supernatural sisters, is slender, and snow-white or sun-bright like a sword. Indeed, it is through her whiteness that she is most often reified. Why might that be so? The white-painted fig-ure on a Greek terra cotta vessel is somebody dead. The white-skinned Scandinavian lady, I suppose, has simply avoided outdoor labor. At any rate, in this category her fair brow and breast get singled out, as does her neck. Surprisingly, her eyes and lips never get described at all. (In erotic *ukiyo-e* prints the revealed bodies of women tend to be whiter than the pinkish-beige bodies of the men who are penetrating them. In American fashion magazines, the advertisements often depict a woman with very very white skin, white teeth, eyes of muted brilliance — for instance, bluish-grey — hair which does not unduly contrast with the skin — blonde, or reddish, or very pale brunette — but then red, red lips!) She is ornamented with gold or silver — very likely arm-rings such

---

[*]To discern beauty, why not also consider its opposite? The Lay of Rig describes the thrall wife, epitome of ugliness: crook-legged, drooping-nosed, dirty-footed, with sunburned arms. Her daughters bear such names as Shorty, Stout-Leg, Stumpy, Dumpy and Cinder-Wench.

as Volund made. She may wear a blue shirt, or a brooch. Contradicting a twentieth-century "zoologist's portrait, celebrating women as they appear in the real world," which asserts that "the arms are the least erotic part of the female body," her most notable claim to beauty is her arms, for in the Eddas they receive more frequent mention — eleven times in total* — than any other feminine attribute. Usually (seven times) the female arm is simply white, twice it is soft, once shining and once gleaming. This last, which occurs in "Skírnismál," renders eerie praise to the giant-maiden Gerth, whose "arms did gleam," so that "their glamor filled all the sea and the air." (In the Younger Edda's retelling, "when she lifted her arms and opened the door. . . , light was shed from her arms over both sea and sky, and all worlds were made bright by her.") The kiss takes a prominent place in my own culture's erotic and romantic narratives, and this must be one reason why Hollywood actresses (like geishas) so often accentuate the redness and moistness of their lips. I suppose that the embrace plays an equivalent role in Eddic poetry; hence the female arm's irresistible powers of beguilement. Odin himself warns: "In a witch's arms beware of sleeping, / linking thy limbs with hers" because she will bewitch a man into isolation and sorrow. The same point gets made in the Lay of Svipdag, which is essentially a love tale. The glamor of its heroine, Mengloth, gets expressed most of all by the eerie journey required to claim her, with the necessity to call up the hero's dead mother in her grave for protective witchcraft, the wall of flame around the heroine, then the happy outcome, like a jewel of gold glowing all the more in darkness. Like Volund's wife, Mengloth is twice described as soft-armed. As for the hero's stepmother who forced him to undertake the adventure, how did she gain her ability to rule him? This anti-heroine, who is evidently as dangerous as the ghost of a Christian woman, is presented to us as "the crafty woman / in her arms who folded my father." It is as if the father were helpless.

So much is the female associated with her white arms that when Loki, who is insulting everyone in Valhalla, arrives at the goddesss Ithun, he cannot forbear from pro forma praise of her most lovely feature: "for thy shining arms on the shoulders lay / of thy brother's banesman."

---

*For a detailed tabulation of Eddic beauty-descriptions, see Appendix B.

To be sure, fair-browed Brynhild, white-armed Guthrún and the various other swan-white ladies become as de-individualized and stylized as Lady Murasaki's blackhaired Japanese beauties. But the power of feminine beauty grows all the more uncanny for its mechanistic invariability. The Valkyrie Sigrdrífa counsels her hero-bridegroom: "Though fair women, / and brow-white, sit on bench: / let the silver-dight one not steal thy sleep." What about them is so dangerously alluring? Doubtless their white foreheads and silver rings contribute. But it may be the stylized invitation itself that comprises the thrilling peril. In the Greenlandish Lay of Atli, a doomed warrior's wife, vainly counseling him not to accept the invitation of the man who will kill him, relates the following dream: "Methought in the darkness came dead women hitherward . . . beckoned and bade thee . . . to their benches forthwith." Who knows whether in death they remain fair and brow-white? The wife fears the power of their beckoning just the same.

Indeed, the beauty of a Norsewoman can be likened to a sort of doom inflicted upon the men who suddenly find themselves in love or in lust with her.* In *The Saga of the Volsungs*, a certain Sinfjotli simply "saw a lovely woman and strongly desired to have her." That suffices. In *Eyrbyggja Saga*, two berserks are lured into a rage and consequent fatal exhaustion by the mockingly silent presence of a woman described only as "gold-adorned." We know that she is dressed in her best and lifts her head high. We know her name, which is Asdis. That is all. And yet this saga, like so many others, does not withhold detailed descriptions of the second most beautiful category in the world, namely, weapons such as the sword of Steinthor whose silver hilt shines and whose grip is wound around with gold-threaded silver wire. Why then should gold-adorned Asdis remain a cipher, unless such was the saga writer's choice?

---

*Mishima would have loved this. It is very characteristic that of his five modern Noh I have in translation, four of them have to do wholly or in part with cruel, controlling women. Naturally, he could not forgo to rework that tale of supernaturally lethal female jealousy, "Aoi-no-Ue."

The eponymous hero of the thirteenth-century "Ivar's Story" breaks his heart over a woman named Oddny Jonsdottir, and although his grief and its remedy — receiving permission to talk about Oddny day after day with the King of Norway — comprise the point of the tale, Oddny herself is not described in any way. It is as if she were an earthquake. Among the romantic motifs in Norse myths and fairytales we encounter love instantaneously induced through sight of the beloved in a picture or magic mirror, love caused by a glimpse of an unknown princess's hair, and, of course, the love that comes from seeing a woman's white arms. If I could see Oddny in a magic mirror, could I resist her? Would the shining of her arms suffice to enthrall me forever, or would I need a glimpse of her magic hair? In *The Saga of Gunnlaug Serpent-Tongue*, a warrior-poet sings his subjection to Helga the Fair: "The woman was born to bring war / between men . . ."* He praises her as "the ring-land's light-Valkyrie," meaning "the land's rings' goddess," which signifies simply and hauntingly *woman*. All this seems in keeping with the appearance of the old Scandinavian figurines of Valkyries or *dísir*: longhaired, silhouetted from the side, almost blank of facial features, stylized, nearly inhuman.

### "THEN I WISH ALL MY LUCK ON TO YOUR HEADS"

What is doom? One summer in Iceland, a man named Hrapp rows out to the narrative, which rides and rocks on the verge of departing for Norway, and he asks to be carried into future chapters. How many unknown characters inhabit the darkness that frames everything we can see in this present instant of our lives? As he so often does, the saga writer with-

---

*About her the saga writer tells us more than is the case with most ancient Norse heroines: "She had such long hair that it could cover her completely, and it was radiant as beaten gold." (She was also, typically enough, the most beautiful woman ever in Iceland.) On the subject of Norsewomen's hair, it is surprising how rarely its color is mentioned in the ancient sources. But I assume that it was usually blonde or golden as Helga's was. The lovely captive in the early-fourteenth-century romance of Bosi and Herraud is another case in point: ". . . never had they seen such a beautiful woman! Her hair was tied to the chair-posts, and was as fair as polished straw or threads of gold."

holds description of Hrapp here; our impression gets conveyed entirely through dialogue. "I suspect," says the captain, "that whoever takes you aboard will have cause to regret it." All the same, Hrapp gets his way. Cheating the captain out of payment for his passage, he next requests to be taken into the household of Gudbrand of the Dales, whose daughter he will seduce, impregnate and abandon, whose son he will murder, and whose temple to the gods he will pillage and burn. Upon meeting him, Gudbrand remarks, "You don't look like a man of good luck." And indeed, Hrapp soon finds it prudent to get out of Norway. "Save me, good people," he cries to the Njalssons, "for the earl is after my life." Helgi Njalsson replies: "It strikes me that you are a bringer of ill luck. It would be wiser to have nothing to do with you." "Then I wish all my luck on to your heads," says Hrapp, and in due course, there it goes.

The lesson read in this is that once Killer-Hrapp darkens anyone's door, there remains no right way to deal with him. Ungrateful, violent, treacherous, he will abuse a kindness as well as avenge a rejection. Killing him outright will merely ensure a different doom. The heroes and heroines of Norse sagas express a cool, brave indifference to each and all such prospects. If one must die, then so be it. Enduring what cannot be helped need not equal submission to it. And in *The Saga of Grettir the Strong*, when the outlawed hero's mother takes final leave of him and his brother, her admonition, whose gloom can certainly not be denied, offers a residuum of proud comfort: "There you go, my two sons, and your deaths will be the saddest of all, but no one can avoid what is ordained. I will never see either of you again. Meet the same fate."

But what if there were some way to avoid doom? In the sagas we also often find a strong shrewd man of moderation, who succeeds, if only temporarily, in containing the violence of his neighbors. Even Grettir has friends, whose support, alas, erodes page by page. Olaf the Peacock in *Laxdaela Saga* declines to act against his son's killer, who happens to be his foster son, and the eponymous protagonist of *Njal's Saga* continually acts to limit hostilities and make settlements between people. When Hrapp's bad luck begins to assault his sons, Njal counsels them: "You should let it be understood that you intend to take action only if you are provoked. But if you had asked for my advice at the very beginning, you would never have raised the matter at all, and so you would never have compromised yourselves." This is truly the voice of rational restraint. All the same, Njal's very next words run: "But now you are already committed to a trying situation; humiliations will be heaped upon you, until you have no alternative but to cut through your difficulties with weapons." And so we descend back to inevitable doom. Olaf the Peacock, who bears advantages of person, deeds, wealth and lineage, does persuade all parties to the feud to settle, however grudgingly, but after his death, the constrained inevitable bursts its fetters just as the Fenris Wolf will do come the end of the world. As for Njal, wise, moderate and careful though he is, even second-sighted, from the very first we find him, like all the others, a hostage to friendship and kinship. He enters the saga by counseling underhanded tactics in a dubious third party lawsuit. He does not initiate this process; nor does the friend who comes to him; nor can either of them derive any good from winning it — on the contrary. No matter. Njal cannot escape getting enmeshed in matters which he knows full well are dangerous. His doom is to be burned alive in his house with his wife and sons.

Who sent Hrapp to ensnare us? Where lay Grettir's fault? On the one hand, Grettir's cruel and sullen nature manifests itself even in childhood, when he flays his father's mare alive; but then, like the late-starting youngest son in many a fairytale, he begins to accomplish great things, and goes far down on the road to renown until he does the good deed of killing the bloated black monster called Glam, who curses him with outlawry and ill fortune. "And this curse I lay on you: my eyes will always be before your sight and this will make it difficult to be alone. And this will lead to your death." What is the morality of providence? Can we give a hero any more credit for being lucky than we can a woman for being beautiful? In *The Saga of the Volsungs*, when Odin appears at a battle that his former favorite King Sigmund has been winning, and raises his spear against him, Sigmund's sword breaks. "Then the tide of battle turned, for King Sigmund's luck was now gone." The expression "favored of fortune" fails in this context. It is one thing when an Old Testament figure transgresses the will of the divine, and then his fortune, or that of his descendants, turns evil. But as Odin himself reminds us in the Eddic poem "Hávamál," the doom of every living thing is to die; no virtue of any mortal is immortal, excepting only renown. Therefore, no matter how hard we try to escape our doom, there will always be other men of rage and violence ready to be drawn into the saga; and even if Hrapp could somehow be avoided, slain or appeased, then Odin must come forth from the darkness with his spear aimed at us.

The grim suspense of *Njal's Saga* does not abate on rereading, because understatement creates its own homeopathic richness of effect, and one never tires of seeing how one laconically described episode gives rise to another. Doom's patterns surpass so much other richness that doom grows beautiful in and of itself. The conflict between the dictates of common sense, or even peacefulness, and one's duty to participate in kinship and therefore to protect the clan by avenging their deaths, or to defend one's lonely honor from sudden assault, simply cannot be reconciled. Such triumphs of self-laceration must surely be universal. Far away from the saga lands, and contemporaneous with the sagas themselves, in the Ashikaga era of Japan, we find in the equally understated Noh play "Kagekiyo" the conflict between the necessity to fight for one's lord in a battle not at all of one's own making, and the Buddhist dictates of nonviolence. But Japanese understatements of doom seem to me to partake more of resigned sadness than their Norse equivalents. I would be the last to deny the horrifying beauty of a *yase-onna*, Dojoji or *hannya* mask; but against these we must set the sad and ecstatic tranquilities of ever so many others. Doom is a frequent result in Japanese literature; it is rarely a cause. In *The Tale of the Heike*, when it comes time to decapitate an eight-year-old son of the defeated side, his wet nurse holds him in her arms, weeping. The chief executioner, after weeping himself, says to her: "Your little lord cannot escape this by any means." Then he orders the swordsman: "Execute him at once!" Why did the child have to die? Why did the Heike fall from power in the first place? They were arrogant, we are told in the very beginning of the tale; but even if they had been otherwise, it would have made no difference, because of the theme of this great work, as of so many others, is *evanescence*. But while the Heike family's doom may prefigure itself through its own sinister tokens and omens, the doom of a Norse saga protagonist is more actively baleful and threatening. The prophecy of doom, personified sometimes in a doom-bringer such as Hrapp, sometimes in a far-seeing, unwilling kinsman as occurs in *Laxdaela Saga* and *The Saga of the Volsungs*, cannot be withstood. Our doom itself, says Odin, cannot die. And in the sagas as in our life, it comes in equal part to the good and the wicked. In *Eyrbyggja Saga* the witch Katla saves her son from vengeance three times, magicking him first into her distaff, then her goat, then her pet hog, but on the fourth occasion the men are accompanied by the rival witch Geirrid, who throws a sealskin bag over Katla's head, and this time the son is found and hanged, the mother stoned to death. As her enemies approach for this final fatal encounter, Katla remarks that a strange feeling has come over her. This feeling must have been similar to Sigmund's when Odin broke his sword. The saga informs us that no one feels sorry over the killings of Katla and Odd, but I myself cannot forbear from pity for people who, however uncanny they might be, share my fate.

Doom will find a way in. Doom will strike us all down. But six and seven hundred years after they were written into life, Sigurth, Grettir, Egil, Njal and the beautiful Gudrid of *Laxdaela Saga* live within my brain. Although their renown, like that of the sagas themselves, and of the earth, the sun and all things, must someday dwindle, within the cross-referential metatext of the sagas together, these people remain as changelessly bright as gold in a barrow's hoard. Njal has outlived his doom triumphantly; his triumph grows all the greater in that he foresaw it and made it his own. The Norse virtue of steadfastness, which in a Noh protagonist would be a sad symptom of illusion and attachment, remains gloriously eternal in him. When Egil Skalagrimsson's brother Thorolf agrees to be separated from him when fighting a battle for King Athelstan, Egil says, "Have it your way, but it's a decision I'll live long to regret." Thorolf lives yet in Egil's verses; Egil himself, that brutal, brave, merciless, enduring, vicious, brilliant word-smith, I cannot dismiss from my horrified regard.

### HILDIGUNN'S GIFT

The voice of doom is often a woman's. In *Njal's Saga*, the lovely, vindictive Hallgerd orders her share of murders, and when her beleaguered husband's bowstring gets slashed by one of his enemies, she refuses to give him two locks of her hair in substitute, remarking: "I shall now remind you of the slap you once gave me." "To each his own way of earning fame," Gunnar replies, and in due course his foes bring him down. Njal's wife Bergthora, who will die bravely beside him, feeds revenge's maw nearly as often. In the sagas, women often assault their kinsmen with the grisly relics of murdered men; and *Njal's Saga* sports a typical case: When the powerful chieftain Flosi dines with her, the widowed Hildigunn opens a chest and withdraws a cloak. "She threw the cloak around his shoulders, and the clotted blood rained all over him. 'This is the cloak you gave to Hoskuld, Flosi,' she said, 'and now I give it back to you.'" Flosi calls her a monster. All the same, he cannot then refrain from avenging Hoskuld; and so, in spite of the efforts of many goodhearted arbitrators, Njal and his sons are doomed to burning.

Norse femininity, like Norse masculinity, can certainly be notable for its aggressiveness. In the Elder Edda, Brynhild and Guthrún are both murderesses; the latter is called by one commentator "demonic." A demonic Japanese heroine would find no rest, but golden-clad Guthrún maintains to the end a grim joy in her vengeance. When she calls her little sons to her side in the bedchamber, they submit to her power even while remarking, much in Gunnar's style, that she will not enhance her reputation by what she is about to do to them. In her next marriage, she sends a new crop of sons to kill and die. They set off, remarking that she will soon be sorry. They are right. Meanwhile, her will is inevitable.

## "THE QUEENLY WOMAN"

The power of the Norse feminine is great not only because it can rule others, but also because it can rule itself. Guthrún may know quite well that she will be sorry when her sons are dead. Alternatively, she may be effective at ignoring or denying it. All the same, she never flinches from harming herself and those she loves in order to carry through her purpose. Neither did Brynhild, when after inciting Sigurth's murder she stabbed herself and commanded that she be burned beside him on his pyre. Self-possessed to the last, she doled out gold to her bondsmaids, offering more if they would die with her. To her unloved husband she remarked: "Thy brow-white wife awaiteth death." She calculated, foresaw and defyingly accepted.

When Sigrún the Valkyrie* enters the funeral mound of her husband Helgi, she says that she is as eager to be with him "as Othin's hawks" are "hungry for meat, / when war they scent and warm corpses, / and dew besprent the daylight see." Having elaborated his pallor and ghastly wounds, she prepares a bed and lies down with her darling. I stand in awe of her brave and ferocious love. In my imagination, the rank darkness of the barrow is illuminated only by her forehead, in whose reflected light shine her golden arm-rings as she slips them off one by one. The dead man praises her as "woman sun-bright" and describes her as "Hogni's white-armed daughter . . . the queenly woman." Then comes that night-long embrace between living and dead, supernatural and human, female and male, beauty and horror, which Sigrún's love alone saves from ghast-liness. Who can she be to me, but every woman I have ever loved? Before cockcrow he goes to Valhalla and returns no more; she soon dies of grief. But they had already lived and died once before; it may well be that their love will be reborn eternally — a tormenting thought in Japanese Noh drama, but to Helgi and Sigrún surely their most luminous hope. As I said, a preeminent Norse virtue for both genders alike is *ruthless steadfast-ness*. No wonder that the phrase "sun-bright" is reserved not for beautiful women alone; they and swords can both shine like suns.


A LADY'S SLEEVE


What if the beauty of women were no more than a simplified, stylized fetish made up of a very few characteristics? I refuse to believe this, but I may be outnumbered. "The nape of the neck is the glamor spot in kimono," advises a modern Japanese publication. (What might the Norse

---

*A number of Eddic heroines are Valkyries. They can be either "hateful and grim," as is a certain Valkyrie in Odin's hall, or white-armed and lovely in the fashion of Sigrún and Sigrdrífa. No matter what, they are proud, brave, meat-hungry. Davidson remarks that Valkyries may have gotten smoothed out into beautiful equestriennes, "but a different, cruder picture of supernatural women connected with blood and slaughter has also sur-vived." But they remain very feminine.

glamor spot be? White arms, of course."* For Kenneth Clark, historian of the Western nude, the glamor spot appears to be the relative distance between the lower breast and the navel. If this is called one unit, then the ideal classical female body, in artistic representation, at least, will likewise measure one unit between the breasts and one unit from the navel to the separation between the legs. In Gothic art, all these figures will remain the same except for the breast-navel distance, which doubles. Clark makes no secret of his feelings about that alteration, writing: "The basic pattern of the female body is still an oval, surmounted by two spheres; but the oval has grown incredibly long, the spheres have grown distressingly small." Of course actual female bodies vary dramatically, and a promiscuous lover such as myself cannot but pity someone such as Clark, whose feminine ideal incarnates itself in a relatively rare number of women.† All the same, I cannot but wish him well when he undertakes "that search for finality of form which, on our definition, is the basis of the nude." Who would not want to know exactly what beauty is? What does a *ko-omote* Noh mask have in common with a great-breasted, great-buttocked prehistoric fertility goddess such as the Venus of Wurttemberg? To me both are beautiful, erotic. Were I to do as Clark did, and choose one over the other, I would be proclaiming that finality of form has been determined to my satisfaction, when in fact I do not wish my search ever to end. Here the beauties of understatement take me into

---

*What is fetish, what is stylization, and what is simple specificity? Thomas Blenman Hare has diagrammed inflection patterns for male and female roles in the play "Hagoromo," which he calls representative. The pitch of the male voice either prolongs itself at a high point much beyond the other three forms of utterance, or else falls slightly, abruptly rises to a peak, then falls off. As for the two female modes, the first is a long, gentle rise with a flattened peak and then the beginning of an equally gentle fall; the other rises more steeply than it falls, but remains smoother in slope than the male forms. Is this more or less meaningful (beside being certainly more abstruse) than the "glamor spot" as a defining characteristic of the back of the female neck? Is a Norse kenning for a lovely woman merely mechanistic, or have I myself failed if I cannot sense the living femaleness in every use of it, just as I can in every living woman? In this attempt to discover the beautiful feminine I sometimes feel as if I am grappling with tissue paper.

†His saddest passage: "Not that the Esquiline girl represents an evolved notion of feminine beauty. She is short and square, with high pelvis and small breasts far apart, a stocky little peasant such as might be found still in any Mediterranean village."

their affectionate embrace. Among her list of elegant things, Sei Shonagon in her *Pillow Book* includes a counterpart to a Valkyrie's sun-white arm: the sleeve of an Imperial concubine-to-be's lady in waiting, deliberately shown to a messenger. She is on the right track, but why couldn't it be any woman's sleeve? I like another of her fancies better: Two lovers grow so well acquainted with each other's particularities that his knock and her sleeve-rustling are mutually identifiable. Meanwhile, I remain free to imagine their faces and dispositions as I will.

The old Norse tales and poems afford me the same pleasure.* Thanks to narrative genius, understatement and subtly chosen discriminations, their formulaic epithets of female loveliness escape vacuity. Rarely individuated descriptions of women do creep in, like serpents in a treasure-cave; I remember Thorgunna of *Eyrbyggja Saga*, who was "a massive woman, tall, broad-built, and getting very stout. She had dark eyebrows and narrow eyes, and beautiful chestnut hair." In *Egil's Saga*, the eponymous, famous and infamous hero's daughter Thorgerd is introduced to us as "a fine-looking woman, very tall, intelligent, and proud, but usually rather quiet." But then we return to the indistinguishable flock of white-armed ones.

In kennings and love poems a woman is customarily the goddess, tree, land, or Valkyrie of the bed,† of nice clothes, of mead, or most often of gold and silver. Whereas the potent man is called *ring-breaker*, meaning apportioner and generous giver of treasure, the worthy woman, although she too is generous, is somewhat more likely to express her relationship to these beautiful things by adorning and being adorned by them. The blonde beauty of gold, so appropriate to Norse women, demonstrates that she is powerful, cherished, or both. She becomes *land of gold*, or more elaborately *land of the serpent's bed*. Among the Younger Edda's recommended kennings for women, we find *dealer of gold*, and *flood-fire-keeping Sif*, which latter can be parsed into "gold-keeping goddess of the golden

---

*For a brief discussion of how beauty and doom in medieval Norway have been treated by a gifted modern Norwegian writer, see the postscript to Appendix B.

†Sexual innuendo rarely grows explicit. An exception, from *Kormak's Saga*: "So dear are you, sea-Freya, / to the sword of the love-hair's island," meaning the sword of the pudendum, namely the penis.

hair." Indeed, Sif's hair is real gold, for in one of his many acts of mean-ness Loki stole the hair she was born with, so Thor made him replace it with something better. (One kenning for gold: "Sif's hair." Another: "Freya's tears." The latter goddess is said to weep tears of red gold.) Gen-erally speaking, the Younger Edda advises, a woman may be referred to "by all female adornment, gold and jewels, ale or wine or other drink that she serves or gives." Thus the lovely Oddny Isle-Candle gets praised by her poet-lover as "the elegant arm-goddess," or goddess of the hand-fire, hand-fire of course being golden finger-rings. (Poorer women must content themselves with *arm-ice*, or silver.) Helga the Fair is called "the fresh-faced goddess of the serpent's day," which is to say of gold, whose radiance is the only sun the "land-fish" sees as it slithers deep in dead men's treasure-barrows. Her lover boasts: "I played on the headlands of the forearm's fire / with that land-fish's bed-land," meaning that he toyed with or caressed the gold-ringed fingers of her gold-ringed arm.

*Laxdaela Saga*, whose bloody plot owes much to the irresistible attrac-tiveness of certain women, leaves them in a more enigmatic invisibility than the faces of the hooded Norns who were engraved on the Franks Casket. The subtlety of the narrative is such that a single adjective inevi-tably portends the future: "Jorunn was a good-looking, imperious woman of exceptional intelligence; she was considered the best match in all the Westfjords." Upon her marriage, the spouses "got on well together, but they were usually rather reserved with one another." No wonder that the husband gets a concubine. "The one sitting at the edge of the tent caught his eye; she was shabbily dressed, but Hoskuld thought her beau-tiful, from what he could see." What the saga writer considers relevant is not the particulars of her beauty, but simply that she was beautiful. I remember seeing in a performance of Kojiro's "Ataka" a fairly young boy in beige, maybe nine, on the very edge of the Noh stage,* standing straight in that eerie immobility from which a sweeping gesture is even more dramatic; it is precisely this method that the Norse tales and poems employ, not least in their portrayal of women. The radiant one waits within the text, understating herself until the time comes for her to make her next gloriously fatal movement. It is her beauty which empowers her

---

*He was the *ko-kata*, young Minamoto Yoshitsune.

to alter the lives of mine. It is thanks to temporarily availing attempts to mitigate effects of the rivalry between her and Jorunn (both of whom are exquisitely realized as characters; one knows them through what they say and do), that the central tragedy gets prepared.

As for the saga's *femme fatale*, Gudrun, "she was the loveliest woman in Iceland at that time,* and also the most intelligent," which commits what Hemingway considered the cardinal sin of telling instead of describing. What does she look like? Her face must be the face of beautiful doom, as brightly hidden to the gaze as the sun's disk. I'm more than willing to suppose that rings of red gold adorned her white arms. *Seid*, the magic art somehow related to females, with which Freya seems to have been associated, is nearly unknown to us; likewise the workings of Gudrun's magic. Her true love and victim, Kjartan, gets a good two sentences of description; we are informed of the colors of certain horses; Gudrun for her part is a *disir* figurine. The only detail we ever learn of her looks and gestures is that when her third husband's murderer wipes his bloody spear on the sash around her pregnant belly, she smiles.† The child inside her will take vengeance in due course.

## IN THE SERPENT'S BED

As Odin says, we are all doomed to die. Doom's strides are as long as Sleipnir's eight legs on an ancient picture-stone — but I prefer to reify doom as Hallgerd, the vengefully irresistible heroine of *Njal's Saga*. "She

---

*Meanwhile, the king's sister Ingibjorg "was the loveliest woman in Norway," and with characteristic ellipticality we are informed of her intimacies with the hero Kjartan (who is Gudrun's intended) by the comments of his foster-brother, which he unconvincingly repudiates, and by the fact that she falls silent when he announces his determination to return to Iceland. When she gives him a gold-embroidered headdress, which will later be destroyed by Gudrun, she remarks: "I want the women of Iceland to see that the woman whose company you have been keeping in Norway isn't descended from slaves." What could be a more elegantly understated way of conveying both her love and her stoic pride?

†Lady Murasaki's diary: "To be pleasant, gentle, calm and self-possessed: this is the basis of good taste and charm in a woman."

was very tall, which earned her the nickname Long-legs, and her lovely hair was now so long that it could veil her entire body." Ketilrid Holmkellsdaughter of *Viglund's Saga*, who is "blessed with beauteous hair" and a "fair white brow," enthralls her own Viking-poet, who praises "the bright lady's nature, like a swan swimming." She dooms him to love her forever. And in the old tales and lays, and in every magic mirror and unexpected darknesses of the world, the white arms of half-known women prepare to ensnare me in ambushes of overpowering glamor. It is not so that they are all alike; they are sisters merely in their blinding brightness.

The white-armed woman holds sway over her gold-adorned hall. She adorns herself in kennings which dazzle my wearied eyes. My bedazzlement is my failure. (Sometimes when I see Noh actors from the back, their strangely flat beetleness, the way their arms can outstretch and freeze; or when I lose my way amidst the music of the chorus in brown plaid kimonos in front of that pine tree, staring straight ahead, then I forget that movement of striped kimono sleeves will extend into wings and grasp something supernaturally black. The real world is stylized into slow neutrality here; for the sake of what will come, it must be so. The boy's pure high voice answers the man who kneels down on the polished floor. In the audience, old couples are following along character by character in well-thumbed or immaculate books. I envy their knowledge. This is the lesson I must take to heart: A perception of monotony is the result either of ignorance or a failure of attention. That may not always be true; sometimes the performer fails; if this book reads monotonously to you the failure may well be mine; but it is in my interest always to make the grandest assumptions about whatever offers itself before me. This boy in his robe and conical hat, he has what Zeami calls the false flower of his youth; let it be his youth, then, not his talent, that I reverence; or rather let it be his youth as tightly controlled by the play and by his training. They adjust his hat for him; they give him a bamboo staff taller than he is. A scowling man in a tapering black hat and a kimono of black, white and gold haunts the stage. Between periods of immobility and silence a sudden shimmering noise beats from a triangle of outstretched hands; I glimpse the child, then get overwhelmed by a line of elaborately identical kimono'd men all pivoting at once.) If I truly wish to see the loveliness of a bygone Norsewoman, then I must gaze at her with all my might, until my eyes burn out. Within their seeming sameness, what do the kennings mean?

The phrase "bright goddess of the serpent's bed" makes me think on Sigrún in Helgi's howe; perhaps the snakes are already crawling across the corpse she holds in her arms, brightly alone in the treasure-strewn darkness. If I were brave enough, I would be the one in there with her. I am sometimes ready to lay myself down in the serpent's bed, believing as I do that love of a woman is the most glorious doom that can befall a man.

# 23

# Passing Light

*Andrew Wyeth's Helga Pictures*

Helga Testorf, or her painted semblance, gazes down into the dark earth. An ominous grove almost silhouettes itself upon the high horizon. The world is wall and grave-core, crooked block of almost-night. Against this darkness, far more richly than the pale scrap of sky, Helga's hair is shining, gold in a serpent's hoard, flickering fire. Although the painter once remarked that he was striving for the "frozen motion" in Rembrandt, wherein "time is holding its breath for an instant — and for eternity," he also said: "I would like to paint so nothing is at rest in my work. Nothing is frozen. I would like people to sense even in those paintings with brilliant passages of sunlight, that the sunlight is not really still but that you can really see the passage of the sun." And indeed, light of some kind (probably more supernatural than the sun) alters upon the back of her head. Each hair is a wire amalgamated from slightly different proportions of gold and copper than its neighbor. Helga's braids shine alternately light and dark. A sliver of reddish-orange collar ends her pale neck. And all around her, the earth has been worked like a dark wool coat. It seems to be made of fibers. The Deputy Director of the National Gallery of Art sees in this painter's textures "a similarity of stroke and surface applied alternatively to field grasses, animal fur, and human skin and hair."

Helga Testorf stands gazing into the weave of the earth, where all of us must go. What does she see? When the *shite* of "Izutsu" stares down into the well, she discovers that her reflection has changed into her lover's. He and she are long dead, of course; perhaps each is the other's opposite. Life looks down into the weave of the earth and sees, I imagine, death. In this painting called "Farm Road," Helga Testorf, bright goddess of the serpent's bed, spies death, or love, or herself, or some other entity — possibly the tuber of the true flower; call it the Unknown. As Kofumi-san replied when I asked what this or that dance-gesture meant, "It's a personal feeling. Isn't it better that you *don't* get anything in advance? It's all up to the viewer." Autumn blazes nakedly, and so the artist veils it by painting in a mist.

Even nowadays I still hope somehow to go "deeper" into art, as if by staring at the reverse side of my reproduction of "Farm Road" I could discover a more chthonic slice of earth. Were I a trifle more intelligent, could I *interpret* beauty instead of merely describing it, then no doubt I would "learn" or "realize" increasingly, in much the same way that a maiko's crimson collar gets embroidered with ever more silver thread, until it comes time for her to give up her youth and become a geiko . . .

Well, I will now try to go deeper just the same.

Do you remember what Zeami said about the expression of demonic roles? Even then the actor should appear to be holding a branch of flowers. And the man who painted Helga so faithfully and secretly is nothing if not a flowery demon. The biographer Meryman sees a connection, as do I, between that famous portrait Wyeth did of his friend and neighbor Karl Kuerner — a sad, absent, hard yet tender-lipped face inspecting us sidelong from beneath two meathooks — and the artist's following admission: "There's grace in my work like spring flowers. But there's some harshness, too. I'm a coarse man, really. I'm a strange combination of delicacy — fragile, in another world — and brutality."

When he first began to notice Helga, she was taking care of Karl, who was dying from leukemia. Her English was accented; and she and Karl sometimes sang German songs together.

"Nobody knows her," Wyeth described her. "She's an enigma. She hovers over the land she lives on."

And he took precautions (at least so runs the legend) that not even his wife knew her — for fifteen years.

In "Letting Her Hair Down," the first Helga nude, which has been described (wrongly in my opinion) as comparable to the nudes of the fourteen-year-old Finnish girl Siri Erickson ("the same slight coarseness" — I see no coarseness at all — "the same strength, the same defiance, but diluted by a feeling of come-hither"), Helga sits against a dark wall which is constituted of the thick woolen fibers which make up Wyeth's earth, and her skin exists somewhere between youth and early middle age; it seems to be altering even as we see it, recapitulating the transience of a Kawabata heroine. She gazes to our left, not quite grimly almost-smiling, perhaps shy or amused. The milky light on her upper breasts gives meaning to the yellow-white blankness of the open window. A solar medallion hangs on a dark ribbon just over her collarbone. Her left breast protrudes freely, while the wristbone of her right arm, folded across the left, cuts into the right breast beneath the nipple. Her hair is a stunning stiffness of yellow and whitish-yellow wires of light. Returning to her face, I now see on it a softer expression of patience and sweetness; her rather thick lips appear to be smiling more — an illusion which perhaps only I experience, unlike the viewer of a Noh mask which changes angle. What caused this impression? First, like most human beings, I sought out the human gaze, which Wyeth has slightly withheld from me. Then the softness of Helga's form gradually made my aquaintance, like the softness of the barn-darkness itself; and so my judgment of Helga's expression was altered.

As for Helga, she said: "I became alive. It shows in the pictures. I became young overnight. I've never done anything more worthwhile."

As for the artist, he recalled: "And now I meet this girl and can right get up to her crotch and really look at it and draw it. With no feeling of, oh, you can't do that."

And again: "She was an image I couldn't get out of my mind."

When Helga undressed for "Overflow," Wyeth "felt the country, the house, Germany, the dreamy, moist, rich female smell — the whole thing."

What *is* the whole thing? Just as paper-thin stage panels painted with flowers sometimes retract, revealing Kabuki dancers arrayed as flowers, so my understanding of female grace may at times draw away, with the same stunning rapidity that a Kabuki dancer's costume can change from green to red or gold before the audience's eyes, from what I think I understand now. And how much might that be? — As Wyeth said of Helga: "Whoever she is to us, we cannot know her infinite other identities."

I cannot imagine any of the geishas and Noh actors whom I have interviewed saying of any aspect of their craft what Wyeth once said about drybrush: "If I control it, it's no good."

Perhaps that was why her identities were infinite to him.

In the painting called "Braids," the black background has grown so rich as to be almost blood-red, and Helga, gorgeously imperfect in the manner of G. M. Hopkins's poem "Pied Beauty," gazes down and to the left, hollow-cheeked, with creases at the inward corners of her eyes, and a full nose with a knife-sharp bridge. Her reddish-blonde eyelashes are sufficiently delicate to die for; her braids shine reddish and goldish with lights on them as they twist neatly down her high-collared sweater, vanishing as they approach her sweet breasts; and speaking of sweet, the face of Helga is a mixture of sweetness and severity, unlike her counterpart, the *fukai* mask, which merely dreams down into the darkness; Helga similarly projects herself into someplace beyond us, but her femininity has been embodied, by her own corporeality and by Andrew Wyeth.

He altered "Braids" after Helga related a certain sexual experience. "I'd painted those braids beautifully coming to the fine end, the fluffy blondness of the hair. I thought, fuck it. This is not it." He sawed off the bottom of the portrait.

There came the year when he was done with Helga, so that it was time to prepare his exhibition to finally show Betsy. "Taking the lids off the boxes . . . they had the odor of the girl, they had the whole — I knew they were not just pretty pictures."

What were they then? "Night Shadow," according to our authorized biographer, "is Wyeth's memory of his father in the coffin, the moment he bent down to kiss the forehead, feeling the cold waxiness on his lips." But what we see is Helga, whose face is paler and softer than we usually encounter it in the corpus of Helga Pictures ("Night Shadow" does not belong to this suite, because Betsy Wyeth kept it and two other Helga paintings), and her familiar half-smile is more of a smile than ever, but her eyes are shut as she lies there on her back, her hair barely surviving the darkness around her, hair braids black, white and honey-gold; a weak-ish shadow bisects her face below the bridge of the nose, so that she is bright —excepting her left shoulder and the narrow dark ribbon around her throat — below her lovely cream-and-peaches breasts, at which point darkness jaggedly breaks her off. I imagine her as Sigrún in Helgi's howe, with her dead lover bending over her. But that is merely what Helga means to me. If I were writing a book about Noh, I might try to refer to fog, jade, water; to Nara's ancient camphorwood statues dim in the rainy darkness. And who knows what Helga would say? For these paintings and drawings of her partake of that mysterious effect based on under-stated description, *yugen*. What did the ends of her braids look like before Wyeth sawed them off, and what would it have been like to hold them in my hand? If Wyeth's father could see from beyond the grave, which if any aspect of himself would he perceive in "Night Shadow"? As for the artist's wife, when the Helga Suite was first revealed to her, her reaction was: "Who the fuck is this woman? Boy, she looks tough as nails in that one — and she's as soft as velvet in that one, and who is she and what's going on here?" John Wilmerding, Deputy Director of the National Gal-lery, emoted in a more consonant spirit: "Now her sturdy features and sober demeanor, reflective of her northern European background, match the somber browns and enduring contours of this Pennsylvania terrain." Wyeth himself said, specifically regarding "Night Shadow": "It's not just anybody lying there. It's that momentary thing — something you'll never see again . . . That's my relationship with Helga. Timeless." He continued, and the past tense made his honesty crueler still, for Helga was (so I've read) bereft once he finished with her: "She epitomized all my German background — all imaginative things embodied in her. I used her for a stepping-stone."

To repeat the words of Kanze Hisao: "It is highly detrimental to a mask to be treated like a piece of antique art, to be shut up in a box or shown only in a glass case. It is only on the stage that it continues to maintain its vitality."

But let me mention a reproduction of a certain *ko-omote* carved for the Kanzes by Deme Yasuhisa — it is a near-perfect copy of one of Tatsuemon's masterpieces, which was once referred to by Zeami himself — and this mask, whose underside has been inscribed in gold and red, lives in a box additionally inscribed. "And thus, this mask is known as a *hako-iri-musume* (girl in a box, meaning a girl brought up with tender care)."

The box opens, offering us a girl's face sleek with baby fat; her U-shaped double chin mimics the curve of her lower lip. As the mask turns rightward it takes on a shy smile of tenderness or perhaps of pride in receiving some compliment from father, husband, suitor, lord; facing left with its chin a trifle higher, its expression becomes bolder, although no less serene; it could be dreaming of an attachment or contemplating the peace which that attachment's death will bring. Vertical streaks of light now gild its eyelids. On the left cheek and above the upcurving right corner of the upper lips, birthmarks or timemarks live their quiet lives. The left eyebrow is a wider cloud of black than the left. Darkness shines out at us from the half-smile beneath the black teeth.

The description continues: "A copy of the Honmen of Konparu. The nose tilted to the right and the flesh on top of the cheekbones are superb. Blemish, beauty mark, cracks, and even the damage on the tip of her nose is accurately copied. The colors are quite unique. It is made from the Japanese cinnamon tree* like the Honmen, and on the back, the nose, eyes, vertical lines from the lower lip to the chin, and the double horizontal cut with a round chisel which interrupts them, are all exactly the same as on the Honmen."

Too old to be represented by a *ko-omote*, Helga would be better portrayed by a *fukai*. Time's damage to her face deserves to be accurately

---

*Could the translator have meant the Kiso cypress?

copied; and although I have never met Helga, I *believe* in her; the flesh is superb; the perfection of her particularity is as fragrant as a cinnamon tree.

Helga is a girl in a box. I keep my book about her pictures carefully on the shelf. When I open it, I turn the pages as gently as I can.

"There's no general beauty in the world," Mr. Kanze Hideo had said to me, and Helga's loveliness is certainly not general. — But what is any *ko-omote*, even this famous girl in a box, but a stylized, hence at least partially generalized representation? How much of its subtle individuality can an audience see as a difference? — Or is this question as ingenuous as an inquiry into whether all women who possess two eyes are more or less the same?

Who is this inside the box? Wyeth must have "known" what he had made, but he lacked the noun to describe it. "Taking the lids off the boxes . . . they had the odor of the girl, they had the whole — I knew they were not just pretty pictures."

She remains on her side of the abyss, her paintings relentlessly immobile and two-dimensional — understated, in short; fascinating and inexhaustible.


"THE GROWTH AND DEPTH OF MY EMOTION"

Noh actors and Inoue School geishas repeat that they strive to feel nothing when performing their roles. Zeami insists that the Perfect Fluency "has no connection . . . with the actor's conscious artistic intentions or with any outward manifestation of those intentions." Meanwhile, here is Andrew Wyeth: "To me, it is simply the question of whether or not I can find the thing that expresses the way I feel at a particular time about my own life and my own emotion. The only thing that I want to search for is the growth and depth of my emotion toward a given object."

Perhaps defensively, he remarked to Thomas Hoving that the Helga pictures were "too real for some people. You have to feel deeply to do this kind of thing."

For years I hoped to meet Andrew Wyeth to ask him how deep into the earth his emotion was growing, toward what; but as I finished this book, at the beginning of 2009, he was freshly dead, his feeling's constellation of image-object as motionless as a lord's retainers in an old Kabuki play. Helga Testorf, so I imagine, gazes down into the place where he has gone. She sees it better than I. When the *shite* of "Izutsu" stares down into the well, when Zeami envisions snow in a silver bowl, and when Suzuka-san meets her own snow-white geisha face in the makeup mirror, are their visions somehow equivalent?

In Kanazawa I have looked down at the Ishakawon Gate, discovering snow on the roofs, the forest silver behind it, as if I have lost myself in an old Genji Picture-Scroll. Ishakawon's gangling walls, gabled roofs, complex of ponds and walks invite enumeration, however unsuccessful such a procedure might be. In "Farm Road" it would be impossible, unless one so far misconstrued coherence as to inspect Wyeth's brush-strokes through a hand lens.

Had I been lucky enough to meet Andrew Wyeth, what holes under the tree-roots might he have shown me? One visitor from 1965 perceived the artist's identity to be "fluid and fluctuating . . . You can feel it changing and altering in a constant play while you talk to him. This makes you think you have got behind the mask, but when you leave you don't know whether you have."

THE ISHAKAWON GATE.

What then; where then? If on a summer's night in Kyoto you watch the mask just when the actor turns away from the torchlight, will you learn where the face goes?

And when Mr. Umewaka dances Yoroboshi at Yasukuni Shrine, his mask grows dreamily downturned, inward-turned into a true blind face; then when he raises the mask it seems startled, attentive to some distant sound. Slowly he swirls his almost closed fan before him as he turns. A gash of light catches on his chin like a tear. He turns, more tear-light kissing his mask just under his blind eye; then a circlet of light crowns his forehead. Presently the fan comes before his face, becomes a knife-edge, then slowly cleaves the air. Later he will fling out his sleeve, collapsing when the voices slow. Then the *waki* comes to face him, but Yoroboshi stares at the ground. The *waki* spreads his golden fan in what I can only inanely describe as "a very dignified gesture," after which absolute silence follows. Mr. Umewaka at a wide remove from the *waki* glides down the bridge, with time itself breaking between them.

Does Helga see what the blind man did? If I could succeed in seeing through darkness, would my vision be one certain and secret thing, or could it be any number of things? When a Noh actor or geisha considers nothingness, what if anything lies beyond this, glowing like a jewel within the earth?

Noh's overt answer to this might recapitulate the Genjo Koan of 1231: *"The individual self striving to realize all things is delusion; all things striving to realize the individual self is awakening. Those who awake to delusion are Buddhas, while those who are deluded about awakening are humanity."* But this is not what I wish to believe. I want to kiss the mask, and when I put my lips against its wooden emptiness, I want to feel a woman's tongue in my mouth.

And when aestheticians refer to the slow rising of a Noh actor's hand as "the gateway to something beyond . . . a symbol not of any one object or conception but of an eternal region, an eternal silence," I can never avoid wondering whether they have been tricked by the Emperor's nakedness. But when I experience the *yugen* of the geisha, or of "Farm Road," or when the woman I love slowly raises her hand to her hair, then I do believe that there is something beyond.

To look at something far away, the Noh actor shades his eyes, and the cognoscenti know. When he outstretches his sleeve with his fan angled outward, the fan becomes a cup; he is scooping up water. But when Helga gestures, what does it mean? Does grace without allusiveness fall into its own category?

"It's not just anybody lying there. It's that momentary thing — something you'll never see again . . ." — Genji might have felt something of this sort when Murasaki died. And so it *is* anybody, and everybody, and all of us who have existed on one or the other side of an alluring mask. I cannot tell you what Helga sees when she stares down into the earth; but I imagine that I can when I am in Kanazawa, at the point of passing through the many stone arches of an ancient castle gate.

# 24

# Who Is the Willow Tree Goddess?

*Snatches of a Play*

On the grounds of old Nagoya Castle, attended by fountain and moat, the rainbow curtain tucks itself up and a heavy figure in turquoise glides out, on its shoulders a bundle of white, in its hands a basket. It stops almost onstage and turns to face another figure, a sprite garbed in the colors of earth, whose hands rest at its breast, the foregrounded sleeve falling below in a long earthern triangle from elbow and wrist. Its face is a honey-colored wig and a Noh mask of something staring and old. This entity begins to chant, and the drums, flute and chorus accompany its song, not a word of which I understand. Then it and the figure in turquoise begin to sing loudly and resonantly to one another from across the bridge.

I could remind you of the functions of the two figures who enter from the little stage door, crossing the mirror-board to kneel at the rear, partially occluding the pine tree. I could explain the plot to you, pretending that even if Mr. Umewaka had refrained from summarizing it for me at the end I would have comprehended the Emperor's command. If I had educated myself more during my interviews with mask-carvers I surely could have dissected for you the illusion by means of which the sprite's gape becomes more and more thoughtful when seen from the side. The chanting and music speeds up and deepens, the flute shudders. Only the sprite moves, and he finally lays down his wand, removes a fan; then throughout a long bout of chanting, he stays still, the light glistening on his level mask, and faces the golden envoy across the stage. Never mind who is the Willow Tree Water Goddess. This performance being mediated by my untrained, incoherent perceptions, I can only serve you up with bits of things. I remember a kimono's white and silver arrows, and a mask thatched with hair and offering us all its gruesomely grimacing wooden lips. Why does the crown have flames on it? The advances and retreats of this being, its dim movements especially, which are as delicately exquisite as horses in an Assyrian hunting relief, its creeping, twirling and stamping, the waving of its fan, the fact that on the bridge it casts a sleeve over its crown and the way its head flickers with ghastly liveliness, have all been choreographed; but even if I were no longer an ape in a cage, and could tell you the significance of each step and syllable, I still could not peer within "the gateway to something beyond"; in fact, I might remain farther away from it, like a darkroom technician whose very skill prevents him from composing interesting photographs. At least, so I reassure myself.

Why Helga is beautiful, whom we are meant to think of when we see a certain pregnant Cycladic marble with a nose like a knife, pointed breasts and a wide flat pubis; why I am bewitched by this geisha's perfect white face which glows in the darkness as softly as a paper lamp (who is she to me? I think of the Jungian concept of the anima, the projection of the feminine within me, but that can't be much of it, because she is *alien*), to these questions the eternal beyondness of understatement gives some answer, to be sure, but if I knew more I could *know* more. In the Nara National Museum there is an eighth-century scroll of the Flower Garland Sutra: silver-dust characters evenly spaced on night-blue paper;

call it a celestial blueprint. I "appreciate its beauty." But I cannot read it. There is too much in this world for me to know. As the *shite* says in the madwoman play "Miidera" (literal translation): "Thinking heart is saddened."

What is grace? The lap drummer cries out; the three golden fans slowly flash.

# III

# BEAUTY'S GHOST

## 25:

# Snow in a Silver Bowl

*An Epitaph for Radha's Grace*

And because femininity has no one true face, because it is modish, living, and hence at every moment ageing, because my loving or lustful or worshipful gaze must itself die, because my male attraction to the female is attachment, which even if it could last would eventually (whether or not I believe it) become torment, it is good for me to think again and again on Zeami's third highest level of beauty: *"The art of the flower of tranquility.* Piling up snow in a silver bowl." The Sanskrit poet Jayadeva celebrates Radha's liquidly moving doe eyes, her black braid, her red berry-lips and perfectly circular breasts; her earlobe is the bowstring of desire and fragrance comes from her lotus mouth. Where is Radha now? The grace of a woman is a snow image; and then the sun comes out from faraway Silla, and there is only water in the silver bowl.

26:

# Beauty's Ghost

*Ono No Komachi in Traditional Noh Plays*

In Hokusai's sketch, high-eyebrowed Komachi stands in a regal bow-like arc of kimono and haughtiness. So many men seek her — unimaginable the future when she will be expelled from the palace! This artist also portrays her in old age, clutching a disk whose upper rim bursts into leaf. And in the ninth of his illustrations to the renowned *Hundred Poets* anthology, in the midst of late spring, an old crone in a pale blue kimono and a red obi grips a cane, her white fist wilting down from its sagging red sleeve; and there she leans, staring at a cherry tree's cloud-white blossoms, which do indeed resemble two-dimensional, multi-lobed clouds clinging to the tree's crooked red arms and fingers. We see her only from the rear. Facing her, and looking at her either not at all or else only out of the corner of his eye, one of Hokusai's typical balding, wry-faced workers sweeps the white path; white blossoms cling to the red bristles of his broom. The poem accompanying this image may be her most famous, the one that puns on rain and senescence; it begins: *Hana no iro wa / Utsuri ni keri na . . .* — "The flower's color / has already gone . . ."

We have looked in on Zeami writing almost obsessively about the various ages in a Noh actor's life, always emphasizing what he should aspire to create. At the age of twenty-four or twenty-five, when both voice and carriage have matured even as the body continues to be youthful, "this is a very dangerous moment for him. This flower is not the true flower . . . Due to his inexperience, he does not realize that this premature flower will fade soon. He must ponder this fact over and over again."

In his effort to explain the meaning of "elegance beyond maturity," Zeami quotes this proverb:

*The flower of a lover's mind*
*Is one that may fade at any moment*
*Without his being aware,*
*Like cherry blossoms*
*Ready to fall.*

Noh most assuredly conveys the flower's readiness to fall, all the more so now than in Zeami's time, when the art's various stylizations were not yet bygone; indeed, Zeami asserted that even Noh itself is transient, decaying; its *hana* declines each century. (Proust: "Whether it is because the faith which creates has ceased to exist in me, or because reality takes shape in the memory alone, the flowers that people show me nowadays for the first time never seem to me to be true flowers.") And so the cherry blossoms come blowing down. — Are they the true or the false? The lovely girl has an old man's feet. And Komachi's poems about her bygone beauty are beautiful as she herself beneath poetry's mask no longer is. "The flower's color / has already gone . . ." Accordingly, what could be more suitable than a cycle of Noh plays about her?

Once upon a time, a transgender woman decided that her desire for other transgender women was most often stimulated by their eyes, in which she read "endless strength and inconsolable sadness; I see a woman who was made to feel shame for her desires and yet had the courage to pursue them anyway."

And the magnetism of young Komachi, on stage one reenacts it by means of a courtier who chants out his longing to kiss the vermilion lips of a *waka-onna* with another man inside. This hidden man possesses the true flower, the *ease in rigidity* of which a geisha who has reached greatness, for instance Kofumi-san, expresses: how could she, living statue, even tire, much less age?

But another cherry petal falls. The solid inkiness of a certain seventeenth-century *zo-onna*'s hair has begun to flake off above the parting. Here and there, the forehead shows age spots. Within that melon-seed face, all is not roundness; the corners of the eyes narrow into the lance-point, and the dark red lips make almost a hexagonal crystal bifurcated by a slit of black teeth. The girl seems to be regarding me from the midst of her own breathless joy — or does she perhaps express the inward-turned wonder which I have seen from time to time on the faces of corpses? Who is she? Suddenly she seems to be the moon. Those flecks and abrasions and freckles which four hundred years have placed upon her brow, they could be the mottlings of the lunar face which are so lovely to me on full moon nights.

## MASK SUBSTITUTIONS

A Japanese Emperor once said: "The most important accomplishment for a beautiful woman is to be able to write poetry." Indeed, *this* beautiful woman (born in about 820 or 830) was one of the Six Immortals. The literary scholar Donald Keene considers her "possibly the sincerest poet of her epoch." I know her only in translation, of course, but to me sincerity seems as peculiar an ascription for Komachi as it would be for the slow rotation through stage-darkness of an ivory Noh mask with diagonal eyebrows; for her poems are as multiply allusive as Noh texts. Trickster of the pivot-words called *kakekotoba*, whose functions and effects I cannot appropriately convey to you, voice of changeability, empress of paradoxes, she performs her femininity with the understated brevity of her time. In one verse, the darkness which prohibits her lover from finding her accordingly illuminates her breast with desperate fire. Is this indeed sincerity, or simply truth? Another poem, more bitter, refers to the way a man's deceitful flower, in other words his heart, can change without fading; he represents himself as unaltered, and pretends fidelity, when in fact he no longer loves the woman. Perhaps these lines were composed in torment; or for all we know Komachi crafted them in utter coolness, under the exigencies of some extemporaneous palace competition. Either way, they express a sadly eternal aspect of this floating world.

Beneath an *ukiyo-e* painting's many-crooked cherry tree we find her, melon-faced and teeny-tiny-mouthed (her presumably blackened teeth hidden), as with her white arms and long white curving fingers she immerses the Imperial Anthology in a black bowl which is decorated with golden flowers. Thus she disproves an accusation of plagiarism, made by the villainous Otomo no Kuronushi, who listened at her door, heard her declaim her poem, and rushed to inscribe it in the old manuscript. New ink dissolves first; thus she cleared her name. The water has gone grey; the pages are a blank pale reddish-orangish-gold. A single comb crowns her hair.

Five more legends about her have been told to me. One is that she became the lover of Narihira, he who wrote the *Tales of Ise*. The second and most famous details her cruelty to Fukakusa no Shoso (or Shii no Shoso), whom she refused to embrace unless he stationed himself outside the palace for a full hundred nights, sleeping on the bench which held up the shafts of her carriage. Some say that he died in the ninety-ninth night; others, that his father did, so that he had to give over the ordeal.

This story haunted people from her near contemporary Sei Shonagon right up to the twentieth-century star geisha Iwasaki Mineko, who mentioned Komachi's name when she told the tale of a certain snow-faced colleague who threw down the gauntlet to a customer, daring him to visit her each night for three years if he truly loved her.

And so it appears that Komachi could do whatever she wanted to her suitors. In the Noh play "Sotoba Komachi" we hear that Komachi "had in her day the blue brows of Katsura" and her eyes were once "like the color on distant mountains." I imagine that she often associated herself with the items which Sei Shonagon's *Pillow Book* lists under the category of "Elegant Things" — for instance, "a young girl's trailing white robe, worn over a lavender chemise."

Many of her tankas express passion and desire for her unnamed lovers, but several are in this vein:

*Surrender to you,*
*is it that you're saying?*
*As ripples*
*surrender to idle wind?*

And then her mask-face began to win its stains and scratches. — Makuzu Tadano, 1818: "It is good for a woman to realize that once she grows old, she becomes useless to the world." Her third and fourth legends approached. She continued gliding across this floating stage; so years rippled about her in just the same way as the slender black calligraphy of the Tokugawa Museum's Genji Picture-Scroll snakes down across an irregularly granulated background of pigments which shade subtly into one another, or get interrupted by mid-tones applied sometimes in wriggling creeks and other times in clouds like the high eyebrows of Noh masks; here and there the scroll has been showered with small squares or smaller irregular polygons of gleaming gold, upon which the black ink-strokes lie flat as if on the surface of some shimmery pond which reflects the hues of earth and autumn leaves; in certain parts of the scroll, the background takes on a jadelike tint, while mid-tone creeks resemble cracks; at times it grows more orange; resembling the bruiselike shadows which can sometimes appear around the cheekbones and under the eyes of ageing Japanese women, the scroll may adopt mauves or blues; it is always muted but never dull. Sometimes it reminds me of one of the ochayas in Kyoto or Kanazawa where I have had the great privilege of seeing the geishas dance: a mat-floored, paper-walled room of various warm beiges and creams, sometimes centered around paper tatami-squares; soon the dancers will come.

By then she must have begun to resemble first (in the fashion of Helga Testorf) a *fukai* mask, then an *uba* or a *rojo*. In her *fukai* state, so I have learned, one fan appropriate to her would have been the Hosho School's *tessenmon-kazura-ouni*, with yellow-centered flowers white and blue on a brownish-grey background.

(It does no good to retreat into virginity; Zeami knows as well as the rest of us that the flower must be shown or it will be lost. Come to think of it, it will be lost in any event.)

I suppose that the first few grey hairs shocked her, as mine did me.

Just as when a Noh chorus, having sat silent in the firelight for half an hour, suddenly howls in unison, then sits silent again, so this or that touch of Death's paintbrush offended the undying youth of the mask I thought I wore, then stopped offending it; I was accustomed to my newest age-spot; I promised to bear it quite cheerfully if only I never got another one!

She is now, if you like, a *toshima*, a woman who emanates "mature charm." When she danced for me, Kofumi-san certainly emanated such beauty. Unfortunately for Komachi, the inmates of the palace prefer the beauty represented by *ko-omote*s and maikos.

Bunya Yasuhide invites her to accompany him into the countryside — but she sniffs out the taint of condescending jocularity, and in her return poem she writes that she would eagerly cut her roots to become a drifting water-plant, if the inviting creek could but be trusted. I can almost see her irises going gold and the corners of her eyes squinting in the almost imperceptible resentment of the loveliest *deigan* mask.

Perhaps she continues her attendance at moon-viewing excursions. To me the full moon resembles a Mycenaean mirror whose verdigrised streaks and patches cause the whole to glow all the more brightly against the void. To her it now perhaps resembles her own face.

Shall we look at her now? Here is a *rojo* carved by Himi, the man who used the corpse of a starved woman as his model for a *yase-onna*: "With the *rojo,* simply being beautiful is not enough. It must deliver very deep thoughts. It must create fear along with elegance. Despite . . . the red lips, the dreadful drama of a woman is carved in this masterpiece . . . This piece is also called Onorojo, since it describes Ono no Komachi . . . Umewaka Rokuro writes that when his grandfather Umewaka Minoru wore this mask in 'Sotoba Komachi,' he could see Komachi's ribs, and when his father Rokuro wore it in 'Obasute,' it expressed the longing to be absorbed in the moon, and in 'Higaki,' when the Hikimawashi was pulled down and the Nochijite appeared, he was so shocked by the mask and costume that he shuddered from the thought of the horrific ending of the woman's life."

The *rojokomachi* mask just described looks as follows: a face bleached like stripped wood, a crack in the arch of the upper left eyelid; the ridge of the nose, which splits off into the elegantly rounded brows, as sharp as anything in an aerial view of the Trans-Antarctic Range. The corners of the faded lips curve down; the eyes stare in fear and misery, unable to see anything but the end. Noh remembers Komachi as the *ruins of allure* — or, to distant Zeami, the bone and breath of it without the flesh. What remains? What is grace hollowed out? For answer, turn your gaze upon a *rojokomachi.*

And by now, as you might imagine, nobody is inviting her to come away on excursions anymore.

Her next legend inspired the Noh play "Sekidera Komachi," in which the ancient beggar, being invited to the Festival of Stars, tries to dance. Representing her in this is of course a great challenge for the *shite* actor, who must gracefully convey her gracelessness. In the instant when she seems to embody her lost youthful elegance, the chorus chants: "How sad! My heart breaks! A flowering branch on a withered tree." And yet this approaches Zeami's definition of the true flower. My thoughts return, as in this context they so often do, to the aesthetic category called *sabi* (literally, rust), which gives to decrepitude the qualities of tranquility and austerity.

In the Noh play "Aoi-no-ue," Princess Rokujo, transformed into a demon by jealousy, laments that "I lack form; therefore I lack anyone to ask after me." Komachi does not yet lack form, but her form has decayed, and the *shite* of "Sekidera Komachi" informs us:

> *The century-old woman to whom you've spoken*
> *is all that's left of renowned Komachi,*
> *is all that remains of Ono no Komachi.*

Certainly she knows the next chapter. She has left us a tanka imagining herself as her own cremated smoke.

Even if she had never loved, but only dallied, her addiction to love-attachment must resemble ours to life.

In the final legend, wind blows through her skull's eyesocket, imitating the moans of sadness she uttered while she was still alive. And so she has achieved parity with Rokujo's formlessness. Doubtless a delicate Noh representation of even this could exude the fragrance of *sabi*.

In short, she came, like all of us, to a bad end; and some tales imply her to be blameable for it; the way she treated Fukakusa no Shoso has been particularly disliked, but at least it shows a sort of discrimination, perhaps even devotion to appropriate hierarchical values, for what if he had been beneath her? A certain poem in the *Tales of Ise* admonishes the exalted and the base not to fall in love, because the disparity will be *bitter*. The *yase otoko* mask through which the Kanze School sometimes portrays Fukakusa is "the face of a man in hell." "This mask, its expression dignified rather than grim, is one of the best-suited of all for the nobility of this thwarted suitor." But to me it seems like an exoskeleton of a face fashioned from almost translucent yellow cartilage, washed in the black water of death, his mouth limply gaping, his moustache somehow resembling a catfish's whiskers; they say that this mask is sometimes used to play the ghost of a fisherman who after betraying a shallow passage to the enemy was stabbed and left to drown; now he swims and swims; the waters of blackness pass through his mouth. Black water shines deep behind his eyes. He bears the mottled complexion despised by Sei Shonagon. His cheek-hollows could have been transplanted from a crab's carapace. He is so far lost, so far down even below Komachi, that he no longer knows who he is. Komachi, his murderer and only friend, draws him toward her head-planet; he comes slowly, a dead yellow comet, drawn on by an erotic gravity which is all that defines him now.

Yes, she refused him. Certainly her behavior differed from that of the heroine of Saikaku Ihara's seventeenth-century cautionary tale about a nymphomaniac who goes mad, runs naked into the street, and sings the words of "a Komachi Dance." What did posterity want of Komachi? How could she be bad in two opposing ways? Perhaps we simply wished to claim her, to embellish our own agonies by comparing them to hers. Here is how Lady Nijo memorializes her: "Yet could she have been as miserable as I was?"

### THE MESSENGER RISES

I said that I knew five legends about Komachi, and you have now read four, including the last, which is to those who still keep flesh in our eyeholes the saddest. The penultimate one takes us near the end of her living decrepitude: By messenger the Emperor sends her a poem. Such is her cleverness that when the crone presents the messenger with a return poem, it is the original with one syllable altered. In Osaka I have seen the late Mr. Kanze play her in this rarely performed Noh play, which is called simply "Ono no Komachi." When she comes creeping out from behind the rainbow curtain, she nearly stumbles; her knees shake. The chorus is singing, more slowly and softly than before: "Yo-o-o-o-oh . . . ooh!"

Komachi wears the mushroomlike greyish cap of travel, leaning on her stick. Then a single chorister's voice soughs like the wind.

When they sing all together, their winter basses remind me of Zeami's vision of the true flower as an old tree with blossoms on it. All the same, how dismal they sound!

I find dozers better represented in this audience than at any other time in my experience: the lady beside me, the lady next to *her*; even my poor interpreter can hardly keep her eyes open.

Komachi halts by the first pine, gazing sadly out at us from the bridge. I have never seen that before.

She begins to sing in her trembling voice, while the men of the chorus chant a background curtain of sound, their voices like the wind. Once upon a time her lips were as red as the fallen autumn maple leaves at the Shoren-in. But colors do change, and one of her tankas reads as follows:

> *What do you now tell me,*
> *I who age*
> *in this tear-rain?*
> *Your words, like these leaves,*
> *have turned color.*

Someday soon, windblown pampas grass will whip across Komachi's skull in much the same way that a maiko's headdress sometimes dangles its fruiting bodies of pearl and tortoise-shell down past her eyes. And like the grassblades, Mr. Kanze's voice is vibrating and wobbling in a strangely lovely almost monotonous melodic portrait of decrepitude.

It has been said that the intensity of her poetic expressions of passion is such that they transfigure the subjective into the seemingly objective; and in Noh's equally poetic envisioning of her elder days, Komachi appears on the verge of blooming again; her dance, like those words and leaves, has turned color; but which color? What is a woman? What animates the stiffness of a golden fan?

In her singing in "Sotoba Komachi" she alludes to her poem of reply to Bunya Yasuhide: Now she would cut her roots and float down *any* inviting stream, no matter how untrustworthy its waters; but no stream invites her anymore. Now what does she sing to the Emperor's envoy?

When the others chant (they are Shingon priests), she halts, lowers her head and seems to sense the chorus, bringing alive Zeami's maxim that for a skilled actor "movement will grow from the chant" because word and thought are superior to since causative of action; "functions grow out of substance and not the other way around." And so it feels as if at the end of her wearily triumphant disputation with the two priests, followed by a paroxysm of her now chronic madness (brought about by Fukakusa no Shoso's vengefully lovelorn ghost), and succeeded at last by her prayer, outcome unknown, for salvation, it were the chant that impels her into that slow creep offstage in her long yellow kimono while they sing for her as for a departed spirit.

MR. KANZE AS KOMACHI.

But at the end of "Ono no Komachi" she simply halts. Slowly she turns back, reaches out toward the chorus, one wrist crossed over the other, and irresolutely creeps back onto the stage.

In one of her poems she describes her misery at perceiving herself cowering away from malicious eyes even in her dreams; but this seems to have been composed back in the days of her love intrigues. I can well imagine what so sensitive a person now feels, to be regarded quite simply as a disgusting object. She cannot yet escape the stage of this floating world; and so she comes to us, performing withered femininity with perfect grace. Holding an invisible branch of flowers, she dances out her weary agony.

I cannot tell you why I so clearly remember the long interval during which Komachi faces the messenger, he gazing at her, she staring down at the ground. Then an assistant comes, carries her hat off the ground and vanishes through the low corner door, adding to my sense that the characters are only half alive and must continually be cared for. The messenger departs to sit amidst the double row of kneelers at stage right.

When Komachi, still seated, bends down to gaze into her cupped hands, we can see the black band of hair on the crown of the mask. She creeps upward, struggling to rise. While one man drums, a second chants and a third plays the flute, three assistants gather around her right there next to the bridge, transforming her so that instead of being in yellow she now wears a burgundy kimono with rich gold splotches resembling leaves. Presently she is on the bridge by the closest pine, gazing out of her yellow skull-like mask. She faces almost to the rainbow curtain, raises her fan, her sleeve hanging open almost all the way to her waist; she creeps a trifle toward the rainbow curtain, then back again, stands on the stage gazing down into the woodgrain, raises her fan slowly; leaning on her stick, she beggar-creeps to the very edge of the stage, her golden fan extending, slowly sweeping up, gold on one side, red on the other. Most of the play has to do with her painfully standing and crouching, coming and partly going, staring down under the stage.

How to describe that mask? Golden-yellow with metallic hair, sunken-eyed, with a dark slit for a mouth, shadow-cheeked and aquiline — an *uba*, perhaps. I am too far away to see it clearly. The weight of it seems to bow her backward.

In some Kanze School performances of "Sotoba Komachi," she incarnates herself in a *higaki-no-onna* mask, which may also be used to portray "a once-beautiful courtesan brought low by haughty arrogance who looks back from the secluded hut in which she lives out her old age, surrounded by a fence of cypress-wood, upon the golden days long ago when she was the toast of Kyoto." The *higaki-no-onna* is perfect for *jonomai*, the slowest Noh dance. In a pair of reproductions, that mask looks at me, straight on in despairing dullness, the skin still smooth but greyed and whited down, and turned to the left, which causes Komachi to lose herself in herself, like the dreamy concentration one sees on the faces of corpses who died peacefully; harvest moon of femininity, this face of Komachi swims alone in outer space, sickly conscious of her disembodiment: She will never again feel a man in her arms — unless an actor ties her onto his face, and then . . . and then she will merely get carried about in a creep. As for "Ono no Komachi," that play is so rarely performed that I have

KAGEKIYO MASK AND *KO-OMOTE*.

no information respecting permissible masks. And Mr. Kanze is dead. Laurel of the moon, human shadow, Komachi, our dying other self, what am I to do with you, you whom I see but cannot touch? Slowly Komachi orbits away from me. Soon she will be back in her box.

The messenger finally rises. Komachi straightens toward him. He stands and waits; then she glides past him and he past her. As it habitually does, the rainbow curtain rises by itself, and the messenger glides into its undershadow. Komachi stands onstage alone, chanting, then a sharp drum-click impels her to depart in silence, limping along the bridge.


## BEAUTIFUL TOMBS

And it was Noh; it was beautiful, like a marble *kore* broken away from the Parthenon. Lacking arms, legs and even her head, this young woman first appears to us as an age- and pigment-stained boulder. Her young breasts are as worn as sea-glass. The incisions of her tunic-folds provide most of her surviving definition, aside from her right thigh, which, says the museum catalogue, "is revealed as she pulls the peplos to one side with her now-missing right hand." Her belt is tight and her waist is narrow. Here stands, on sturdy modern pins, a chipped stone garment with someone inside it who is living yet incomplete. Before Lord Elgin conveyed her away, before his predecessors mutilated her, and the centuries abraded her paint into something less than a suggestion, who was she? Beneath the blue brows of Katsura, Komachi's gaze once looked out. If we peer into her eyesockets, can't we find it? Can't we believe in the Elgin Kore's right hand? If we can see old age and ruin as understatement in their own right, masked performances of a beauty in which we never could have imagined we would believe, then actor and audience together have won a victory.

In "Sekidera Komachi," even as we are led to pity the vanity of worldly attachment, of Komachi's longing to remain young and beautiful, we are simultaneously advised that poetry remains immortal and green like pine trees, that words of poetry will never fail.

To what extent could this possibly be true? During successful performances, Noh's insistent disjunction between the lovely or at least artful mask and the actor's flabby throat permits the former to triumph over the latter or at least to make it irrelevant: the adam's apple moves without shame. And in the Komachi plays, the pathos of the heroine's lost past (her present sad, her future worse) is beautified by her memories of her youth:

> *My rooms shone with tortoise shell,*
> *Golden flowers grew from the walls,*
> *And in the door bloomed crystal bead strings.*

More clear-eyed than Murasame and Matsukaze (after all, she is not yet a ghost), Komachi admits to herself that the past is past. But grace dwells yet in her bones. As Zeami remarks, "white jade, even in the mud, will retain its real appearance."

As for those artifacts of yellow jade called skulls, why, don't those also remain as they are?

One summer dusk on the bamboo-shaded hillside above Choraku-ji Temple I am surprised to discover myself a guest of death. The narrow tomb-pillars, as pleasingly proportioned as packaged sweets, the trembling ferns, air and light shimmering through the tall bamboo, the loveliness of this world, which has put on a costume of shade, the bright white backdrop of sky through, beyond and behind like a theatrical backdrop of radical simplicity, my own joy, and the workings of my mentality (I have just realized that in this place, near the conclusion of the *Tale of the Heike*, a certain sad Empress took the tonsure) protect me from the reality: Someday, unless I get turned into smoke, wind or ants will pass through the eyeholes of *my* skull. Crows croak. Sitting on the ground, I cannot see Kyoto below me.

# 27

# Urashima's Box

*A Few Thoughts About Time*

The grace of a woman is indeed a snow image. A snow-faced onnagata gazes sadly out at this floating world from the corners of her eyes, whose over-and-underlining thickens as it departs the nose, so that their inward edges are points and the outward ones rounded like raindrops; her crimson heartshaped little mouth takes on all the more beauty above her sky-blue collar and below her purple-black wig and eyebrows; with long white fingers she holds her striped robe just open or just closed at the breast, showing off the milky river-patterns on her slate-blue obi. Within a few hours at most she will be washing off her paint.

Katy might fall asleep with her makeup on, but tomorrow she too must slough off her female skin.

A Noh actor plays Komachi. Then in the mirror room an *uba* mask goes back into its box, and an old man goes home.

Once upon a time, Urashima of Mizunoé married the Sea-God's

daughter and lived immortally with her amidst the octopi until he fool-
ishly decided to visit his parents, who of course had long since risen up in
funeral-smoke; so, standing alone on the shore, he opened the casket she'd
warned him never to open, and out came a white cloud that returned to
the Sea-God's palace without him; he immediately died of old age.

The grace of Noh is one more snow image, and likewise Kabuki, in
which the faded block prints and paper screens of the past are reborn
into stunning brightness. How easy it is to live delusionally beyond time,
until the performance ends, the beautiful face returns to its box, and I
swirl out of mine, joining the effervescence of salarymen in dark suits
who march along with me all the way to Shinagawa Station, their heads
high, only a few of them yawning, most of them resolute even when they
bear dark hollows under their eyes, almost all proceeding in one direction, which is the same taken by the shoals of miniskirted high heeled
schoolgirls in uniforms which vary the sailor suit theme; these people are
concentrating sometimes on some intermediate point ahead of them in
the night, sometimes on something within their skulls, or on the screen
of an illuminated cellphone held at arm's length, but hardly ever on each
other; they resemble a school of fish, wide-eyed and together forward,
passing solitary from womb to grave. As it gets later, the clothing grows
more varied, the faces less resolute; one even spies grubby people. But
every now and then a lovely face streaks across my horizon, always rightward, and, like all the others, rounds the corner and passes through the
ticket gate. I reach my coffin hotel. It is time to hang up my wilted suit.
The crowd continues on toward the Sea-God's palace. I brush my teeth
and say goodnight to my ageing face.*

That ageing isn't all bad I know from the time-scarred buttocks of
various marble Aphrodites, not to mention those lovingly used Noh
masks. Besides, as my late grandfather always used to say, in evident
disagreement with Komachi, "well, Bill, it's better than the alternative."
One such alternative is conveyed by this letter from Oda Nobunaga to
Murai Sadakatsu, 1575, with vermilion seal: "The town of Fuchu is nothing but corpses . . . I'd like to show it to you! Today I shall search every

---

*The plastic wrapper on the plastic bathroom mug reads: "DISINFECTED. Maybe I've
been hoping too hard. But I've gone this far. And it's more than I hoped for."

mountain and every valley, and I shall kill them all." Accordingly, just for today I will permit myself to get a trifle older, being not quite ready to choose death, as Mishima did. And next time I go to Kyoto and ask Kofumi-san to dance for me, the lines at the corners of her mouth will have lengthened. She will be no less beautiful to me for that, and perhaps more so: *Sabi* not merely enriches but defines the open fields painted by Andrew Wyeth, who called their implied loneliness "natural for me." In *Snow Country*, that master of *aware*, Kawabata, takes note of a certain woman as follows: "It was such a beautiful voice that it struck one as sad." This may well be the most characteristic sentence in his oeuvre. (Did this man not write a book called *Beauty and Sadness*?) The sadness, for him at least, comes from transience. Whenever his artistic gaze met schoolgirls in blue uniforms, green lanterns, red walls, necklaces of wisteria spilling down the tree-trellis, it was as if he remembered rather than perceived them. Mishima's consciousness for its part would have sniffed them all anxiously for indications of decomposition. Urashima preferred to avoid them, and dwell — at least until his guilt or yearning prevented him — in a changeless place which I only *imagine* that I can imagine because it must be very old, and even if the gems remain in their sockets, the black calligraphy still frozen in rainstrings superimposed on the greyish cloud-shapes and grass-shapes of the palace screens, all the same, black must have flecked out of the courtiers' hair, their faces decayed and flaked half away, their sea-flowers long since scattered and devoured by snails — unless, of course, Zeami is incorrect, and the true flower can in fact endure forever, like some precious mineral concretion in an E. T. A. Hoffmann fairytale.

The Sea-God's daughter must have been perfect; her mouth must have been as cool as a mosquitoey afternoon exhaling from a moss garden in Kyoto. Beneath the cold waves on edge of which the saltmakers of Suma gathered seaweed to burn, the palace might have presented, like so many of Kyoto's old temples, a curving roof of wavelike tiles, beneath which white panel walls and fragile wooden pillars stood multiply open to reveal a grid of paneled walls and tatami floors. Perhaps black snails kept them clean. And I imagine an open vermilion structure with silver-white rails from which Urashima and his wife could gaze down from the crest of a hill of tea-green shrubs — really more seaweed, but after his

IMPERIAL PALACE GATE, KYOTO.

first thousand years of residence he might have forgotten the appearance of terrestrial plants, whose flowerings false and true would have been as lost to him as the changes of the moon.

Now that I think of it, the palace could just as well have resembled Mishima's house, whose courtyard's tile path winds among statues and urns. Mishima smiles widely in the old photos, drifting in or hiding from the shoals of guests who were allured by his talent, family, money, power, celebrity, physical appeal. He poses Napoleonlike on the stairs, with a painting of a three-masted sailing ship behind him. The house is a museum now. His Parisian clock, which in its swirling rococo intricacy resembles a hunk of tropical coral reef, no longer tells the time.

Mishima sometimes liked to pose amidst his statuary, which emanated masculinity. Well, and what is a statue to you? I myself prefer to meet imperishable femininity. From 350 B.C. or thereabouts, a winged nude goddess stares stolidly ahead, her dark and mottled skin its own armor, her breasts and nipples their own breastplates, her V-shaped pubis one more facet or plane which might perhaps open from within, like the air vent of a tank, her pupil-less eyes equally impenetrable surfaces flecked with greenish-gold. She is, apparently, Lasa, an approximate Etruscan equivalent of Venus. The alabastron she holds in her left hand is a perfume vessel. Her right hand visors her gaze. Her hair resembles swirling sun-rays. She is hard and slender. Call her a true flower incarnated forever. She allures me, but I can scarcely pretend to know her as an Etruscan would. Devoting the remainder of my life to learning to love her through her context might bring me joy, but I would be decaying ever farther from her with every instant; moreover, who would she be, if anyone? At least the mask sometimes has a living being inside it. If my feelings for her fulfilled me, how would they differ from autogynephilia? Wouldn't it be more appropriate simply to set her beside another statue?

I remember two figures together on a Noh stage, the demon whirling, the goddess still and composed. Isn't this how the marriage of a human with an immortal would go?

The Tokugawa Museum displays a scroll depicting Ono no Komachi: The eyebrow-lines painted high on her forehead, the arrowhead face, narrow eyes, and long, black hair could almost have represented any lady in a Genji Picture-Scroll — not quite, for her cheeks were not as chubby as theirs, but she had been analogously understated into feminine elegance; she dwelled with the Sea-God's daughter in that realm where each eye is one stroke of the brush and all women have wide cheeks and small mouths, regardless of age and sex, and where, furthermore, they are depicted always in profile or half-profile, never with any expression, in the late Heian style of "female picture" called *yamato-e*. Why shouldn't such entities endure for eternity? Komachi's kimono opened at the neck in a series of nested outward-curving V's like waterfalls or rainbows springing apart from the same root, revealing the zigzag dark-on-green of the inner kimono, and then a faint arc of snow-white inner kimono where multitudes of desperate lovers must have directed eyes, caresses and poems.

Was it this realm that Fukakusa no Shoso, he who failed to win Komachi on the verge of achieving his hundred faithful nights, truly wanted to enter? Would he have been content to live eternally in expressionless profile? Perhaps his soul was disordered from the beginning. In "Sotoba Komachi," he possesses his enfeebled antagonist in order to announce through her lips: "She sent no answer, not the merest trifling word; accordingly for punishment she has grown old. She has lived a hundred years. I love her; how I love her!" — Thus Noh insists once again on the insanity of attachment.

That attachment is insane is, of course, no strike against it. (Andrew Wyeth again: "The only thing that I want to search for is the growth and depth of my emotion toward a given object.") And for me the point of Komachi's story is not that she was cruel, if indeed she was, but that she was thoughtless, as most living beings are and might as well be. She got old, then regretted the days when she had been thoughtless. In "Sotoba Komachi" the priests sorrowed for her. Why not for you and me?

If Kawabata had written about her, I think he would have concentrated in the days just before her mask began to get scratched. Mishima did take her up. He rewrote "Sotoba Komachi."

Were this a more "literary" book I would have spent much of it on Kawabata, who was not, as Mishima is, the bitter victim of beauty, but its mourning celebrant. If you want to see what he saw, look at the youngest faces in the girlie magazines. Or go to the hot springs of the Snow Country. Or visit the Hiragiya Ryokan in Kyoto. This inn offers the paying guest a certain lovely tatami room with walled garden all around: stone lanterns, ferns and moss. The blinds are a trifle down and there is a lacquered table. So much of this inner world is soothing and beige. I remember the latticed sliding screens with snow-viewing windows at the right height for seeing when sitting. Kawabata used to stay here with his wife — although it is said that he rented another place to write in.

As for Mishima, when I think of him I remember Urashima's box. Mishima might have married the Sea-God's daughter, but, suspecting the treacherous limits of everything, even the immortality her profiled kiss would have offered him, he took that casket and immediately smashed it on the rocky beach.

# 28

# The Decay of the Angel

*Komachi in the Noh Plays of Mishima Yukio*

Like most novelists, Mishima writes principally about himself. In each volume of his *Sea of Fertility* tetralogy, which shines ever more obviously as one of the great works of the last century, the protagonist appears to have been reincarnated into a different body. First he is Kiyoaki, a sensitively self-destructive young dreamer who falls in love with the one woman he has been expressly prohibited from loving, and from that love he catches his death at age twenty. Next we see him as a *kendo* athlete with "a face like new-fallen snow, unaware of what lies ahead," who matures into a rightwing suicide terrorist. In the third novel he's reborn as a Thai princess who also dies young, of a snakebite; in the last, as a handsome, cruel young lighthouse keeper. The reincarnated person can always be identified by a certain birthmark, and the identification gets accomplished by the other protagonist, Shigekuni Honda, who is a judge — perfect profession for a soul whose task it is in the tetralogy to decide what might or might not be true, and what existence means. In the first novel, he muses about Kiyoaki: "Up until now I thought it best as his friend to pretend not to notice even if he were in his death agonies, out of respect for that elegance of his." Certainly Honda never suceeds in *preventing* anybody's death agonies. Scrupulous, empathetic, intelligent, aching to understand, and ultimately impotent, Honda might as well be — a novelist.

In effect, then, there are two main characters in this long work, the observer and the observed. Is the observed really one soul who comes to life four times, or, as the final volume hints, has Honda deluded himself (as I perhaps would) out of yearning for supernatural coherence?

Mishima was both Honda and Kiyoaki, the one and the myriad. As an artist, he could create, but creation can never substitute for action. Action, on the other hand, may be powerful but cannot transcend ephemerality. Action dies as does Kiyoaki, and as did ultimately Mishima himself, whose carefully politicized, aestheticized suicide was not only rabidly absurd, but a failure on its own terms: The troops refused to rally to his call for Emperor worship. At least Isao, the *kendo* athlete of the second book, succeeds in assassinating somebody before he cuts his belly open. Mishima was ultimately more like Honda than like Isao, which is hardly a terrible thing: while he may be sterile in the sense that he will not bring about any "great event" (he will not murder any ministers), his empathy will endure. Honda's seeking, his sincerity, his fidelity to that not necessarily well founded belief in Kiyoaki's reincarnations, here are the strands of perception, conceptualization and devotion which sustain patterns of recurrence into something permanent and precious. Without Honda, the four young men and one young woman who share nothing but a certain birthmark and a predilection to secret self-absorptions would not have added up to any collective thing. Thanks to him, they embody a sacred mystery. That is why Honda can be likened to the immense display case in the Mishima Yukio Literary Museum, where our author's books shine as colorfully frozen as any collection of immaculate butterflies.

So Honda is Mishima; and the butterflies, the various versions of Kiyoaki, are also Mishima, whose strangely plastic features — and this is a quality more often pertaining to women, because more of them know how to dress the part and put on makeup — seem capable of forming themselves into any number of vastly dissimilar faces. Sometimes in the photographs his very head appears elongated, as though he were Cambodian or Vietnamese; at other times it's rounder, like the clay head of some Assyrian idol; that frequently very sensitive and delicate face, Kiyoaki-face, can on occasion appear bleached and bleak like an ageing prisoner's, or harden into the stereotyped clay vulgarity which I have seen in the attitudes of tattooed Yakuza gangsters posing for my press camera (this, perhaps, was an attempt to embody himself as Isao the suicide-terrorist). We have Mishima the suit and tie man, Mishima the flashy dancer (caught from above and grainily, à la Weegee), Mishima the artful poser in the dark kimono polka-dotted with light, and they are all his expressions of self, his legitimate incarnations, but only the Mishima called Honda sits down to the desk on which the bronze or brass letter-opener surmounted with the medallion of a Caucasian's head (a certain Emperor Napoleon, I believe) lies beside a miniature sword; two very Japanese looking metal fishes and a metal lizard bask eternally by a golden Parker pen; it is none other than Honda who, perhaps wishing that he could be Isao, writes at the end of *Runaway Horses*: "The instant that the blade tore open his flesh, the bright disk of the sun soared up and exploded behind his eyelids."

This defines Mishima's agony. As he writes in his eerie confession *Sun and Steel*,

In the average person, I imagine, the body precedes language. In my case, words came first of all; then . . . came the flesh. It was already . . . sadly wasted by words. First comes the pillar of white wood, then the white ants that feed on it. But for me, the white ants were there from the start, and the pillar of plain wood emerged tardily, already half eaten away.

Regarding Ono no Komachi one sees the white ants in retrospect. But in her heyday, no doubt, one saw only the white wood of her perfect flesh, the white arms, black teeth, black hair.

Kiyoaki has the body, of course, and Honda the words. And the words despise themselves, knowing that their own fulfillment necessarily spoils the body with sedentariness. But without the words to define and cohere, the body lapses into its own separate incarnations; and even its most dramatic self-expressions, its mutilations and orgasms, cannot win to the *understanding* which words make possible and which will keep the body's consciousness whole. For all his athletic poses toward the end, the mere existence of the Mishima Yukio Literary Museum suffices to prove that the body was not enough for our novelist, that like Kiyoaki he became too restless to stay in one body, that he wanted to be the man of a thousand faces even if the close-cropped hair, the half-smoked cigarette failed to remove him as much as he thought it did from kinship with any small boy who dresses up as a sailor. Yes, incarnation is restless, and so in some photographs, Mishima, whom my Japanese translator thinks of as "definitely gifted, but somehow not really sure how to cope with the 'gift,'" wears a radiant if at times hysterically radiant smile, the white teeth tight together; in other images he's trying to look stern. In the body-builder portraits, Mishima appears rounded and drawn in on himself, transformed into clay, a stolid corporeality which expresses itself more loudly than the inner spirit; but I suspect that the spirit, which accentuated that corporeality because it loathes itself, feels tormented by that loudness and dares not confess it. Could that be one reason that Mishima chose death?

About that death, or at least about its supposed inevitability, a little more should be said. In *Sun and Steel* he bitterly complains about the fact that men cannot objectify themelves, and from the context it's evident that he means *objectify their bodies as women can*. I ask his ghost: What about the spectacularly objectified feminine beauty of the male Noh actor? Not answering, Mishima hurries on: "He can only be objectified through the supreme action — which is, I suppose, the moment of death, the moment when, even without being seen, the fiction of being seen and the beauty of the object are permitted. Of such is the beauty of the suicide squad." Mishima wrote those words in that languorously white house of his, which might be considered a little peculiar for the abode of a Japanese nationalist given those white urns, Greekish statues and European horoscope mosaic, that house which serenely bides and forebodes behind its high white wall; if anything, it makes me think of the residence of the minister Kurihara in *Runaway Horses*, whom Isao stabs to death in punishment for the crime of sacrilege. Kurihara is, among other things, another Honda. The body hates the words (so, at least, the self-hating words say). The body freely, guiltlessly kills and copulates, marches, overthrows, dances, allures, inspires, makes history. It can do everything. But what's it made of? The white ants are already eating it. When Mishima, naked but for his loincloth, sits on the tatami mat for yet another photograph (if you knew him by only this image, you wouldn't suspect that he lives amidst French engravings of nineteenth-century experimental balloons), when Mishima leans on the staff of his sheathed sword, his face, which to others, including himself, may evince resolution, to me betrays resignation, even vacancy, as if it cannot escape its own clay.

And yet that house with its erotic luxury and hallmarks of foreign possibilities, that cosmopolitan palace which Isao would have hated, what a perfect womb for a creative mind! To be sure, he could have become soft and fat living in that house (and suddenly I think with more sympathy of Urashima, immortal so far, dwelling endlessly underwater with the Sea-God's daughter). In his study stand Japanese brushes in a lacquerware cylinder, an elegantly slender calligraphy box, a block of scarlet ink for what I think is a stamp or seal; with those objects perhaps he could have incarnated himself into a living exemplar of the Japanese tradition which he imagined that he had to die for. He might have chosen any number of fates. And it may be significant that the tense, gruesome *Runaway Horses*, whose hero kills himself more or less with Mishima's method, is not the final novel of the tetralogy, but the second. What if Mishima, like the ghost-*shite* of many a Noh play, had outlived his own death? Honda himself is condemned to outlive Isao's *seppuku* for two more volumes in which nothing nearly as dramatic will occur. In the third volume, *The Temple of Dawn*, he witnesses what he believes is Kiyoaki's reincarnation in the person of a beautiful, mysterious Thai princess. Mishima's mood becomes richly tropical here, and the discourses into Buddhist theology, which irritate some readers, to me evince a last flowering of intellectual excitement on Honda's part as he continues to attempt to find, and Mishima to convey, perhaps to feel, the meaning of existence. But halfway through this novel, the famous aridity has already set in. Lovesickness, ideological rapture, and divine mysteries are done. The final book, *The Decay of the Angel*, exudes a suffocatingly existential quality. It's all about waiting for death — not the joyfully fanatical death of *Runaway Horses*, which Mishima tried unjoyfully to die, but the death of the white ants. Unable to move forward to oblivion, the *shite* chants out nausea and putrefaction. Reading *The Temple of Dawn* always makes me feel that the tetralogy's end, and Mishima's corresponding finish, were not preordained.* The enigmatic little Thai princess offers the prospect of something different, something not only almost as erotic as suicide, but perhaps more elusive, something worthwhile enough to warrant not killing oneself while one tries to uncover it. Very possibly, if *The Temple of Dawn* is any indication, this something could have been religion or philosophy. I wonder how feverishly Mishima hunted for it in his wood-clad study with the bookshelved walls.† He failed to find it, and that is why every year on 25 November, the white-clad Shinto priests lay down their prayer-streamers on the altar, which resembles a tabletop model of a round-towered castle, and the blood-red disk of the Hinomaru flag hangs above them in the darkness beside Mishima's portrait.


## MISHIMA'S KOMACHI

In the shade of his sensational end, Mishima's Noh plays often go overlooked.

Of the five which I have been able to read in translation, three fall considerably short of their originals. Only his "Hanjo" is clearly superior. All of them gleefully defy Zeami's edict that "one must not copy the vulgar manners of common people."

In shocking contradistinction to the classical Noh aesthetic of *yugen*, Mishima begins his "Sotoba Komachi" as follows: "*THE SET is in extremely vulgar and commonplace taste, rather in the matter of sets used in oper-*

---

*You may recall that Zeami believed that an actor was at his peak at about thirty-five. Mishima's suicide occurred at forty-five, the age when in Zeami's opinion a Noh actor's "own natural beauty of carriage and the appeal of his performance (which is so attractive to the audience) will fade gradually away," *unavoidably*, he insists. For this reason he advises most fifty-year-old Noh actors to retire, but then immediately offers the example of his father, the great Kanami, who continued to perform up to his death at fifty-two. Although the old man left more difficult roles to others, and eschewed ostentation, "his flower looked better than ever. As his was *shin-no-hana* it survived until he became old without leaving him, like an old leafless tree which still blossoms."

†Most of the books are in Japanese, but here and there lurks a two-volume monograph on Dutch painting from the National Gallery, or Günter Grass in English, or *Fiesta Brava*, or *La peinture manièriste*.

*ettas.*" In other words, "the white ants were there from the start." One of Mishima's hallmarks, like Poe's, is *nastiness*.

In the original, as in the sister Noh plays, Komachi is a pathetic character whose echoes of her past beauty and arrogance render her grandly pitiable — and more, for having outlived the false flower of her youth she may win through to enlightened non-attachment. But in Mishima's version she becomes, as women so often do in his work, an impure devourer whose weapons include ambiguity and hypocrisy. Mishima's hero-protagonists are resolute. His heroines are the enemies of resolution.

One could write a diverse catalogue of the little avarices which occur when poverty marries old age. But when this ant-eaten Komachi of his counts over her hoard of cigarette butts, this seems not only appropriate to an aged beggar, but germane to the younger Komachi whose absence shines from behind the rainbow curtain — for didn't she collect from Fukakusa her utmost toll of those hundred fatal nights? Mishima recapitulates her tale on a gruesomely petty scale. I, glorifier of my attachments, reject to my utmost power Noh's assertion that clinging to whatever moves becomes torture — but Mishima's Komachi is a horridly convincing argument against me. What makes her horrid is that he has stolen her grace away.* In this anti-Noh of his, the Poet who stands in for Fukakusa insists: "The park, the lovers, the lampposts, do you think I'd use such vulgar material?" Mishima uses it with glee; Komachi embodies it, all the while assuring us that nothing was not vulgar once. The Poet, who himself lacks any sweetheart, loves lovers because they seem to each other more beautiful than they are. To this Komachi replies that those who keep such illusions are actually dead: Boredom and disgust prove that one has come back to life.

Here is an example of Mishima's typically morbid version of *aware*. Komachi looks around her at the loving couples in the park and remarks: "They're petting on their graves. Look, how deathly pale their faces look in the greenish street light that comes through the leaves."

---

*Mishima might reply: "What grace?" or, more likely, "Isn't grace the same as death?" — Who could deny the Heian snobbery of Komachi's day, which Mishima skewers by having a lady explain: "There's always something slightly crude about a dress made by a Japanese?"

And presently one even finds a tiny bit of *yugen*, although it reminds me of some grim voyage to Hel in the Norse Eddas: "Shadows are moving over the windows, and the windows grow light and dark by turns with the shadows of the dance. So wonderfully peaceful — like the shadows cast by flames."

Mishima continually implies that the beauty of femininity's mask is not merely delusory, but dangerous, distracting, voracious: the ruination of male energy. (As it happens, he forgives the loveliness of the onnagata who gazes demurely down while the red-painted outer corners of her eyes curve impossibly up.)

Did Fukakusa no Shoso die a worthwhile death? In *Spring Snow*, Kiyoaki fruitlessly visits again and again the woman who, her virginity stolen by him, has been led to take the tonsure and renounce him forever. Like Komachi's lover, he dies at last of exposure. There is, to my mind at least, an element of self-destructive stupidity in Kiyoaki's doings; but what I interpret as the author's accomplished irony may be something else, given how he ended his life (how horrible if he had felt "ironic" even then!). And Captain Fukakusa in Mishima's "Sotoba Komachi" has certainly been warned by the old witch herself not to let himself be allured. He seems to inflict the spell upon himself, and therefore to be more self-aware, profounder, than his exemplar in the traditional texts. As for Komachi, like so many Mishima heroines (although certainly not all of them), she is not much more than evil, and therefore far inferior to her original. When Mr. Kanze portrayed Komachi in her old age I could almost see the white triangles of snow in the joints of the bamboo-grove at the Shoren-in, or the way that in late spring the moss of the Shoren-in mottled and marbled with fallen cherry blossoms;* whereas Mishima's Komachi is simply an ogress — or is she? The rule is this: Call her beautiful and you die. She sportingly warns the Poet of this again and again even as she entices him to dance. But is he perhaps already dead? He promises to meet her *here* in a hundred years, when she will have grown

---

*Zeami writes in his treatise on "finding gems and gaining the flower" that an ideal performance can be accomplished when the actor somehow translates the musical atmosphere he has created into its visual expression; and Mr. Kanze's Komachi was first of all a wobbling voice and then the tremulous physical representation of that voice; he trembled as gracefully as does shimmering water.

old as he will not. So could he be the ghost of Fukakusa? Tonight has dreamily become the hundredth night, so Komachi must give herself to the Poet, at which prospect he feels simultaneously happy and disheartened. But then he says: "If I think something is beautiful, I must say it's beautiful even if I die for it." And so he dies, and Komachi calmly sits counting up her cigarette butts.

As a matter of fact, Fukakusa's character is hardly otherwise in the traditional Noh plays. In "Kayoi Komachi" the *waki* comes to the grass to pray for the release of her moaning skull. Fukakusa no Shoso's spirit also exists here; but he at first refuses to accept the Law of Buddha and be enlightened. Clinging to his love and resentment, he goes so far as to menace the priest. Presently, however, he finds himself, in the accustomed pathetic fashion of ghosts, reenacting the hundredth night, on the verge of winning of Komachi's favors, and this somehow enables him to reach the better consummation of enlightenment.

I see Komachi young and alone in a certain snowy landscape, at the bottom of a narrow vertical *ukiyo-e* painting, one branch of a leafless tree poised over her head, then far above her the scribbly rain of calligraphy. With her pale, stylized face she could have been anyone. I feel a trace of boredom; trapped in the Sea-God's palace, I find myself preferring Mishima's Komachi — but only for an instant, because what ruined Urashima was that his attachment became a trap, and Mishima's tale ends no better; his attachment merely happened to be to death itself.

When I compared him to Poe, I was thinking precisely of the horror which stained their separate but not dissimilar thanatophilia. In Mishima's fantasies, *seppuku* may come voluptuously, and the man's corpse may allure other men, but *there is no branch of flowers*. In any good Noh performance of "Aoi-no-Ue" the goldenfaced horned monster of hatred and jealously lowers its mask-face, glowering and grinning, horrible, advancing upon the exorcist, yellow-eyed and almost cheerful but also dead and rotting, the reincarnation of the lovely woman who did not know how envious she was; whenever it lowers its head, it seems to be snarling and cowering like a dog; when it raises it, it embodies evil on the verge of triumph; and still it is beautiful with the severe beauty of a marble Artemis who has scarcely aged.

Meanwhile, Mishima's Komachi scrounges cigarette butts. This act of vandalism refreshes me; it brings me out of the Sea-God's palace; but then the decay I see in her brings me only grief. I feel in Mishima's Noh plays the violence of a man who attacked his tradition because he hated himself.

The black cracks and wrinkles in even a Kamakura Buddha's gold-skinned face can certainly inspire any number of unhappy sensations, but there do remain to us three strategies for overcoming such feelings. The first is to make decay into something piquant, as I have done when making love with extremely aged women. The second is to obscure those signs of deficiency, as the Urashimas among us strive insistently to do (or, as Mishima does, to insist on them, which is almost the same thing). The third is to project and animate the material shell in such a way that its beautiful essence claims our immediate perception. Naturally this requires distance and deception. Or perhaps it simply requires under-statement. We need not state the wrinkles to state the Buddha. In any event, it requires transient life to animate the mask.

What Kawabata says in opposition to Mishima, and many Noh texts also imply this, is that a recollected attachment can outlive the decay of the lovers, like the violet blossoms blooming reclusively on the ancient maple tree at the beginning of Kawa-bata's novel *The Old Capital*. "As time passed," he writes in *Beauty and Sadness*, "the memory of their embrace was grad-ually becoming purified within Otoko, changing from physical to spiritual . . . When she recalled what he had taught her, and imitated it in making love to Keiko," her lesbian protégée, "she feared that the sacred vision might be stained," as it always is in Mishima's pages. "But it remained inviolate."

The white pillar lists and rots; white ants attack it; they are as snowskinned as an image of a dancing courtesan on gilded paper. Mishima feels no *sabi*, or at least denies that he does. But neither does Komachi herself. Like him, she is less a teller than a protagonist of the tragedy. It is not that his art is any less "true" than Zeami's. It is merely less neutral, "unattached" and self-observed. The Heian court poets might have best understood it in relation to *ushin*, conviction of feeling.

In the photographs of him he always appears "sensitive," sometimes clearly on purpose, sometimes, as in the body building portraits, in spite of him. His lower lip frequently protrudes a trifle, like that of a *ko-omote*. His pale face is narrow, his handsome mouth occasionally a trifle twisted. Who is this person?

Mishima fears the white ants, and fears to fear (also fearing boredom), and so he offers himself to them. The result is a combination of bravery and cynicism: "To wash oneself clean of one sin that was permeated with sacrilege, one must commit another. In the end, the two would cancel each other out . . ." This is what I love Mishima for most of all. If he can only screw up his courage in this childish and twisted way, still, he dares; he strives to be "realistic." Attachment without grace! How the Heians would have blanched! — And yet, Noh's spiritual emphasis may be summed up by none other than the following sentence in *Runaway Horses*: "He was always thinking of death, and this had so refined him that the physical seemed to fall away, freeing him from the pull of earth and enabling him to walk about some distance above its surface." Rereading this sentence, I seem to see Mr. Kanze gliding in beautiful agony across the bridge toward the rainbow curtain.

# IV

# THE MOON MAIDEN
# GOES HOME

# 29

# Sunshine on Silla

*The Unknown*

I n Silla at the dead of night, the sun shines brightly." Thus Zeami describes the highest of his nine levels of beauty. This is the flower of peerless charm. "The meaning of the phrase Peerless Charm surpasses any explanation in words and lies beyond the workings of consciousness . . . the Grace of the greatest performers in our art . . . gives rise to the moment of Feeling that Transcends Cognition, and to an art that lies beyond any level that the artist may have consciously attained."

What Silla "means," therefore, even Zeami could not say. Sillan sunshine, which I imagine to be as still and white as a geisha's face powder, may in fact be less visible than snow in a silver bowl, or even pine trees ornamented with balls of snow. In the words of the eighteenth-century aphorist Lichtenberg: "The metaphor is much more subtle than its inventor, and so are many things. Everything has its depths. He who has eyes sees all in everything." — And so I propose that Silla, that far away monarchy whose dominion over Korea's Three Kingdoms collapsed more than four centuries before Zeami was born, is the place where the objects of our attachment live, and therefore the place where we can never go.

The Romantic poet Novalis wrote a novel whose protagonist wondered: "Do I not feel as I did in that dream when I saw the blue flower? What strange connection is there between Mathilda and that flower?" We know what Mishima would have replied: "That's easy. They both equal death!" But how that connection would have played out we will never know, for Novalis died two years after Lichtenberg, with *Henry von Ofterdingen* unfinished. Meanwhile, Rodin's "Psyche" waits for nothing, veiled by her own half-formlessness in the marble, the vagueness of her stone features haunting, almost shocking because what we can in fact see of her is perfect. The subtlety of *that* matter might have been likewise saved by the death of the inventor. I myself could hardly hope to rescue Psyche with a chisel, nor to definitively diagram Mathilda's relation to flowerhood.

In the Noh play "Hagoromo" a man goes in quest of his vanished celestial wife. In such a situation, how high should be *my* expectations of success?* Wandering between Kyoto's tall and narrow severally-decked pagodas, I encounter merely one more industrial sunset whose concrete-walled stage becomes blue in the fading light.

In the Tokyo National Museum, Kannon prays for me, her plump face all gold, her slender, tapering fingers pressed together at her chest, ever so many smaller jointed arms at her sides; she is the lobster or crab of mercy, holding many small bottles and other objects in her hands, perhaps charms or medicines. Can even she help me find the gold at the end of the rainbow, the place to which the metaphor points? The rainbow curtain goes up by itself; the bridge faintly creaks beneath a *kyogen* actor's unusually rapid step.

But perhaps Silla awaits even in tonight's dead of night! From the fifteenth century, in his "Errant Cloud Collection," Ikkyu Sojun reports upon the *arhat*, or Buddhist saint who has expunged himself of the passions:

---

*It is this text to which Mishima's *Decay of the Angel* is indebted for its title. In the original Noh play, which may predate Zeami, a man refuses to return an angel's celestial cloak, and she accordingly displays the fivefold signs of corruption.

*In this polluted world an* arhat *dwells far from Buddhaland;*
*A single visit to a brothel, however, will arouse his great wisdom.*

Then again, an evening at the Noh theater might do just as well. A flame flickers at Yasukuni Shrine and the chanting goes on, each chorister's mouth a square when he chants; and Yoroboshi, who is Mr. Umewaka, comes slowly, slowly creeping, his stick ahead of him at the perfect angle, because he's blind; he's chosen yellow-beige to wear and his mask is paler than anything which has ever existed. He sings, his long, long hair spilling down in two thin waves upon his breast. Slowly he turns, his voice so resonant and tuneful; and a cold mist of rain comes down on us and the drum begins to tap as the blind figure extends itself. The *waki* puts the golden fan over his head. Silla is the stately immobility of Mr. Umewaka, and the ethereal way in which he turns, his blind man's cane never varying in angle, his hair tapering precisely down his back, cherry blossoms glinting in the torchlight and chorus-voices swelling into dreams.

I remember an eyeless Noh mask like a pupil-less marble Aphrodite; and the snowy-faced concentration of the *ukiyo-e* lady who with tilted head scissors away the stalk of a flower in just the right place to fit it into a formal blossom arrangement. I recall the overwhemingly beautiful curtains at the Kabuki-za glowing from behind like lantern slides; I especially remember one of that theater's stage: Mount Fuji peaks above the clouds, accompanied by a blood-red sun; the light simmered behind it as if the sky were going overcast. These inspire me with visions of the Sillan sun, which, granted, I can discover only indirectly, as when I realize that in Wyeth's paintings Helga is so often looking at something that I can never see, sometimes something between trees but more frequently something in the darkness.

In the British Museum I have seen many-grooved silvergolden bracelets from Silla. Who wore them I lack the education to imagine. Did those long-dead princesses shine in the dead of night as sun-brightly as Valkyries? — Since I cannot quite envision such a shining, please permit me to call it peerless charm.

Floating in a cracked and mottled heaven of gold, a certain Roman Muse touches her wreathed head while raising up the oversized and gaping mask of Tragedy, whose eyesockets are as melting craters. If I got too close to those (not to mention the mouth), I would fall into nothingness. I cannot believe in this fresco's verisimilitude; but if it *were* true, I'd be better off keeping my distance. Anyhow, I can't go there; I'm *here* in the noodle shop which is so narrow that when the sliding glass door closes there barely remains room to sit on the three little stools between it and the counter where the hoarse-voiced woman in black and her mother and husband make *udon* whose noodles are as thick as fingers with broth beautiful yellow from raw egg yolk. (They laughed with white teeth and clapped their hands when I said it was the best eel in Osaka.)

What is grace? — Two geishas view plum blossoms in the snow. Everything is pinkish, as in the sunset-infused winterscapes of Kawabata's *Snow Country* — and against this "everything," the snowy branches and the geishas' skins stand out. How otherworldly, how Noh-like the way the ladies turn away from each other, each admiring her own chosen blossom! Their long, brocaded robes almost touch the snow. — This *ukiyo-e* print by Torii Kiyonaga (1752–1815) exemplifies the true flower. Those geishas, if they ever actually existed, departed beyond the rainbow curtain centuries ago. And yet here they continue their shining, like the sun from the night of Silla. — Needless to say, for me at my long remove of ignorance, the Edo era itself, from which *ukiyo-e* was meant to be a semi-fantastic escape, has become a province of Silla; for I can see it only as the prints show it to me: as a time and place when everybody was melonfaced and wore robes of yellow and of lead-vermilion faded almost to yellow, and everyone was rushing, bearing burdens, buying and selling, seducing, sitting folded-kneed on bamboo porches, flirting in doorways, paying mouth obeisance to the samurai while dreaming of Kabuki

ROCK GARDEN AT THE REIUN-IN SUBORDINATE TEMPLE.

evenings, new silk kimonos, visits to the pleasure quarter. Which sun do you suppose shines there at night? Here is an early-eighteenth-century black-and-white *ukiyo-e* print of a plump courtesan with a maple leaf hairpin who is raising up her many-crested surcoat with her little hand in order to step toward the righthand edge; we can see one miniature foot, and we can tell that she is gazing at something through her sleepy little eyes, but to find out just what, we will have to board a discreet boat to Yoshiwara. And since all such boats have rotted, burned or sunk, what shall I do but listen to snow in a silver bowl, or, if I lack the wit to do that, watch a Noh performance?

Isuien Garden in Nara is a rolling Arctic moss-scape whose pools tease the gaze, going in and out of view. I remember an islet made of a single rock whose shape resembles a tortoise shell; its moss-spots, which possess the brilliant pallor of green tea, shine against the darker green of that rock-ringed pool whose reflections of sculpted pines seem to grow downward like roots; really there is no down; each reflection lies *across* the surface, which can be crossed by an irregular array of stone cylinders whose tops are almost level with the water; what does it mean to go from here to there across the water? What could be more simple? On that mossy islet-rock is a single feather. What does that mean? The stone steps are still; the water moves ceaselessly, so gently that ripples but rarely mar its representation of the green, green world of upside trees; but a water-strider, having rested, suddenly kicks its back left leg and sends concentric circles across the jade-tinted reflection of a cloud. Beyond that insect, the trembling reflections of the many leaves comprise a complexity whose magnitude, like that of a Noh kimono's brocade design, overwhelms perception-all-at-once, and thereby achieves at least one order of infinity. By "perception-all-at-once" I mean the opposite of consciousness's systematic trolling: the data banks of a corporation, or the memories of a lifetime, may add up to any number of items; this leaf, that leaf and any number of others may be brought back into consideration; an artist may carefully represent each leaf in the reflection, but when all's said and done, the result is more than we can take in all at once. Meanwhile, thanks to the breeze on the water, that totality alters at every instant, which increases infinity by another order. And all this is but a semblance acted out upon the skin of the water: the relationship between the reflected and the so-called "real" add another order of infinity, what goes on beneath the surface of the water, what stories the ancient carp enact, there's another order; and beyond this vaguely heart-shaped pool, whose shape can almost be recorded by perception-all-at-once, lies "the world." Never mind all that. Cross the stepping-stones from here to there and perhaps you are in the other world. In that case, what does the island signify?

The silhouette of a carp slides by and vanishes behind or under the green-gold reflection of that pine tree. Just then the wind blows, and the reflection breaks up into myriad prismatic ovals of light green and white, pine needles duplicated, replicated, distorted.

Grace is under the water, or reflected on the water. I can see it; why can't I touch it?

# 30

# Pine Tree Constancy

*"Takasago," "Izutsu" and "Matsukaze"*

In an anonymous fan created sometime during the middle Tokugawa period (1742–91), pine trees express their peerless charm as ovoid needle-clouds in a sky of pure gold, rent along the fan-curve by two crimson irregularities studded with gold leaves and insects, and also by a very stylized blue shard of water with green lilypads. The pines offer Japanese asymmetry in all its grace. Their needle-clusters have been embellished into fans of rays within each cloud-lobe, and eyelashes-like constructions along the edges. The Noh actor who employs this fan represents a shrine priest. What could be more appropriate to his station? After all, the pine remains *evergreen*. In defiance of my epoch's botanists, Zeami asserts that pine blossoms appear every thousand years, ten times in all — a span which for humans practically equals eternity. "So, awaiting this occasion, the branches of the pine / Bear leaves of poetry, shining with dewdrop gems." — This marriage of the eternal with the transient expresses much of lies within Noh's mysterious heart. The old man transforming himself into the young female, the stillness that frames passion and delusion and violence, the constant endeavor to neutralize opposites, all these can be expressed in the trope of the flowering pine. No wonder Zeami writes that the Noh actor who successfully impersonates an old man becomes "like blossoms on an ancient tree!"

It would not be going too far to ascribe divinity to the pine. When I asked the Noh actor Mr. Mikata Shizuka what it signifies on the Noh stage, he began with the surprising information that "before the Edo period, we didn't have that pine tree," I suppose because in the past the plays were usually performed outside;* then he said: "The god has to come to something, and it is to a pine tree where the god comes. Toward the tree we dedicate our art."

### TAKASAGO

One of the best known Noh plays is called "Takasago," and indeed the fan just described was fashioned for use in this very drama, which portrays two pine trees. Zeami informs us that they "grew up together," although their residences, Sumiyoshi and eponymous Takasago, lie three days' journeying apart. The enigma solves itself when we learn (as the play's original audience knew quite well) that they are god and goddess.

Hokusai offers us a simple line-image of this old couple, the man with a rake over his shoulder, the woman with a broom below and behind her. This is how we first see them in the play, in the typical Noh mode of unassuming mortal disguise. It is, after all, as exemplars for humans that they are best known. The song beginning "O Takasago!" is still sung at most Japanese weddings, which would please Zeami the populist entertainer. And apparently this song or a similar one once opened the year's Noh repertory. Fenollosa's notes inform us: "And while the cup of the Shogun is poured out three times, Kanze sings the 'Shikai-nami' passage from the play of Takasago, still bowing." The play is a lovely evocation

---

*The fourteenth-century stage lacked both back walls; and the bridge lay where the pine tree now presides.

of conjugal fidelity,* and its last lines are especially beautiful: "The pines that grew together dance in the wind, / resounding with the rustling voice of joy."

I myself, a product of skeptical individualism, have never been impressed by "Takasago's" pieties, which must have been cliché'd before Zeami was born. In the late tenth century, we find the author of *The Gossamer Journal* penning such poems as

> *The pine-clad mountain*
> *will never be inconstant*

and I wonder how many times I have read this before. The Gossamer Lady's husband, who ultimately will prove quite inconstant indeed, has already written her father a promise-poem comparing the length of his fidelity to the long-lived pines at Sue-no-Matsuyama. She wryly supposes him incapable of sleeping alone "even if you were dwelling near the peak at Takasago." Even then, it would seem, the allusion had become sufficiently well worn to permit irony without impiety.

But although I cannot feel, much less believe in, the mystical dimension of this play, I admit that others can and do. After seeing a sequence of his plays I asked Mr. Umewaka what his most challenging role had been, and he replied: "Today's 'Takasago,' because it portrays a god."

## ETERNAL GREEN, VAIN THOUGHTS

What *is* inconstancy, really, but time itself? I quote from *A Tale of Flowering Fortunes*: "On the Day of the Rat, the pines at Funaoka impressed everyone with their eternal green . . ." That happened almost a thousand years ago now. Even if Zeami is correct, and those pine trees have up to nine thousand years more of life, someday they will be gone. As we read in an eighth-century poem from the *Manyoshu*, "the maiden's crimson

---

*Hare reminds us that it likewise expresses allegiance to the sovereign. Here for instance is a couplet of Zeami's: "I celebrate my lord in the aged pine, / expecting him to live ten thousand years."

face is gone forever with the woman's three duties to obey, and young white flesh is destroyed forever with the wife's four virtues." To whom, then, is her husband being faithful?

In Nara a five-tiered pagoda stands almost obscured by a pine tree, and as dusk comes on, its greenish-grey tiled roofs increasingly come to resemble the pine needles in hue; its wooden walls resemble the tree; only the white panels, subdivided into hexagram-like patterns by the wooden railings, stand out. Someday this too will be gone.

Through March's bare branches, a pine tree's swaying can be seen. When spring comes, new leaves of other trees will hide this view; the pine will be lost.

In the Nara period, a noncommissioned officer of the frontier guards likens rows of pines to "my own people! / They stood just so / As they came out / To bid me farewell." — Then what? The farewells end; isolation begins.

A woman loves a man and marries him. They promise to keep faith with one another. Someday death will end their faith even if they lie together in the same grave — or is this not so? Why not insist that it is not so? Once both parties have reverted to soot and dust, how can it do any harm to call their fidelity eternal? (Even Komachi was eternally faithful — to herself.) In the spectacular "Izutsu," the *shite*, ghost of a dead man's multiply betrayed woman, grieves for the love she cannot forget. Her lover was Arihira no Narihira, who composed the poetic core of *The Tales of Ise*. "His name alone lives on," sings the chorus in "Izutsu." And we hear that the temple named after him has long since collapsed into the mold. "An ancient pine is rooted in the mound." Hare sees the pine as ironic, given that Narihira's bone-dust lies beneath it; I am not so sure.

In Kawabata's typically understated novel *The Old Capital* (1962), twin sisters separated almost at birth discover each other when they have become women. Chieko has been raised by foster-parents in the refined culture of Kyoto; Naeko is a peasant girl in the mountains. A young man in love with Chieko mistakes Naeko for her. After recognizing his mistake he nonetheless proposes to Naeko, who remarks (and it is precisely this that Mishima's Noh plays react against): "Even when I'm an old woman of sixty, won't the Chieko of his illusions still be as young as you are now? . . . The time never comes when a beautiful illusion turns ugly."

Of course by symbolizing attachment the pine tree necessarily represents imprisonment also. The *shite*'s situation, which is to say ours, is grounded in yearning for an inconstant illusion. Hence the fundamental contradiction of life itself. About her ex-lover a geisha writes: "I couldn't break the bonds of my insane attachment to him . . . I was writhing and squirming like a snake left for dead but alive." How does this differ from the anguished constancy of a widow? How is it inferior to the loyalty of Takasago?

In the museum in Kanazawa I see a vermilion-and-pale-green checkerboard undergarment from the Edo period, the vermilion squares enclosing cloud and treasure-ring patterns, the green ones containing cranes in diamonds. This robe was worn by the *shite* in the second act of "Takasago." The farewells ended centuries ago. The men who wove and acted in this garment are all dead. Surely even Takasago must feel bereft in time. Why wouldn't *she* writhe like a snake? Malraux writes that "all art is a revolt against man's fate," and even when Noh advises submission to fate, revolt being attachment, all the same, Takasago stands firm, and Mr. Umewaka worries that today's kimonos will remain usable for the merest hundred and fifty years! Is that or is it not insane attachment? If not, what is it?

The pines that grew together dance in the wind — and one of them falls, then the other. Why? Every literary critic has his theory as to what brings actors and spectators together in the Noh theater. As Pinguet says in his essay on Japanese suicide, "love is a madness, but therein it is pure, like flame, empty and transparent . . . the most touching truth is the supreme innocence of gratuitous suffering and gratuitous love, which takes fire and burns away unexplained . . ."

The instability of human love is fundamental to the *Tale of Genji*, and to Komachi's verse, not to mention "Matsukaze" and "Izutsu." The abyss between us can be bridged only provisionally. The feminine grace that I long for and, if I am lucky, consume may not suffice to maintain my decency and responsibility to the woman I love. Such was the case with *Genji*'s eponymous hero, whose myriad women could count on his support but not always on his attentive presence in their lives. And so a twentieth-century scholar concludes, perhaps a trifle glibly, that "there are fundamental barriers created by society and the marital system" of Heian times "which even the most devoted, sensitive, and well-intentioned lovers cannot cross." Accordingly, "it is the women" in the novel, not Genji, "who come to a deeper, albeit bleaker, vision of love and marriage." It is certainly true that in the period when the *Genji* and the various Noh plays under consideration were written, women enjoyed far less power than men. All the same, the women to whom I am drawn seem no less likely to break my heart than I to shatter theirs; and even Genji grew sad at the end.

As a man and a woman chant together in the Noh play "Nishikigi," "Perhaps with love it is always so: vain days, vain thoughts unnumbered, and no way to forget."

Another Noh play ("Aya no Tsuzumi"): "The anger of lust denied covers me like darkness."

But attachment, in its epiphanies, at least, can approach the oblivion of Nirvana. In "Izutsu" we hear this about the lovely and loving *shite*: "At nineteen I first pledged love with him, she said, and vanished in the shadows of the well curb . . ." Of course her fate is to haunt her lover's tomb, which sometimes becomes the well into which he and she once gazed; now she is immortal because her loneliness cannot die. But must this be the human situation? In the Greek myth of Baucis and Philomen, a poor but contented old couple ask the gods for nothing but to die at the same time. When their moment comes, they turn into a pair of trees. If death is, as I hope it to be, oblivion, they will certainly be spared the vain thoughts unnumbered; if there is postmortem consciousness, then hopefully their proximity will be a comfort.

What about the rest of us? Our story tells itself in the drama I find most affecting of any: "Matsukaze."


### SALTMAKERS' TEARS


Although the play was performed even earlier, as a *dengaku*, much or most seems to have been written by Zeami, with one sequence near the beginning credited to his father. In that epoch, "Izutsu" was considered to express the highest artistic level, that of "peerless charm," while "Matsukaze" achieved merely the "flower of profundity." I disagree.

The plot has already been summarized: A travelling priest comes to Suma, and finds a pine tree bearing a wooden memorial tablet and a poem. — Suma is, like any other spot on this Noh stage that we call the world, rich in ghosts. It especially epitomizes loneliness. In the Genji Picture-Scrolls we see the Shining Prince himself seated with two male companions in a thatched-roof pavillion, watching the black moon rising through a hole in the dark-flecked goldness above the pines of Suma. When, if ever, will he be permitted to return to the capital? And so he writes poems and seduces a young lady in nearby Akashi. — But this memorial tablet discovered by the *waki* relates more overtly to other ghosts; for a villager now informs him that here is the grave of the sisters Matsukaze, "Pining Wind,"* and Murasame, "Autumn Rain." Night is falling. The priest sees a salt shed, and asks for shelter there. It belongs, of course, to the two ghosts, who finally overcome their shame and let him stay. They tell him the story of how the exiled courtier Yukihira† chose them for his own. (Genji himself makes allusion to Yukihira. Hokusai has left us a sketch of his own imagined Yukihira, who huddles over his outdoor writing table, his eyebrows high painted dots in Noh mask style, and in the background, no doubt in reference to the sisters, we find a steep hill of pine trees and rain.) "He changed our saltmakers' vestments for damask robes, scented subtly with fragrance." Three years later, he was recalled to grace, and died, "so young! . . . Now the message we both pined for would never come."

He had condescended to cross the abyss to them; they had gratefully crossed the void to him; now he was not merely beyond them but *gone*, right out of this crazy-edged world, which is tipped and tilted, above all, broken, with the long twisted snow-flesh, clouds and lichened blocks of it spilling down like milk from a shattered pitcher. Where did he go? Perhaps he now dwells with Yokihi, better known as Lady Yang.

---

*In "Hanjo" a similar pun on pining and pine trees is offered by the *shite*, the prostitute Hanago.

†He was the elder brother of Narihira, the clever acrostic poet and situational acrobat of eros, whose verses about irises imparted to the Eight Bridges of Mikawa a poetic glow that lasted a thousand years; Narihira as we have just seen, lives on in Noh.

The two tokens he left them, his cloak and hunting hat, increase the torment. Matsukaze drops the cloak, picks it up, as unable to forget as that lovelorn geisha who squirmed like a snake. And so the play's sadness grows as lush as snow on the roofs in the zone that Kawabata called Snow Country. Presently Matsukaze's insanity makes her mistake a pine tree for Yukihira. In the end, the two sprites beseech the priest to pray for their rest. Then they fade away.

The site of Yukihira's exile, and Genji's, also encompasses Atsumori's stupa, where the nighttime sea shows itself across railroad tracks as a row of yellow lights underlined by their funneling reflections. Atsumori's eponymous Noh play informs us that the defeated Heike warriors took on the lives of saltmakers for a time, awaiting the last battle. Meanwhile, Atsumori's spirit masquerades as a grasscutter during the first act. In the second, the Honsho School sometimes employs a *juuroku* mask; I have seen one from the sixteenth century that is very white-skinned and infantile, the expression of the mouth similar to a *ko-omote*'s, the eyes perhaps a trifle more open and the lower lip definitely fuller, like a true girl's, but in place of long womanly locks wrapping around his forehead and cheeks, his bangs go ruler-straight across his forehead. His thin eyebrows slope up and out.

The yellowish clatter of a local train rushes behind Atsumori's stupa, almost bisecting it. Crickets and leaves gild this diminished thing with whatever *sabi* can be obtained in its courtyard with cars before it and the train behind it. It stands still and sad, a forgotten giant in five stone parts.

The walk is short from there to Suma-dera Station, which can feel lonely with its late night electric humming, cigarettes, beer and coffee glowing in the vending machines; crickets; a man's singing voice, recorded or not, coming from the Pony Coffee Shop, no sea smell at all, but a plenitude of asphalt, concrete, lights and gratings; and from there it is an even briefer walk to Matsukaze-do, the memorial for Matsukaze and Murasame.

Here a sculpted pine whose leaves are as clouds inclines itself before three cages, before the middle of which hangs a thick braided rope ending in a bamboo knocker. Behind the latticework, twin bouquets in twin vases may perhaps represent the two sisters; my interpreter does not know. Behind them stands another latticework window whose dark-

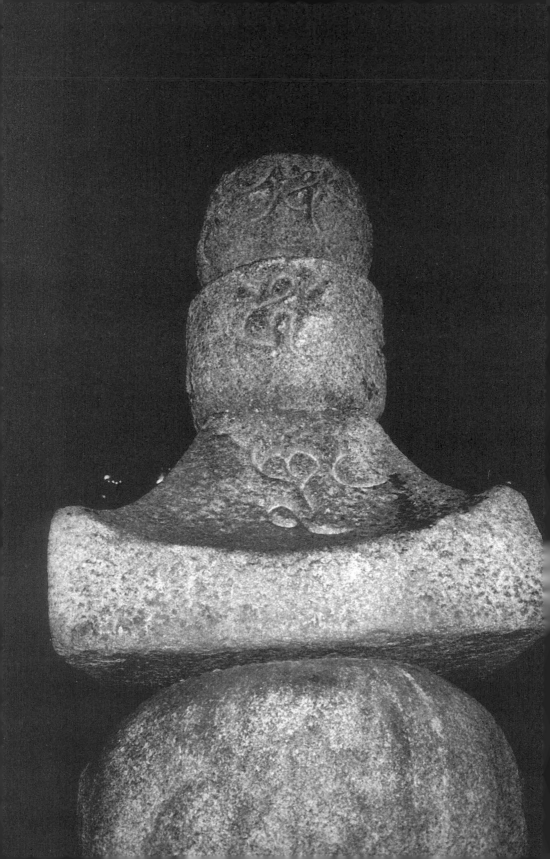

ness occasionally blooms with reflected headlights. As for the righthand cage, bulbous rock objects and one feminine-seeming doll stand arrayed in bibs behind another more slender rope. In front of the cage is a teapot, which may for all I know be a dipper of purifying water. And in the lefthand cage, behind the sculpted pine that I first mentioned, remains an impressive stump, supposed to be the remains of the pine tree on which Yukihira hung his clothes. The sculpted pine is the one he planted. Here he supposedly lived and met the two sisters. Then they moved away to die, somewhere up the hill. I could not find their tombs, but I did go to Suma-dera Park, where from a pavilion on a black pond streaked with ovoid pillars of pale light I watched a hotel's orange window-lights and especially the consecutive lobby or restaurant brightnesses of its first level bleeding greenish-orange onto the black ripples of the pond; to the north I could see the silhouette of hills, and somebody thought that the two sisters might be buried there.

## MASKS OF FEMININITY

Donald Keene insists: "It makes no sense whatsoever to imagine Matsu-kaze's height or coloring, or even to ask if Yukihira was equally in love with both sisters or favored Matsukaze over Murasame. Such matters are not mentioned in the play and therefore, almost by definition, they are irrelevant." All the same, being an ape in a cage, I will imagine what I choose. For the most enduring incarnation of the true flower is that of the image, or the ghost. If I were a Norseman, my vision would give them both white arms. Were I Japanese, they would have black hair; and had I lived in old Egypt I would have likened their hair to lapis lazuli. — Now that we have gotten all that out of the way, why not imagine Matsukaze in a *waka-onna* mask? So the Kanze School portrays her. The mask carver Ms. Nakamura imagined that a *waka-onna* would be more appropriate for Matsukaze than the younger *ko-omote*, because she must still be beautiful but had already begun to suffer. Indeed, this is the mask now commonly used for performances of the play. But until sometime in the seventeenth century, Matsukaze was considered sufficiently careworn to be expressed by the *fukai* instead.

The rarer *fushikizo* mask, which closely resembles a *waka-onna* and is sometimes considered to be one, can also be employed. I have seen a photograph of a *fushikizo* used for this role. It partakes of the narrow oval of an *ukiyo-e* beauty's face, although the latter's lips are much tinier, her nose more angular and pronounced, her willow brows more elongated. Its carver describes it thus: "*Yuki* style with the nose tilted to the right. The cheekbone on the right is lifted sharply like a *yase-onna*'s, while the left cheek is full and round. Therefore, the lips are round like a *ko-omote*'s and with a smile on the left, but are noble like a *zo-onna*'s on the right. Left and right should not be made the same."

This amalgamation makes me envision Matsukaze rather differently than I would have otherwise. You may recall that the *yase-onna*, skinny woman, portrays the pathetic aspects of vengeful female ghosts; and the pathos of Matsukaze's situation is all too evident, I resist considering her as vindictive; she seems too gentle and literally unworldly for that. But this only goes to prove yet again the correctness of Mr. Umewaka's dictum that "the mask is most important always." What is grace? What is a woman? Why should the tilt of a *fukai* mask's nose determine what that mask best performs?* And so what signifies the lift of a cheekbone? Since the old Native American lady with high cheekbones whom I once met on a Greyhound bus was not, insofar as I could tell, a sadly vindictive ghost; since, in short, the predictive and diagnostic virtues of physiognomy have been discredited, recognizing the hint implied by a specific choice of Noh mask, and allowing our interpretation, and resulting aesthetic pleasure in it, to be guided accordingly, will always unsettle me a trifle. But just as Claudio Arrau's performance of Chopin's "Nocturnes" and fugues is so profoundly warmer and more hushed than Daniel Barenboim's that we could almost be listening to two different compositions, so a Matsukaze whose madness has literally split her face, like the ghost of Yokihi danc-

---

*This is no exaggeration. The carver Hori Yasuemon writes: "Kanzesoke has the beautiful *tsuki* and *yuki fukai*. This mask," an original by Echi, and literally soaked in Zeami's sweat, "is *a tsuki* and has the nose tilted left. The expression on her eyes is very gentle and full of love. Ideal for expressing the loneliness of losing a child or beauty in sadness. The other *fukai*, 'Snow,' has the nose tilted to the right, and is highly effective in scenes like 'Neya wo nozokunayo' in 'Adachigahara'. . . . It must have been made for special effects and scenes."

ing out the everlasting pain of "Rainbow Skirts" in a moon-style *ko-omote*, is alien to a Matsukaze who incarnates the perfect coherence of sweet sadness.*

In any event, narrower than a *ko-omote*'s face, the *fushikizo*'s offers its audience dark red lips parted in a smile of knowing submission to pain. Turned to the left, the face expresses a readiness to smile even as the lower lip seems on the verge of trembling. Angled right, it seems more resigned. (Doubtless other viewers would see it differently.) Knowing as I do that this *fushikizo* can represent madness, I find myself elongating the eyes and mouth-slit in my memory, haunted by, and yes, I confess it, allured by that smile, that smile of pain.

When I asked Mr. Mikata which masks he might consider using to play each of the two sisters, he replied: "Procedurally both are *ko-omote*, but it can be up to the actor; one could use any woman mask."

"Would you consider a *fukai* or must each woman always be very young?"

"In the case of 'Matsukaze,' the hardship is not really related to the age. Time is not conspicuous in this matter. Our information says thirty years. In "Izutsu" it is also eternal, since in childhood they got married. Both have others and got separated and still they are in love."

"Which gestures would you use to differentiate Matsukaze from Murasame?"

"Basically when you show a distant scene, both are lined up like this" — and his hands went out. "When you want to put focus on the *shite*, the other players stand still and do this, while only the *shite* moves. What is interesting is, there is a scene where you scoop seawater. In the Kanze School, just the *shite* and the chorus does it, because the focus is on the elder sister, the *shite*. Even if you are looking at distant scenery, focus is on *shite*. In the Kita School both sisters sing together, and focus will be on both. That is in first half, but in second half, their feelings are in conflict, and the procedure alters."

---

*Some Japanese poets and essayists have argued that *sabi*'s implicit pleasure in the yearning for past beauty may be still deeper than the pleasure of seeing the beauty still incarnated; and it has always been in just this way that I prefer to experience "Matsukaze," the grief (which in its raw form is for any empathetic observer ghastly to witness) at least partially purified into beauty, as in Kawabata's most exemplary novels.

Who then is Matsukaze? How does this ape imagine her?

A poem in the *Manyoshu* remarks that the fisher-girls of Shika, who could not have been too dissimilar to those of Suma, almost never find time to comb their hair, so busily must they drudge at seaweed-gathering and salt-burning. I imagine that they often stank of smoke and sweat. Much later, Hokusai illustrates a thirteenth-century poem about burning seaweed on the beach of Matsuo, which faces Suma. Two men are stacking bundles of kelp; a man blows on the fire and a woman feeds it; meanwhile, two other women depart with their double buckets of salty ashes on poles across their shoulders. One leans forward, her feet splayed, and the other throws her shoulders back, gazing upward. How then could Matsukaze and Murasame not have had red, callused hands, sooty faces and unloosed, matted tresses? The translator Tyler insists, however, that some fisher-girls were entertainers and prostitutes. Lady Nijo mentions meeting on the isle of Taika some nuns who had once been such: "They would perfume their gowns in hopes of alluring men, and comb their dark hair, wondering on whose pillows it would become disheveled. When night fell they would await lovers, and when day broke, grieve over the separation."

These were very real women, to be sure, with real boxwood combs, and my book-acquaintanceship with them encourages me to imagine Matsukaze's height *and* coloring, thus:

One hot sad night I lay tormented by the indifference and evasiveness of the woman I loved, who had once cleaved to me with wild passion. She now communicated with me at rarer intervals and more superficially; when I asked her what was the reason for this change in her she irritably closed the subject. On various occasions she told me that she was tired, that she hardly knew whether we were lovers or friends, that she reserved the right to refrain from saying *I love you* whenever she liked. She had gone away, found a perfectly practical reason not to see me on her return, then gone away again. I telephoned her and she did not answer; once she would have answered immediately. It seemed only too clear that our attachment must soon end. And so that night, having stayed up late in hopes that she would call, I slept very little, mostly trying to find a comfortable way to dispose my body, wondering how to endure the aching of my heart. And then into the room there drifted someone in a pale nightgown, someone tall, with long hair; and I realized that she had come to me. In a single graceful motion she slowly pulled the nightgown over her head and was naked. Then she lay down beside me. All this had happened before, especially in recent months when we had frequently grown silent and bitter with one another, so that I went to bed alone; waiting rigidly on my back in the darkness with a child's hurt pride until she finally came silently in to me. And so this new visitation was not exactly surprising. All the same, there had been an instant when she first came in when I had not known who she was; and then there was the *silence* of her silence, the luminous pallor of her nightgown, and the way she approached me without seeming to move her feet, just as a Noh actor could have done. And when she got into bed with me, that, too, was all in one motion. Now she had come to me, and the grief in my chest was instantaneously relieved. Then in the next instant I awoke, with her far away, of course, and at once my heart ached as if a sledgemallet had struck it. Until dawn I lay in misery, but also in gratitude at the loveliness of the visitation, during which I had not even seen her face as more than a pale blur in the darkness. Her phantom caused me pain, as Matsukaze's vision of her absent lover did for her; yet how glorious it had been to see it, like watching the Noh play itself . . .

Zeami has said that the flower does not exist in and of itself; and perhaps another of attachment's errors is to feel that it does, in which case, even though "the mask is most important always," it remains nothing without the actor to animate it. She had been my flower. Now what was she?

After our final quarrel, which I desperately precipitated and angrily concluded because I wanted a resolution (she told me that I could keep her even now if I would only stop making demands; but the way I saw it, I was already losing her, and what I asked was merely for her to become again to me what she had once freely and passionately been), I exchanged the desperation of losing her for the anguish of having lost her, and *that* was as reliable as a friend. When I was younger I would have done almost anything to ameliorate this feeling, but now that I was older like a ghost, I realized that anguish is constancy.

But what was it I was longing for? I still think I did right, when she began to turn away from me and many efforts could not win her back; to leave her of my own accord before she glided entirely off the stage. Glide away she did, to a better place where she need not think of me; and all I could do was wait on my side of the rainbow curtain, imagining the joy she felt on ascending into this resplendence; nearly her last words to me were that she had no time to open the conversation.

As the days without her passed, my anguish naturally deepened. So did my constancy. But I remained merely human.

The constancy of Matsukaze and Murasame is as white as cherry-blossoms; their agonies give off the fresh smell of the wind in Nara.

Only a mask can be utterly constant. The mask possesses the true flower — as also, I suppose, does a ghost.

"Now the message we both pined for would never come." But love itself remains, in much the same way as a Noh mask floats in the darkness like a Tanizaki heroine's face, while a living woman has a neck — and, by the way, "as a last step," advises *Marie Claire* magazine, "always blend around the jawline and down the neck — just blurring the line between fact and fiction." In the *ko-omote* mask called "Flower," carved, so they say, by Tatsuemon, and one of his Three Treasures, that pallid face, ever so dreamily smiling, gazes through me, the face of a red-lipped, black-toothed, high-eyebrowed girl who has just climaxed, I see darkness in the pupils of her half-closed eyes. Flower's face widens toward the chin, like a firm pear from the moon's best tree; her pinkish-pale cheeks are shining at me, and the parting of her hair is very white. On the other side of her face the lips seem a darker scarlet against the dark wood; the eye-holes are simple goggling roundnesses, above which, in characters of gold, the following has been written: "Received from Lord Hideyoshi, the *ko omote* 'Flower' . . . among the three best masks in the world, an original."

# 31

# Kagekiyo's Daughter

## *"Semimaru" and the Plays of Separation*

And so constancy is attachment, which condemns us *shite*s to mistake perishable manifestations of this floating world for our already perished fellow ghosts with whose beautiful heart-flowers we remain enthralled, anguished — but in some Noh plays, as in life, constancy to a principle requires us to detach ourselves from people we love. Unfortunately, even then, unless we withdraw from the world as monks and nuns, our principled constancy merely resolves into another form of attachment. For instance, *bushido*, the way of the warrior, which requires the utmost loyalty, self-discipline, uprightness, courage, endurance of pain, will still, as Mr. Umewaka has told us,* consign a man to hell for having taken life. All the same, the plays assert that steadfast defense of the lord, or of honor itself, remains equivalent to faithful love; and they honor it accordingly. Noh's critique of attachment is far more

---

*See above, p. 20.

ambiguous than it pretends. And how could matters be otherwise? A seventeenth-century treatise explains that "the Way of Heaven has no love for" the fighting man, "yet has to make use of him."

Once in Nara when I saw the play "Ebira," which means *quiver*, Kofuku-ji's white-clothed priests came clicking onstage in their wooden clogs; one bore a sword in a red lacquered scabbard; and presently the *shite* was extending his fan of many metallic colors as the musicians played faster; his kimono consisted of filigreed golden diamonds upon blackness; his soul was a bearded, moustached mask which wore a white headband and an immense black axehead of hair, the rest of its locks spilling almost to the navel and down the middle of the back. With its immensely wide golden legs and arms it sometimes seemed inhuman, especially when it flashed fan and sword so fiercely. What I felt resembled my sensations on seeing my own era's soldiers on the rubble-stage of this half-ruined world; they patrol from one burnt pine tree to the next, wearing wide-flaring helmets, swollen-shouldered uniforms, cartridge belts and heavy guns. — Who are they? What have they done? — "Mission accomplished!" crows the President.

In his eponymous play, the exiled, senescent warrior Kagekiyo rejects his daughter's care: "The end is near: go to your home; pray for my gone soul." We are informed that love of woman scarcely ever prevented the Japanese warrior from doing his duty as he saw it; and even though he calls her "candle to my darkness, bridge to salvation," this man, like other warriors defiled by blood and death, can hardly expect his daughter to save him from hell. Perhaps he is truly better off alone. Did the affections of Matsukaze and Murasame do *them* any good? Their pine tree fidelity reminds me of the old poem by Ariie about being in one's rainy garden, one's sleeves wet from pine tree wind so that one almost wonders whether tears from some secret grief have dampened them — or, still more to the point, the nightmare image in an equally ancient Shunzei poem of a dead wife lying eternally under the moss, listening to the pine-winds of midnight.

But what about what would have been best for Kagekiyo's daughter? Well, never mind her.

"What should he have done?" I once asked Mr. Mikata, who replied: "The pride of a Japanese man at that time was this: When you were a strong warrior you should not think about any woman or girl. But this Kagekiyo has humane sentiment, and when the Heike declined, he did not want to see the Genji's prosperity, so he damaged his own eyes, became a beggar and relied on local people, living in a shabby hut. There at this time, his daughter visited him. Of course he wanted to see her. But his pride that remained in his bone said that this is not my daughter."*

In the play itself, the chorus sings that this once great man who hosted multitudes now feels shame at exposing to her his wretchedness; moreover, he wishes to spare his "flower so delicately tended," his girl in a box, the humiliation of being known as a beggar's daughter. And so poor Hitomaru, who voyaged all the way from Kyoto, only to be dismissed, literally pushed toward the bridge and the rainbow curtain, departs with "no remembrance other" between them than his "I stay" and her "I go."

No matter how attachment incarnates itself, says Noh, the finite will continue hatefully toward infinitude; the soul will be unable to die. Like erotic attachment, the love between parent and child must also be dissected by death or separation, and then what? Every human bond is a trap.

In the Noh play "Michimori," we watch the eponymous Heike hero (played by Mr. Mikata) drinking with his wife for the last time, and then the Genji attack increases; so he must leave for war, all the while thinking of his wife, but fighting hopelessly until the end. We see the actor slowly, darkly gliding in a middle distance between the lamps and the void where the audience sits, his golden fan a subdued flash in the darkness. He seems to rise up to an immense height, then to shrink down to the level of the chorus, folding away his fan. Later I will remember how the yellow cylindrical torch-lamps, two open flames, made the stage a soft golden beige. Then came silence, all still except for the flickering of the two flames . . . and suddenly sang the flute, followed by the first beat of the hollow drum.

What could Michimori have expected? — Nothing but death. — Did he put his wife out of his mind, then? — I hope not; in fact, I hope that he loved her as he died, leaving her with understanding.

---

*I inquired as to which position or gesture was appropriate when Kagekiyo first saw his daughter, and the answer caught me off guard as usual: "There is no particular move."

Accordingly, Michimori, like the Inoue geisha, had better "prepare a mind of mirrorlike emptiness." Indeed, it has been said that "the hieratic calm and simplicity" of Noh is "in absolute harmony with the *bushi* ethos, the life of a samurai swinging like a pendulum between sudden and violent action and quiet, contemplative repose."

## DEAD WHITE LIGHT

Noh's violence has most often to do with severance of ties.

The typically loss-centered Noh play "Semimaru" portrays two cast-off Emperor's children, the sister having been expelled because she is mad, the brother because he is blind. A functionary shaves the brother's head and makes him a priest. He consoles himself that his life in either a palace or a hut would be short-lived in any case. He tries to believe that in abandoning him to this wilderness, his father is helping him to atone for whichever sin from his former life made him blind. His sister Sakagami meets him accidentally, hearing the Imperial beauty of his lute-playing. It is never explained why it is that she must leave again, but she does, and both weep at their parting.

Semimaru may never have existed, but if he did, his hut would have overlooked Lake Biwa, in the borderpoint called Otsu, which receives two mentions in *The Taiheiki*. Meanwhile, on the south shore of Lake Biwa, Choan-ji is the site of "Seki-dera Komachi." Otsu is not called Otsu anymore, but if you go there you will find a Semimaru Shrine proclaiming itself by means of a grimy torus on the far side of the railroad tracks, followed by a curtain of worn and flaking moss, the remnants of a fence with roof-tiles on them all in an ugly heap, a rusty shed, stone lanterns, a small platform, probably for dancing, the central room or *honden* with its pallid bell-pull and its latticed windows, to which written wishes are attached (help my son pass his exams; help my aunt recover from her illness), written on the shingle-like pieces of wood called *ema* (literally, picture-tablets). Around all four sides of the *honden* runs a roofed walkway. It is dank and dark. Within the *honden* stands another platform with "paper hair" hanging for purification and a curious table which in shape and position resembles an altar.

In a Hokusai drawing, which was never colored and printed as a woodcut, we see the blind man as strong and youthful, with long black hair and a black moustache and beard. His biwa projects from behind his back as if he were carrying a living turtle. Travellers come and go on the road before him that he cannot see. He leans backward, resting on his stick, dreaming and perhaps even smiling, with his hut lushly thatched behind him and a tree in leaf as a doorpost.

But in the Noh play, Semimaru wears such a glossy white dead masked face!* He stands in a pale yellow robe and a longer blue-crested underrobe, gazing down through the audience's feet into blindness. Two attendants follow behind, holding a slanted framework box over his face, a red square in the middle of it. It must represent a palanquin.

What is there to say about his mask? It is dead white light itself. But I think this only because I know it represents a blind man. If it were a *ko-omote* I would enthuse about its milk-white beauty. It *is* beautiful, and delicate.

The two men vanish with the litter-frame. No one will convey him anymore.

The green-clad old messenger in the tall hat kneels before Semimaru, who stands still, listening.

Two members of the chorus strip off his whitish-yellow cloak, revealing the greyish undercloak. Then they place a poor man's pointed hood on his head, while the messenger stares sadly into space.

Semimaru stares straight ahead, while the chorus gazes at his hands. Now comes the melodiously sorrowful, slightly wobbling male singing of Semimaru in dialogue with the equally sad and deeper bass of the messenger, who presently advances to bestow upon him the wide conical hat of priesthood. Semimaru feels this object, then sets it gently onto the stage; and the messenger brings him a slender staff of blindness, at which the hip drummer begins to chant "*Whooh!*" and taps his drum. Presently the cho-

---

*In the performance I saw at the National Noh Theater in Tokyo, Mr. Umewaka was in the chorus, being one of many kneelers in dark robes gazing past Semimaru's hut while the blind man himself, led by an attendant, slowly came across the bridge. (The *tsure* Semimaru was played by Kanze Tetsunojo.)

SEMIMARU'S SHRINE IN OTSU.

rus begins to sing together, magnificently grieving, while the hip drummer chants, "*Whooh! Whooh!*" and the two protagonists face each other.

And so his messenger and attendants leave him alone forever at Otsu.

We see the white flash of Semimaru's skullish mask from within the bamboo skeleton that his well-wisher Hakuga no Sammi has built for him. We see Semimaru in his cage as the rainbow curtain rises and the rainbow-lovely sister glides gorgeously forth, bearing a branch of madness in just the same way as any expresser of Zeami must carry a branch of flowers. Her name means "upside-down hair." The gleam of the electric stage-light rests upon her white forehead and upon the darkness of her human throat. The chanting man in the female mask (a *zo-onna* or *masugami*) is the lovely girl in the shining robe, gliding on her white-*tabi'*d feet. Her costume is peach-golden and metallic.

SEMIMARU IN PALANQUIN.

The Kanze family owns a certain fifteenth-century *masukami*\* mask by Yasha; it is "the face of a woman possessed by a god." We are informed of its appropriateness for the role of Sakagami among others. The face, which is of a pale terracotta color, cannot be called beautiful; to me it even seems a trifle coarse. Two diagonal creases roof off each side of the nose-bridge; dimples "convey the faith of this character in the gods." Thin and crooked strands of hair twist down the cheeks. Simultaneously smiling and grimacing, gazing right through this floating world, perhaps even seeing beyond the rainbow curtain, this rather squat-nosed face seems perpetually on the verge of laughter or tears.

In the performance which I now describe, the face was much whiter.

Semimaru stares sightlessly at her from his cage while she sings on the bridge. Precisely when he becomes aware of her we cannot tell; we

---

\*The same as a *masugami*. What can we do in this floating world, but let the transliterations fall where they may?

have already heard Zeami define fascination as a sensation experienced prior to the consciousness of the sensation, and no doubt understatement is nicely conducive of such effects. When a Noh mask gazes at me just after its embodiment has crossed the pine tree bridge into my world, or when a woman whom I feel for studies me and I do not know what she will do, then I most certainly tend to be fascinated. Semimaru, of course, is not a person at all, but the representation of certain aspects of regal patience, poesy, filial loyalty, disempowerment and death. But because it is my nature to want to kiss the mask, invading it with my passion and my belief, I wonder all the same just when he senses the presence of his sister?* He wonders aloud if it is Hakuga no Sammi whom he hears. Sightlessly he gazes at the rainbow curtain from behind which she came and behind which she will go. She arrives on our side of the bridge, glides and whirls about (in decorous Noh stillness, of course), then raises her branch and begins fencing with it. The white mask leans forward at the very edge of the stage as if the madwoman it portrays will let herself fall off into the dry moat of white stones. It dances almost all the way back across the bridge — a rare sight, which I recall seeing before only in a Komachi play — and slowly returns. It comes and goes. It is the *shite* Sakagami,† played by Kanze Kiyokazu. Like

SAKAGAMI.

her brother, Sakagami has been cast out. The rainbow curtain will not rise for her, but she stares at it for a long time. And this is what I remember most from that slow sad performance: the eerily smiling mask of the crazed sister.

---

*As an American dance critic remarked: "You become really absorbed at a play when Romeo is not only distinct and spontaneous, but also makes you recognize the emotion of love, which has nothing to do with the actor personally or with acting in itself or with words in themselves."

†Sometimes transliterated Satagami.

Finally Semimaru begins to sing from his cage, the shining sister frozen on the bridge, holding her green branch, gazing away.

When they meet, they each kneel, facing one another, each echoing the hand and face gestures of the other.

He cannot see her grace, which she herself may well be barred by her insanity from knowing. And so her beauty is a gift to us alone, to us, the audience, who do not exist. And this is "Semimaru": the transient conjunction of two loving and damaged attachments. Grace is a branch of flowers; flowers die.

The chorus sings out the turn their lives have made: from jade pavilions to straw mats and rattling doors. What finally happened to Komachi in possible retribution for her cruelty to Fukakusa no Shoso has struck these two in their youth, and they suppose that perhaps they, too, are being punished for misdeameanors committed in their previous incarnations. But although at the play's beginning Semimaru bravely insisted to the Imperial messenger who left him in the wilderness that his father has treated him lovingly in expiating his karmic burden, we can scarcely celebrate the Emperor's kindness. "Denied the moon," chants the chorus, "in a straw hovel that closes out even the sound of rain, day or night, my mind runs on grief and misery."

The two masked exiles sit very still on the stage, not quite side by side, gazing out at us that we might contemplate them.

A long chant endures. Semimaru gazes down, wearing his tall bishop-like hat; the sister likewise gazes down, half smiling.

Why must she go away? One might as well ask why flowers must die. The chorus informs us that he longs for her black hair.

The play approaches its end. Semimaru bows in agony, outstretching his grey sleeves as the lovely mask of Sakagami vanishes forever behind the rainbow curtain.


WILD GRASSES


I will never forget a performance of "Sumidagawa" which I saw in the Kawamura Theater in Kyoto in 2004.

The chorus traverses the long bridge with nearly unseemly casualness.

Then two assistants come, bringing a large green-curtained box draped with greenery. They carefully position it. The flute begins to shrill. From the unknowable realm on the far side of the bridge creeps a man on his knees, or so it seems, for behind his heels stretch two long tails of his crested, wave-patterned robe. His head is cropped. He begins to sing, his ageing face staring straight into space. He is the *waki*, the boatman of Sumida River. Then he reaches his position and stops in it, gazing away from everything. Silence falls. Then the chorus howls: "*Yooooooooooo — oooooo.*"

A merchant traveller appears in this world. A madwoman comes behind them. The merchant and the ferryman agree to wait for her, so that her ravings may entertain them. When we see her face, we may well find her in a certain brooding Edo period *fukai* mask, which has flatter cheeks than the *ko-omote* but is still smoothskinned excepting the dimple-like wrinkles around the mouth. Her forehead and chin project slightly forward. The corners of the mouth do not turn upward like a *ko-omote*'s; and the eyebrows are thicker. This mask is often used for a mother who has lost her child or, as we know, for a lonely wife, for instance in "Kinuta," and indeed we are now informed, mostly by the chorus, that her son was stolen away by slave-traders from the east, and that she has lost her way while searching for him.

The golden mist-patterns of the fan she holds, at least when this play is performed by the Hosho School, are indicative of strength; and so I see her as desperate but not yet broken by despair.

And so they begin to cross the Sumida River, where long, long ago the nameless young gallant of the *Tales of Ise* declaimed a sad poem about his lady back in Kyoto, center of the world — a poem which made everyone weep. Yes, they cross the abyss; they cross the river, whose various floating, swimming and sinking lives, of course, are far too self-absorbed to be much moved by her concerns. For instance, a faded picture scroll of "Sumida in Autumn" by Chobunsai Eishi depicts passengers on a boat admiring the moon. There are faint torii in the distance. And in a woodblock by Isoda Koryusai, *circa* 1770, we see a man and a courtesan seated on a veranda overlooking the pale-green-inked Sumida River, on which a fishing boat rests, one fellow in the act of poling, the other drawing up his net; and on the far side, small figures, some of children, wander across the street-plain of Edo beneath what might be the "gazing-back wil-

SAKAGAMI AND SEMIMARU.

low," the spot where this courtesan's customer may well stand tomorrow, looking back across the river into Yoshiwara and perhaps even seeing the same lady who now leans on her elegantly sleeved elbow, facing the river, her eyes closed as the man drapes her white leg over his shoulder, entering her oysterlike vulva with an organ whose many parallel wrinkles, especially in the testicles, recall the rocky mountains of traditional Chinese painting.

Soon the crossing will be completed. Already they can see on the far bank a crowd around a willow tree. The mother asks what they are doing, and the ferryman answers that they are marking the first anniversary of a child's death. The child was, of course, her son, whom the kidnapper cast away when he became weak.

In 2005 I visited this spot. The Buddhist temple to the child, Umewaka, was destroyed in 1870; a Shinto temple replaced it. The building was saved by chance from Allied air raids. One can see a few black-ringed bullet-holes. In an apartment complex, the stele's eight characters —

three small, five large — descend within a niche of concrete wall to two geranium planters side by side, and then the shrine itself, a nondescript modern glass-and-steel cupola (which fire regulations require) enclosing the old fish-scale gable roof.

The young boy lost his father early, we read, and was deceived by kidnappers. He sickened and died at age twelve. A priest was moved by his deathbed poem, and accordingly erected this stele, planting beside it a willow tree, whose Japanese name is *umewaka*. (A young plum is a *waka-ume*.)

We see a young willow, a rope, a wrapped heap of volcanic rocks before the triple-storey freeway on whose lowest level the blue-tarped houses of the homeless focus the eye; then runs the Sumida unseen, above which the roofs of the far side call out.

Stepping away from the stele, one discovers a lovely spot in the blacktop, with the noise of children playing baseball unseen beneath the trees which rise partway up the height of the apartment monoliths, steel bridges and the milky-grey Sumida.

And so the merchant, the ferryman and the madwoman disembark. The chorus asks the crowd to disinter the corpse, so that the mother can see her son one last time.

All of them call upon Amida Buddha for his sake; even the madwoman summons the strength to do it.

Then they hear the child's voice.

Zeami, ever favoring rarefication, opined that the play would have been still more effective without a child actor in the mound, but his son Motomasa, who wrote or completed the text, thought this would needlessly increase its difficulty. It seems to me that Motomasa was correct. When I saw this performance I did not know the story at all, but the instant the child began to sing, my eyes grew damp and my throat choked up without my knowing why. As I looked around the theater, I saw tears in the eyes of many others.

The effect now closely resembles the final exchange between father and daughter in "Kagekiyo," for mother and son each ask: "Is it you?" She tries to embrace him; he goes away. The chorus chants: "What appeared to be a dear child is wild grasses thick on the tomb . . . Oh, sorrow! Nothing else remains. Oh, sorrow! Nothing else remains."

# 32

# Behind the Rainbow Curtain

*Going Home Beneath the Skin*

Once a man met, courted and won a woman who lived in Yamato.
After a time, he had to return to the capital . . .

THE TALES OF ISE

I n that archetypal Japanese romance, *Taketori Monogatari,* a lovely
moon maiden, sent down to our unworthy realm to atone for some
unnamed sin (and simultaneously to help her adoptive father, the
meritorious old bamboo cutter), gets recalled at last to the place where
she belongs. The Emperor himself cannot prevent her departure. Upon
the arrival of the radiant moon entities, his two thousand guardsmen
lose all will to shoot their arrows. Her foster parents grow pitiable with
grief, but the moon entities disdain their uncleanliness. Against her will,
Kaguyahime must take leave of them. And so one of the lunar attendants
dresses her in a celestial robe of feathers. "No longer did the maiden
consider the old man pitiful or pathetic, for one who dons such a robe is
emancipated from sorrow. She entered the carriage and soared into the
heavens, escorted by one hundred heavenly beings."

She might as well have put on a Noh robe.

In "Hanjo," the prostitute Hanago, crazed by attachment to her absent lover, quotes the old proverb that "a jewel is stitched in our robes," meaning that enlightenment lies nearer to us than we imagine, "but the sting of love makes us forget." Kaguyahime pulled the stinger out. She donned better garments. Then she remembered who she was.

Once upon a time a certain woman loved me, and my faith in our mutual attachment resembled my belief in the immortality of that ecstatic moment when the actor in the Noh mask glides out of nothingness, moving more slowly than a geisha although more rapidly than his colleague Mr. Umewaka. When Kofumi-san dances for me in that teahouse in Gion, she gazes into my eyes, so that I feel, in part deludedly, that she *sees* me; and this woman who loved me said that she saw me, truly; her face used to descend by sweet degrees onto mine as we lay together in the darkness. One morning she arose and went away. Once I comprehended that she was emancipating herself from me I entreated her to open her heart, but she had become enlightened, which must be why it is that my memory of her face has now become like my vision of that Noh actor's mask turning slowly like a hanged man in the wind, *shite* of a ghost, lovely mask of a woman offering herself to be looked at, naked in the same sense as Kofumi-san is when she dances, yet singing with a man's voice. What do I possess now but my memory of the last slow angling of Kaguyahime's face? She has returned to her native place. And Kofumi-san and Konomi-san have both gone home; they've washed away their white paint, which is called *shironuri*. As for that Noh mask turning almost imperceptibly through various jewel-degrees, hasn't that gone back to bed in its dark box?

But I remember when the mask was still vital. It was during Mr. Mikata's chamber production of "Michimori," performed in a certain temple in Kyoto. The doomed Heike warrior enters slowly, bearing the white skeleton of a boat about his waist; he sets it down on the floor within the glimmer of firelight, and the righthand torch flickers over the chorus. The woman with the man's voice is his wife, with whom of course he must soon exchange the last cup of parting, for the Genji are pressing the attack, which is to say that this is our life: Some of us die; others, stung by love, mourn them, then soon or late must follow them. The warrior now stands beside his wife within the boat. Everything is wan in the torchlight; the face of the lady in the audience beside me has grown as ivory as a Noh mask. The man stands frozen; the fan swoops; all goes grim; then the woman slowly begins to rotate and diminish. The man also kneels. He wears a gorgeous checked costume the tail of whose white sash hangs down; and in the dimness there appear to be four chrysanthemums on it. His long queue is very dark and glossy. They sit together in profile, he and she, utterly still, bloodless but for the low, trembling chants which recapitulate the sound of wind blowing across wide-mouthed earthen jars; these wind-songs are issuing from the two masks.

In time they rise. She raises her hand and he his, at the same place and rhythm.* What is she now, but a pale mothlike figure? What is he, but her morbid memory? They both pivot and freeze, with their elbows extended at the same angle. They draw apart, each one isolated in the light of a single flame.

A chilly night-exhalation has crept in, pushing out the sickening smell of ginkgo trees. The flames twist up brighter, the long silences between chants punctuated by the flickering of flamelight. Soon Michi-mori will enter on his fate more rapidly, and the bamboo quality of the drums will grow somehow more pronounced. The darkness will deepen behind him as he slowly pivots to face his wife from far away. The music will increase in pitch, volume and rhythm.

A mask gazes sideways at me, narrower than the head and wig it parasitizes, the flame behind it imparting the flicker of life to its hard flesh. The warrior mask gazes down, very pale against its crest of dark hair; and from the side its mouth is almost sad and almost cunning. Then it advances toward wife and flame, the closed fan thrust before it like a

---

*Later I asked Mr. Mikata about this gesturing in unison: "Does this symbolize unity between the couple or something different?" — "It means that both of them felt the same way," he replied. "About this move to show the sadness, for instance, both of them were about to go into the water, so they were both sad. The two of them perform the same move, so that the same movement accumulates for the audience. It's not that the timing has to be completely the same, but the fact that they do the same move which shows that both of them feel the same. So when I play a role, of course the timing is important, but rather than the superficial move, the *emotion* is most important; that has to come first, if you want to achieve expression. The superficial stage of Noh ends once the hands move or it looks beautiful or like that. We must go beyond that."

lance. According to Mr. Mikata, a fan conveys no directional meaning whatsoever. It can be a whip; open and extended it can become a sake cup, and there exists a stylized gesture for pouring the sake, but the figure that a fan-gesture makes defies deconstruction into any element but beauty itself. What then is Michimori doing with his fan? Shall we just say that he is reaching toward the one he loves while sternly pushing her away?

When the tempo increases, he must gaze away from her. She gazes after him from her flame, and then he has departed. He has set out for the capital.

The chants swell almost into shouts; the flute is now frenzied, the drumbeats as rapid as battle itself; soon it will be time to sink into Michimori's death when the chant slows and the flute blows. Then they will all go to a place I do not know. This place, like the face of a geisha, of a *ko-omote*, or of the woman who used to love me, excites my desire in part because I cannot attain it.

(Kawabata, 1934: "For me, love, more than anything else, is my lifeline. But I have the feeling that I have never taken a woman's hand in mine with romantic intentions." And perhaps the same is true of life itself, he continues; perhaps he has never taken life by the hand.)

In the *Tales of Ise*, that nameless courtier-poet whom we think of as Narihira weeps for the capital, and for his beloved there — who may be one or many women. Whenever he woos rural beauties, he condescends (in the archaic sense of the word) to bestow on them the same exquisite courtesies as he would have done for a lady in Kyoto. "Even in the provinces," the narrator enthuses, "this man did not depart from his customary behavior." There shines one more indication that someday he will return to the capital. Then all the country maidens he seduced will pine eternally, like Matsukaze and Murasame. As for him, I hope that he will achieve some measure of Kaguyahime's emancipation from sorrow — although, being a Heian noble, he would surely not forgo that bittersweet, poetic melancholy called *aware*.

As a spectator of Noh, which is to say a man of the provinces who loves beautiful women (which category includes all women), I am a backwater sort on whom grace has been occasionally bestowed. I want to hold onto my life but cannot. Year by year, it flies away up to the moon. Disobedient to my plans and wishes, my hair has gone grey. I want to keep my loves in my heart's treasure-box, but those likewise dissolve into moonbeams, either through losses and endings or through familiarity, which is of course a gain as well as a loss, but most definitely a loss! I want to understand every Noh gesture, to recognize each Chinese box of nested textual allusion; but, as I so often complain to you, I will never know either the language or the canon. Even if I could, I could never follow the *shite* behind the rainbow curtain at the end of the final act. He goes home to the moon, the capital, long lost Kyoto.

What *is* the capital? For Kawabata it can be signified by red weeping cherry trees, not to mention schoolgirls and maikos. For the lovely concubine in "Yuya" it must be the home of her dying mother. For a certain poet in the *Manyoshu*, it is youth itself; the sight of it, so he pretends, would restore his best years. For me, so I infer, it is all the women whose love I have lost, and the woman whom I love now and with whom I wish to merge utterly, but cannot, thanks to the abyss between man and woman, soul and soul. Lady Nijo and Lady Sarashina expressed kindred formulations. For Mishima the capital can be reached by means of a homoerotic violent death. For Ono no Komachi, home is youth regained. And now the capital moves to Edo, where pagoda-compounds peer out between golden clouds of ink, and Fuji lords it over the horizon across the bridge all along the avenues of booths and houses, and peering between the shoulder-poles of palanquin-bearers I covetously spy all the many inkstained woodblocks hanging in Edo's bookshops; lovely ladies sport *katsuyama* hairdos; I see the heartstopping dark blues of *ukiyo-e* skies, the courtesans of Yoshiwara; in one theater I am gladdened by the red-outlined eyes of a pale-faced Kabuki beauty; in the next, by a Noh actor in a white and gorgeous mask and a silver-turquoise kimono with gold embroidery; and then another figure, even more fantastic, comes down the bridge in a higher, narrower golden crown, like the first wearing both long dark hair and a golden fan, but its kimono is dark purple and its undergarment is yellow-gold. — Each of us who is the *shite* perceives the capital in terms of his own attachment. Never mind that; as we glide about within our world's polished wood, with a stylized pine tree as the backdrop, the chorus will remind you, our audience, what forms our particular delusions take. Here they sit, a half-dozen men, with sharp grey shoulder-winged vests over their black kimonos, and pale medallions over their breasts. In deep, stern, mournful voices, in chorus thrillingly inhuman, they sing a Shinto song.

In exile at Suma, Genji tells his best friend of his fear that he will never glimpse the capital again. As Mr. Mikata once said to me, "Suma's image is loneliness." The woman he seduces and impregnates there (she will become one of his less distinguished concubines) torments herself thus: "Born at Akashi! What a hideous thought!"

I was born at Akashi. I will never go to the capital.

Worse yet, I do not want to. When I learn that the *Kokin Shu* anthology, which first appeared in about 905, walled in for centuries the entire permissible vocabulary of poetic diction, I feel sad and stifled. I would not care to express that sadness only in whichever gestures Noh approves. Were I a woman, I would never choose to be constrained in the garments and gestures of a geisha. I prefer what Mr. Umewaka would call the easy choice.

But the *idea* of the capital as a heavenly home allures me as much as the fantasy embodied by a maiko or a man in a woman's mask.

Whenever we seek to peer into our own lives and those of others, we place ourselves in a neutrally perfect imaginary place: the capital. Only there can we discern attachments accurately.

In the ancient times of the Genji Picture-Scrolls there were the *fukinuke yatai*, the roofless houses, so that we could look in and see in stylized drawings Heian aristocrats diverting themselves. In the seventeenth-century woodblocks made to accompany Saikaku's tales we could spy on, for instance, the courtesan-turned-letter-writer, who has nearly completed her first column of calligraphy, kneeling beside her customer on the tatami mat while the maid brings a single cup of tea in her left hand. We saw their lives; they could not perceive us; we existed while they were but fictions; they were provincials, and we, residents of the capital.

Or am I dead wrong? We, the audience in the Noh theater, may possess a certain knowingness about the story, which pretends to occur uniquely but which to us may be familiar and more; we may even feel superior to the *waki*, who fails to recognize the *shite* in his first humble contemporary manifestation. All the same, we who watch are here to receive and be moved, to be, as the cliché goes, elevated. If anyone is perfect, it is Yuya or Matsukaze, not us. The mask slowly, slowly turns, beautiful, ancient and virginal. It is of the capital, and I am of Akashi. The stage radiates vital superiority in the costumes, gestures, etcetera that it bears. Some of its interest derives simply from its availability to the gaze. From a dark wooden-floored brasserie in Paris I look past the shiny brass railing which is dabbed milk-white with fingerprints, and into the stage beneath the dripping awnings — a street with ripples in the puddles on the white crosswalk, and across it, another red-awning'd café much like the place in which I sit; I see old men gesticulating, married couples slowly eating, pretty girls crossing their long white legs, and I want to watch everything. That girl in the hooded black raincoat paces in the foreground, her pale hand clenched against her ear; she must be talking on her cell phone. She finishes, deposits her hand in her pocket and goes away. Where is the privileged place? My voyeurism makes me forget that the world is in fact not a stage. But the Noh stage is truly a world set apart from mine, an island world in a moat of white stones. And that bridge over which this higher order of beings comes and goes leads not to Akashi, but to that unknown realm behind the rainbow curtain.

Is it the capital or is it something else? The antique treatise of Pound and Fenollosa informs me that the three pine trees besetting that wooden bridge from stage to curtain symbolize, in increasing order of distance, heaven, humankind and earth. Shouldn't it be the other way around? Why can't this ape understand?

I sit in a private room in the ochaya, and at last the geisha comes to me. She is so lovely I can hardly describe her. She dances for me until I begin to worry about being able to pay. I thank her; she goes; I return to Akashi. That private room, like the Noh stage, was a way station, a temporary representation of the capital.

The woman I love comes to me. She promises to be with me forever. She says that no one can *see* her as I do, that she *sees* me. Then her love departs. We leave one another. I know where she lives; I used to sleep there in her arms. No matter. I have also seen Mr. Umewaka in the mirror room behind the rainbow curtain. The far side of the painted curtain is dull. Then, from behind its dimmed down colors — I remember this from the Omi Noh Theater in Kyoto — a gap between fabric and doorway shows the crowd, the people from Akashi: the audience now waits.

But that is merely what I have seen; I have failed to see the unseeable. And that woman who used to love me, I could visit her house, but would never find her there, merely her semblance; she has departed for the capital.

> *Clutching this transient life*
> *I survive on the seaweed,*
> *Which I, soaked by waves,*
> *Gather at the isle of Irago.*

What did she do for me? She showed me how beautiful heaven is. Her flesh was red and white, like the azaleas at the Shoren-in. And what did I do for her? My plainness helped her loveliness shine all the better. The Noh actor Mr. Mikata once remarked to me that for "Kinuta" a *fukai* mask "is almost a rule. You don't use a *ko-omote*, nor a *waka-onna* either. That is because the servant of her husband wears a younger mask That way the audience will have an image that the husband may now love this younger woman." I was a *fukai* from Akashi; she was a *waka-onna* from Kyoto.

Had I been sufficiently educated in courtly custom to attach a faded chrysanthemum to my poem of resentful love, thereby expressing the neglect doubly, she might have despised me less.

I go home to Akashi, where my losses live. With every step I take away from the theater, I diminish all the more into my loneliness. Even Semimaru's palanquin-bearers are affected by this phenomenon, which resembles the falloff of sunlight according to the inverse-square law — and they know that they will be able to return home as soon as they have completed the formal abandonment of the blind prince. "I was not intended for a world in which women shackle themselves in garments that are not even made of cloth," complains Proust, who also laments the substitution of motorcars for horse-drawn carriages. "My consolation is to think of the women whom I knew in the past, now that there is no elegance left." This is likewise one of Noh's consolations. The masks bring back the Heian capital, most of which perished in the Onin Wars of the mid-fifteenth century. The capital remains as still as leaf-shadows on the white panels of the Shoren-in, where each breath of camphor afternoons is cooler and more refreshing than the last. But being from Akashi, I wander through the weedy outskirts of time, interviewing men who sit in grass or plastic lean-tos, men who gaze red-eyed and yellow-eyed at their cigarette stands which hardly anyone patronizes. I have no objections to a world in which women wear garments of metal, or shoot machine-guns. (*InStyle* magazine, January 2008: "Trend Watch: Metallics. No need to gloss things over this season — make them shine in rose gold, silver or copper." Here's a little vinyl purse, a clutch, they call it, metallically blushing at a discounted price.) I try to make the best of the fact that I was never intended for the capital, and could not expect to be welcomed there. My companions are grey water, clouds, slatey wave-shoulders, and, should I ever be so foolhardy as to seek out the capital, seasickness. (*Tales of Ise*: "The sea her world, / the fisher-girl can but gather / her dreary seaweeds . . .") All the same, I feel; I love; I perceive; hence I sincerely believe that my life here is or can be as fantastically lovely as the snake-necked cranes on a faded vermilion *nuihaku* Noh robe, each crane different, some with their triple-taloned feet open, all yellow-beaked and golden-eyed, the tops of their heads crimson like setting suns; the centers of their bodies are green-feathered in butterflylike shapes, and they wear underskirts of black feathers.

I go away, because the Noh-masked Heians have gone away. The play is over. *They* are the ones who were not intended for this world.

Not every personage in a Noh play departs by means of the rainbow curtain. The *koken*, the assistants, often leave through the tiny door at the base of the main stage, and in "The Sought-for Grave" the two *tsure* who play the roles of village maidens do the same. Because I am from Akashi, I cannot say whether they return to the same district of the capital as the *shite*. To me the capital understates itself, keeping its secrets.

The actors' costumed reflections appear in the worn gloss of a Noh stage. Then they depart across that bridgeway, whose function and appearance remind me of what the *Tale of Genji* calls "the bridge of dreams," the frail connections between man and woman, soul and world. It must be this that the shaman crosses on the Emperor's behalf when he visits Yokihi and is regaled by her dance of everlasting pain. In his journey, he recapitulates Teika's thirteenth-century tanka about the traveller who is crossing a bridge over a deep gorge: the autumn sunset lights of the far side of the chasm with loneliness, and his sleeves whip about in the wind.

How could she have stopped loving me? Why must Yuya's dance come to an end? And what is it like behind the curtain? Is it a realm of more dances, ever more exquisite, like those in Dante's *Paradiso*, or does it partake of the pallid severity of a Zen rock garden in Kyoto: raked gravel, tall narrow rock, long rock laid down, cloudlike rock, all enclosed in bright summer ivy? Surely there is a path behind the rainbow curtain to the mountains of Hagai, a place which contemporaries from our age gloss as "unidentified; but presumably it was a hill near Kasuga." Long, long ago a poet's wife died, and he wrote in the *Manyoshu* that he had been told she was in Hagai's mountains. "Thither I go, / Toiling along the stony path; / But it avails me not"; he found not even her shadow. — Somewhere behind the rainbow curtain lives her shadow and more.

To any and all of these conjectural forms, Akashi remains strikingly inferior. I suppose that when Kaguyahime dons her moon robe and then gazes on her foster parents with indifference, the home they gave her disgusts her. In *The Taiheiki* this note is sounded so frequently that it almost becomes ludicrous. For instance, one exile's "eldest daughter alone was suffered to remain in the capital, but eighteen daughters departed from the city weeping, to go to wearisome Tsukushi. How pitiful it was!" The narrator repeatedly applies this last ejaculation to ritual suicides and battle-deaths. Can exile really be on the same level as those? If so, how sad for us inhabitants of Akashi and Tsukushi!

How could she have stopped loving me? She saw a chance to escape from wearisome Tsukushi.

Of course she did not depart instantaneously; for a brief time I could witness her grace while she stood upon the bridge. All summer, until I pressed her at our final meeting, she would not say that she no longer loved me. After all, in both Noh and Kabuki the actor continues to perform while protractedly entering and leaving the stage-world by means of a special bridge or passageway. Zeami specifically advises that after leaving the mirror room at the commencement of a Noh performance, the actor ought to stop one-third of the way across the bridge, study the audience; and precisely when their expectations of his entrance song have reached the maximum, he should sing it. This he called "matching the feelings to the moment."

Akashi and Tsukushi are dreary enough. But other points of exile are even worse than these.

"And Lord Suketomo they banished to the land of Sado, making his death sentence one degree easier." Thus *The Taiheiki*. As it happens, it was to Sado that Zeami also went. In 1424 he composed *Kakyo*, that just quoted treatise which defines "matching the feelings to the moment." Some people say that it was his refusal to divulge these secret writings of his to the Shogun that caused his punishment; others speak of rivalries and vanities; no one knows anymore. In 1429 he was prohibited entry to the Sento Imperial Palace. And in 1434 they dispatched him on what must have been an exceedingly long, wearisome, perilous and sorrowful journey by land and sea, crossing the abyss. Again I think of the Noh play "Yokihi," of the Emperor's sorcerer crossing space to find the isle where Lady Yang's ghost grieves endlessly over her attachment. No doubt Zeami has played many female roles in his time; who knows whether he played Lady Yang in some lost play? Now he must play her for life.

Yes, he crosses the abyss, in keeping with Basho's haiku:

*The rough sea —*
*Extending toward Sado Isle,*
*The Milky Way.*

so that, like the infant Kaguyahime at the beginning of her parable, he has departed the true world to which he belongs, the realm of such complete perfection that the very rustling of a plebeian woman's gowns will be detected as loud and coarse; so he gets rowed through outer space, until Sado appears beneath the clouds like a long sea-mountain, an icy leaden amethyst with white snow-grooves.

Will his kindred moon beings ever descend to Sado bearing a celestial robe of feathers for him? Sado has become his mirror room. He sits enshrouded in bitterness and old age, waiting to be masked so that his performance can begin. But onstage it's only one *kyogen* after the other. Perhaps he will never again be called past the rainbow curtain.

The *shite* of the eponymous Noh play "Shunkan," left alone on Devil Island* when his two companions in exile have been recalled to the capital, chants out his situation: " 'Wait awhile and you'll come home to Kyoto,' say the voices coming faint from far away, and faint his hope . . ." He will die alone there, of course. I see a seventeenth-century Shunkan mask, carver unknown: The mask bares its teeth, in the tranquilly resigned manner of its kind; its sculpted bony prominences of cheek and chiseled forehead-wrinkles render it something between a burlwood contortion and a skull. The narrow eyes are almost flat at their lids. The mask remains caught between this world and the other; wait awhile, wait awhile. But why not hope? At very rare intervals an envoy in gorgeous robes may indeed come to us from behind the rainbow curtain, which follows its own celestial laws of permeability. Once upon a time, a lady-in-waiting of the Nijo Empress finally agreed to receive her suitor, but with curtains between them. The poem he uttered in reply contains these lines:

> *Please put aside*
> *the River of Heaven,*
> *that barrier between us.*

"Struck with admiration," the *Tales of Ise* reports, "she accepted him as her lover." And so he was permitted behind the rainbow curtain, although for how long no one knows. So why should not Shunkan, if he were patiently loyal, have been carried home across the River of Heaven?

I waited for my lover as long as I could. Unable to bear the alternative, I kept faith that she would come for me. How ordinary! The longing of the wife for the absent husband in the play "Kinuta," the yearning which the geisha song "Sekare sekarete" expresses for more than rare secret nights together, the temple bell ringing out another separation at dawn, what are any of these but drip-drops in the water-clocks of Akashi? "Wait awhile and you'll come home to Kyoto."

From *The Taiheiki*'s description, Zeami's punishment nearly recapitu-

---

*Which could have been any one of three prison islands in southeastern Japan.

lates Shunkan's, Sado being likewise "a dreadful island, unfrequented by human beings." Here Lord Suketomo's death sentence will presently be carried out after all. "The cutting is like a gust of wind. And indeed the wind of Sado is like an executioner's blade."

Standing on Sado's snow-striped sand, watching a column of snow approaching over the brownish-grey water, I find that the mountains are now nearly charcoal-dark. A cormorant flies furtively overhead. Wind chills my back; snow-devils devour ever more of the sky.

All the same, Sado's winters are no worse than Kyoto's; moreover, Zeami encountered any number of human beings there.[*] In the courtyard of Ho Sho Ji, the second temple where he reputedly lived, a haiku concerning him has been cut into a rounded boulder; and on the cemetery's edge a bamboo fence encloses a rounded stone on which he is supposed to have sat. Here, in deference to the laws of *iki* and *miekakure*, white gravel discreetly betrays itself beneath the white snow. Somewhere on the grounds (due to the shrinekeeper's absence I could not see it) resides the many-wrinkled wooden mask which they say he brought from the capital, on one occasion successfully employing it in a dance for rain.

From the gable's downspout, melted snow runs down a chain of bell-like metal cups and into the snow. Slide aside the wooden panels and you will smell incense. Gold-lettered dark pillars frame an altar-centered darkness.

In Sado there is an ancient agricultural shrine, which Lord Suketomo's executioner later dedicated to his victim. And here one also finds an outdoor Noh theater, one of thirty-three on the island, so I am told; this one is at least as old as the Edo period; of course Zeami never lived to see it. In fact even Sado's one indoor Noh theater postdates him. — Perhaps Zeami wandered to this very place, in order to visit the shrine. I imagine the refrain of his bitter blood: "To die at Akashi! What a hideous thought!" — But I, a good Westerner, believe in Progress. Now that we

---

[*]So did Shunkan. The *Tale of the Heike* reports that "there were, of course, some natives, but their speech was incomprehensible." And do you remember the two heroines of the Noh play "Matzukaze," whom Yukihira played with during his exile from the capital? Five centuries after him, Lady Nijo writes: "when I learned that we were passing Suma, I thought of the courtier Yukihira," who "had 'lived alone with tears and dripping seaweed.'" Such is the snobbery of the capital.

have thirty-four Noh theaters in Sado, I refuse to say that we're in Akashi anymore.

The pine tree, repainted in 1978, appears not on the bridge but on the rear wall of the main stage, and for some reason it is accompanied by a red sun. Leaving my shoes in the snow beneath the first step, I stand upon those grey pine boards in an ocean of white. I tread the bridge, which lacks that rainbow curtain of the thick pastel stripes, and come into the mirror room. Here the wickerwork bell of "Dojoji" awaits its next performance. Then through the door that the musicians and *koken* use I reemerge onto the stage, and gaze out from my pine island, with the painted pine at my back. Here the world begins. A white rope hangs in the dark entryway of the shrine, whose name is Dai Zen Jin Ja. Behind two snow-shouldered stone lanterns the red paint is busily flaking off a torus. Then come snowy trees. This silent silver-grey stage reminds me of snow in a silver bowl. After all, exile does not lack its own charms, categorized by the entity called *wabi*, or "desolate beauty." After awhile I begin to hear the dripping of the eaves; then when a crow caws I see and hear farther, although not yet far enough to reach the wet snow in the shade of the bamboo groves, the shining white grass-dyked rectangles of rice fields, the high northern mountains, which are lightly glazed with white; the milk-glow of waves beneath the white sky, white rain dripping from the pines; the roughly conical "Married Rocks" at the sea's edge; one of them is grooved; in this area the rock-lilies bloom in May; they die if they are taken away.

No one is sure if Zeami died on Sado. There is a tomb for him next to Kanami's, in the old capital; it may be a mere cenotaph.

It is said that he once heard the cuckoo singing on Sado, and remembered the flowers of Kyoto, because when the cuckoo sang there, the flowers were in bloom.

"I can't help thinking about the capital today," we overhear voyagers repeating on a certain New Year's Day in the tenth century. "I wonder how it all looks — the straw festoons, with their mullet heads and holly, at the gates of the little houses." And just before performances start, I myself, hearing through the curtains of Euro-American theaters what Proust compares to the sounds within an egg just before it hatches, am compelled to wonder who and what I will see. Thus likewise the moment when the geisha is giggling at the bottom of the teahouse stairs and the musician is tuning her shamisen. Will Kaguyahime herself appear to me, or shall I make do with some imitation? No doubt Zeami treasured his own anticipations.

In a Noh theater, of course, not a sound passes through the rainbow curtain. How could I have ever expected to perceive anything but silence? As a human being in a world of gods, as a lover where my beloved is, a deaf and blinking spectator in Noh theaters, I am *base*. The mask gazes at me without seeing me. It is incomparably above me.

In Kanazawa I see a shrine tree overlined with snow, people clapping three times and throwing their coins into the box with a dry rattling sound, the sky grey and yellow, in the snow a dark puddle trembling with pale gold reflected fire. What happens to those coins? Do their Platonic forms reach the capital?

Spying snow on bamboo leaves, I try to imagine snow in a silver bowl. Well, I'm a good ape; I know it must be as white as a koto's thirteen strings—

In Sado I live and breathe, my progress of inhalations and exhalations as steady as the pond of blue sky in the thunderheads above the ocean.

I see a crescent of perfect snow upon the beach's leaden sand, colored along one side, as if eyelined, with rusty grass. The bay is calmer, hence bird-ridden; the ice is hard. A line of birdprints on the snow seems to have been made by a single foot. What would it mean to tread this stage? Where could I go? Where can I go on this prison island, this world?

## THE PROPER ENVIRONMENT

What is the capital, but the abode of grace? And what is grace? What does Kaguyahime possess that a denizen of Akashi lacks? Her robe must be equivalent to one of those Edo-era Noh costumes of gold thread and silk embroidered with flowers, which outshine anything I could ever hope to wear. One would need connections in the capital to obtain such treasures. But more fundamentally, grace must derive from the woman's inner being — although the proper environment brings it out, of course. "Thus by living in the capital" and performing before refined specta-tors, writes Zeami in "Kakyo," "the actor is in the proper environment, and the insufficiencies in his art will naturally disappear." I suppose that when she departs the capital to take up residence with me in Akashi, insufficiencies in her art will naturally reappear.

Nara-era maidens combing their morning hair, will their combing slowly lose its grace once they get married and carried off to Akashi?

Gazing at my female self, quite mindful of Yukiko's categorization of her clients as narcissists, I nonetheless feel excited into joy. Have I crossed the abyss, then? Was there an abyss at all, or was the gulf, as some transgender people would have it, the merest figment of prejudice and ignorance? Who is this woman in the mirror?

When Mr. Umewaka becomes Yuya in the mirror room, who is he? Noh actors and Inoue School dancers aim to feel nothing; Odori dancers do the opposite. When the sorcerer in "Yokihi" travels through space to meet Lady Yang, when Zeami departs for Sado, when I face my own death, or myself as the opposite gender, or some biological woman whom I desire or love or whose love I have lost, or some mask of beauty, what is common to all of these?

Whatever that commonality might be, it surely lives within me already. Mr. Umewaka is his own Yuya; he cannot become entirely alien to himself. And when I first emerge into a traditional garden in Kyoto, the shrine's wooden overhang forms a space partway between inside and outside. The air touches me but my gaze continues to be framed within a rectangle, so that, to borrow from Shakespeare, the world becomes a stage. And there I am, character and audience.

The tiny eyes and lips of an Utamaro beauty bejewel the old print, and I regard their stylized grace. Utamaro and his model have both long since turned to smoke; anyhow, the woman represented by this *bijin-ga* must have been more individual than this. So has my attachment merely been tricked forth? Is deception the common element of allure in this floating world?

A beautiful woman named Nancy sits in church in Provincetown, Massachusetts, gazing diagonally, as do the congregation's other members, out of the black and white photograph; her large hands are clasped in her lap, and if she is in her middle thirties then her face is a trifle worn for a woman's but smooth for a man's. In a sweet color photograph from the following year she stands in a meadow beside her Aunt Ida May, both of them holding uprooted plants, Nancy with her left hand, Ida May with the right, and Ida May is saying something just to her while Nancy in her pink blouse and floral slip gazes again diagonally beyond us. In church Nancy had wavy hair. Now she has straight hair and bangs. The year after that, Nancy stands nude in her home in Cambridge, with her hand on her hip, looking younger than ever, large-eyed and small-breasted, so beautifully feminine, slim-bodied like an adolescent girl, and a penis hangs between her legs. In this portrait only does she gaze directly at us. Who is she? Is the mystery of who she is any more enigmatic than yours or mine, or Mr. Umewaka's? A mask is a lie, of course, but by virtue of being so, it leaves behind many of flesh's native-born accidents, asserting a specific being, and hence, if you believe that we can make our destinies, truth. All the same, who is Nancy? What does it mean to desire her as a man desires a woman? Who would Nancy be to me if I had never seen her nude, if I never knew that she possessed a penis?

I quote again in full Shun'e's advice to Chomei that

> when one gazes upon the autumn hills half-concealed by a curtain of mist, what one sees is veiled yet profoundly beautiful; such a shadowy scene, which permits free exercise of the imagination in picturing how lovely the whole panoply of scarlet leaves must be, is far better than to see them spread with dazzling clarity before our eyes.

And I also quote the seventeenth-century Chinese writer Lu Yu: "A man's true feeling for a woman does not arise from the bodily contact, but from the eye contact that precedes it."

Would Nancy prefer me not to know about her penis? Would she rather be half-concealed by a curtain of mist? If so and if not, what does her posing for a public portrait signify? Who is she? Is her womanhood substantially other than Mr. Umewaka's? If she lived in the capital and performed only before refined spectators, would I never guess that her body was partly male? If I were attracted to her without knowing, then found out, would my reaction be disappointment, revulsion, or an awed grief that someone beautiful and plausible in her grace, the half-existing biological woman whom I had believed in, was now flying away forever to the moon? Or would my attraction be unchanged? — If I never desired her, if I loved her only as a friend, then I would be indifferent if my conception of her gender changed. I know that I could continue to treat her as I would treat any woman, employing appropriate pronouns and compliments. In fact, I might admire her performance. — But what is grace? Perhaps (this also I resist) it is the space between fascination and fulfillment. Fascination, as you may recall, Zeami defined as the sensation before the consciousness of that sensation. Fulfillment, he says, is the union of becoming and of settling in place. The cherry blossom falls. Sakagami departs, and Semimaru completes his tale forever in the blind immobility which might almost be death.

I see the mask of beauty, and I want to kiss it. Then what? I taste wood.

Drawn to the mask of love, I give myself. My fulfillment will be separation. One will stop loving the other; or one will die. Wait awhile; wait awhile.

No, I reject that! I want grace that lasts forever . . .

Then down with me to the Sea-God's palace! Having married an immortal, I wait awhile, wait awhile, but then I long for life, the out-stretched red and gold fan whirling, the figure so fantastic, spectacular and immobile even as it moves. If I get desperate I'll open Urashima's box. The actor's right arm rises to the crown, and suddenly . . .

A face is a mask; a lovely face is a lovely mask; even if I kiss it I can never "possess" it even though my desire insists that I can; but because desire is hunger, then if possession were actually possible than it would partake of consumption; therefore, how excellent a thing is a mask! My eyes drink of it without depleting it.

Is the heterosexual attachment of a man to a woman who unbe-knownst to him retains some of a man's attributes any more of an illusion than any other attachment? Noh asserts that all attachments are equally useless, even harmful. I myself cannot help but feel that Kaguyahime's abandonment of her foster parents was cruel. But it was cruel because they were still attached to her. — Well, then, should they have stayed in exile on the dull side of the rainbow curtain, eternally declining to perform their roles and be attached?

Grace creates attachment. Would it be better, then, to remain an ape in a cage, incapable of appreciating grace?

All attachments must end. A famous poem in the *Tales of Ise* asks the moon why it must disappear so rapidly, leaving us unslaked. Already the actor has gone behind the rainbow curtain to remove his mask! Well, then is it preferable to absent myself from the performance? I could remain unattached in Akashi, determinedly distant, ironical, dreary and irrelevant, like some fading Noh under-kimono dedicated primarily to the representation of foreigners and warriors in light armor (purple, with eight-feathered fans between waving golden lines); awaiting my end without anticipation or fear; they'd call me beauty's teetotaler . . . If I see only insufficiencies in art, will I have maintained myself in the proper environment?

In the Gnostic Scriptures we find a writing called "The Thunder: Perfect Mind," in which God is female: wife and whore, barren mother of all contradictions. She says: "For many are the pleasant forms which exist in numerous sins . . . and fleeting pleasures, which men embrace until they become sober and go up to their resting-place. And they will find me there, and they will live, and they will not die again." If I withhold myself from sin in Akashi, will I finally be able to attach myself to beauty once she invites me into the capital? Just as a kimono pulses around a woman's white ankles when she goes upstairs, so the robe of Kaguyahime allures me as she ascends to her lunar home. Should I blind my recollections to it until I am called, if that ever happens? But what if I am no longer fitted for beauty by then? Doesn't it take a lifetime to comprehend the flower of peerless charm? Even then, how much can this ape hope to learn when grace so often follows the model of one family's Noh theater which I saw reconstructed in Kanazawa: partitioned chambers for the elite enclosing the open tatami space for mass audiences? — Where would I be? Since I'm from Akashi, they'd surely show me to my proper environment.

Even an Edo dweller might be able to visit the theater only once a year, perhaps dressing one's hair in a special way, awaiting the moment of passing through the "mouse gate" and entering another world: To the seductive, almost leering wavering of many shamisens, a snowfaced Kabuki warrior throws back his head and raises his parasol! Upon the stage bridge begins a slow parade of a Kabuki courtesan with her retinue. — And then? — Back to Akashi.

There is a geisha song about a pair of butterflies tied to each other by dreams which cannot come true; they flutter to "the end of the end." The commentary explains that two lovers who could not be together in this floating world killed themselves, and became butterflies. What then? Why, at the end of a butterfly's life they reach the end of the end.

All attachments must end. And every time I see a performance of "Matsukaze," I will see it end in the same way, down to the very last gesture. About this fact, Mr. Umewaka once remarked: "It's more difficult to always do the same thing than to change; we chose to do the difficult thing."

And I, too, would rather do the difficult thing. I prefer to experience grace even though I must lose it and fall back down to my death in Akashi; I defy my proper environment. My dream is over; last night's autumn rain has ceased; now nothing remains but the wind in the pines. But I remember when Komachi's throat was as white as a new tatami mat, and someone who proved cruel and treacherous still loved me. My proper environment may soon be a waste of pampas grass where the wind sings through my eyesockets, but I'll turn away from that while I can; why not listen to the song of the capital bird?

Indeed, it seems to me, perhaps because I am not a *shite* but a *waki*, that my way was never a sliding path upon the polished stage of a Noh theater, but a pilgrimage through places far more irregular than the stepping stones in the gravel paths of the Shoren-in Temple; and on many of the occasions when I have passed into Japan, I have visited spots where ghosts in various guises have told me of the past. Against all Noh's warnings, I have always sought out attachments. I seek to know these ghosts so that they can allure me all the better. The dances of Kofumi-san and the faces of all the maikos of Gion who shine like jewels in the darkness, the loveliness of Suzuka-san as she transforms herself, the sweet happiness in the dances of Masami-san, the flashing golden fan of Mr. Mikata, the slowly, slowly turning head of Mr. Umewaka in a *ko-omote* mask, the warmly neutral eyes of Konomi-san, the shadow of Konomi-san's neck and wig upon the wall of the teahouse, they tell me stories to which I cling far more than a true courtier from the capital would find needful; for all that I, a man, client, spectator, reader, foreigner can grasp is a single instant; whereas their performances exist far before and beyond me. Although you may see me as a sliding, passing consciousness upon the smooth stage of these printed pages, I believe that I have actually been places. Once in Pakistan I heard the muezzin calling in the darkness as rain flowed down — rain? No, it was the simultaneous ablutions of the faithful, running down pipes in walls all around me. The street lay crisp beneath the full moon. A horse canter-clopped by. Then the chorus of prayer-song arose from the mosque, more unearthly to me than the raptures of a Christian choir because the tonal scale was so different; it reminded me of the wind-soughs and river-music I've sometimes heard alone in my tent in the Arctic. It echoed weirdly; it might have been a crew of sailors singing far away on a storm-tossed ship. And all these things that I thought I heard were in reality a Noh chorus which sings to you what it is that I, a mere construction of words, claim to perceive.

### KISSING THE MASK

"To see with the spirit," writes Zeami, "is to grasp the spirit; to see with the eyes is merely to observe the function." What lies beyond function? Is it what lies behind the Noh mask? If so, are we supposed to see it?

If her face is a mask, then perhaps the vulva of the woman whom I love is a square lacquered box whose white butterflies resemble both pointed-tipped hearts and the black-ribbed fans of women; these insects browse on silver-gold brier roses in a blue-muted darkness, reminding me what a certain lady wrote in 1818: "Those who dedicate themselves to pleasure realize that they are like insects playing in the flowers, but find it difficult to forsake these frivolous habits." Meanwhile, every one of this box's decorations is misted toward silver, as in Shun'e's advice to Chomei.

Voltaire insisted that "an allegory carried too far or too low is like a beautiful woman who wears always a mask." But when I kiss a woman I love, I am kissing her skull.* The tiniest distance separates me from her blood-bathed brain. If her skin and flesh became transparent, would I still love and desire her? What kind of lover would I be if I did not? As

---

*In his modern version of the Noh play "Kantan," Mishima has the hero say: "I feel as if a mask kissed me." The beauty replies: "That's what women's kisses are like." — "You really are pretty," he says. "But if you strip away the skin, what have you got but a skull?"

I said, familiarity is indeed a gain. Shouldn't true love engage itself with the entire beloved, including even her excretory system? For what indeed lies at the heart of beauty? We are all coelomates, meaning that like worms, our predecessors and inheritors, we are built around hollow gut-tubes lined with epithelial cells and filled with matter in various stages of digestion. When the woman I love dies, shouldn't I love the gases of her decomposition? If it could, if *I* could, I would receive admittance to the capital at last. I'd sleep forever in perfection's arms.

Behind the rainbow curtain reigns death, to whose peace the *shite* now returns. Like Mr. Umewaka in the mirror room brooding over his mask, like the carvers chiseling dull wooden crystals which someday, if their hands do not slip, will become *ko-omote* heads, like a transvestite fitting his breasts on, a woman painting her mouth, a dancer preparing to incarnate the idealized Heian soul, coelomates wait to mask themselves in loveliness. (That Takigi-Noh lady-face so vivid white — how *can* it be so smoothly white and still alive? Isn't it a mask as hard as a skull? But then once again the firelight warms it back to flesh — but it is more perfect than flesh . . .) As for what lies beneath the skin, to admire *that* we might need, as Zeami surely did on Sado Isle, the peculiar Japanese solaces of lonely beauty and rusty beauty, *wabi* and *sabi*.

### SMEARS OF HAIR OIL

Pursuing this subject, I sometimes regret that in this book about feminine stateliness I have forgotten the vibrant vulgarity of biology, the "real" world of the floating world we float through, as exemplified by the hilarious pompous grotesqueries of *kyogen* masks, like fungi and potatoes, the rapid movements of the actors within them, the brighter atmosphere of *kyogen* nights, the players proverbially more easygoing, the audience readier to laugh, the craft of maskmaking perhaps more open to newcomers (one old lady in a *kyogen* audience in Kyoto told me that this deceased mask maker whose creations, animated by actors, we were now watching, was once her chemistry teacher; he started learning mask making, and so did his friends); this is far from Noh and nearly as far from the Inoue School, but it approaches the coarser, jollier, more grasping and desperate world of the geishas in Kafu's novels. (The geisha Kikuyo: "Her face, ordinarily covered with thick make-up, was now mottled with spots where the liquid powder had cracked and crumbled. This, together with the grayish smears of hair oil on the back of her neck, made it look as though she hadn't even taken a bath . . .") These skits about arguments, drunkenness, thievery, the parodies of hierarchy are in this world; but every now and then a *kyogen* actor stops to declaim, almost as a *waki* would. And in this world I argue, get drunk, steal, fornicate and declaim just as much as anyone. I am a lady from Akashi. I am an exiled courtier from the capital. I, seeker of beauty and pleasure, have written for you these things that I have seen in the floating world; because it is my will to preserve the evanescent and because it is my duty to send you a remembrance;* I am the ghost called Attachment-to-Nothingness; here where I live out my death it is so cold and dark that I am dazzled by the shining of snowballs cupped in pine branches; but it is my pride that once and more than once I have been to Kyoto to see the geishas dancing; and with equal pride I now impart to you the secret and expensive knowledge (never mind; I'll make you a gift of it) of exactly how beneath unpainted globular paper lanterns and before folding gilded screens the geishas of Kanazawa dance on tatami mats in those square rooms with glowing latticework paper doors. Behind the dancing-rooms of the very old ochayas there may be territories of the country beyond the rainbow curtain, which is to say narrow rush-floored corridors screened with reed blinds; more modern geisha houses allow the night's streetglow to shine in; in either case proprietress and the guest will fill each other's sake cups and drink to one another. The ivory-tan hue of tatamis will resemble the cheeks of old Noh masks in torchlight. A shamisen will always lie ready, and often in the corner they will keep the long harp called the *biwa*; once you have seen its shape you will know how Lake Biwa got its name. Occasionally there might even be a big *tsuzumi* drum, as in the song which invites crop-eating insects to visit the fire in the next village, then the village after that, and so on until they have been lured into the fatal sea. The geisha wraps her

---

*In her eleventh-century *Pillow Book*, Sei Shonagon advises that a letter from the provinces should arrive accompanied by a souvenir. A letter from the capital, of course, needs nothing else, being its own souvenir.

sleeve to show that she is a working peasant girl, and begins banging happily on the *tsuzumi* (which, so she tells me, was in the old days actually used to scare insects away with vibrations). Her wrists flash. Sometimes her singing resembles the cries of a Noh shoulder-drummer. And her drumbeats fly into the cold night, perishing long before they could ever cross the snowy moat of dark-stoned Kanazawa Castle.

Higashi, formed in 1818–30, is the most prestigious of the three pleasure districts, so I will bring you back there, returning to the ochaya where I watched Suzuka-san change from a young woman into a snow goddess. I'll never forget her snow-white lips before the red went on; I can never get enough of being wounded by the painful whiteness of snow. Upstairs, Masami-san's sky-blue sleeves rush in toward one another as she beats the drum, her pale twin hairpicks upright, her eyes lowered, her expression less concentrated or smiling than meditative, her kimono perfectly outstretched on the red mat all around her. Nothing she does ever betrays effort, much less strain. The musician Fukutaro-san is smiling sweetly at the geisha while she sings, her young throat erect, her dark brown hair a discrete mass as if carved, the shamisen at a forty-five-degree angle to her body, the long slender wooden handle between the thumb and forefinger of her left hand, the body of the instrument on her right thigh, the plectrum widening like a scoop as it comes out of her right hand. I have read that geishas sometimes use their own fingernails in place of plectrums in order to set a more intimate tone. But I have never witnessed this, perhaps because I am a woman from Akashi, an ape in a cage.

Now it is ended, but I remember that when Masami-san danced, the asymmetric folds and zones comprising her reminded me of the lobes of one of those fantastic rocks in a Japanese garden: shoulder, elbow and wrist, the latter bent in front of her throat in parallel to her tilted face; then the several folds of her wide sleeves, her knees, and the various ripple-like swirls of her hem; and at each instant, that boulder of her flowed into something else: a girl-figurine; then into a pond with leaves and flowers floating on its surface.*

---

*The space between musician and geisha is still another abyss to cross. Those two create a world together, but the musician merely upholds it without existing in it; the geisha exists alone.

In Kyoto they dance Inoue style, *mai* style. Here they follow the less austere fashions of *odori*. Their faces and bodies move more; their kimono-patterns are more realistic, partaking of the mode called *kaga*.

When Masami-san tilted her head and raised the half-opened fingers of her right hand before her chin, her left hand hid within the long fold of her right sleeve. She curved at the left hip, then again at the right knee, her form then arcing back again down to her left heel, and her hem encircling her on the floor like a statue's base.

She let her left sleeve spill down from the central band of her obi to her lower calf; while the fingers of her right hand gestured upward at the level of her forehead.

I do not know, but I want to know, so when their performance is finished I inquire: "What makes a woman beautiful?"

Hachishige-san, the ochaya's proprietress, replies: "In our generation, experience of life will make the beauty come out. Other people might value only physical beauty."

Says Masami-san: "We just want to be beautiful, and for that our inside self must be beautiful; we must take something from the heart. We begin by imitating others."

And Fukutaro-san says: "There are many beautiful Elder Sisters, fortunately. I was frequently scolded. The Elder Sister reminded me that the customers always watch you, how you move."

I ask the musician what she was thinking of when she performed, and her reply is quite unlike anything I ever heard from practitioners of the Inoue School.

"I am still a beginner," she begins modestly. "I try to visualize what the music seeks to express. In that second song, which is a sad song, I try to feel sad. But every time I perform, I hear something new. I was lucky that my Elder Sister taught me the tricks. For instance, it is very difficult to sing properly to make the right sound. The posture is like this: Sit straight, looking down with chin up, so the voice goes better. Breast should push forward, buttock backward."

I ask the geisha: "When you dance, do you feel or are you trying to keep your mind blank?"

"I am trying to be the heroine. In this occasion, I try to imagine that you are the lover I left."

"To what extent is beauty a performance?"

Fukutaro-san says: "Regardless of age, it should appear easy and smooth."

"Is there anything a woman can do that an onnagata cannot?"

"Give birth," laughs Fukutaro-san. There it is again, that answer I so often hear.

Masami-san tells me: "In a dance whose theme is longing for the other sex, in that case a woman can really think and feel that."

She hesitates, then continues: "When I was turning my back to you and trying to look sad, trying to look most defenseless, the key, which I learned from my Elder Sister, well, it's kind of embarrassing. You can be careful of the shoulders and other parts. The trick is to make the vagina tight. That affects your appearance, particularly when you show the back."

## THE MOON IN CUPPED HANDS

Could I ever possibly have discerned it, had Masami-san in her kimono and obi, with her back turned to me, actually clenched her vagina? If I could not, what does that say about my gullibility as I pay out money all through this floating world? And if I could, as I sincerely believe that Masami-san considers to be within a habitué's capability, then might understatement contain still more universes than I suppose? What if I simply trust that I *might* someday learn to perceive such subtleties? ("Wait awhile and you'll come home to Kyoto.") Wouldn't the possibility enrich me just as much as if the mask actually kissed me back?

Masami-san dances. The Higashi Eastern Pleasure Quarter may not be the old capital, but from my point of view (I now remember it several summers later, in another country) it might as well be the moon. — I feel the impulse to tell you about Masami-san's faintly smiling dark red lips, not to mention the hairpieces and ornaments frozen in her wig like candy statuettes in the frosting of a fancy cake, her throat still young and her face just beginning to coarsen, although she was a good fifteen years older than she looked. When her dark eyes actually gazed into mine, she remained detached, and her sky-blue sleeves drew together in her lap. — Better not to miss her too much! In the Noh play "Nishikigi," a suitor sets out unavailing love charms before a woman's house for three years, and finally dies; his grave is called the Brocade Mound. When she hears this news, the woman also dies, and is buried there also. The two ghosts call each other husband and wife. Their attachment torments them until the arrival of the usual priest. — Why ask to feel that? And so farewell to Kaguyahime and Yuya and Matsukaze; I will not desecrate the rainbow curtain; wait awhile, wait awhile. Hence this book resembles the deathbed poem of Ki no Tsurayuki, who wonders whether the world he now departs could ever have been any more real than moonlight reflected in water in his cupped hands. Where, if anywhere, dwells the Noh play's *shite* who has been released from attachment by the priest's prayer? And where does she go when the actor who expressed her removes his gown, wig and mask? We will never know before we follow Tsurayuki behind the rainbow curtain. We might not find out even then. So for now, why not click little sake-glasses with whomever in this floating world I can love? Why not kiss the mystery's blackened teeth? "We had been fussing about with our dress and powder since early dawn," writes Murasaki in her diary. She seeks to control how she is seen: a swiftly glimpsed or never-glimpsed face, masked by long black hair and an elegant fan which sprouts from her gorgeous sleeve. Now she is ready. Now the play will begin.

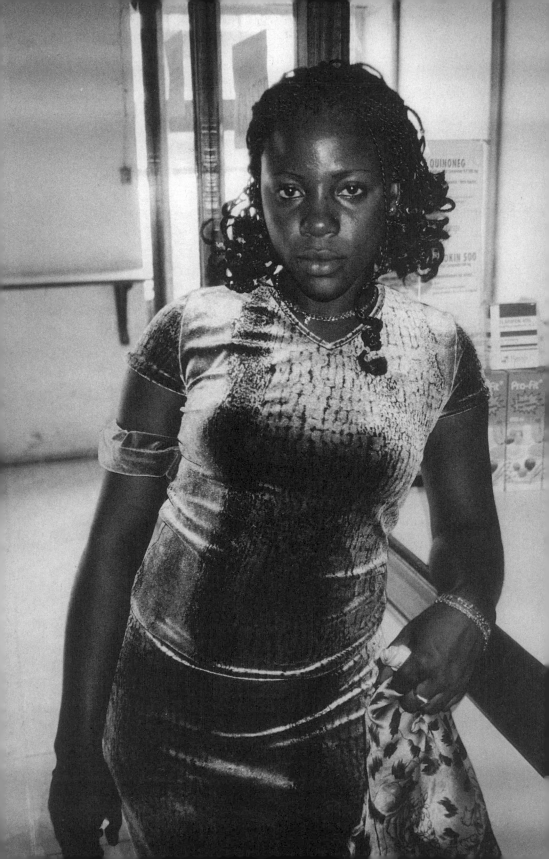

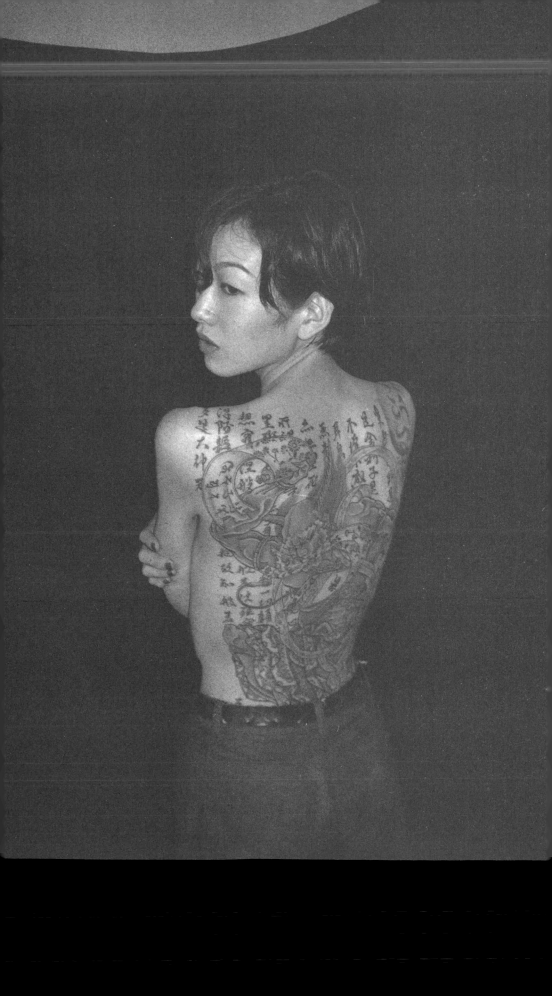

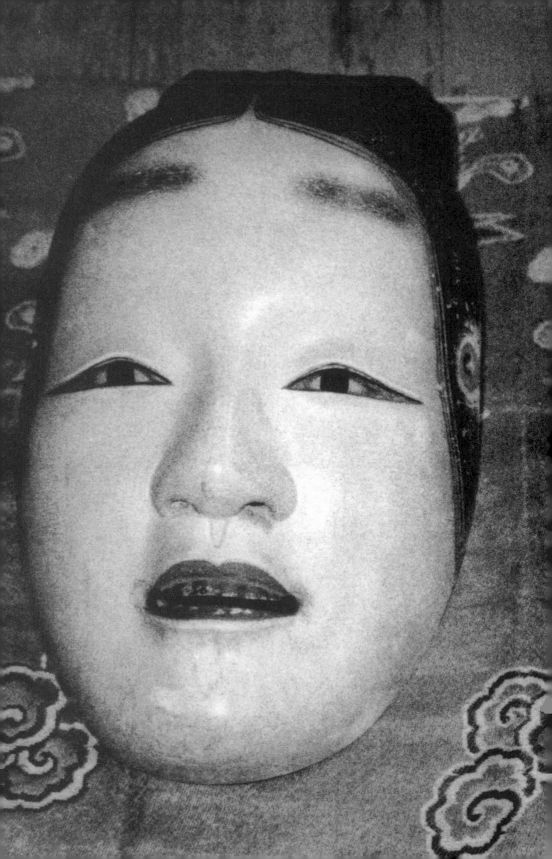

# APPENDIX A

*Descriptions of Feminine Beauty in*

The Pillow Book of Sei Shonagon (ca. *1000–1010*)

Citations by Shonagon of the opinions of others have been omitted unless she expresses approval of them.

| PAGE | BEAUTY | UGLINESS |
|------|--------|----------|
| 22 | | dark skin showing patchily through under face powder |
| 26 | | disorderly hair |
| 60 | longhaired young woman lying abed in an orange robe and crimson skirt, covered in a mauve and violet robe | |
| 71 | | ugly-haired in white robe lower class, in scarlet trouser-skirt |
| 85 | many-layered clothes visible through bright curtains of state beneath green bamboo blinds | |
| 94 | young, with long hair over her shoulders | |
| 113 | contrast between Empress Sadako's white forehead and glossy black lute | |

| PAGE | BEAUTY | UGLINESS |
|------|--------|----------|
| 129 | Empress Sadako's complexion, which harmonizes with her three-layered scarlet silk dress and two plum-red robes | |
| 130 | an Imperial concubine's robes of plum-red, deep red, dark red and an over-robe of light green embroidered silk which makes her look young even though she conceals her face behind a fan | |
| 131 | the concubine's young attendants in loose, cherry-colored coats, underskirts of light green and plum red, and long trains | |
| 163 | Court ladies dressed "with their robes, skirts and Chinese jackets perfectly matching the season," the colors being tawny yellow, light violet, purple, deep red | |
| 167 | pretty hair | |
| 172 | beautiful shoulder-length tresses | |
| 174 | Court ladies in light grey skirts, Chinese jackets, matching dresses of unlined silk, scarlet petticoats | |
| 186 | the light pink hue of the Empress's hands | |
| 189 | | a mottled complexion |
| 194 | "a natural beauty" in a tawny unlined robe and a light robe over a dress of dull purple. "With her long hair being blown about and gently puffed up by the wind, she was a truly splendid sight." | |
| 201 | neat short hair in a woman of the lower classes | |

| PAGE | BEAUTY | UGLINESS |
|---|---|---|
| 231 | the Empress's red Chinese robe above a willow-green damask robe, five unlined grape-hued silk robes, a robe of blue and white gauze, a ceremonial silk skirt | |
| 231 | her hair's front parting, "which was combed at a slight angle pointing towards the ornament that held up her hair over her forehead" | |
| 240 | "an attractive woman, whose hair tumbles loosely over her forehead" | |
| 170 | | "I cannot stand a woman who wears sleeves of unequal width" |
| 171 | "Once I saw a girl of about eighteen with magnificent hair that hung in thick tresses all the way to her feet; she was nicely plump and had splendid white skin," had a toothache; her hair was disordered and her face wet with tears; she pressed her flushed cheek to her hand; a charming impression | |
| 258 | a lady in an unlined white silk gown, a crimson trouser-skirt, a faded dark robe | |
| 262 | | "women in travelling costumes who walk in a great hurry" |
| | | a thin ugly woman with dark skin and a wig |
| | | a darkskinned person in an unlined robe of stiff silk |

# Appendix B

*Descriptions of Feminine Beauty in Some Old Norse Sources*

I

Descriptions of feminine beauty in the *Elder Edda* (Hollander trans.). Non-visual descriptions such as "good" and "loving" (e.g. "Hávamál," p. 30: "the good maiden, in whose loving arms I lay") are omitted. So are non-concrete visual descriptions such as "winsome" ("Helgavitha Hjorgarthssonar," p. 170: "the winsome women of the war leader").

| PHRASE | SOURCE |
|---|---|
| ARMS (11 REFERENCES) | |
| gleaming | "Skírnismál," p. 66. |
| shining | "Lokasenna," p. 94. |
| soft (2x) | "Svipdagsmal," p. 151. |
| white | "Atlakvitha," p. 290. |
| white | "Hábarzljod," p. 79. |
| white | "Hávamál," p. 40. |
| white | "Helgavitha Hjorgarthssonar," p. 171. |
| white | "Helgavitha Hundingsbana II," p. 201. |
| white | "Volundarkvitha," p. 160. |
| white | "Volundarkvitha," p. 161. |

| PHRASE | SOURCE |
|---|---|
| *BROW (5)* | |
| brow brighter than whitest snow | "Rígsthula," p. 125. |
| brow-white | "Hymiskvitha," p. 85. |
| brow-white | "Sigurtharkvitha hin skamma," p. 260. |
| brow-white | "Volundarkvitha," p. 167. |
| fair-browed | "Brot af Sigurtharkvitha," p. 245. |
| *BREAST (1)* | |
| breast lighter than whitest snow | "Rígsthula," p. 125. |
| *COLOR IN GENERAL (6)* | |
| fair | "Volundarkvitha," p. 161. |
| snow-white | "Alvíssmál," p. 111. |
| sun-bright | "Hávamál," p. 28. |
| sun-bright | "Helgavitha Hundingsbana II," p. 200. |
| sun-bright | "Svipdagsmal," p. 151. |
| swan-white | "Atlakvitha," p. 293. |
| *FINGERS (1)* | |
| dainty-fingered | "Rígsthula," p. 126. |
| *HAIR (2)* | |
| fairhaired | "Helgavitha Hjorgarthssonar," p. 170. |
| fairhaired | "Rígsthula," p. 126. |
| *NECK (1)* | |
| whiter than whitest snow | "Rígsthula," p. 125. |
| *SHAPE (2)* | |
| slender | "Alvíssmál," p. 111. |
| slender | "Hávamál," p. 40. |
| *CLOTHES AND ORNAMENTS (8)* | |
| blue-shirted | "Rígsthula," p. 125. |
| brooch-breasted | "Rígsthula," p. 125. |
| gold-dight | "Hábarzljod," p. 79. |
| gold-dight | "Hymiskvitha," p. 85. |

| PHRASE | SOURCE |
| --- | --- |
| gold-dight | "Helgavitha Hjorgarthssonar," p. 175. |
| in golden weeds | "Fafnismál," p. 231. |
| ring-bedight | "Helgavitha Hjorgarthssonar," p. 171. |
| silver-dight | "Sigrdrífumál," p. 239. |

2

Descriptions of feminine beauty in *Laxdaela Saga*. Gudrid, the heroine, is never described in any specific terms. The hero, Kjartan, gets a good two sentences of description.

3

Descriptions of feminine beauty in *Njal's Saga*. The heroine, Hallgerd, is frequently described when she makes her dramatic entrances onto the stage. The author devotes more description to her than to anyone else. I have omitted non-specific descriptions such as "a woman of great beauty."

"She was a tall, beautiful child with long silken hair that hung down to her waist" (ch. 1, p. 39).

"She was very tall, which earned her the nickname Long-legs, and her lovely hair was now so long that it could veil her entire body" (ch. 9, p. 55).

"She had put on a woven blue cloak over a scarlet tunic and a silver belt. She wore her hair hanging loose on either side of her bosom and tucked under her belt" (ch. 13, p. 66).

"The one in the lead was the best dressed of all . . . Hallgerd was wearing a red, richly-decorated tunic under a scarlet cloak trimmed all the way down with lace. Her beautiful thick hair flowed down over her bosom" (ch. 33, p. 93).

# POSTSCRIPT: A NOTE ON SOME NOVELS
## BY SIGRID UNDSET

That great twentieth-century envisioner of medieval Norway, Sigrid Undset, bestows upon us spacious treasuries of description, so that at first she seems to deny the Eddic tradition of understated love-doom. Here, for instance, is her most famous heroine, Kristin Lavransdattir: She was "small-waisted, with slender, fine limbs and joints, yet round and plump withal. Her face was somewhat short and round, her forehead low and broad and white as milk; her eyes large, grey and soft, under fairly drawn eyebrows. Her mouth was somewhat large, but it had full bright red lips, and her chin was as round as an apple and well-shaped. She had goodly, long, thick hair, but 'twas something dark in hue, almost as much brown as yellow, and quite straight." A few pages later on, when Kristin is getting ready for a certain fateful dance, Undset has her "spread her masses of yellow hair out over her shoulders and back" — a simple, powerful act of much the same enthralling character as the display of a legendary heroine's shining white arms. When at that dance Kirstin encounters Erlend Nikulaussön, who will be the love and torment of her life, the scene is underplayed with great skill. She smiles, gazes into his eyes; finally she accompanies him into the herb-garden in the darkness. She "knew that this was madness," writes Undset. "But a blessed strengthlessness was upon her. She only leaned closer to the man and whispered softly — she knew not what." At dawn they vow oaths to one another, although she was promised to another. After that, no one can pull Kristin back from the doom she craves, not even her sorrowing father, who is perhaps the most lovingly drawn of any character in either of Undset's great trilogies. "She burst into weeping," we read. "But she wept because she had felt in his caress and seen in his eyes that now he was so worn out with pain that he could not hold out against her any more." He has himself been doomed by his compassionate love for his daughter, which overcomes his equally loving concern for her best interest as he sees it. As for Kristin, in her we find the resolution of an ancient Norse heroine, but overlain with Christian compassion and guilt. Her world remains in most respects the supernatural one of the Eddas. At the very beginning of the trilogy, when she is still a small girl, the reflection of a grey-eyed dwarf-maiden or elf-maiden bends toward her, seeking to lure her into the mountain with a wreath of flowers. Although this scene foreshadows the eventual tarnishment of Kristin's bridal crown, it has been so skillfully realized that the elf-lady lives in her own right. She has been delineated in more detail than we would have found in the sagas, but even so, some reserve remains in the description; something is lacking or mysterious about her. She appears specific and even beautiful enough, but her reflected image must be wavering slightly in the dark pool; her form possesses less fixity than Kristin's; she might be the reflection of bushes and a rock, and her nostrils strangely resemble a horse's. This dangerous other world obtrudes itself upon us from time to time throughout the novel; and one of the last experiences Kristin has in her old age before entering a convent is hearing a stone roll and a door shut beneath the mountain. What would have happened had she followed the elf-lady? We never hear of the mountain letting anyone go; and at one point a mendicant monk informs us that the damned cannot be saved because they are addicted to their torment.

Certain dooms are more inescapable still. In the last volume of the trilogy, when Simon Darre, Kristin's fiance from long ago, jilted by her and accordingly doomed to a loveless marriage with her sister, breaks up a fight and gets a knife-cut for his pains, his friend Vigleik dreams "an ugly dream" that Simon's dead cousin Simon Reidarssön asks the injured man to come with him; and the next day the wound is infected, and Simon keeps seeing Simon Reidarssön. Then he understands that he is fey. And indeed he dies, although Kristin does her best to heal him. In this episode, doom expresses itself, as in the Eddas and sagas, with the neutral inevitability of a physical law. One thinks upon the ancient tale of Sigurd, who knows that he will slay the dragon, win the gold and the maiden, and after that be rapidly murdered. There is nothing to do but take his fate upon himself. And Simon Darre behaves with a similar clearsightedness, overlain with modern emotional explicitness, arranging the lives of his dependents as best he can, dying calmly, and sincerely speaking his heart. There is no vain and cowardly struggle against the end.

But in the second volume of the trilogy, when Kristin and Erlend have been married for several years, love-doom gets defined through quiet comparison with its changeling, for Erlend now embarks on a disastrous affair with another married woman, Lady Sunniva. At each step of his ensnarement, he persuades himself that he could not have done anything else. Sunniva and her maid are menaced in the street by a band of drunken Icelanders. Erlend approaches, his sword in his belt, and they fall back. Here the reader recalls that he and Kristin became acquainted when he saved her and a companion from being robbed and raped in Oslo. Erlend is a natural rescuer of women, a brave and skilful fighter, and the tragedy of his life, as was the case for Grettir the Strong, is that he was born too late to be a hero of the Saga Age. Sunniva simpers: "Can you believe it, Erlend? — old a woman as I am, maybe I like it not ill that some men think I am yet so fair, 'tis worth while blocking my way—" Undset pens the next sentence in calm irony: "There was but one answer that a courteous man could make to this." She skips a line, then resumes: 'He came home to his own house the next morning in the grey of dawn . . ." Here we have the doom of a man who is not in fact resolute, but impulsive.

In the Eddas, and to a lesser degree in the sagas, doom is written from the beginning, and the only choice people have is how bravely or loyally they meet it. In Undset's trilogies, the two inevitable dooms of death and original sin have been laid upon us; but we are at times given grace to avert evils from ourselves and others. This grace is another better doom; we cannot will it into being, but we are free to basely reject it. Undset finally says, in words of half-equivalence to those of Odin the High One in "Hávamál": "The good you have done cannot be undone; though all the hills should crash in ruin, yet would it stand—" As for the evil one has done, Odin and Christ differ as to whether that can be undone. In Undset's novels, love partakes of any and all of these various dooms and their contingencies. The greatest compliment that I can pay her is that her work thus continues, and in a way completes, the effects of such great forerunners as *Laxdaela Saga*.

# APPENDIX C

*Descriptions of Feminine Beauty in Sappho and Miscellaneous*

*Greek Lyric Sources*

All from Barnstone, whose edition contains the complete poems of Sappho and a smattering of other Greek lyric poets from the Greek period through the Byzantine.

I

Descriptions of feminine beauty and its opposite in Sappho (b. *ca.* 630 B.C.)

| PAGE | BEAUTY | UGLINESS |
|------|--------|----------|
| 76 | "Graces of the pink arms" | |
| | "Muses of the splendid hair" | |
| | "a soft girlfriend's breast" | |
| 77 | "honey-voiced women" | |
| | limbs like violets | |
| 78 | honey-soft eyes | |
| 80 | supple Cretan dancers | |

| PAGE | BEAUTY | UGLINESS |
|---|---|---|
| 81 | "slender-ankled girls" | |
| | loud and heavenly singing | |
| 82 | | a farm-girl who does not know the proper way to lift her gown over her ankles and who wears "farm-girl finery" |
| 84 | Gonglya in her milk-white gown | |
| 85 | a Lydian-embroidered gown extending to the toes | |
| | "the soft fine linen robes of Amorgos" | |
| 86 | a lover (presumed) who exceeds a fine robe's softness, gold's hue, a lyre's sweetness, an egg's whiteness | |
| 87 | a tender girl | |
| 88 | a soft girl | |
| 89 | blonde Helen | |
| | S.'s little daughter, "who is beautiful like a gold flower" | |
| 90 | | wrinkled flesh and black hair aged to white |
| | "pink-armed Dawn" | |
| 91 | a quiet girl in beautiful garments | |

## 2

Descriptions of feminine beauty in Archilochos (late eighth century B.C.)

| PAGE | BEAUTY | UGLINESS |
|---|---|---|
| 36 | "Her breasts and dark hair were perfume . . ." | |

## 3

Descriptions of feminine beauty in Alkman (mid seventh century B.C.)

| PAG | BEAUTY | UGLINESS |
|---|---|---|
| 50 | goldenrod hair | |
| 51 | floral gold chain | |

## 4

Description of feminine beauty in Anakreon (b. *ca.* 572 B.C.)

| PAGE | BEAUTY | UGLINESS |
|---|---|---|
| 122 | blonde hair (of Artemis) | |
| 123 | "warm women" | |
| 124 | "colorful sandals" | |

## 5

Description of feminine beauty in Pindar (d. 438 B.C.)

| PAGE | BEAUTY | UGLINESS |
|------|--------|----------|
| 161 | "Helen of the lovely hair" | |

## 6

Descriptions of feminine beauty in Bachkylides (fl. 476 B.C.)

| PAGE | BEAUTY | UGLINESS |
|------|--------|----------|
| 166 | "white-armed Iole" | |
| 167 | violet-braided Marpessa | |
| | white cheek | |
| 168 | "violet-wreathed" | |
| | "white-armed bride" | |

## 7

Description of feminine beauty's opposite in Asklepiades (fl. *ca.* 270 B.C.)

| PAGE | BEAUTY | UGLINESS |
|------|--------|----------|
| 161 | | black skin (but A. pleads for her beauty regardless) |

Descriptions of feminine beauty and its opposite in Meleagros (fl. *ca.* 270 B.C.)

| PAGE | BEAUTY | UGLINESS |
|------|--------|----------|
| 202 | perfumed hair | |
| | unspecified glow | |
| 203 | "erotic mouth" | |
| | aquamarine eyes | |
| | eyes like fire | |

Descriptions of feminine beauty and its opposite in Philodemos the Epicurean (*ca.* 110– *ca.* 40 B.C.) His lover, Charito, is in her sixties.

| PAGE | BEAUTY | UGLINESS |
|------|--------|----------|
| 211 | dense hair | same woman's old age (but P. says this is no handicap) |
| | high-pointed, conical white breasts | |
| | ambrosia-fragrant, smooth flesh | |

## 10

Descriptions of feminine beauty's opposite in Marcus Argentarius (early C.E.).

| PAGE | BEAUTY | UGLINESS |
|------|--------|----------|
| 214 | | scrawniness (but can be overlooked by love) |

## 11

Descriptions of feminine beauty in Rufinus (*ca.* 50 B.C. – *ca.* 50 A.D.).

| PAGE | BEAUTY | UGLINESS |
|------|--------|----------|
| 215 | silver ankles | |
| | milky breasts like golden apples | |
| | round hips (from pregnancy) | |
| | swelling belly* | |

## 12

Descriptions of feminine beauty in Nikarchos (*ca.* first century A.D.).

| PAGE | BEAUTY | UGLINESS |
|------|--------|----------|
| 219 | plumpness | |
| | "beautiful limbs" | |

---

*Content leaves it ambiguous as to whether or not the poet considers this beautiful.

## 13

Description of feminine beauty in Paulus Silentiarius (*fl. ca.* 560).

| PAGE | BEAUTY | UGLINESS |
|------|--------|----------|
| 238 | silver neck | |

## 14

Anonymous description of feminine beauty.

| PAGE | BEAUTY | UGLINESS |
|------|--------|----------|
| 257 | snowy breasts | |

# Appendix D

*Proportions of Feminine Beauty in Some Classical and Western European Sources*

(After Kenneth Clark, pp. 75, 20–21.)

1. Female nude, "Esquiline Venus," pre-classical Greek bronze (which now exists only in 2 marble copies)

Length of head = 1/7 height of body. Distance between breasts = 1 length of head = distance from lower breast to navel = distance from navel to division of legs

2. Female nude, classical [Greek] canon and its imitators until the first century

Distance between breasts = distance from lower breast to navel = distance from navel to division of legs

[p. 70, 2 wall paintings from Pompeii: "The distance from the breasts to the division of the legs is three units instead of two; the pelvis is wide, the thighs are absurdly short, and the whole body seems to have lost its structural system."]

3.  Female nude, Gothic ideal

Distance between breasts = distance from navel to division of legs[*] = ½
distance from lower breast to navel

"The basic pattern of the female body is still an oval, surmounted by two spheres; but the oval has grown incredibly long, the spheres have grown distressingly small."

---

[*]Clark does not give this distance explicitly but seems to imply it, as does the image of the Gothic Eve he reproduces.

# APPENDIX E

*Noh Play Groups, and Plays Mentioned*

Noh dramas are divided into six groups, if we give "Okina" its due. Formally there are but five groups, and "Okina" is a peculiar subcategory of the first. Never mind that Zeami, the most important of Noh's founders, specified only three categories. A full traditional program would include one play from each (usually excepting "Okina," which is performed under special circumstances), and in the following order:

0. "Okina"

1. **Waki Noh** [god plays]:
   Takasago
   Seiobo

2. **Shura Mono** [ghost or warrior plays]
   Atsumori
   Ebira
   Kanehira
   Kiyotsune

3. **Katsura Mono** or **Kazura-mono** [wig plays or woman plays]
   Ashikari
   Eguchi
   Izutsu

Matsukaze

Obasute

Sekidera Komachi

Sotoba Komachi

Yokihi

Yuki

Yuya

4. **Kyojo Mono** or **Yonbamme-mono** [madwoman plays; Tyler simply writes that this category cannot be described usefully in a few words; Keene remarks that this group paradoxically includes "realistic" plays; "Shunkan" offers crazed loneliness but no women at all appear in it]

Ataka

Dojoji

Hanjo

Kagekiyo

Kayoi Komachi

Kinuta

Miidera

Motomezuka

Nishikigi

Shunkan

Torioi-bune

Yoroboshi

5. **Kichiku Mono** [demon plays]

Aoi-no-Ue

Kasuga ryujin

Kokaji

Taniko

The current Noh corpus actually contains two hundred forty plays. Thus one source. Another says "only a few hundred." Hundreds more are no longer performed. Waley claims that eight hundred plays from before 1868 survive. Mr. Jeff Clark writes me: "Actually thousands have been written . . ."

# Glossary

*For definitions and descriptions of relevant Noh mask types, see chapter 3.*

**Atsuita**  Robe made of a certain thick cloth; generally used for male Noh roles.

**Aware**  The beauty and harmony beyond direct expression which shines uniquely from various entities in their own occasion. In pre-Heian times it was simply joyous; then it became tinged with pathos; now it has connotations of wretchedness. The capacity for appreciating it is sometimes associated especially with the feminine.

**Bijin-ga**  Portraits of beautiful women. Used to refer to *ukiyo-e* woodcuts and paintings. Hokusai and Kaigetsu are two masters of the form who are mentioned in this book.

**Biwa**  A kind of lute. Lake Biwa has a *biwa* shape.

**Bushido**  The "way of the warrior," exemplifying self-discipline, readiness for death, loyalty, chivalry and aesthetic spirituality.

**Daimyo**  Feudal lord.

**Dan**  Section. Used not only for each of the five subdivisions of a Noh play, but also for the chapters of other works, for instance *The Tales of Ise*.

**Dharma**  An object of perception.

**En**  Charming, or visually beautiful. For example, the decorative virtue of a picture-scroll.

**Eri**  The scarlet collar of a **maiko**.

**Floating world**  Not at all a uniquely Japanese conception. For instance, an ancient Egyptian love song advises: "Enjoy pleasant hours, and weary not thereof . . . Behold, no one departed will return again."

---

*Definitions and examples of *aware*, *en*, *miyabi*, *okashi* and *yugen* are indebted to De Bary et al., pp. 197–99, 365.

**Fue** A kind of Noh flute.

**Fukinuke yatai** Roofless interiors in the Genji Picture-Scroll illustrations and later pictures as well, such as the seventeenth-century woodblocks accompanying the books of Saikaku.

**Geiko** [Kyoto term.] A full-fledged geisha; hence she has advanced beyond the **maiko** stage. First used at the end of the seventeenth century by dancing girls who wished to distinguish themselves from prostitutes and therefore called themselves "gei-ko" (literally, "arts-child").

**Hako-iri-musume** Girl in a box, meaning a girl brought up with tender care. Although it has been said that Noh masks are meant to be used, not kept in boxes, this term was applied to a certain *ko-omote* carved by Deme Yasuhisa (a copy of a masterpiece by Tatsuemon).

**Haori** A protective jacket worn over a kimono.

**Hayashi** The musicians on a Noh stage.

**Hikime kagibana technique** Used in Genji Picture-Scrolls and elsewhere to portray faces with stylized understatement. Women's faces are generally expressed as *urizane-gata* (winter melon shaped). Such stylized Genji figures are (at least to my mind) recapitulated in almost any of Hokusai's calligraphic from-the-back sketches of a court beauty: a black hair-oval whose inky tail curves down toward us almost to the floor, an opened fan, subdivided into rectangles and peering over the left shoulder; the nearly semicircular arc of kimono sleeves and shoulders — an ovoid figure, in short, built out of arcs, of kimono-train.

**Hikizuri** A maiko's kimono.

**Hon'i** The decorum appropriate to the expression of a given subject. For instance in a Heian court poem about the approach of the cherry blossom season, *hon'i* required the expression of a stylized impatience for the flowers to arrive.

**Honzetsu** The source or "seed" of a Noh play (or of a poem).

**Iki** Chic, dressy, sexy in the usual understated Japanese way. A band of red in a kimono-sleeve, or, if you like, the red sole of a black high-heeled shoe, are both *iki*.

**Kabuki** A more flamboyant form of theater than Noh, using the rapid, agile *odori* dance rather than **mai**. The original meaning meant something like "beyond the pale," or "avant-garde." Some stories, such as "Dojoji," are performed in both Noh and Kabuki modes.

**Kaga** Kanazawa-style kimono pattern, less "fancy" and more "realistic," geishas say, than that of Kyoto.

**Kara-ori** Small-sleeved brocaded Noh costumes.

**Kotsuzumi** Small hourglass Noh drum.

**Kyogen** Comic drama which is often played between intervals of Noh, and also presented in its own right. Sometimes in Noh a non-comic *kyogen* part is provided for an actor to explain to the audience the circumstances of the play. *Kyogen* masks can be more whimsical and fantastical than their Noh counterparts.

**Maeshite** Shite of the first part, or act, of a Noh play.

**Mai** The slow and stately form of dance most germane to Noh. Also practiced in some types of Kabuki.

**Maiko** An apprentice geisha. (Lit.: "Dancing girl," or "dance-child.") This readily distinguishable individual is found only in Kyoto.

**Mehari** Red makeup applied around an **onnagata**'s eyes.

**Miekakure** The art of enhancing beauty through tantalization, concealment or delay. Example: a bit of garden seen behind a wall.

**Miyabi** Courtliness; often associated with Chinese culture or the capital. An example might be the erotic allure of a Heian noblewoman's sleeve.

**Muga** Self-effacing repetition of a task or performance until a perfect and egoless accomplishment is achieved.

**Nochijite** *Shite* of the second part. [Also: "Mojijite."]

**Nokan** A kind of Noh flute.

**Nuihaku** A kind of small-sleeved satin Noh kimono with embroidery and *surihaku*, used mainly for female roles.

**Nyotai** Feminine mode of Noh dance.

**Obi** Kimono sash. Often very ornate and expensive when used to perform beauty.

**Obi-age** Silken obi support. More ornate and colorful for **maiko** than for **geiko**.

**Obi-jime** Braid of an **obi**. Closed with a **pocchiri**. More ornate and colorful for maiko than for geiko.

**Ochaya** A geisha teahouse. Traditionally, dancers and musicians perform in the *hikae-no-ma*, the waiting room or stage, while guests sit in the adjacent *zashiki*, or eating room. In Kanazawa, the Ochaya Shima in the Higashi Kurawa district displays such features and is currently open to visitors.

**Okashi** Cheerful, amusing, delightful. For instance, *kyogen* humor; or the witty spitefulness of Sei Shonagon's *Pillow Book*.

**Okawa** See **Otsuzumi**.

**Onnagata** A female impersonator in Kabuki. Also called *oyama*, but the latter is much less respectful.

**Oshiroi** White makeup worn by geishas and Kabuki actors. Once worn more generally among denizens of the Floating World.

**Otsuzumi** Large hourglass Noh drum. Also called an **okawa**.

**Ozashiki** Geisha entertainment.

**Pocchiri** Clasp for the obi of a woman's kimono. More ornate for **maiko** than for **geiko**, who sometimes do not wear them at all.

**Sabi** Pleasant decrepitude not necessarily associated with melancholy. An example might be a fallen leaf or an old peasant hut.

**San-san-kudo** Ceremony binding a new **maiko** to her **geiko** "elder sister." Generally characteristic of wedding ceremonies.

**Sarugaku** The precursor to Noh. Literally, "monkey music." A concatenation of juggleries, dances, etcetera. This word was frequently used by Zeami and his successors to refer to Noh.

**Shinto** One of the two Japanese religions, coeval with Buddhism. It is difficult to describe briefly and accurately. Shinto has to do with agriculture and the links between Japanese and the land with its indigenous spirits. These links may be strengthened through purification ceremonies or weakened through such defilements as blood, sickness and death. See endnote to "the sin of human beings," pp. 437–38. Mr. Mikata insisted to me that in the time that Noh dramas were written and set, "Shinto and Buddhism were very interrelated, with no conflict. It was in the Meiji era that Shinto and Buddhism were clearly separated."

**Shironure** The white makeup on a geisha's face.

**Shite** Principal role in a Noh play.

**Shunga** Erotic pictures, especially in *ukiyo-e*.

**Shura** Damnation.

**Surihaku** A kind of Noh kimono (or usually under-kimono) characterized by short sleeves and foiled stenciling. Often employed for female roles.

**Tabi** Split-toed white socks worn by Noh actors, geisha dancers and many women in formal kimono.

**Taiko** A type of Noh drum, more rarely used than the others.

**Takigi-Noh** Torchlight Noh performance, usually on a summer night on the grounds of a shrine. Said to have been practiced as early as 875 A.D., before Noh itself existed in its present form. One version (now often performed at Yasukuni Shrine in Tokyo) is *yozakura-Noh*, nighttime Noh beneath the cherry blossoms.

**Toshima** A woman who emanates "mature charm."

**Tsuki** One of the three sub-styles of certain young female Noh masks (*ko-omote*, *waka-onna*, *zo onna*, etc.), *tsuki* means Moon. The other two variants are *yuki* (snow) and *hana* (flower). *Tsuki* masks tend to have their noses tilted a trifle to the left. *Yukis'* noses tilt to the right. One actor describes a certain *fushikizo* thus: "It has a nose tilted to the left, which is the basic 'Tsuki no Koomote,' describing the characteristics of a *waka-onna*. On the back, the left eye is carved double, while the right is triple, which is unique and attractive . . . My late father Sakon loved it and used it every occasion he could. The details are concrete rather than abstract. The way the lower lip is positioned farther forward than the upper lip, and the gentle look of her almond eyes make her look like a modern beautiful woman."

**Tsure** The companion or subordinate role to the *shite*.

**Tsuzumi** Hourglass-shaped shoulder drum employed both by geisha and by Noh musicians.

**Ukiyo-e** Literally, "floating world picture." Paintings and especially block prints of the pleasure quarters, theaters, kimono fashions, ephemeral beauties of nature, and suchlike subjects calculated to appeal to the escapist tendencies of the Edo period.

**Ushin** Conviction of feeling or of spirit. A more directly emotional style of classical poetry.

**Wabi** The beauty of loneliness, desolation, isolation, infinity. One design example given by Boyé Lafayette De Mente is a gold-flecked lacquered box that gives the impression of stars in the night sky.

**Waki** The witness, whose perception frames and introduces the **shite**'s story as the narrator does the story of *Wuthering Heights*.

**Yamato-e** A stylized form of door- and screen-painting from the late Heian and Kamakura eras. It first came into being around 999. Women thus portrayed appear in expressionless profile or semi-profile, with small mouths, plump cheeks and simplified brush-stroke eyes.

**Yonbyoshi** Collective term for the flute and three kinds of drums in the "Noh orchestra." [Also transliterated: "Yonnbyoushi."]

**Yugen** Ineffable beauty, often relating to the gaze. This term is often employed in descriptions of Noh. At first it was a Buddhist word meaning "obscure." In the Heian period it became a poetic virtue.

**Yujo** Prostitute. The eponymous heroine of the Noh play "Yuya" was one of these. [Sometimes this word is transliterated "yuujo."]

**Yuki** See **tsuki**.

**Zashiki-Noh** "Drawing room Noh." Performances held in intimate settings — temples and the like. Cf. **ozashiki**. The brief discussion of "Michimori" in this book is based on a *zashiki-Noh* performance at Jumenji Temple.

# CHRONOLOGY

## ASUKA PERIOD 552–645

552   Buddhism comes to Japan. De Bary et al. give the date of 538, and no doubt what little of this Chronology actually gets read will meet with a variety of disagreements.

## EARLY NARA PERIOD 645–710

**Late 600s**   Mention of the itinerant female entertainers called *saburoko* (serving girls). They have sometimes been interpreted as proto-geishas. See entry for *odoriko* in 1680s.

668   In Korea, the monarchy of Silla (founded in 57 B.C.) forcibly unifies the Three Kingdoms. In a trope for the highest level of beauty, Zeami will say: "In Silla at the dead of night, the sun shines brightly."

## LATE NARA PERIOD 710–794

710   Foundation of Kofuku-ji Temple (which had two prior incarnations at two other sites outside of Nara). Capital established at Nara.

752   Bronze Buddha (largest in the world) dedicated at Todai-ji in Nara.

755   An Lu-shan Revolt in China, which leads to the execution of Lady Yang Kuei-fei (718–56). Her beauty and attachment will be expressed in Komparu Zenchiku's Noh play "Yokihi."

759   Date of latest poem in the *Manyoshu* anthology.

767   Foundation of Kasuga Shrine, a place since associated with the Noh play "Kasuga ryujin."

772–846   Life of the Chinese poet Bo Ju-yi, who wrote the "Song of Lasting Pain" about Lady Yang.

794   Capital moved to Kyoto, then called Heian-kyo. (Some sources date the move 10 years earlier.)

806   Tendai Buddhism brought from China by Saicho.

*ca.* 820–30   Birth of Ono no Komachi.

825–80   Life of Arihira no Narihira, who wrote many of the poems in *The Tales of Ise.*

**Late 9th/early 10th century**   Composition of the *Tale of the Bamboo Cutter.*

*ca.* 905   Publication of the *Kokinshu* anthology of poetry.

905–951   Completion of *The Tales of Ise* by an unknown author.

935   Collapse of Silla in Korea.

*ca.* 935   Ki no Tsurayuki completes *A Tosa Journal.*

*ca.* 970–78 — *ca.* 1015   Life of Lady Murasaki Shikibu.

*ca.* 970s   The Gossamer Lady (Mitchitsuna's mother) completes *The Gossamer Journal.*

*ca.* 1000–1010   Sei Shonagon completes her *Pillow Book.*

1008–1010   Period covered by Murasaki's diary.

*ca.* 1009   Murasaki completes *The Tale of Genji.*

1030–1045   Akazome Emon completes the "main portion" of *A Tale of Flowering Fortunes*; an anonymous supplement is completed *ca.* 1300.

1114–1204   Life of the poet Shunzei, whose poem of the dead wife under moss is mentioned on p. 355.

1155–1216   Life of Ariie, whose poem about the sleeves dampened by a pining wind is mentioned on p. 355.

1160–1180   Known life-dates of the priest Shun'e, whose "curtain of mist" metaphor is referred to several times in this book.

1162–1241   Life of Teika, whose poem about the bridge over the deep gorge is mentioned on p. 375.

*ca.* 1120   Completion of *Tales of Times Now Past.*

1180–1185   War between the Heike (Taira) and the Genji (Minamoto), won by the latter.

## KAMAKURA PERIOD 1185–1333

*ca.* 1210   Compilation of the *Shin Kokinshu* anthology of poetry.

1235   Fujiwara no Teika completes the anthology *One Hundred People, One Poem Each*, which will be illustrated by Hokusai 600 years later.

1241–1350   "Late classical period" of court poetry.

*ca.* 1300   Composition of "The Lady Who Admired Vermin," which appeared in the anthology *A Riverside Counselor's Stories*. See p. 108.

1307   Lady Nijo writes her memoir, *Towazugatari*.

*ca.* 1330   Completion of *The Tale of the Heike*, perhaps by the courtier Yukinaga. The Noh plays "Atsumori" and "Shunkan" are among those derived from this source.

*ca.* 1330   Time of events in *The Taiheiki*, written not long after this.

1333   Kamakura Shogunate thrown down.

## ASHIKAGA (MUROMACHI) PERIOD 1333–1573

14th century   Appearance of the samurai code of etiquette called the Ogasawara style, prescribing how to bow, how to enter a room, etc. Geisha still follow much of this code in their formalized movements. Some Noh gestures also derive from it.

1333–84   Life of Kan'ami.

Mid 14th century   Active career of Komparu Gonnokami.

1363–1443   Life of Zeami.

1394   Yoshimitsu begins construction of the Golden Pavilion.

1395–1432   Life of Motomasa.

1400   Zeami composes *Kadensho*.

1405–68   Life of Komparu Zenchiku.

1423   Zeami composes *Sando*.

betw. 1423 and 1430   Zeami writes "Izutsu."

1424   Zeami composes "Kakyo."

1429   Zeami prohibited entry to the Sento Imperial Palace.

1434   Zeami exiled to Sado Island.

1434–1516   Life of Kanze Nobumitsu (Kojiro).

1467–78   The Onin Wars destroy most of Kyoto.

1482   Yoshimasa builds the Silver Pagoda.

1530–69  Active career of Tosa Mitsumoto, to whom the *Tale of Genji* illustrations in the Burke Album are attributed.

## MOMOYAMA PERIOD 1573–1615

1582  Hideyoshi Toyotomi takes over the capital and environs.

1589  Hideyoshi permits a pleasure quarter (called Yanagimachi, "Willow Town") to be licensed in Kyoto.

1590  Foundation of Edo (now called Tokyo).

## EDO [TOKUGAWA] PERIOD 1615–1867

1644–94  Life of Basho.

1647  Actresses banned from public performances after too many samurai brawl over their favors. Other sources give the date of 1629.

1680s  First mention of itinerant dancing girls, *odoriko*. To differentiate themselves from prostitutes, they begin to call themselves geiko, "arts-child." In Kyoto this is still the word for a geisha who has graduated from the maiko stage.

*ca.* 1700  Kabuki and woodblock arts get popular.

*ca.* 1700  First (male) geishas appear.

1742–91  Middle Tokugawa Period.

*ca.* 1750  Kiku from Fukagawa is the first woman to call herself a geisha.

*ca.* 1760  Female geishas establish themselves.

[1789  Beginning of Kansei Period.]

1760–1849  Life of Katsushika Hokusai.

1765  Kanze Motoakira publishes the *Meiwa kaisei utaibon*, which (at least for the Kanze School) narrows the Noh canon and restricts the choices of masks and costumes for given roles.

1780s  Geishas begin to perform in ad hoc festivals called *niwaka* which express "the ideals of the Floating World."

## MEJI PERIOD 1869–1912

1868–70  Noh performances abandoned in Japan.

1871  Mr. Umewaka Minoru resurrects Noh in Tokyo.

1871  First annual Miyako Odori or Cherry-Blossom Dance in Kyoto.

1873  The Empress appears in public without blackening her teeth.

1899–1972  Life of Kawabata Yasunari.

## Showa Period

1918  Kafu Nagai publishes *Geisha in Rivalry*.

1925–70  Life of Mishima Yukio (Hiraoka Kimitake).

1948  Umewaka Rokuro born.

1952  An American Occupation censor writes: "Today, the Umewaka school may be forced to cease its performances" due to "intrigue and pressure" by the Kanze School.

1954  After several decades of separation, the Umewaka School rejoins the Kanze School.

1958  Prostitution becomes illegal in Japan.

1988  Mr. Umewaka succeeds his father to become Rokuro Umewaka the fifty-sixth.

# NOTES

All sources are cited in short form (e.g.; "Ze-ami" and "Zeami"). The bibliography immediately follows. When quoting from Rimer and Yamazaki, I have not capitalized "Flower," "Grace," etc., since the other Zeami translation I cite did not.

Epigraph: "What am I to do with you . . ." — *Manyoshu*, p. 86 (poem 248: "Addressed to a Young Woman"), slightly "retranslated" by WTV. In his modern version of the Noh play "The Damask Drum," Mishima has an old janitor rhapsodize about his cruel young beloved: "She's the princess of the laurel, the tree that grows in the garden of the moon" *(Five Modern No Plays*, p. 40). And why not? In the original, the old gardener says: "They talk of the moon-tree, the laurel that grows in the Garden of the Moon . . ." (Waley, *The Noh Plays of Japan*, p. 172; "Aya no Tsuzumi").
Epigraph: "Dresses make the lady . . ." — Von Mahlsdorf, p. 109.
Epigraph: A woman never imitates herself." — Zeami, p. 142 ("Shugyoku tokka").

## 0: UNDERSTATEMENTS ABOUT THIS STRING-BALL OF IDLE THOUGHTS

Epigraph, p. 1:  "His colleagues gave their leisure to various pastimes . . ." — Mishima, *Runaway Horses*, pp. 5–6. Kafu (p. 108) refers to the same phenomenon less contemptuously in his lovely description of an aesthete's observations of nature during "an idle life in a kind of watery world whose loneliness he relished."
2:  Footnote: The poem about the book of Noh lessons — Ueda, *Light Verse*, p. 172 (*senryu* "retranslated" by WTV).
2:  "Can't a man praise the woman he loves?" — In a trope which Mishima must have liked, Zeami compares the actor who is not also a playwright to "a brave warrior who is on the battlefield without arms" (op. cit., p. 41 ["Fushikaden"]). I similarly compare to this unarmed warrior the observer of feminine beauty who has not loved women much.
2:  "Can't he describe her?" — In the ancient Welsh *Mabinogion* a raven lands on a duck's corpse. "Peredur stood and likened the exceeding blackness of

the raven, and the whiteness of the snow, and the redness of the blood, to the hair of the woman he loved best, which was as black as jet, and her flesh to the whiteness of snow, and the redness of the blood in the white snow to the two red spots in the cheeks of the woman he loved best" (p. 178, "Peredur Son of Efrawg").

## I: "THE MASK IS MOST IMPORTANT *ALWAYS*"

10: Footnote: Comments of Noh expert in Umewaka lineage — Clark corrections, unnumbered p. 2.

10: Mr. Umewaka Rokuro as a candidate for best living Noh actor in Japan — For instance: "Unanimously called a genius, Umewaka Rokuro is arguably the best dancer/actor alive." — Yokoyama Taro ms., p. 2 of 3.

10: Footnote about kimonos — Brazell (pp. 120–21) gives the nomenclature, and all of the following derives from her. She notes that "the basic garment" is "similar to the modern kimono." She provides the names for the materials used to fabricate kimonos for male and female roles; these I omit. The outer brocade robe is called a *kara-ori*. Such garments as hunting cloaks have their own names. The stiffened pleated skirts are made of *okuchi* if plain and *hangiri* if satin with gold or silver weft. Brazell goes on to detail wigs and other aspects of Noh and *kyogen* costuming.

11: Remarks of Mr. Umewaka Rokuro — Interviews in Tokyo and Osaka, April 2002. The Noh actress Yamamura Yoko was interviewed in Tokyo at the same time, on the premises of Mr. Umewaka's school.

11: The stink of Noh kimonos — Jeff Clark objects (correction to ms. p. 3) that "they're freshened with sachets, incense and an occasional venting. So it's misleading to say that they stink. The undergarments that get the most sweat etc. are washed." All the same, the kimonos brought to me by Mr. Umewaka's apprentices did stink.

17: Zeami: "All the exercises must be severely and strictly done . . ." — Ze-ami, p. 16. His name is sometimes also transliterated "Seami."

18: One observer: "A religious and sober atmosphere of almost suffocating intensity" — Ze-ami, p. 4 (foreword).

19: Dr. Yokoyama Taro: "Unlike most other music/dance performances . . ." — Tokoyama Taro, trans. by Sato Yoshiaki, p. 1 of 3.

20: Footnote on *shura* — Jeff Clark corrections, note to ms p. 9.

20: Excerpt from *Taiheiki* — De Bary et al., p. 291 ("The Loyalist Heroes").

20: Footnote: Sins washed away by the Great Exorcism — Ibid., pp. 34–35. Another peculiar sin listed is "woes from creeping insects."
Same footnote: "The Mahayana Precepts" — Ibid., p. 143.

20: "The sin of human beings" — When I remarked on the sadness of a similar Noh drama, Mr. Umewaka said, "After all, he got involved in war, so that's the tragedy of the human being. Tsunemasa is talented; he loves the lute so much, and because of his love of the instrument he returns as a ghost. He was involved in the war without his intention. But it is a sin nonetheless." Here it may be worth remarking on the Shinto notion of sin as *defilement*. In the records for The Great Exorcism of the Last Day of the Sixth Month (recorded in 927 AD), we find enumerated among the heavenly and earthly sins to be washed away by the Great Exorcism of the Last Day of the Sixth Month such evil choices as violating one's child or violating a mother and her child, then such ambiguous acts as killing animals, covering up ditches and double planting, which survival itself might necessitate, and finally unavoidable consequences of biology itself — for instance, defecation. What is guilt in this context? Indeed, some Buddhists might say, what is guilt in *any* context? Evil and delusion burdens us as does biological necessity. Only sacred mercy can save us. But save us it can. "The Mahayana Precepts in 'Admonitions of the Fanwang Sutra'" go so far as to guarantee that all of us defecators from kings to prostitutes to supernatural beings can be named "most pure ones" if we accept the Buddha's Admonitions of the Law.

21: Kagekiyo: "The end is near . . ." — Waley, p. 133.

21: *"Late dewdrops are our lives . . ."* — Loc. cit.

21: One scholar: "In the time of Tokugawa (A.D. 1602 to 1868) . . ." — Pound and Fenollosa, p. 7 (Fenollosa writing; my italics). I would have quoted from my other copy, which contains the original introduction by Fenollosa, but since Umewaka Minoru is mentioned in it so extensively I gave it to Mr. Umewaka.

22: Zeami: "The impersonation of old men is the most important thing in Noh. . ." — Ze-ami, p. 27.

23: Zeami: "He must not bend too much at the waist or at the knees . . ." — Ibid., pp. 26–27 ("Fushikaden").

23: Information on the meaning of "Tosaka" — Tochigi Reiko to WTV, 2009.

26: Footnote: "Until the Edo period, Noh was a popular art form . . ." — Clark corrections, unnumbered p. 5.

27: Footnote: "As for the portrayal of high ranking officers and noblemen, or of natural things . . ." — Loc. cit.

30: Noh performances by women in Muromachi period — Rath, p. 9.

30: The three greatest masks of Tatsuemon — Re: "Snow" the following may be of interest: "I have been requested to repair and copy the Honmen of 'Yuki' from its owner, and I have also seen the Hako-iri-musume *ko-omote* . . . which is a detailed copy of the Honmen 'Yuki' kept by Kanzesoke [and evidently itself a copy of Tatsuemon's 'Yuki,' mentioned on p. 36; plate 4]. With these in mind, I focused on creating an accurate copy. The bone structure, such as the nose tilted to the right and the chin towards the left, which are characteristics of 'Yuki,' could be done perfectly from my long years of experience. However, the colors from Muromachi-period . . . were difficult. 'Yuki' is a prime example of the subtleness and profoundness of Noh, and has a slight blue color. In modern stages, the 'Tsuki' whose nose is tilted left delivers more emotion to the viewers, but with 'Yuki,' the nose is tilted to the right. It is a difficult mask requiring a higher level of performance" (Hori, Masuda and Miyano, trans. for WTV by Yasuda Nobuko, p. 35); English slightly rev. by WTV.

30: Zeami: It is "really easy" for the Noh actor to "play the part of an ordinary woman . . ." — Loc. cit.

33: Remarks of Otsuka Ryoji — From an interview in his studio in Shimada City, Shizuoka Prefecture, 2004.

34: Atsumori — In the source version in *The Tale of the Heike* (vol. 2, p. 562), he was 17, not 15.

34: Footnote: Zoology of high female eyebrows — Morris, p. 32.

36: "Izutsu": "A frail dream breaks awake; the dream breaks to dawn." — Brazell, p. 157 ("Izutsu," trans. by Karen Brazell; for clarity I have slightly altered the wording).

37: Footnote: " 'How tall you have grown since last I saw you!' . . ." — Lady Murasaki, *The Tale of Genji*, pp. 178–79. Kawabata once said: "It is almost inconceivable that I should ever feel deep love for a woman who is completely adult" (quoted in Keene, *Dawn to the West*, p. 805). The Japanese interest in extreme youth, which sometimes makes Occidentals uncomfortable, may be seen in the following movies from the twenty-four-hour Rainbow Channel (2 Hour Adult Channel schedule, inner sheet): "The Memorial Love of School Girl 2," "Conquest Amateur School Girs [*sic*] 1", "The Nude of Anonymouse [*sic*] School Girl." — "On the Sister's Body" and "An Exhibitionist Sister Special Version" may deal with incestuous couples who are still young enough to live together. My favorite title, alas, has nothing to do with the themes of this book: "Honey Wife in an Apron on the Naked Body."

38: Footnote: "Their *hos* and *yas* indicate where they are in the score . . ." — Jeff Clark corrections, ms. p. 28.

39: Footnote: Mr. Umewaka's acquaintance with Mishima — Jeff Clark corrections, unnumbered p. 6.

41: "It's like praying to the god, wishing for good harvest." — Mr. Kanze Hideo, same interview.

41: Sexual continence of the Okina actor — "When I was a child, you had to purify yourself," said Mr. Kanze Hideo (interviewed in the lobby of his hotel in Kyoto, May 2005). "You couldn't eat together with others. You had to eat specially prepared rice for a week. You have to use different water from others just to make tea. We were so strict when I was a child! Nowadays it's not that strict. But still when we perform "Okina" we make a kind of thing in the waiting room and display Okina's mask and dedicate it to the god. Before the *shite* starts, all the performers have sake. Even if you can't drink, you just pretend that you drink."

41: Sexual continence of the Okina actor (cont'd). — In this connection it is amusing to see a woodblock from Isoda Koryusai, circa 1770, depicting a courtesan being penetrated by an Okina actor whose mask she has partially pushed aside. The editor's caption (Uhlenbeck and Winkel, p. 101) mistakenly calls "Okina" a New Year's *kyogen* play.

41: Footnote: Experience of the Kongo School's head when performing "Okina" — Ibid., p. 18.

## 2: SCHEMATICS

43: "In making a Noh, he must use elegant . . . phrases" — Zeami, p. 69 ("Shikado").

43: "*Sarugaku* is the occupation of beggars . . ." — Diary of Go-oshikoji Kintada; quoted in Hare, p. 16. It must have been wildly popular in those days. *The Taiheiki*, written not long after Zeami's career, relates (p. 131) that "around that time in the capital, men made much of the dance called field music," namely *dengaku*, "and high and low there was none that did not seek after it eagerly." The fancy garments that the lords heaped upon the actors they patronized resembled mountains; they gave them gold and silver and jewels.

44: Increasing lengths of Noh performances — Tyler, p. 13.

44: Evolving spoken parts into songs — See Hare, pp. 56–57.

44: Footnote: "Originally it was considerably more natural . . ." — Bowers, p. 23.
Same footnote: Rath's claims about Noh's ritualization — Op. cit., pp. 222–27

44: Noh's combination of verisimilitude and elegant movements — Zeami, p. 51 ("Fushikaden").

45: A "feeling one has the words right . . ." — Brower and Miner, p. 213.

45: "When one gazes upon the autumn hills . . ." — Brower and Miner, p. 269.

45: Auerbach on the Scriptures — Op. cit., p. 110.

46: "To call her to the curved bow's tip . . ." — Tyler, p. 167 ("Kinuta").

47: "A *waki* fulfills his function . . ." — Zeami (Rimer and Yamazaki), p. 165 ("Shudosho").

47: The *waki*'s determined immutability — After Pinguet, p. 113.

47: A scholar's discussion of Basho's *Narrow Road* — Ueda, *Basho*, p. 42. It has been remarked by Donald Keene (*Twenty Plays of the No Theatre*, p. 792) that Kawabata's narrator in "The Izu Dancer" resembles the *waki* of a Noh play. Keene pushes this insight farther, claiming (*Dawn to the West*,

p. 805) that "this is true of the men in other works by Kawabata, who serve mainly to set off the women . . . they are . . . hardly more than the waki who induces the shite to appear before us."

47:     "These generally have little to say." — Tyler, p. 8.

47:     Ghost story from *The Taiheiki* — Op. cit., pp. 332–33.

48:     Brief explanations of the masks mentioned for "Kinuta" — Takaoka et al., unnumbered p. in ch. "A way into another world . . ."

49:     "From the fact that earthly life has ceased . . ." — Auerbach, p. 192.

49:     "The only wine a valley stream . . ." + "Wait a while . . ." — Brazell, pp. 186, 192 ("Shunkan," trans. Eileen Kato).

49:     Footnote: Alternate end of Shunkan — *The Tale of the Heike*, vol. 1, pp. 190–91.

49:     Same footnote: Hokusai's Shunkan — *Men and Women*, p. 231. p. 7 (Shunkan, Buddhist priest . . . exiled to Kikaiga-shima).

49:     "The dull thud of the fulling block, in the chill of night." — Keene, *Twenty Nō Plays,* p. 309 ("Torioi-bune"). This sound exerted a similar effect upon Lady Nijo, who (p. 29) found herself weeping at "the bleak sound of wooden mallets beating silk" not long after her father's cremation.

49:     The *shite* of "Izutsu," and her alteration into her lover — Hare, pp. 150–52.

50:     "We who dwell in dark delusions . . ." — Keene, *Twenty Nō Plays*, p. 93 ("The Brocade Tree").

50:     Zeami's five parts of a Noh play — Hare, pp. 49–51.

52:     Attainment by the demonic *shite* of "Aoi-no-Ue" of Buddahood "free of delusion" — Bethe and Emmert, Noh Guide 7, p. 55 (words of chorus).

53:     Facts about the Noh stage — Pound and Fenollosa, pp. 34–35. The original Kabuki stage was similar (Gunji, pp. 20–22).

54:     Separation of stage by white sand suggests Shinto origins — Hoover, p. 150.

54:     "The music and dance of noh have always been the central concern . . ." — Hare, p. 55.

54:     Props "always" supplied based on the music (lit. "have been always equipped based on all different music") — Tokugawa Art Museum, p. 121; trans. for WTV by Keiko Golden.

54:     Information on flute and drums — After Bethe and Emmert, Noh Guide 3, pp. 65, 67 (notes 4–5); also after Tokugawa Art Museum, p. 131; trans. for WTV by Keiko Golden (English grammar slightly corrected by WTV).

54:     "A sharp, urgent click" + "a muffled, funereal boom" — Hoover, pp. 151, 150.

54:     Use of the flute to begin "Atsumori" — After Bethe, Emmert and Brazell, Noh Guide 5, p. 6.

54:     Information on *jo, ha, kyu* — After Keene, *Twenty Plays of the Nō Theatre*, p. 13.

55:     "Rhythmically unobtrusive." — Hare, p. 53.

55: "Improvisation in Noh is probably closer to that of Sviatoslav Richter . . ." — Clark corrections, unnumbered pp. 3–4, 6.

56: *Kotoba* and other modes of singing — After Brazell, p. 122.

56: "Pitch in noh is relative . . ." — Bethe and Emmert, Noh Guide 7, p. 60.

56: "The importance of the music is in its intervals . . ." — Pound and Fenollosa, p. 32.

56: "Contrary to the principles of our art." — Zeami, quoted in Waley, *The No Plays of Japan*, p. 30.

56: Footnote: "Noh music probably entered its present incarnation around the beginning of the sixteenth century." — Information from Takeda and Bethe, pp. 29, 32.

56: Skill in Noh singing was widespread among the samurai class — After *Guide to Edo-Tokyo Museum*, p. 14.

56: "A truly fine play involves gesture based on chanting." — Zeami (Rimer and Yamazaki), p. 44 ("Fushikaden").

56: "Intelligent dancing — which might as well be called correct dancing . . ." — Denby, pp. 146–47 ("How to Judge a Dancer," 1943).

56: "All the exercises must be severely and strictly done. . . ." — Zeami, p. 16.

57: "Noh is for the warrior . . ." — Mr. Ichikawa Shunen, interviewed in Tokyo, January 2008; translated by Kawai Takako.

57: Admonition for performing "Matsukaze" — Zeami (Rimer and Yamazaki), p. 184 ("Sarugaku dangi").

57: Umewaka Minoru's "roll" for dancers — Pound and Fenollosa, p. 30.

57: "All I am able to do is teach you the form . . ." — Iwasaki and Brown, p. 297.

57: "There is no room here for my own thinking." — Zeami, p. 69.

57: Mr. Mikata Shizuka — Interviewed in his studio in Jumenji Temple, Kyoto, 2004.

57: Footnote: "It is . . . possible for an actor to deliver a line perfectly . . ." — Keene, *Twenty Plays of the No Theatre*, p. 2.

59: Description of *mai* style — Cavaye, Griffith and Senda, p. 52.

59: Mr. Kanze Hideo — Interviewed in the lobby of his hotel in Kyoto, May 2005.

61: "Their movements become dreamlike glosses . . ." — Bowers, p. 17.

61: "She was instantly recognized as a geisha of the very first class . . ." — Kafu, p. 52.

61: Meanings of red brocade robe, under-kimono's colored neckband and diamond-fish-scale design (this I have extrapolated to the "sword and mountain" design) — Brazell, p. 121.

61: Colors associated with middle-aged women — Interview with Hagashi Sumiko, curator, Kanazawa Noh Museum, January 2008.

61: Madwomen *shite*s let their right sleeves slip— Information from Takeda and Bethe, p. 246 (checklist of the exhibition).

61:     Descriptions of Noh costumes — Mitsui family, trans. for WTV by Yasuda Nobuko, pp. 19, 56, 46, 1–15 (summary, from which I take information on fabric-dyeing and the air raids), 25, 21. Interpretations (except for that of the Chinese monster, which is spelled out in the text) are mine.

62:     "Merely since the middle of the Edo period." — Information from Takeda and Bethe, pp. 118–19 (Kawakami Shigeki, "The Development of the Karaori as a Noh Costume").

63:     Precedence in age of the Komparu School's mask — Rath, p. 11.

63:     Relative newness of Kita School — From same interview with Mr. Kanze Hideo.

63:     "Kanze has the reputation of being on the flashy side . . ." — Clark corrections, unnumbered p. 5.

64:     Kanze's preference for *ko-omotes* to play *shite* roles — Just to remind you of the infallibility of my understanding, I report from Hori, Masuda and Miyano, trans. for WTV by Yasuda Nobuko: "*Ko-omote* is often used for *tsure* in Kanze-ryu" (p. 32).

64:     Footnote: Remarks of Mr. Umewaka, Jeff Clark and Dr. Yokoyama Taro — From first Umewaka interview, from Clark corrections (unnumbered p. 6), and from Dr. Yokoyama Taro's communication to WTV, p. 3 of 3.

64:     Brighter Noh pieces should be performed at night — Ibid., p. 39.

64:     "The more intense the emotion, the more regular the metre." — Tyler, p. 9.

### 3: MALIGNANCE AND CHARM

65:     "Noh was supposedly born out of sacred Shinto chants . . ." — Information from Pound and Fenollosa, p. 30.

65:     "Masked court dances also seem to have been already on the scene . . ." — Information from Rath, p. 12.

65:     Footnote: Evolution of masks — After Nakanishi and Komma, pp. 102–3.

65:     Miraculous origins of masks; ability to bring in a good rice crop — Ibid., pp. 18–21.

66:     Motoyoshi on masks — Zeami (Rimer and Yamazaki), (pp. 230–31, 236–38).

66:     Definitions of "Sarugaku dangi" + "Noh was considered the property of the government . . ." — Prof. Nishino Haruo, Director, the Nogami Memorial Institute for Noh Studies, Hosei University, Tokyo, October 2006, Tochigi Reiko interpreting. Prof. Nishino showed me a two-volume work in German, copiously illustrated, by Friedrich Perzynski, which he thought to be the best treatment of this subject in any language. Unfortunately, he said, the original was extremely rare, and the English translation was poor. He was in the process of translating it into Japanese.

66:    "But by the late sixteeth century . . ." — All information in this sentence from Rath, p. 29.

66:    "There are now sixty main types . . ." — Information from Rath, p. 14. My translator Yasuda Nobuko summarizes Hori, Masuda and Miyano thus (pp. 17–24): "The number of Noh masks differs largely depending on where the line between basic masks and variant masks is drawn. Considering various theories, most of the current programs can be performed with 60 masks. The author divides the masks into groups A to U, with male masks and female masks as the major categories (Okina masks are treated separately). The latter half of this section explain the use and effect of masks, with examples from various programs. In many of them, different masks are used for the first part (Maeshite) and the latter part (Nochijite). In modern days, unique combinations of masks and costumes are used, bringing in fresh ideas to Noh theater." I remain far too ignorant to attempt to categorize the variation in masks and other Noh accoutrements over time. One Tokugawa collection of these items, so the catalogue informs me, "shows a splendid Edo period Noh spirit that is far different from that of Meiji period Noh collections" (Tokugawa Art Museum, p. 51; trans. for WTV by Keiko Golden. English grammar slightly corrected by WTV). I saw the exhibition and admired it, but certainly could not distinguish Edo from Meiji.

66:    Types of masks — Takaoka et al., unnumbered p. in ch. "A way into another world . . ."; also, Kodama, pp. 151–53.

66:    Footnote: Utamaro's three best types of vulva — Uhlenbeck and Winkel, p. 119.

66:    Ochie of Koiseya — Utamaro (Sato Takanobu), trans. Yasuda Nobuko. Picture 6: Edokoumeibijin; Kobikichoushinyashiki; Koiseya Ochie, around Kansei 4–5 (1792–93). Large Nishikie. Chiba City Museum of Art.

67:    The way that old women in their late twenties arrange their hair in the *oomarumage* style — Ibid. Picture 11: Kasenkoinobu Fukakushinobukoi. Around Kansei 5–6 (1793–94). Large Nishikie. National Museum of Asian Art-Guimet.

67:    The shaved eyebrows and *shimadakuzushi* hairstyle of a certain Utamaro beauty — Ibid. Picture 10: Kasenkoinobu Monoomoukoi. Around Kansei 5–6 (1793–94). Large Nishikie. National Museum of Asian Art-Guimet.

67:    Description of the *kohime* — Hori, Masuda and Miyano, trans. for WTV by Yasuda Nobuko and slightly rev. by WTV; p. 28. My visual description comes from the accompanying plate.

67:    Kanze Motoakira and the Noh canon — Rath, pp. 199–203.

68:    Other remarks of Mr. Mikata (excepting the fn. remark on the maidservant's mask in "Kinuta," which took place in 2006) — From the 2004 Kyoto interview.

68: Mr. Mikata Shizuka's choice of masks for "Michimori" — Interview in Jumenji Temple, Kyoto the day after the performance (October 2006).

68: Ms. Nakamura Mitsue's remarks about masks in this section — From an interview in her studio in Kyoto, October 2006.

69: The plump-cheeked, snow-skinned girl in the Genji Picture-Scroll — *Genji Monogatari Emaki*, Tokugawa Museum version, p. 182

69: The "hard" *ko-omote* — Kanze, Hayashi and Matsuda, pbk. commentary vol., p. 24.

69: Otsuka Ryoji — Interviewed in his studio in Shimada, 2004.

69: "In what I do, beauty is about millimeters." — *New Beauty*, winter-spring 2008, p. 200 (advertisement for Dr. Daniel Shapiro).

69: Mr. Kanze Hideo — Interviewed in the lobby of his hotel in Kyoto, May 2005.

70: *Waka-onna* in "Izutsu" and "Eguchi" — Kanze, Hayashi and Matsuda, pbk. commentary vol., p. 23.

70: Miscellaneous other characteristics of same mask — *Dictionary of Japanese Art Terms*, p. 594.

70: Use of the *magojiro* to play Yuya — Nakanishi and Kiyonori, p. 123.

70: "Both his acting and his singing should probably be classed at the rank of the tranquil flower." — Hare, p. 30.

70: "The delicate red on the cheeks of this mask . . ." — Hori, Masuda and Miyano, trans. for WTV by Yasuda Nobuko and slightly rev. by WTV; p. 58 (words of Katayama Kurouemon).

71: *Maeshite* of "Kinuta"'s representation by a *fukai* — Mr. Mikata Shizuka remarked that the mask representing her "has to be an old lady, and we have only have three here. Among them, we have to choose." In another interview he spoke of the maidservant, saying that her role would be well served by a *ko-omote* mask in order to delicately express the possibility that the absent husband had transferred his affections to her.

71: Choice of masks for "Miidera" — Bethe and Emmert, Noh Guide 3, p. 5.

72: "Eyebrows convey different emotions" — Aucoin, p. 115.

72: Description of the *masukami* mask — After Nakanishi and Kiyomori, p. 76 (plate 81; attributed to Tatsuemon). Hori, Masuda and Miyano speculatively derive the name from Masuho, meaning the hair is like grass waving in the wind (p. 72).

72: Description of the *manbi* mask — Ibid., p. 78 (plate 83, by Shimotsuna Shoshin).

72: "How can charm be expressed? . . ." — Hori, Masuda and Miyano, trans. for WTV by Yasuda Nobuko and slightly rev. by WTV; p. 40.

73: "*Uba*" as used by Hokusai — Hokusai, *One Hundred Poets*, pp. 7, 9 (introduction).

73: Use of *uba* or *rojo* to portray Komachi — Rath, p. 15.

73: "Inner elegance" of *rojo* — Takeda and Bethe, p. 253 (checklist of the exhibition).

74: Employment of a *deigan* in "Kinuta" — Kanze, Hayashi and Matsuda, pbk. commentary vol., p. 34.

74: Description of the seventeenth-century *deigan* by Genkyu Mitsunaga — After Tokugawa Art Museum, *Noh Masks and Costumes*, p. 39 (plate 74).

74: "Particularly famous as a mask embodying a woman's hatred and sorrow." — Kodama, p. 153.

74: "The hannia in Awoi no Uye is lofty in feeling . . ." — Pound and Fenollosa, p. 32.

75: Footnote: *Ja, hannya* or *omi-onna* mask for "Dojoji" — Nakanashi and Komma, pp. 122–23.

75: Use of *ryo-no-onna* to represent Unai-otome — Kanze, Hayashi and Matsuda, pbk commentary vol., p. 25.

75: "Calm, almost rectangular pupil openings" of *yase-onna* — Takeda and Bethe, p. 253 (checklist of the exhibition).

75: Cited use of *yase-onna* — *Dictionary of Japanese Art Terms,* pp. 629–30.

75: *Yase-onna*: Anecdotes of Himi, Kanze Hisao — Hori, Masuda and Miyano, trans. for WTV by Yasuda Nobuko; p. 74.

75: Footnote: "A young male role that has both secular and religious aspects." — Kodama, p. 151.

76: Use of the *higaki-no-onna* — Kanze, Hayashi and Matsuda, pbk. commentary vol., p. 35.

## 4: A BRANCH OF FLOWERS

85: Characteristics of a successful play of the first rank — Zeami (Rimer and Yamazaki), p. 44 ("Fushikaden"). Such terms as "Flower" and "Grace" are capitalized in these translations. I have elected not to follow that usage, since other translations I cite do not.

85: Seasons of the flower; flower, charm and novelty; "a flower blooming in the rocks" — Ibid., pp. 52–54 ("Fushikaden").

86: Deliberate reintroduction of impurity — Ibid., p. 67 ("Shikado").

86: "The flower does not exist as a separate entity." — Ibid., p. 62 ("Fushikaden").

86: "A flower blooms by maintaining secrecy." — Ibid., p. 59 ("Fushikaden").

86: "Stage characters such as Ladies-in-Waiting . . ." — Ibid., p. 47 ("Fushikaden").

86: "Dignified and mild appearance . . ." — Zeami (Rimer and Yamazaki), p. 93 ("Kakyo").

87: "Roles requiring great taste and elegance . . ." — Ibid., p. 65 ("Shikado").

87: The five skills of dancing — Ibid., p. 80 ("Kakyo").

87: Rules for performing a woman's role — Ibid., p. 76 ("Kakyo"); p. 227 ("Sarugaku dangi").

87: "It should seem as though each were holding a branch of flowers in his hand." — Ibid., p. 94 ("Kakyo"). In 2005 I asked Mr. Mikata how he carried his branch of flowers, and he replied: "For example, in 'Fushikaden' it tells how to play a demon. To express your demon, you must be not only just strong but even a rock," he said, spreading his hands, "as if a flower comes out of rock. An old person, it's as if a flower is coming out of an old tree." — "So if you were portraying a very ferocious demon," I asked, "would you make the demon less harsh?" — "No," he replied. "Well, of course you play to your utmost, but your core strength and your real strength are different. Although you subdue your movements, the real strength can still be expressed. Strongly performing those actions is not the best."

87:     Footnote:    Renoir: "For a battle piece to be good . . ." — Malraux, p. 353.

88:     Footnote on the demonic grace of Lady Rokujo — Bethe and Emmert, Noh Guide 7, p. 64.

89:     "He must not fail to retain a tender heart." — Zeami (Rimer and Yamazaki), p. 58 ("Fushikaden").

89:     "If the motion is more restrained than the emotion behind it . . ." — Ibid., p. 74 ("Kakyo").

89:     Surface brilliance and heart — Ibid., pp. 100–101 ("Kakyo").

89:     Appearance of doing nothing — Ibid., p. 94 ("Kakyo").

90:     Forget the details, etc. — Ibid., p. 102 ("Kakyo").

90:     *"The art of the flower of tranquility . . ."* — Ibid., p. 121 ("Kyui").

## 5: THE DRAGONS OF KASUGA

91:     Description of "Kiyotsune" — from a Takigi-Noh performance on the grounds of Kofuku-ji Temple, Nara, May 2005.

92:     The Venerable Myoe's visions and their revision — Based on Tyler, pp. 142–45 (introduction to "Kasuga ryujin").

92:     "The face is long . . ." — *Dictionary of Japanese Art Terms*, p. 177 (entry on *Kurohige).

93:     Kofuku-ji as "older and more prestigious than Kasuga" — See Aoyama, pp. 16, 24.

93:     The Venerable Gedatsu of Kasagi and the Seven Great Temples: Ibid., pp. 148, 151.

93:     Footnote: Gedatsu's supernatural vision — *The Taiheiki*, pp. 368ff.

93:     Affiliation of Zeami's troupe with both Kasuga and Kofuku-ji — Rath, p. 37, who notes that they were also affiliated with Tonomine Temple in Nara.

93:     Zeami: "One must not permit this art to stray . . ." — Op. cit., p. 15.

94:     Footnote: Fenollosa on Kasuga as the origin-site of Japanese drama — Pound and Fenollosa, p. 59.

94:     Kanami's promise of Takigi performances at Nara in perpetuity — Zeami (Rimer and Yamazaki), p. 245 ("Sarugaku dangi").

94:     Remarks of Mr. Kanze Hideo — Interview in Kyoto, May 2005.

95: First definition of *yugen* — Indebted to a beautiful passage in De Bary et al., pp. 365–66.

95: *Yugen* as the highest principle of Noh — Ibid., p. 369 (Zeami, "Entering the Realm of Yugen").

95: Immediately following three sentences (some prerequisites of *yugen*): Ibid., pp. 369–71; paraphrased and abbreviated by me.

95: Noh's nine stages of excellence — Ibid., 372–76 (Zeami, "The Nine Stages of the No in Order").

95: Footnote: The silver bowl must be oxidized — De Bary et al., p. 367.

96: Tanizaki on Noh, Japanese flesh and darkness — Lopate, pp. 349–51.

96: Bowing of the vegetation before Myoe of Mikasa Grove — Tyler, p. 149 (chorus of "Kasuga ryujin").

97: The man who went hawking in Kasuga — *Tales of Ise*, pp. 35–36 (Dan I).

97: "Matsukaze"'s links to *The Tale of Genji* and *The Tales of Ise* — Tyler, op. cit., pp. 184, 186–87.

97: Muromachi illustrations to *The Tale of Genji* — Murase, chaps. 11, 45.

97: Footnote on Muromachi Period — Zeami, p. 8 (intro.).

98: The Hokusai woodblock drawing of Kofuku-ji — *One Hundred Poets*, p. 157 (ill. to # 57, Fujiwara no Mototoshi).

98: Lady Han's poem about Kasuga moor — Keene, *Twenty Plays*, p. 135 ("Hanago").

98: Yukigeshiki Uji no Ukifune — *Miyako Odori* program, 2005; trans. for WTV by Sumino Junko.

99: Some other miscellaneous textual allusions to Kasuga — Brower and Miner (p. 208) cite an ancient poem about "the green fields of ancient Kasuga," with erotic overtones of girls waving their white hempen sleeves. Zeami's father Kanami was said to have been taken to Kasuga as a boy and dedicated to the god Kasuga Myokin, who is sometimes equated with the Dragon God (Hare, p. 13). It was only at Kasuga and the Shogun's court that the enigmatic "Yumi-Ya" canto of Noh could be sung (Pound and Fenollosa, p. 8). Kasuga is mentioned in a poem in the classic *Tosa Journal* (McCullough, p. 91), and Abe no Nakamaro made a poem to the Chinese when departing (ibid., p. 87): "I see the same moon / that appeared above the hills / of Mikasa at Kasuga." In the Noh play "Motomezuka," the chorus chants an invocation to the watchfire guardian of Kasuga (Keene, *Twenty Plays*, p. 42). In the play "Taniko," pilgrims remark on Mount Mikasa in Kasuga as they pass it (ibid., p. 322).

99: Proposal that Lady Nijo become the Emperor's concubine — Lady Nijo, p. 265, n. 3.

99: Kasuga's tree carried to the capital — Ibid., p. 146.

99: The lover's dream of Kasuga — Ibid., p. 105. For a brief description of the place in her day, see p. 202.

99:  The concubine's flawless recitations from the *Kokin Shu* poems — Shona-gon, pp. 37–39.

99:  Arthur Waley on the relative meagerness of Noh's allusions — *The No Plays of Japan*, p. 41.

100:  "A nerve, a wire, a roadway . . ." + "The chief work of literary men . . ." — Fenollosa, pp. 22–23.

100:  Utagawa Kunimori I's erotic parodies of *Genji* — Uhlenbeck and Win-kel, p. 209 ("A Critical Study of the Charms of Women," figs. 82a–b). The attribution is not completely certain; the artist may be Utagawa Yoshikazu.

100:  "The *shite*'s parts are more reliable than the *waki*'s . . ." — Hare, p. 58.

100:  "About the instrumentation and the dance choreography less can be said." — Again, see Hare, pp. 58–61.

100:  ". . . more visually explanatory and possibly centered on *yugen* . . ." — Bethe and Emmert, Noh Guide 7, p. 76.

100:  Revised coloration of Rokujo's robe — Ibid., p. 70.

100:  "Then you should take lines from well-known poems . . ." — Zeami, *Sando*, quoted in Hare, p. 54. Many Noh plots are derived from folktales (see for instance Ikeda, pp. 175, 236–37). However, Donald Keene opines *(Twenty Plays of the No Theatre*, p. 2) that "the allusions that are so troublesome to the translator could not have been entirely clear even to the first audiences."

101:  Ivan Morris on "false exoticism" — Shonagon, p. 17.

101:  "All that remains of Aeschylus is his genius." — Malraux, p. 46.

101:  Footnote on *hon'i*: "Express impatience in waiting . . ." — Brower and Miner, p. 254. Not mere books, but leviathan-encyclopedias ought to be devoted to cherry blossom symbolism in Japan. In his youth, Zeami him-self was compared with "a profusion of cherry or pear blossoms in the haze of a spring dawn; this is how he captivates, with this blossoming of his appearance." — Nijo Yoshitomi, quoted in Hare, p. 17. Sometimes I sympathize with Princess Shikishi (died 1201), who wrote in a tanka about cherry blossoms: "Coldly they fall; coldly I watch" (Sato and Wat-son, p. 182).


6: SUNSHINE AT MIDNIGHT

102:  Interview with Mr. Mikata — In the temple chamber where he had per-formed "Michimori" the previous night, Kyoto, October 2006.

103:  Proust on Madame Berma — Vol. 1, p. 485 ("Madame Swann at Home" section of *Within a Budding Grove*).

103:  Footnote: Thirteenth Case on snow in a silver bowl — Hsien and Ch'in, pp. 88–91. In the verse appended to this koan we read the following typi-cally cryptic lines: "He knows how to say, 'Piling up snow in a silver bowl.'

The frog can't leap out of the basket. A double case. Quite a few people will lose their bodies and lives." And here is the pointer to the Thirty-Seventh Case (p. 226): "Some people lower their heads and linger in thought, trying to figure it out with their intellect. They hardly realize that they are seeing ghosts without number in front of their skulls."

## 7: PERFECT FACES

106: Epigraph: "Someone once said that black hair is a 'shunga' . . ." — Miyata Masayuki, p. 5 (excerpt from the art book *Rafu* [naked woman]); trans. for WTV by Sumino Junko; English substantially revised by WTV.

107: Footnote: Chao Luan-Luan's encomia, and remarks on the same — Weinberger, pp. 118–19, 233.

107: Frequent image in the *bijin-ga* of Kaigetsu — *Moronobu to Shoki Ukiyoe*, trans. for WTV by Sumino Junko. Figure 12: Kaigetsudo, Ando. "Tachi-bijin zu" (A standing beauty). Idemitsu Museum.

107: "As their 'ruby' lips parted . . ." — Hawks, p. 395. This took place in Yokohama. Here is a British reaction to geishas in the same period: ". . . some gorgeously dressed singing and dancing girls, their face painted ghastly white, their lips green, and their teeth black . . ." (Peabody Museum, p. 58 [Allen Hockey, "First Encounters — Emerging Stereotypes, " quoting the *Illustrated London News*, 1874]). That this disgust was less ideological than aesthetic is suggested by the following kinder observation, noted in Simoda (p. 397): Among the Japanese, in distinction to other Asian nationalities such as the Turks, "woman is recognised as a companion, and not merely treated as a slave."

108: "Her eyebrows look like furry caterpillars . . ." — McCullough, p. 258 ("The Lady Who Admired Vermin", *ca.* 1300).

108: Court ladies blackening their teeth for the New Year's banquet of 1025 — McCullough, p. 228 *(A Tale of Flowering Fortunes)*.

108: Further piquant examples of black teeth: In *The Taiheiki* (p. 60) we encounter "the painted eyebrows and blackened teeth of a boy of fifteen years." *The Tale of Genji* (p. 207) details the charm of a boy's decayed teeth. Interestingly (p. 127), those of the heroine, Murasaki, are not blackened.

108: Black teeth of some geishas in last month of maikodom — Gallagher, p. 159.

108: Tanizaki on black teeth — Lopate, pp. 352–53 (much condensed).

108: "Like a jeweled hairpin . . ." — *The Tales of Ise*, p. 61 (Dan XXI).

109: The woman with boils on her body — *The Tales of Ise*, p. 137 (Dan XCVI).

109: "The moon was so bright that I was embarrassed to be seen . . ." — Lady Murasaki, *Diary*, p. 36.

109: "Her hair falls just about three inches past her heels . . ." — Ibid., p. 47.

109: "The contrast between her pale skin . . ." — Ibid., p. 48.

109: Ichirakutei Eisui's print of "The Courtesan Karakoto of the Chojiyu House" — Seen at the Ota Ukiyo-e Museum in Tokyo, 2006. Tochigi Reiko suggests that "Chojiya" would be a better transliteration.

110: "Her tresses black as a mud-snail's bowels . . ."— *Manyoshu*, p. 310, poem 986. See also p. 201 (poem 615).

110: The black hair is so common a stock epithet that it is mocked by Mishima in his twentieth-century version of "The Damask Drum" *(Five Modern No Plays,* p. 41).

110: The lovely woman is often compared to a mirror — For instance, *Manyoshu*, p. 168 (poem 513: "An Elegy").

110: Osaka Port (Mitsu) compared to the mirror on a girl's comb-case — Ibid., p. 93 (poem 273: Tajihi Kasamaro, "On His Journey to Tsukushi").

110: "When I visited the abyss of Tamashima . . ." — Ibid., p. 258 (poem 793, one of the "Poems Composed on a Trip to the River of Matsura").

110: "On the Death of an Uneme . . ." — Ibid., p. 45 (poem 112).

110: "Of the Maiden Tamana . . ." — Ibid., p. 216 (poem 614).

110: "Lovely eyebrows / Curving like the far-off waves" — Ibid., p. 128 (poem 402: Lady Otomo of Sakanoe, "Sent to Her Elder Daughter from the Capital").

110: "The young moon afar" — Ibid., p. 135 (poem 430: Otomo Yakamochi, "On the New Moon").

111: Direct and indirect quotations in the subsequent paragraph — Lady Murasaki, *Diary*, pp. 6, 7, 20, 19, 25. Other passages bearing on this subject may be found on pp. 15, 17, 47, 65.

111: "As long as the character is mysteriously beautiful . . ." — Hare, p. 132, excerpt from *Sando*.

111: Women depicted in the Tokugawa Museum's Genji Picture-Scroll — *Genji Monogatari Emaki*, Tokugawa Museum version, p. 142.

111: Footnote: Description of the *hikime kagibana* technique — Ibid., pp. 157–61, trans. for WTV by Yasuda Nobuko; revised by me for grammar and style, and slightly abridged.

112: Genji has relations with women he cannot see — For instance, *Genji*, p. 149.

112: Screened reclusiveness of *The Taiheiki*'s heroines — Op. cit.; e.g., pp. 53, 330.

112: Definition of *miekakure* — De Mente, pp. 78–79.

112: "Make your sensibility the basis of your acting . . ." — Ibid., p. 133.

112: Himi Munetada's mask and its model — Kanze et al., *Omote*, commentary volume; remarks on plates 20–21.

113: Description of a seventeenth-century courtesan — Saikaku, pp. 137–38 ("The Life of an Amorous Woman").

113: Kamo no Chomei: "A beautiful woman . . ." — Quoted in Brower and Miner, p. 268.

113: Interview with Kanze Hideo — In the lobby of his hotel in Kyoto, 2005.

113: Extract from *Dr. Zhivago* — P. 247.

114: Footnote: "The transsexual's position consists of wanting to be All . . ." — Millot, p. 42.

115: Public appearance of the Japanese Empress with unblackened teeth (1873) — Blomberg, p. 202.

115: "The ideal feminine face must be long and narrow" — Bacon, pp. 58–59 (fn).

115: "That reminds me of *The Tale of Genji* . . ." — Ms. Kawai Takako, interviewed by telephone, January 2006.

115: Footnote: "Chinese girl beauty is large eye . . ." — My interpreter "Michelle" (Wei Xiao Min), interviewed in Nan Ning, summer 2002. She appears at greater length in my book *Poor People*.

115: "I totally disagree! That is *so* weird! . . ." — Mrs. Keiko Golden, interviewed by telephone, January 2006.


## 8: AYA KUDO AND THE *ZO-ONNA*

117: Photographs of Aya Kudo — Saiki Hiroyoshi, unnumbered pp.

118: "A slender, oval face of the classic melon-seed type . . ." — Tanizaki, p. 144 ("The Bridge of Dreams").

118: "A face well-rounded in the modern style" — Saikaku, p. 132 ("The Life of an Amorous Woman").

118: The *zo-onna* and *waka-onna* masks — Nakamura Mitsue postcards.

120: Footnote: "The crease lines between the eyebrows on statues of male Shinto gods. . ." — Takeda and Bethe, p. 65 (Tanabe Saburosuke, "The Birth and Evolution of Noh Masks").

121: "On the last night of the year . . ." — Lady Murasaki, pp. 44–45.

121: Preference for young, symmetrical and composite faces — Nehamas, pp. 64–65.

121: Various masculine and feminine facial lengths, widths and distances — Heath, pp. 44–45.

121: "Extend the whites." — Aucoin, p. 37.

121: Footnote: Alteration by angle of perceived expression of *magojiro* mask — Lyons et al.

122: "Female masks, whether *ko-omote* . . ." — Hori, Masuda and Miyano, trans. for WTV by Yasuda Nobuko and slightly rev. by WTV; p. 39. Hori continues: "When 'Tsuki' or 'Yuki' is worn for the *shite* role, 'Hana' can be used for the *tsure*. The nose is not tilted, but carved straight."

123: Mr. Mikata Shizuka on the subject of Ms. Nakamura's masks — Interviewed in his studio in Jumenji Temple, Kyoto, 2004.

123: Interview with Nakamura Mitsue — In her studio in Kyoto, 2004. "Why did you decide to make masks?" I asked her. She replied: "In the beginning, I just liked Noh masks. I started learning. As I trained, the more I worked on them, the more I loved them. I studied in art school at university. I was doing oil painting. And I liked to paint human faces. I was very good at sketching. I was very good at grasping shape. So, from hindsight, it was a very good decision." I inquired (tactlessly, I suspect) whether she could support herself easily, and she modestly replied: "Generally speaking, I'm not known."

## 9: HER GOLDEN LIPS SLIGHTLY PARTED

126: The parted lips of Kate Bosworth — *Marie Claire*, vol. 15, no. 4 (April 2008), pp. 108–13 (cover story, "Pieces of Kate," photographed by Mark Abrahams).
127: Place of Kannon in Esoteric Buddhism — De Bary et al., p. 176.

## 10: CROSSING THE ABYSS

128: Footnote: List of things that are near though distant — Shonagon, p. 181.
130: Hilary Nichols — Interviewed in Sacramento, July 2005.
131: Footnote: The young boy in Berlin who likes dusting — Von Mahlsdorf, p. 22.
133: How the harlot's embrace changed the wild man — *Gilgamesh*, pp. 63, 65.
136: "Sachiko" — Interviewed by phone (she was in Tokyo), August 2005.
136: The Japanese-American lady — Mrs. Keiko Golden, interviewed by phone (she was in San Francisco), July 2007.
138: Marina Vulicévic — Interviewed in Beograd, October 2007.

## 11: WHAT IS GRACE?

141: "Some Japanese women have fair skin glowing with femininity . . ." — Kawabata, *Beauty and Sadness*, p. 142.
141: Descriptions of Komako — Kawabata, *Snow Country*, pp. 18, 32, 73, 101, 168. Typically, Kawabata mentions Noh only in passing (p. 149). By the way, it is not as if the grace of Kawabata's heroines is necessarily fulfilling or even wholesome. In *Beauty and Sadness*, the woman's allure is mere bait for a pathological revenge. In *The Izu Dancer*, the heroine is discovered in her nudity to be still a child, and no consummation occurs. In *Snow Country*, the anti-hero, Shimamura, is certainly incapable of loving the geisha Komako except with his eyes and penis. Nor is it clear, in spite of the attachment to him that she most certainly demonstrates, that she, prisoner of drunken anguish and reticent participant in another murky love triangle, could love anybody wholeheartedly.

142:  "From the hollow / Of her throat . . ." — Chrétien de Troyes, p. 28 (lines 839–42), "retranslated" by WTV.

143:  Footnote: Sordamour's hair and thread — Ibid., p. 38 (lines 1158–62), "retranslated" by WTV.

143:  Yeats's poem to Anne Gregory — Op. cit., p. 263 ("For Anne Gregory").

143:  Collarbone as "arguably one of the most feminine parts of the body" — *InStyle* magazine, vol. 15, no. 1, January 2008, p. 89 ("Style File: Figure Flattery").

143:  Desirability of high cheekbones — *New Beauty* magazine, winter-spring 2008, p. 135 ("Face" section).

143:  "Talons dyed with the blood of lovers . . ." — Saadi, p. 184 (VII.19).

143:  Pontano's enumeration of feminine charms — Op. cit., pp. 13, 69 (I.4, I.23); pp. 21, 103, 109, 121, 125, 129, 131 (I.8, II.4, II.7, II.12, II.14, II.16, II.17); pp. 105, 179 (II.5, II.34); pp. 115, 119, 135, 177 (II.10, II.11, II.19, II.33).

144:  Body proportions in female *vs.* male — Morris, p. 177 (belly), 224 (back), 225 (buttocks), 248 (feet). Waist and hip information from Morris is cited separately below.

144:  Replacement of onnagata's acomplishment by actress's anatomy in Meiji era and after — Kano, esp. pp. 7–8.

144:  Feminine character of the mirror in ancient Greece — Geoffrey-Schneiter, p. 22.

144:  Female impersonation in Niger — Hanna, p. 54.

145:  "She is sumptuously arrayed in ornaments . . ." — Jayadeva, p. 99 (VII, stanza 13, "retranslated" by WTV).

145:  Footnote: Jennifer Finney Boylan.

145:  Recollections of Sharon Morgan — *Transgender Tapestry* magazine, issue no. 112, summer 2007, p. 21 (Sharon Morgan, "The Confession of a Cross-dresser").

145:  The boy who put on his sister's clothes — Kane, pp. 4–7.

145:  Krafft-Ebing case study — Ames, p. 12 (name of patient withheld). In 2008, the neurologist V. S. Ramachandran reported that when the penis was lost, either to surgery or accident, fewer male-to-female transsexuals than straight men reported the sensation of a phantom phallus. Far more straight women than female-to-male transsexuals reported phantom breast sensations after mastectomy (*The San Francisco Chronicle*, Sunday, April 13, 2008, "Insight" section, p. 9; Sandra Blakeslee, "Human Sexuality: Gender Identity and Phantom Genitalia").

146:  "All transsexuals rape women's bodies . . ." — Janice Raymond, *The Transsexual Empire* (1979), quoted in Rudacille, p. 169.

146:  "Gender varies over time and place." — After Stryker, p. 11.

146:  Gender- and demon-specific shapes of Noh mask eyeholes — Takeda and Bethe, p. 255 (checklist of the exhibition).

146: "They are not mystical processes . . ." — Simon Baron-Cohen, *The Essential Differences: The Truth about the Male and Female Brain* (2003), quoted in Rudacille, p. 273.

146: "A pretty face and dresses of brocade . . ." — Saadi, p. 162 (VI.2).

146: The transsexual who wondered what made a face female — Kane, p. 95.

147: "The transsexual does not exist without the surgeon and the endocrinologist." — Millot, p. 142.

147: Footnote on the four gender identity categories — Simplified (and hopefully not distorted) from Serano, pp. 77–93, 105–13, 164–65, 190–92. This otherwise thoughtful author demands, by the way, that people who are not transsexuals "put their pens down, open up their minds and simply listen to what we have to say about our lives." Artists and academics are not to "appropriate intersex and transsexual identities and experiences" (p. 212). But I have never seen why anyone else on earth can tell me what not to write. For another interesting conceptualization of gender identity, see Millot, pp. 55–60, summarizing Stoller's tripartite model.

147: Use of embellished collar to hide an imperfect figure — *InStyle*, same issue, p. 88.

147: Femininity coach's advice to hide mannish hands — Danae Doyle Productions, vol. 1.

147: "With a man, preferably one whom you do not tower over . . ." — Rose, p. 35.

148: "Anything around the eye that can make it look brighter . . ." + "You have to treat your hair like it's a baby" ("your hair" in brackets in original) — *Sophisticate's Black Hair* magazine, May 2008, p. 48 ("Telisha Shaw, Hot Hollywood Actress You Need to Know, Now!").

148: Failure if a woman "connives" to beautify herself — Zeami, pp. 143, 142 (Shugyoku tokka").

148: "Beautiful nails are a constant reminder of the feminine you." — Veronica Vera, p. 21.

148: Footnote: "Even the gentlest, most modest and best of girls . . ." — Lichtenberg, p. 219 (notebook L, no. 41).

148: Kanze Hisao: "It is highly detrimental to a mask . . ." — Nakanishi and Komma, p. 99.

149: "The interchangeable instruments of a pleasure that is always the same" — Proust, vol. 1, p. 172 ("Combray" section of *Swann's Way*). Only the reader can decide whether the following offering of grace for sale does or does not bear Proust out: "Sophisticated neat wives' secret time. The serious play of the amateur wives starting from kisses. D-kisses. Fellatio. Second round . . . We promise for beautiful figure and deep service that you will never get disappointed" (small porn pamphlet, pp. 17–18. Trans. for WTV by Keiko Golden).

149: Love-tropes of the ancient Egyptian poet — Simpson, p. 309 ("The Love Songs of Papyrus Harris 500," no. 3).

149: "Just as the golden hairpicks of bygone Japanese courtesans occasionally resemble the haloes of Byzantine saints" — In, for instance, the following: Ota Memorial Museum of Art, 1988, plates 26–27 (Utagawa Toyoharu, "A courtesan and her attendants parading under cherry blossoms," "A courtesan and her maid under cherry blossoms").

149: A cherry blossom seems "appropriate to a highly cultivated audience." — Zeami, p. 131 ("Shugyoku tokka").

151: "Expressed his joy at being able to openly take up female verses . . ." — Munakata, p. 75 (no. 49, "Nyonin Kanzeon Hangakan"); trans. for WTV by Sumino Junko, English slightly rev. by WTV.

152: "The possession of *either* a vagina that nature made . . ." — Stryker and Whittle, p. 64 (Harold Garfinkel, "Passing and the Managed Achievement of Sex Status in an 'Intersexed' Person").

152: "Let the glow of Radha's breasts endure!" — Jayadeva, p. 35 (Miller's intro., citing the *Siddhahemasabdanusana* of Hemacandra (A.D. 1088–1172).

152: Haiku on the old-lady cherry — Quoted in Ueda, *Basho*, p. 38.

152: "Is this Komachi that once was a bright flower?" — Waley, *The No Plays of Japan*, p. 156 ("Sotoba Komachi"), excerpt slightly abridged.

152: Footnote: "I suppose a fool like you thinks every beautiful woman gets ugly as soon as she grows old . . ." — Mishima, *Five Modern No Plays*, p. 13 ("Sotoba Komachi").

153: "Never again will I come as an angry ghost." — Waley, *The No Plays of Japan*, p. 189 ("Aoi no Uye").

153: "Blossoming sleeves . . ." + "Pine winds tear plantain-leaf-frail dream . . ." — Brazell, pp. 155, 157 ("Izutsu," trans. Karen Brazell).

154: Basho's haiku on cloth-pounding — Quoted in Ueda, op. cit., p. 53.

154: The wise Sanskrit poet's advice to his heroine — Jayadeva, p. 92 (V, stanza 8).

154: "A flower shows its beauty as it blooms . . ." — Zeami, p. 130 ("Shugyoku tokka").

154: Masami and Fukutaro — Interviewed in Kanazawa, January 2008.

155: " . . . not actually people . . . " — Tyler, pp. 190–91 (introduction to "Matsukaze").

155: Malraux: Artists are "conditioned" by works of art — Op. cit., p. 281.

155: "The art of female impersonation has refined feminine beauty . . ." — Toita and Yasuda, p. 110.

155: Zeami's prohibition of strength in female impersonation — Hare, p. 33.

155: "Abandon any detailed stress on his physical movements . . ." — Zeami, p. 141 ("Shugyoko tokka").

155: Remarks of Tamura Toshiko — From Kano, p. 19.

156: Conversation with the Kyoto geisha — Interview with Kofumi-san, at Imamura-san's teahouse in Gion, Kyoto, October 2006.

156: Yamamura Yoko — Original interview of 2002.

156: Prohibition on actresses for "Okina" — Rath, p. 230.

157: The transsexual's insecurity which once led him to "hyperfeminise" him-self — Kane, pp. 128–29.

157: "She's calling attention to a shapely ankle . . ." — Hanna, p. 153 (quoting Marcia Siegel).

157: Effect of bulkier female pelvis on hip swing — Ibid., p. 158.

157: Simulation of the human female's greater elbow angle — Morris, p. 118.

158: Shared octave of male and female voice, and strategy for making the former approximate the latter — Deep Stealth Productions, disk 1, about minute 37. The male-to-female transsexual is recommended to pitch his voice an octave higher.

158: Footnote: "After you've hit puberty . . . that's when your vocal chords thicken, and it's irreversible." Ibid., approx. minute 18.

158: Footnote: Source of "Izutsu" — *Tales of Ise*, p. 64 (Dan XXIII).

158: "Fundamentally elusive fantasies of the imagination." — Feldman and Gordon (introduction, by Gordon and Feldman). A biologist who spent more than nine hundred hours in singles bars and other venues of courtship classified the following "distinct steps in male-female attraction: approach, look, turn, touch and synchronized movement" (Hanna, p. 157). I believe this simply because it is *prosaic*; it might even be what some insects do. Can grace be dissected into these components?

159: "The life and spirit of Noh . . ." — Zeami, p. 64.

159: Footnote on "Venus rings" — Information from Getty Museum, p. 30.

159: Remarks of Mr. Mikata on neutrality in playing female roles — From Kyoto interview of October 2006.

159: "The true heart is not masculine . . ." — Shirane, p. 31 (Motoori Norinaga, *Shibun yoryo*, 1763).

160: "I love refinement" + "And beauty and light are for me the same . . ." — Barnstone, p. 91 (Sappho, "Age and Light").

160: Description of the voluminous S-shape of a standing courtesan in a narrow vertical *ukiyo-e* print — After the Ota Memorial Museum of Art (2006), p. 38 (34: Utagawa Toyokiyo, "Standing Courtesan").

160: Description of Stiff White Ladies — After Gimbutas, plate 14; p. 187 ("the symbol closest to death . . ."), p. 198 ("supernatural vulva"), pp. 199–207, p. 316 ("nothing to do with sexuality").

160: Footnote: " 'Superfeminine' . . . supersoft . . ." — Feldman and Gordon, p. 35 (James Davidson, "The Greek Courtesan and the Art of the Present").

161: Description of Tyche — From Getty Museum, pp. 28–29.

161: Description of seventeenth-century *ko-omote* mask — From a specimen seen in the Kanazawa Noh Museum, January 2008.

161: Footnote: "But she was without question a beautiful woman . . ." — Lady Nijo, pp. 84–85.

161: Kanze Hisao: Noh woman-masks pass "beyond all specific human expression . . ." — Nakanishi and Komma, p. 99.

162:   "The beauty of the Noh lies in the concentration." — Pound and Fenollosa, p. 69.

162:   Remarks of Bando Tamasaburo — Peabody Museum, p. 139 (Peter M. Grilli, "Geisha on Stage and Screen").

162:   "Savage cacao . . ." — *Marie Claire*, vol. 15, no. 4 (April 2008), p. 47 (Sephora ad for Ojon Tawaka Ancient Tribal Rejuvenating Cream, $65).

162:   "First you have to be that role yourself . . ." — Mr. Kanze Hideo, same interview of May 2005.

162:   Recapitulation of *mai* dance, and Noh posture, especially for female roles — After Cavaye, Griffith and Senda, pp. 53, 179.

163:   Footnote: Walking-steps of seventeenth-century courtesans — Saikaku, pp. 80 ("The Almanac Maker's Tale"), 138 ("The Life of an Amorous Woman"), 306 and 339 (notes 105 and 377).

163:   Bando Tamasaburo on the erotic quality of feminine discomfort — Hanna, p. 80.

163:   "Mincingly and decoratively . . ." — Ibid., p. 162.

163:   Similar requirements for geisha dance — Feldman and Gordon, p. 233 (Lesley Downer, "The City Geisha and Their Role in Modern Japan: Anomaly and Artiste?").

164:   Remarks in text and accompanying footnote on Style A and B Cycladic figurines — Getz-Gentle, p. 38.

164:   The drawing instructor — Michael Markowitz, interviewed in San Francisco, July 2007.

164:   "Movement metaphors distinguish male from female." — Hanna, p. 77.

165:   Table of "stereotypical nonverbal gender behavior" — Ibid., pp. 160–61. When I asked the Japanese-American woman quoted in "Crossing the Abyss" for her definition of grace, she replied: "It may come from spirit or soul. When you look at somebody's face, you can figure out the personality, kind of. A soul is something very fundamental. Personality is something acquired later. Personality changes from time to time, based on age and environment. But soul may not be affected."

165:   "Completed only when beauty has nothing more to offer." — Nehamas, p. 105.


12: RAINBOW SKIRTS

166:   "Tresses like a cloud, face like a flower" — Owen, p. 442 (Bo Ju-yi, "Song of Lasting Pain").

166:   "As lovely as jade . . ." — Feldman and Gordon, p. 80 (Judith T. Zeitlin, "'Notes of Flesh' and the Courtesan's Song in Seventeenth-Century China").

166:   "His Majesty knew that it could not be avoided . . ." — Owen, p. 450 (Chen Hong, "An Account to Go with the 'Song of Lasting Pain'").

168:   Lady Yang's "helplessness so charming" — Loc. cit.

168:   Bo Ju-yi's descriptions of Lady Yang's charms and accoutrements — Ibid., p. 444 ("Song of Lasting Pain"). But near the beginning of the twelfth century, the Chinese poet Li Ch'ing-chao compares the loveliness of white chrysanthemums to "Yang Kuei-fei flushed with wine," Lady Yang being the loser. — Owen, p. 15 ("The Beauty of White Chrysanthemums").

168:   Du Fu's lament — Loc. cit. (Du Fu,"Lament by the River").

168:   Citations from Pu Songling — Op. cit., pp. 51 and 508 n; 281 and 542 n.

168:   Stateliness of "Rainbow Skirts" — Ibid., p. 443.

169:   Footnote on the Whirl — Ibid., p. 458 (Bo Ju-yi, "The Girl Who Danced the Whirl").

169:   There was already a renowned melody "Coats of Feathers, Rainbow Skirts" — Ibid., p. 448 (Chen Hong).

169:   "A young girl's fluttering sleeves well express her heart." — Keene, *Twenty Plays*, p. 217 ("Yokihi," "retranslated" by WTV).

169:   "The sky-robe flutters . . ." — Waley, *The No Plays of Japan*, p. 223 ("Hagoromo").

169:   Remarks of Yamamura Yoko — Same interview of April 2002.

169:   *Aware* and its darkening, + "The court lady who in the past . . ." — De Bary et al., pp. 197–99, 365.

170:   References to Lady Yang in *The Tale of Genji* — Op. cit., pp. 7, 13, 14. She is also mentioned much later on in the novel, when Genji is longing for his dead Murasaki.

170:   The tenth-century tanka about the Emperor and Lady Yang — Brower and Miner, p. 198 (poem from the *Daini Takato Shu*). Meanwhile, Sei Shonagon likens Lady Yang's face to a pear-blossom (op. cit., p. 63).

170:   "My own nostalgic memories" — Lady Nijo, p. 229.

170:   "While the emperor listened to the song of 'Rainbow Skirts' . . ." — *The Taiheiki*, p. 286.

170:   Allusion to Lady Yang in *The Tale of the Heike* — Vol. 2, p. 624.

170:   Tanizaki's allusion to Lady Yang — Op. cit., pp. 279–80.

170:   "I seek a way to a world unknown." — Keene, op. cit., p. 211 (same play; "retranslated" by WTV).

171:   Footnote: "Those of the Heike who cherished honor . . ." *The Taiheiki*, p. 312.

171:   "The fundamental aspect of 'Tsuki' . . ." — Hori, Masuda and Miyano, trans. for WTV by Yasuda Nobuko and slightly rev. by WTV, p. 39. My visual description is based on the accompanying plate. Regarding the use of the *zo-onna* to play Yokihi, the same source remarks in regard to one specimen by Zoami himself (p. 58): "As with Tatsuemon's *ko-omote*, it is incredible how such a perfect piece can be created . . . Even a master of the Edo period could not carve the bone structure in the way Zoami did. The *zo-onna* is that difficult. The high rank must show in the mask. . . . the way the upper and lower parts of the nose is carved is superb with extreme sex appeal. This mask can be used in various scenes including 'Hagoromo,' 'Yokihi,' and 'Eguchi.' The red on the cheeks complements the white skin. It is not only beautiful, but also shows a strong core, clear bone structure, and is large-scaled, making it the original *zo-onna*" (words of Kanze Kiyokazu).

172: "Your visit only multiplies the pain." — Keene, op. cit., p. 213 (same play).

172: Footnote: Mr. Umewaka plays Yokihi — Osaka Festival Noh brochure, 2002, unnumbered p. (Mariko Hikawa, "Two Flowers Reflecting One Another").

172: Chen Hong on the golden hairpin — Owen, p. 448 (Chen Hong).

173: Yokihi's golden kimono and phoenix headdress — Takeda and Bethe, p. 119 (Kawakami Shigeki, "The Development of the Karaori as a Noh Costume").

173: "Human feelings are rooted in the genitals . . ." — Makuzu, p. 25.

173: Possible echo of the "Song of Lasting Pain" in the Noh play "Miidera" — Bethe and Emmert, *Noh Performance Guide 3*, pp. 63 (text) and 79 (note 35).

173: "Oh, this futile parting! . . ." — Keene, p. 217 (same play, "retranslated" by WTV).

173: "Heaven endures, and the Earth . . ." — Owen, p. 447 (same poem; "retranslated" by WTV).


## 13: JEWELS IN THE DARKNESS

174: Kawabata's mention of the Shoren-in's camphor trees — *The Old Capital*, pp. 113–15.

174: Footnote: Information on Shoren-in — *Sho-Ren-In*.

174: "While this garden is not considered one of the major examples of landscape art . . ." — Treib and Herman, p. 164.

176: Zeami's definition of fascination — Op. cit., p. 133 ("Shugyoku tokka").

177: "A young girl's fluttering sleeves well express what is in her heart." — Keene, *Twenty Plays*, pp. 216–17 ("Yohiki").

177: Gion Shrine in *The Tale of the Heike* — I have been repeatedly told that the Gion referred to is in Kyoto. However, the English translation in my possession claims (vol. 1, p. 6, n. 1) that the *Tale's* Gion was the Jetavana monastery in Sravasti, Indonesia.

177: Descriptions of works by Utamaro, Chobunsai Eishi — As seen at the Ota Ukiyo-e Museum in Tokyo, 2004, 2006.

177: Geishas performing alongside prostitutes in the Yoshiwara — Utamaro (Sato Takanobu), trans. Yasuda Nobuko. Picture 1: Seirouniwaka Onnageishabu; Oomando Ogie Oiyo Takeji; Tenmei 3 (1783). Large Nishikie. Tokyo National Museum.

177:  "Even highly reputed maiko . . ." — Saikaku, p. 128 ("The Life of an Amorous Woman").

177:  Scene from the "Sleeve Scroll" — Uhlenbeck and Winkel, p. 119.

177:  Scene from Keisai Eisen's woodblock album — Ibid., p. 165 (Fig. 58b).

177:  Scene by Utagawa Kunisada — Ibid., pp. 186–87 (Fig. 70, "Games Inside a Bathhouse, Year of the Boar").

178:  "A world where love is bought and sold like merchandise." — Goossen, p. 85 (Okamoto Kanoko, "Portrait of an Old Geisha"). Struggling to interpret the old geisha's kindness for him, the hero of this story wonders if she might be seeking to expiate her heartlessness to bygone lovers.

178:  Peabody Museum's generalized description of geishas — Op. cit., p. 44 (Andrew L. Maske, "Identifying Geisha in Art and Life: Is She Really a Geisha?").

178:  The mid-twentieth-century photograph of a geisha in a straw hat — Bristol, p. 115 ("Geisha with straw hat," 1947).

178:  *Miyako Odori* program, April 2005 — Trans. for WTV by Sumino Junko.

178:  Excerpt from *Snow Country*: Geishas as call girls — op. cit., pp. 20, 26, 28.

178:  Footnote: The strident person on Kawabata — Feldman and Gordon, p. 249 (Miho Matsugu, "In the Service of the Nation: Geisha and Kawabata's *Snow Country*").

179:  Saikaku on speech of Kyoto ladies — Saikaku, p. 312 ("The Life of an Amorous Woman").

179:  Geisha-related citations from Kawabata's final novel — *Beauty and Sadness*, pp. 104–6.

179:  ". . . the dress of the geisha now far exceeds that of noble ladies . . ." — *Monumenta Nipponica* (Pastereich), p. 215.

180:  The "superficial purity" of geishas — Kuwano Toka, quoted in Kano, p. 26.

180:  Geishas as "interchangeable, rather commonplace companions whose association with carnality is the rule" — See, for instance, Goossen, pp. 50 (Nagai Kafu, "The Peony Garden"), 74–75 (Satomi Ton, "Blowfish"), or Tanizaki, *The Makioka Sisters*, pp. 268–69.

180:  Positioning of geishas between artists, prostitutes and mistresses — Kuwano (but Kano herself this time), p. 44.

180:  Footnote: Geishas require new kimonos all the time — Iwasaki and Brown, p. 264.

180:  Same footnote: Cost of kimono at two million yen ($20,000) — Cobb, p. 17 (Mayumi, Tokyo geisha).

180:  Same footnote: Cost of obis and wigs — Gallagher, p. 8.

180:  Interviews with Kofumi-san, Konomi-san, Danyu-san, Mr. Mikata — All in Kyoto, October 2006. All except the one with Mr. Mikata, which occurred in the temple where he had performed "Michimori" on the previous night, took place at Imamura-san's teahouse in Gion.

180: Print of Shakkyo dance — Utamaro (Sato Takanobu), trans. Yasuda Nobuko. Picture 9: Touseiodorikozoroi. Shakkyo. Around Kansei 5–6 (1793–94). Large Nishikie. Henri Vever Collection.

181: Description of the Getty cult statue — After Getty Museum, pp. 104–5 ("Cult Statue of a Goddess, Perhaps Aphrodite").

181: "The Inoue style is noted for its ability . . ." — Iwasaki and Brown, p. 281.

181: Mr. Kanze on the origin of Inoue dance — Interview of 2005.

182: Inoue School as "most prestigious" style of geisha dance — Gallagher, p. 64.

182: Footnote — Mr. Mikata on the lack of meaning in comparing Noh and Inoue dance — Interview of October 2006.

183: Ogasawara style as precursor to geisha gestures — Gallagher, p. 100.

183: Footnote: Remarks of Masami-san on opening a door — Interview in Kanazawa, January 2008. Kawai Takako was the interpreter. (N.B.: Iwasaki and Brown [p. 93] give a detailed description of how to enter a room properly.) Percival Lowell, who believed in that equally beautiful, plausible illusion, the Martian canals, wrote in his *Soul of the Far East* (Strauss, p. 126) that a certain Japanese maiden's "voice was only too human for heaven. Unconsciously it made the better part of a caress." The way she poured tea resembled "some beautiful rite."

183: Definition of transgender "passing" — Bornstein, p. 20.

183: Role of bush warbler droppings in whitening a geisha's face — Peabody Museum, p. 113 (Andrew L. Maske, "Performance and Play: The Art and Accomplishments of Geisha").

183: "Radiant as enamel" — Goossen, p. 87 (Okamoto Kanoko, "Portrait of an Old Geisha").

184: Kawabata's description of a prospective maiko: — *The Old Capital*, pp. 95–96. Another geisha of twenty is "sloping-shouldered, seemingly gentle." Her "teeth were like white beads in her beautiful mouth." In *Beauty and Sadness* he mentions the "rich color" of nipples never suckled by any baby (p. 118).

184: Meaning of one undecorated shoulder: senior maiko status — Gallagher, p. 214.

185: Kyoto geisha: Red symbolizes female pubescence — Cobb, p. 74.

186: Mr. Kanze on dissimilarity of geisha face to Noh masks — Interview of May 2005.

186: Ms. Nakamura on the same topic — Interview of 2004.

186: "A maiko in full costume approximates the Japanese ideal of feminine beauty . . ." — Iwasaki and Brown, p. 157.

186: "A Fan for You" (or "Fan to You") — The syntax and calligraphy of this song (and also "Black Hair") as written out by the ochaya-san Ms. Imamura, were both so archaic that my interpreter-translator Takako, a highly educated woman in late middle age, needed to enlist her mother's help to modernize the words in Japanese she could understand and translate. One must admire Kyoto's hold on the past. About this song Takako remarks: "A fan is considered a happy item, because its widening shape implies an ever more prosperous future." The lyrics (slightly revised by WTV) run something like this:

> You and I resemble the pivot-point of a fan whose leaves are bound together.
> In the era of Han {ancient China}, a lover of the Emperor placed a
>     flower-patterned fan by their pillow.
> Holding that fan, I feel leaves falling on my sleeve.
> But the patterns drawn on the fan will not fall, which makes me happy.
> Forever gracefully turn, pinwheel made with three fans!
> Forever until the eighth generation.
> You are mine, my dear you.

187: "Only fifty or sixty maiko remain in all Kyoto." — Based on Gallagher, p. 158 ("as of the early 2000's"). In Kanazawa, when the geisha Masami-san made her debut, there were more than eighty geishas in the Higashi pleasure district. When the musician Fukutaro-san made hers, there were more than seventy. In 2008, when I met them, there were fewer than fifty.

187: "Black Hair" — The meaning of the song is approximately (as written out by the ochaya-san, modernized by Takako's mother, then translated by Takako, and slightly revised by me):

> My black hair is linked to various memories of you.
> When I comb my hair in my bed alone, I feel so desolate.
> Although I am a wife with tight sleeves, I feel like complaining,
> but I'm just a weak woman.
> Beneath the quiet night sky comes the temple bell's low sound.
> Waking from a dream of last night, I fondly remember the happy
>     memories,
> But at the same time feel disconsolate.
> Snow lies thick, not knowing my sadness.

Takako notes: "Black hair implies something that can easily come loose, suggesting that the happy memories may perhaps loosen and disperse. Accumulated snow here implies that the woman has much feeling for the man."

187: Mention of "Dark Hair" in *Snow Country* — Op. cit., p. 74.

187: Mention of same in Tanizaki's *Makioka Sisters* — Op. cit., pp. 164, 384.

Once it is a dance performed by an unmentioned pupil, probably a geisha; once it is a piece of koto-music practiced by a housemaid.

188:  Izumi Shikibu's black hair poem — Keene, *Seeds in the Heart*, p. 296.

188:  Footnote: "I hacked off at the roots the waist-length hair . . ." — Masuda, p. 121.

189:  "Lovers, if you flee not from hot desire . . ." — Barnstone, p. 211 ("An Ageless Lover"). See Appendix C, No. 8 for a list of her charms.

190:  Footnote: Purpose of red outlining of eyes (she seems to assert that the eye is red all around, with no black) — Buisson, p. 96.

190:  Mr. Mikata on Inoue the Fourth's "practice, practice and still practice" — Interview of October 2006.

191:  "If the *shite* dances and acts with elegant speeches . . ." — Zeami, p. 65.

191:  "Secrecy is the essential art of geisha." — Cobb, p. 17 (Mayumi, Tokyo geisha).

191:  "I don't want to know their tricks." — Ibid., p. 96 (Kyoto client).

191:  Use of the fan to represent joy — Cavaye, Griffith and Senda, p. 180.

192:  "He did not reduce his characters to a mechanism . . ." — *The Nibelungenlied*, translator's afterword, p. 314.

192:  Erotic allure of black high heels' red soles — *InStyle*, January 2008, p. 109 ("Your Most Stylish Year Ever: 365 Star Style Secrets," no. 8: Lindsay Lohan).

193:  Meaning of makeup on the back of a geisha's neck: genitals — Cobb, p. 60 (unnamed geisha); photo of this makeup being applied is on p. 61. Gallagher simply remarks (p. 146) that there is "much to say" about this decoration of "the sexiest of all parts of the decently clothed body."

193:  Geisha makeup as "electrifying" — Gallagher, p. 144.

193:  Mr. Mikata on Noh training — Interview of October 2006.

193:  Mr. Umewaka's grandfather and the loveliness of imaginary cherry blossoms — Umewaka Rokuro, "On the 45th Anniversary of My Stage Career."

199:  "Genuine Perfect Fluency in fact has no connection with the actor's conscious artistic intentions . . ." — Zeami, p. 135 ("Shugyoku tokka").

199:  Chobunsai Eishi, Chokosai Eisho — Seen at the Ota Ukiyo-e Museum in Tokyo, 2006.

200:  Reason for white makeup in Heian times — Iwasaki and Brown, p. 159.

201:  Lady Nijo at the Shoren-in and Gion Shrine — Op. cit., pp. 17, 160.


## 14: "SHE CANNOT DO ANYTHING ELSE"

202:  Remarks of Kofumi-san and Danyu-san — Same session of October 2006.

202:  "A gentleman would place a handkerchief . . ." — Hanna, p. 180.

204:  "As early as eleven." — Cobb, p. 17 (Mayumi, Tokyo geisha).

204:  "The romanticization of geisha life . . ." — Masuda, pp. 6–7.

204: The tale of Takabayashi Ginji — Rath, pp. 1–4.

205: Footnote: "Women exist for the sake of men. . ." — Makuzu, p. 25.

206: "The actor will be able to discern clearly . . ." — Zeami, pp. 139–40 ("Shugyoku tokka").

206: Mishima's resolution to cultivate his body — *Sun and Steel*, pp. 7–8.

206: Procedures of Molly Sims — *InStyle,* January 2008, pp. 109 ("Your Most Stylish Year Ever: 365 Star Style Secrets," no. 23), 119 (no. 233).

206: Mr. Shozo Sato's abstention from water before performing — Information by him, given at a Kabuki costuming and makeup demonstration at the Asian Art Museum, San Francisco, 23 February 2008. This form of preparation is also common among Noh actors. Regarding a *ko-omote* carved by Yamato, the actor Katayama Kurouemon reports: "I once performed Kenreimonin in "Oharagoko" with this mask. Since the colors are very delicate and I wore a flower hat on my head, I didn't drink any water from the day before so that I would not sweat" (Hori, Masuda and Miyano, trans. for WTV by Yasuda Nobuko and slightly rev. by WTV; p. 36).

206: The Goodbye Cellulite, Hello Bikini Challenge — *Marie Claire*, vol. 15, no. 4 (April 2008), p. 59 (Nivea advertisement: "Ready for the Challenge?").

206: "We've all been there . . ." — *Allure*, January 2008, p. 32 (advertisement for CoverGirl TruBlend).

206: Vaginal rejuvenation + balancing ethnic features — *New Beauty*, winter-spring 2008, p. 172 ("Vaginal Rejuvenation & Aesthetic Surgery"); p. 149 ("Balancing Your Ethnic Features") + p. 141 ("The Details About Rhinoplasty").

207: Reoperation rates for breast augmentation and reconstruction — *Allure*, January 2008, p. 54 (safety addendum to ad for the Natrelle Breast Enhancement Collection).

207: Description of the buttocks lift — *New Beauty*, winter-spring 2008, p. 111 ("Remove Excess Skin").

207: Danger of Brazilian hair-straightening treatments — *Allure*, January 2008, p. 44 ("Letters from the Editor: January '08: Vanity Cases").

208: Details of vaginal graft and dilator — Ames, p. 239 (Aleshia Brevard).

208: "Literally melts away fat . . ." — *New Beauty*, winter-spring 2008, p. 87 (advertisement for "Smartlipo Laser Body Sculpting").

208: "It's no fun being a geisha . . ." — Goossen, p. 48 (Nagai Kafu, "The Peony Garden").

208: "Ultimately, ours is a journey of anguish." — Ames, p. 236 (Aleshia Brevard).

208: Noh lessons of Mr. Mikata Shizuka — Observed in his studio in Kyoto, 2004.

209: Dilation of neovagina with plastic stents — Rose, pp. 150–51.

209: Definition of *muga* — De Mente, pp. 47–49.

209: Remarks on Agnes — Stryker and Whittle, pp. 83, 82 (Harold Garfinkel, "Passing and the Managed Achievement of Sex Status in an 'Intersexed' Person").

211: Iwasaki Mineko's punishment and self-discipline — Op. cit., pp. 224, 231.

211: "More of a painted doll than a woman . . ." — Peabody Museum, p. 25 (Lesley Downs, "A World Behind Closed Doors").

211: "The truth and what looks like it are two different things." — Zeami, p. 146 ("Shugyoku tokka").

211: The tale of Charlotte von Mahlsdorf — Op. cit., pp. 46, 44, 92, 102.

## 15: SUZUKA'S DRESSING ROOM

212: Remarks of Suzuka — From an interview in Kanazawa, January 2008; translated by Kawai Takako.

215: Morris on ideal waist-to-hip ratio — Op. cit., pp. 160–61.

215: Footnote on average female hip width — Morris, p. 169.

215: "The tightly laced young woman . . ." — Ibid., p. 164.

215: "Compactness and stability . . ." — Clark, pp. 85–86.

216: Maikos and the wooden pillow — Information from Masami-san, same ochaya, same month and year.

## 16: "THEY JUST WANT TO LOOK IN THE MIRROR"

222: Makeover — Interview with Yukiko, January 2008.

225: Desmond Morris on long hair and puffed-out lips — Op. cit., pp. 18, 79.

226: Sei Shonagon's list of things that have lost their power — Op. cit., p. 145.

228: Footnote: Morris on blonde hair — Op. cit., p. 18.

228: The Vimalakirti Sutra — De Bary et al., pp. 60–61.

## 17: "I SIT WITH MY LEGS CLOSED"

230: Breasts created with padded apron; paragraph on elongated kimono sleeves & c; immediately following paragraph on types of feminine movement — Information by Mr. Sato Shozo, Kabuki costuming and makeup demonstration at the Asian Art Museum, San Francisco, 23 February 2008.

231: Remarks of Mr. Ichikawa Shunen — From an interview in Tokyo, January 2008; translated by Kawai Takako.

231: Footnote: Mishima on onnagatas — *Five Modern No Plays*, pp. 298, 297, 293.

234: "Grasp the logic of the fact that the eyes cannot see themselves . . ." — Zeami (Rimer and Yamazaki), p. 80 ("Kakyo").

236: Visible and interior effects of waist constriction — Kunzle, pp. 15, 30–31.

## 18: "THERE'S NO UGLY LADY FACE"

239: "A double of the super ego" — Bellmer, p. 66. In the same work (pp. 28–29), he describes a paralytic in love with a young girl: "Gradually her physical reality superimposed itself over his own . . . internally at prenatal depths he became the woman he was preparing to possess . . . he transformed into his opposite," namely a woman.

239: "Never created or annihilated by themselves . . ." — De Bary et al., p. 138 (Huisi, "The Method of Calming and Contemplation in the Mahayana" [sixth cent.]).

## 19: THE PHALLUS OF TIRESIAS

244: "Entertainment enacted by a loosely defined occupation . . ." — Rath, p. 10.

244: The ancient Hungarian figurine — Depicted in Gimbutas, p. 231.

245: "By this unnatural differentiation . . ." — Zweig, p. 73. See also pp. 71–72.

246: Tomimoto Toyohina and her two colleagues — Utamaro book, trans. Yasuda Nobuko. Picture 7: Toji-sanbijin; Tomimoto Toyohina, Naniwaya Kita and Takashima Hisa; around Kansei 5 (1793). Large Nishikie. Museum of Fine Arts, Boston.

247: " . . . with a view to maintaining women in the conventional, subordinate role . . ." — Millot, p. 14.

247: Tips on feminine-style self-touching, on walking and on sitting — Danae Doyle Productions, "Feminine Movement Basics Vol. 1," DDP & Feminage, 2007.

247: "A woman's nature is such . . ." — De Bary et al., p. 404.

248: Description of Amelia — Maxwell, p. 60 (*Bright Center of Heaven*, 1934).

248: Reshaping procedure for lip line — Aucoin, p. 45.

248: As depressing as an out-of-season red plum-blossom dress — Shonagon, p. 40.

249: "Now all at once he realized what the repulsive aura was . . ." — Böll, p. 199 (*Der Zug war pünktlich*, 1951).

249: Tale of the transvestite at Caesar's house — Cicero, vol. II (vol. XXII in the works), p. 35 (I.13, Cicero to Atticus, Rome, Jan. 25, B.C. 61).

249: Poem of love separation from the year 1232 — Brower and Miner, p. 271 ("Next Morning Love," by Teika, slightly "retranslated" by WTV).

250: Description of Vanesa Lorena Ledesma — Amnesty International, p. 58. This case occurred in Argentina in 2000.

250: "If we eliminate the pressure to pass . . ." — Mattilda, p. 19 ("Reaching Too Far: An Introduction").

250: The collection of mid-twentieth-century snapshots — In Hurst and Swope.

250: "One might say that the grace of them is not derived from avoiding strain . . ." — Denby.

250: Bone, flesh and skin — Zeami (Rimer and Yamazaki), pp. 69–70 ("Shikado").

250: "Let there be brought to me twenty women . . ." — Simpson, p. 17 ("Third Tale: The Marvel Which Happened in the Reign of King Snefru").

250: "All I am able to do is teach you the form . . ." — Iwasaki and Brown, p. 297.

250: "A fan must be carried . . ." — Ito and Inoue, p. 99.

250: "This is a higher-level mask with strength . . ." — Hori, Masuda and Miyano, trans. for WTV by Yasuda Nobuko and slightly rev. by WTV; p. 54.

251: "Many, if not most women are the wrong shape . . ." — Anders.

252: "Sexual difference, which owes much to symbolic dualisms . . ." — Millot, p. 15.

252: "A smoldering smoky eye." — *Harper's Bazaar*, January 2008.

## 20: A CURTAIN OF MIST

255: A *waka-onna*, *fushikizo* and *manbi* seen all together — Tokugawa Art Museum, *Noh Masks and Costumes*, p. 24 (plates 36–38).

256: "Empowering interpreters with expertise . . ." — Rath, p. 81.

256: "Okina is not a pine tree spirit . . ." — Jeff Clark corrections, to my ms. p. 30.

256: "Poetry is finer than prose . . ." + "Poetic thought works by suggestion . . ." — Fenollosa, pp. 23, 28.

257: Representation of Genji's dying wife by means of a folded robe — In the Noh play "Aoi-no-Ue."

257: The tale of Sen no Rikyu's ocean-view garden — Treib and Herman, p. 23.

257: Utamaro's *yuujo* from 1794 — Utamaro book, trans. Yasuda Nobuko. Picture 31: Nouryoubijinzu. Around Kansei 6–7 (1794–95). Colored silk book. Hitono (=unit for counting fabric size) 39.5 x 65.6 cm. Chiba City Museum of Art.

257: Remarks of Mr. Mikata — Interview of October 2006.

257: Description of Utamaro's round-cheeked white geisha faces — After Utamaro (Tadashi Kobayashi), pp. 25–29 (geisha series from "A Collection of Portraits of Reigning Beauties").

258: Matisse drawings — Op. cit., various pages.

259: "The waste of a woman is in not knowing her carnally." — Simpson, p. 521 ("The Instruction of 'Onchsheshonqy [P. British Museum 10508]," 20/20).

259: "The 'fetish-object' in the history of courtly love is a surrogate . . ." — Kunzle, p. 7.

259: Description of the Queen of the Night — After Collon, pp. 6 (as she looks now) and 8 (digital reconstruction).

260: Understated clothing and breast forms sometimes protects the male bodies of transgender women from being recognized. — Information from Rose, pp. 34–35.

260: Footnote: "The extruding animal breast . . ." — Clark, p. 130.

260: "The one thing that women share . . ." — Serano, p. 52.

260: Description of "Venus" figurines — After illustrations in Gimbutas, pp. 163–65. One example sports what the author calls "double-egg-shaped buttocks."

261: "In punchy shades of purple, green and blue . . ." — *Allure*, August 2008, p. 181 (Cara Litke, "Crossing the Line").

261: Footnote: "It is usually said that a woman should keep everything in her heart . . ." — Makuzu, p. 22.

262: "Although they are peasants, they embody the refinement of a centuries-old courtly aesthetic . . ." — Takeda and Bethe, p. 21 (Tom Hare, "Rituals, Dreams, and Tales of Adventure: A Material History of Noh Drama").

## 22: SUN-BRIGHT LIKE SWORDS

264: "They saw a large band of shield-maidens . . ." — *The Saga of the Volsungs*, p. 50.

265: The three "fair southron maids" — "Volundarkvitha," in Hollander, p. 160.

265: "For the white-armed woman he waited long" + "her white arms" — Ibid., pp. 161, 160.

265: The lovely Norsewoman — What about domestic beauty? Concerning the brooch-breasted, blue-shirted highborn wife of "Rígsthula," "was her brow brighter, her breast lighter, / her neck whiter, than whitest snow." Her son married a girl who was "dainty-fingered, fairhaired and wise."

265: Footnote: Description of the thrall wife — "Rígsthula," in Hollander, p. 122.

265: Sun-bright like a sword — For instance, Odin extolls Billing's daughter, "the sun-bright maid" ("Hávamál," in Hollander, p. 28); in "Voluspa" (p. 10) we read that "the war god's sword like a sun doth shine." We might also mention that Svipdag's "sun-bright maiden" Mengloth shares her appellation with a man; Sun-Bright was also the name of Svipdag's father (Hollander, p. 152).

265: *Shunga's* whiter bodies of women than of men — For instance, Clark et al., p. 102 (Torii Kyonobu I's early eighteenth-century *ukiyo-e shunga* "Erotic Contest of Flowers" [detail].)

266: Denigration of arms in the "zoologist's portrait, celebrating women as they appear in the real world" — Morris, pp. ix., 117.

266: Gerth's "arms did gleam . . ." — "Skírnismál," in Hollander.

266: "When she lifted her arms and opened the door. . ." — Sturluson, p. 31.

266: "In a witch's arms beware of sleeping . . ." — "Hávamál," in Hollander, p. 31.

266: Dangerous as the ghost of a Christian woman — "Svipdagsmal," in Hollander, p. 143.

266: "The crafty woman / in her arms who folded my father" — Ibid., p. 142.

266: "For thy shining arms on the shoulders lay . . ." — "Lokasenna," in Hollander, p. 94.

267: "Though fair women, / and brow-white . . ." — Sigrdrífumál," in Hollander, p. 239.

267: "Methought in the darkness came dead women . . ." — Greenlandish Lay of Atli, in Hollander, p. 298 st. 25.

267: Norsewomen as doom — These examples could be multiplied at tedious length. When Bjorn Brynjolfsson meets Thora Lacecuff, he takes a great fancy to her, says the saga, but does not say why; he abducts her (*Egil's Saga*, p. 81). When Egil Skallagrimssson falls in love with his brother's widow Asgerd, his love poem mentions nothing about her characteristics (ibid., p. 132). In *The Saga of Bjorn, Champion of the Hitardal People* we meet Oddny Thorkelsdaughter, "an exceptionally beautiful" woman whose exceptional beauty is not described, but on account of it she is called Oddny Isle-Candle (*Sagas of Warrior Poets*, p. 154).

267: Sinfjotli "saw a lovely woman . . ." — *The Saga of the Volsungs*, p. 50.

267: Femme fatale of *Eyrbyggja Saga* — P. 78.

269: "Ivar's story" — In *Hrafnkel's Saga*, pp. 129–31.

269: Encomia of Helga the Fair — *Sagas of Warrior Poets*, p. 141 (*The Saga of Gunnlaug Serpent-Tongue*).

269: Footnote on Helga — Ibid., p. 117.

269: Same footnote: Description of the bound captive — *Two Viking Romances*, p. 21 ("Bosi and Herraud").

269: Description of figurines of Valkyries or *disir* — After illustrations in Lindow, p. 96.

270: Citations from *Njal's Saga* — Pp. 184, 185, 189, 198.

270: "There you go, my two sons . . ." — *The Saga of Grettir the Strong*, p. 158.

271: Glam's curse — Ibid., p. 85.

271: "Then the tide of battle turned . . ." — *The Saga of the Volsungs*, p. 53

272: Decapitation of the eight-year-old boy — *The Tale of the Heike*, vol. 2, p. 700.

272: Heike arrogance, evanescence — Ibid., vol. 1, p. 5. The book is rife with such passages.

273: The dooms of Katla and Odd — *Eryrbyggja Saga*, pp. 62–63.

273: "Have it your way, but it's a decision I'll live long to regret." — *Egil's Saga*, p. 126.

273: Other citations from *Njal's Saga* — Pp. 171, 239–40.

274: Guthrún called "demonic" — Hollander, p. 285.

274: Final doings of Brynhild — "Sigurtharkvitha hin skamma" (short lay of Sigurth), in Hollander, p. 260.

275: Sigrún and Helgi in the mound — "Helgavitha Hundingsbana II," in Hollander, pp. 200–201.

275: Footnote: The "hateful and grim" Valkyrie in Odin's hall — "Helgavitha Hundingsbana I" (First Lay of Helgi Hundingslayer), in Hollander, p. 186. Same footnote: "A different, cruder picture" — Davidson, p. 64.

275: "The nape of the neck is the glamor spot . . ." — Ito and Inoue, p. 64.

276: Footnote: Thomas Blenman Hare's diagram of gender inflection patterns — Op. cit., p. 3.

276: Remarks of Kenneth Clark — Op. cit., pp. 75, 20–21.

276: Footnote: "Not that the Esquiline girl . . ." — Ibid., p. 75.

276: "That search for finality of form" . . . — Ibid., pp. 74–75.

277: Citations from Sei Shonagon — Op. cit., pp. 110, 84.

277: Description of Thorgunna — *Eyrbyggja Saga*, p. 130.

277: Description of Thorgerd — *Egil's Saga*, p. 202.

277: Gold- and jewel-related kennings for women, Sif, Freya, etc. — Sturluson, pp. 114, 115, 96, 30, 94. By puns, women are also referred to with feminine names of trees such as willows, birches, lindens (pp. 94, 116). Women used to wear chains of stones around their necks, so stone, gem and the like is another kenning for women. Women can be called forests, floodfire-keeping Sifs, mead-Hrists (p. 115).

277: Footnote: "So dear are you, sea-Freya . . ." — *Sagas of Warrior Poets*, p. 49.

278: Praise of Oddny Isle-Candle — *The Saga of Bjorn, Champion of the Hitardal People*, in *Sagas of Warrior Poets*, pp. 160–61 (in the second citation she is actually "Hrist of the hand-fire").

278: Praise of Helga the Fair — *The Saga of Gunnlaug Serpent-Tongue*, in *Sagas of Warrior Poets*, pp. 139, 135.

278: Citations from *Laxdaela Saga* — Op. cit., pp. 60, 61, 64, 118, 109, 156, 188.

278: Description of Kojiro's "Ataka" — After a performance I saw in 2002.

279: Footnote: Lady Murasaki's diary — Op. cit., p. 56.

280: Hallgerd "was very tall . . ." — *Njal's Saga*, p. 55.

280: Extracts from *Viglund's Saga* — *Sagas of Warrior Poets*, pp. 254, 261.


## 23: PASSING LIGHT

282: "Frozen motion" + "nothing is frozen" — Wyeth (Wilmerding), pp. 172, 174 (Wyeth's words).

283: "A similarity of stroke and surface . . ." — Wyeth (Wilmerding), p. 23 (John Wilmerding, "Andrew Wyeth's *Helga Suite*").

283: Description of "Farm Road" — Ibid., pp. 138–39.

283: "There's grace in my work like spring flowers . . ." — Quoted in Meryman, p. 232.

283: Wyeth's first acquaintance with Helga — Ibid., p. 324.

284: "Nobody knows her . . ." + "the same slight coarseness . . ." + "a picture of a whore sitting there . . ." — Ibid., p. 330.

284: "Letting Her Hair Down" — Wyeth (Wilmerding), p. 35.

284:  Helga: "I became alive . . ." — Meryman, p. 336.

284:  "And now I meet this girl . . ." — Ibid., p. 338.

284:  "She was an image I couldn't get out of my mind." — Ibid., p. 339.

285:  "I felt the country, the house . . ." — Ibid., p. 355.

285:  "Whoever she is to us . . ." — Wyeth, p. 338.

285:  "If I control it, it's no good." — Corn, p. 85 (E. P. Richardson, "Andrew Wyeth's Painting Techniques").

285:  "Braids" — Wyeth (Wilmerding), p. 147.

285:  "I'd painted those braids beautifully coming to the fine end . . . " — Meryman, p. 354.

285:  "Taking the lids off the boxes . . ." — Ibid., p. 369.

286:  "Wyeth's memory of his father in the coffin . . ." — Ibid., p. 224.

286:  Description of "Night Shadow" — After the plate in the same book, p. 343. Since this painting is not part of the Helga Suite it is not reproduced in Wilmerding.

286:  "Who the fuck is this woman? . . ." — Ibid., p. 370.

286:  "Now her sturdy features and sober demeanor . . ." — Wyeth (Wilmerding), p. 22 (Wilmerding's words).

286:  "It's not just anybody lying there . . ." — Meryman, p. 348.

287:  Description of the *ko-omote* copied by Deme Yasuhisa — Hori, Masuda and Miyano, trans. for WTV by Yasuda Nobuko (and slightly revised by me), p. 32. (The visual description, of course, is mine.) After mentioning the "girl in the box," when I say that the description "continues," in fact I have misstated for rhetorical purposes, for in the original the "girl in the box" bit comes second, not first. "Kanze Kiyokazu says, 'Typical female masks used in our performance style express young women, but we use this when we want some lovely and light look. This perfect *ko-omote* mask can withstand the role of *shite*, such as the tidy and pure Tennyo in "Hagoromo." Actually, if this is used for the *tsure*, its presence might overwhelm the *shite*.'"

288:  The Perfect Fluency "has no connection . . . with the actor's conscious artistic intentions . . . " — Zeami, p. 135 ("Shugyoku tokka").

288:  " . . . the thing that expresses the way I feel at a particular time . . ." — Wyeth (Wilmerding), p. 39.

288:  "Too real for some people . . ." — Wyeth, *Autobiography*, p. 114 (re: "Overflow").

289:  "Fluid and fluctuating . . . " — Corn, p. 14 (Brian O'Doherty, "A Visit to Wyeth Country").

290:  "The individual self striving to realize all things . . ." — De Bary et al., p. 325 (Dogen, "The Fully Apparent Case" [Genjo Koan], 1231). Italics mine.

290:  "The gateway to something beyond . . ." — Ibid., p. 265.

## 24: WHO IS THE WILLOW TREE GODDESS?

294: "Thinking heart is saddened." — Bethe and Emmert, Noh Guide 3, p. 8 (literal translation).

## 25: SNOW IN A SILVER BOWL

297: Description of Radha's charms — After Jayadeva, pp. 84–85 (III, stanzas 12–15).

## 26: BEAUTY'S GHOST

298: The two sketches of Ono no Komachi — Hokusai, *Encyclopedia: Men and Women*, p. 216, no. 3 (Ono no Komachi and Noin, poets in Heian period, both included in the 36 major poets); p. 234, no. 3 (Sekidera Komachi, one of seven legends around Ono no Komachi).

298: Illustration from Hokusai's version of the *Hundred Poets* anthology — Op. cit., p. 42.

299: Zeami's remarks on the "flower" — Op. cit., pp. 20–21, 51, 60.

299: "Whether it is because the faith which creates has ceased to exist . . ." — Proust, vol. 1, p. 201 ("Combray" part of *Swann's Way*).

299: "Endless strength and inconsolable sadness . . ." — Serano, p. 280.

300: Description of a seventeenth-century *zo-onna* — Tokugawa Art Museum, *Noh Masks and Costumes*, p. 26 (plate 41).

300: "The most important accomplishment for a beautiful woman is to be able to write poetry." — Lady Nijo, p. 113.

300: Biographical data on Komachi — Keene, *Seeds in the Heart,* pp. 234–35.

300: Komachi's poem about the breast illuminated with desperate fire — Brower and Miner, p. 206 ("*Hito ni awan . . .*")

301: The *ukiyo-e* painting of Komachi — Ota Memorial Museum of Art, 1988, plate 10 (Matsuno Chikanobu, "The poetess Komachi washing the anthology to disprove false charge of plagiary" [*sic*]). In another version of the same scene, the background is a sandy gold and the surface of the water in the basin is also gold with parallel wiggles of ink, as if in preparation to marble paper. — Clark et al., p. 138 (Okomura Masanobu, "Ono no Komachi Washing the Manuscript," *ca.* 1711–36).

301: Sei Shonagon's reference to Komachi (Fukakusa no Shoso's death) — Op. cit., p. 243.

301: Description of Komachi's charms in "Sotoba Komachi" — Pound and Fenollosa, p. 14.

301: "A young girl's trailing white robe, worn over a lavender chemise." — McCullough, p. 167.

302: "Surrender to you . . ." — Sato and Watson, p. 113 ("retranslated" by WTV).

302: "It is good for a woman to realize that once she grows old . . ." — Makuzu, pp. 174–75.

302: Description of background pages of a Genji Picture-Scroll — Tokugawa Museum, *Genji Monogatari Emaki*, pp. 78, 38, 24.

303: Komachi's reply to Bunya Yasuhide — The poem appears in full in Brower and Miner, p. 222.

304: "With the *rojo*, simply being beautiful is not enough . . ." — Hori, Masuda and Miyano, trans. for WTV by Yasuda Nobuko and slightly rev. by WTV; p. 76. My visual description of the mask derives from the accompanying plate.

304: "How sad! My heart breaks! A flowering branch on a withered tree." — Keene, p. 76 ("Sekidera Komachi").

304: Qualities of *sabi* — De Mente, pp. 31–32.

305: "I lack form . . ." — Bethe and Emmert, p. 22 (my "retranslation" of the extremely literal word-for-word gloss).

305: "The century-old woman to whom you've spoken . . ." — Keene, p. 76 ("Sekidera Komachi"), "retranslated" by WTV.

305: Komachi's tanka imagining herself as her own cremated smoke — Sato and Watson, p. 116.

305: The poem in the *Tales of Ise* which admonishes the exalted and the base not to fall in love — McCullough, p. 66. Even more apposite to Komachi is the following: "Kenshi's remains vanished without a trace into smoke — a dreadful sight" (ibid., p. 250 [*A Tale of Flowering Fortunes*]). Kenshi had been an Empress.

305: Description of *yase-otoko* mask — After Kanze, Hayashi and Matsuda, paperback commentary vol., p. 55; hardback vol., plates 138–39.

306: The nymphomaniac's "Komachi Dance" — Saikaku, p. 164 ("The Life of an Amorous Woman").

306: "Yet could she have been as miserable as I was?" — Lady Nijo, p. 187.

307: "What do you now tell me . . ." — Sato and Watson, p. 115 ("retranslated" by WTV).

307: "The intensity of her expression of passion . . ." — After Brower and Miner, p. 29.

307: "Movement will grow from the chant . . ." — Zeami (Rimer and Yamazaki), p. 46 ("Fushikaden").

308: Komachi's poem of cowering away from malicious eyes — Brower and Miner, p. 188 ("*Utsutsu ni wa . . .*").

309: Description of the *higaki-no-onna* mask — After Kanze, Hayashi and Matsuda, paperback commentary vol., p. 35; and hardback plates 64–65.

310: "Revealed as she pulls the peplos to one side . . ." — Getty Museum, p. 19 ("Statue of a Kore [The Elgin Kore]").

310: The pine tree immortality of poetry — Keene, *Twenty Plays*, p. 71 ("Sekidera Komachi").

311: "My rooms shone with tortoise shell . . ." — Ibid., p. 74 ("Sekidera Komachi").

311: "White jade, even in the mud, will retain its real appearance." — Zeami, p. 136 ("Shugyoku tokka").

## 27: URASHIMA'S BOX

312: The tale of Urashima — *Manyoshu*, pp. 216–18 (poem 656: "Urashima of Mizunoe").

313: Concerning my ageing face — One late afternoon in a former Heike village, now a hot spring among whose attractions one counts bear sashimi, steaming sulphur-smelling water spewed from hotel pipes into snowy gulleys. The sun was low, the river blackish-green. A man stopped his truck, threw aside the netting from his reservoir, and caught a pair of immense carp for dinner. That low sun on the dark and snowy river reminded me most sadly of my younger times (never mind that I was ten years younger then). I felt oppressed by my own history. But from the crescent moon bridge I could see pressed against steamy panes the wrinkled breasts of old women; these attracted me with all their wise experiences which stratified them into golden sandstone. I wanted to place my forehead against those sulphur-dripping bulwarks of gentleness and drink their sweat as pilgrims do the holy water of Lourdes. Palms pressed against the glass, wide, affectionate buttocks, these performed cleanliness and steadfastness. When I took the waters myself that evening, I tried the outdoor pool. The cold wet air made my sore throat ache. Stripping, I eased myself into the water, which almost scalded me at first, then uplifted me. I gazed at the purple night, with steam from the pipe obscuring the stars.

313: "The town of Fuchu is nothing but corpses . . ." — De Bary et al., p. 448.

314: "Natural for me." — Corn, p. 66 ( Richard Meryman, "Andrew Wyeth: An Interview").

314: "It was such a beautiful voice . . ." — Kawabata, *Snow Country*, p. 5.

316: Description of Lasa — After Getty Museum, pp. 129 (closeup), 136 ("Patera Handle in the Form of a Nude Winged Girl").

316: "She sent no answer . . ." — Waley, *No Plays*, p. 158 ("Sotoba Komachi," slightly "retranslated" by WTV).

## 28: THE DECAY OF THE ANGEL

318: "A face like new-fallen snow, unaware of what lies ahead" — Mishima, *Runaway Horses*, p. 26.

319:  "Up until now I thought it best as his friend . . ." — Mishima, *Spring Snow*, p. 193.

320:  "The instant that the blade tore open his flesh . . ." — Mishima, *Runaway Horses*, p. 419.

320:  "In the average person, I imagine . . ." — Mishima, *Sun and Steel*, p. 8.

321:  "Definitely gifted, but somehow not really sure how to cope with the 'gift'" — Reiko Tochigi to WTV, personal communication, 2001.

321:  "He can only be objectified through the supreme action . . ." — Mishima, *Sun and Steel*, p. 55.

323:  Footnote: Zeami on the vicissitudes of Noh actors at various ages — Op. cit., pp. 22, 24.

323:  "One must not copy the vulgar manners of common people." — Zeami, p. 25.

323:  "*THE SET is in extremely vulgar and commonplace taste . . .*" — Mishima, *Five Modern No Plays*, p. 3 ("Sotoba Komachi," italics in original).

324:  Footnote: "There's always something slightly crude about a dress made by a Japanese?" — Ibid., p. 16.

324:  "The park, the lovers . . ." — Ibid., p. 7.

324:  "They're petting on their graves . . ." — Ibid., p. 9.

325:  "Shadows are moving over the windows . . ." — Ibid., p. 19.

325:  Footnote: Zeami on translating musical atmosphere into visual expression — Op. cit., p. 128 ("Shugyoku tokka").

326:  "If I think something is beautiful . . ." — Ibid., p. 3.

326:  The *ukiyo-e* painting of Komachi — Ota Memorial Museum of Art (2006), p. 11 (1: Iwasa Matabei, "The Poetess Komachi").

327:  The violet blossoms on the maple — Kawabata, *The Old Capital*, pp. 1–2.

327:  "As time passed, the memory of their embrace . . ." — Kawabata, *Beauty and Sadness*, pp. 122–23.

328:  Description of *ushin* — Brower and Miner, p. 271.

328:  "To wash oneself clean of one sin that was permeated with sacrilege . . ." — Mishima, *Spring Snow*, p. 258.

328:  "He was always thinking of death . . ." — Mishima, *Runaway Horses*, p. 131.

## 29: SUNSHINE ON SILLA

331:  Description of the Flower of Peerless Charm — Zeami, p. 120 ("Kyui").

331:  "The metaphor is much more subtle than its inventor . . ." — Lichtenberg, p. 87 (notebook F, no. 41).

332:  "Do I not feel as I did in that dream . . ." — Novalis, p. 104.

332:  Description of Rodin's "Psyche" — Seen in the Musée Rodin. Sculpture *ca.* 1905, *marbre inachevé*.

332:  Footnote on "Hagoromo" — After Waley, *The No Plays of Japan*, p. 221 ("Hagoromo").

332: Description of Kannon — Standing thousand-armed Kannon Bosatsu No. 504, wood with gold leaf by Ruen, Kamakura period, 1251–66, Tokyo National Museum.

333: "In this polluted world . . ." — De Bary et al., p. 335 (Ikkyu Sojun, 1394–1481, "The Errant Cloud Collection").

334: Description of the Roman Muse — Melpomene the Muse of tragedy, seen at the Getty Villa in Santa Monica. Her mask was as large as from her head to her breast.

334: Description of the two geishas viewing plum blossoms in the snow — *Ukiyo-e* print by Torii Kiyonaga (1752–1815), on view at the Tokyo National Museum.

336: The eighteenth-century black and white *ukiyo-e* print of a courtesan — Clark et al., p. 120 (Torii Kiyomasu, I, "Standing Courtesan," 1705–7).

## 30: PINE TREE CONSTANCY

338: Description of the "Takasago" fan — After a reproduction in Chiba, pp. 24–25.

338: "So, awaiting this occasion . . ." — Zeami, "Takasago," excerpted in Hare, p. 89.

339: "Like blossoms on an ancient tree" — Zeami, "Fushikaden," quoted in Hare, p. 65.

339: Mr. Mikata Shizuka — Interviewed in his studio in Kyoto, April 2004.

339: Footnote: Characteristics of the fourteenth-century stage — Pound and Fenollosa, p. 35.

339: Knowledge of ancient audiences about the pine tree god and goddess — For example, the much older *Tales of Ise* contains an episode about the Sumiyoshi god (p. 152; Dan CXII).

339: Hokusai's line-image of the old couple — *Encyclopedia: Men and Women*, p. 107, no. 9 ("Takasago: Noh play celebrating prosperity and longevity"). This is not Hokusai's only reference to "Takasago." In his *One Hundred Poets* (p. 81), he illustrates an early tenth-century poem by Fujiwara no Okikaze. The poet laments the solitude of old age; even Takasago's pines, he complains, cannot replace his bygone companions. Hokusai's illustration, done more than nine hundred years later, defies Okikaze's self-pity: People sit contentedly beneath the spreading branches of an immense pine. Some faces gaze upward; others look at the schematized sea. In one endearingly and typically down-to-earth touch, a tea-seller hunches over her apparatus.

339: "And while the cup of the Shogun is poured out three times . . ." — Pound and Fenollosa, p. 7.

340: Footnote: "I celebrate my lord" — Zeami, "Takasago" (quoted in Hare, p. 70).

340: "The pines that grew together . . ." — Zeami, "Takasago" (quoted in Hare, p. 102).

340: "The pine-clad mountain / will never be inconstant." — McCullough, p. 148 (*The Gossamer Journal*).

340: Poem of the Gossamer Lady's husband — Ibid., p. 108.

340: "Even if you were dwelling near the peak at Takasago" — Ibid., p. 105.

340: "On the Day of the Rat . . ." — McCullough, p. 214 (*A Tale of Flowering Fortunes*).

340: "The maiden's crimson face is gone forever . . ." — Keene, *Seeds in the Heart*, p. 141.

341: "My own people! / They stood just so . . ." — *Manyoshu*, p. 255 (poem 785, Mononobe Mashima, "Those pines standing in rows . . .").

341: "His name alone lives on" + "An ancient pine is rooted in the mound." — Hare, p. 140 (excerpt from "Izutsu").

341: Hare's interpretation of the pine — Ibid., p. 141.

341: "Even when I'm an old woman of sixty . . ." — Kawabata, *The Old Capital*, p. 155.

342: "I couldn't break the bonds of my insane attachment . . ." — Masuda, pp. 138–39.

342: The vermilion-and-pale-green undergarment used in "Takasago" — From the Kanazawa Noh Museum, seen by me in January 2008.

342: "All art is a revolt against man's fate." — Malraux, p. 639.

342: "Love is a madness, but therein it is pure . . ." — Pinguet, p. 177.

343: "There are fundamental barriers created by society," etc. — Shirane, p. 119.

343: "Perhaps with love it is always so . . ." — Keene, *Twenty No Plays*, p. 86 ("The Brocade Tree").

343: "The anger of lust denied covers me like darkness." — Waley, p. 176 ("Aya no Tsuzumi").

343: "At nineteen I first pledged love with him . . ." — Hare, p. 146 (trans. of *rongi*).

343: Authorship of "Matsukaze" — See, for instance, Tyler, p. 183 (introduction to this play); Takeda and Bethe, p. 21.

343: Ancient precedence of "Izutsu" over "Matsukaze" — Zeami (Rimer and Yamazaki), p. 214 ("Sarugaku dangi").

344: The loneliness of Suma — In his *One Hundred Poets*, Hokusai's illustration to a twelfth-century poem about just this becomes, in a typically cheerful inversion, a portrait of three buxom sake-makers (p. 162).

344: Genji Picture-Scroll illustration re: Suma — Murase, ch. 12. Genji's three sad years of exile have become so emblematic that *The Taiheiki*'s Emperor Go-Daigo en route to his own exile refers to it as if it were real (op. cit., p. 106).

345: Footnote: Kindred "pining" pun in "Hanjo" — Keene, *Twenty No Plays*, p. 139 ("Hanjo").

345:   Footnote: Effect of Narihira's poem on the Eight Bridges of Mikawa —
       Keene, *Seeds in the Heart*, p. 230.

345:   Genji's reference to Yukihira — p. 241 (Waley trans.). For the convenience
       of the reader I also give the following: p. 229, beginning of Suma chapter;
       pp. 246–47, description of Suma; p. 339, pathos of Suma depicted in a
       picture competition. Pages 11, 221, 595 and 604 refer to Takasago, 609 to
       Sumiyoshi and 253 to a pine tree screen. See also *Tales of Ise*, p. 128 (Dan
       LXXXVII).

345:   Hokusai's Yukihira — *Men and Women*, p. 205, no. 5 (Ariwara no Yuki-
       hira, poet in Heian period).

345:   "He changed our saltmakers' vestments for damask robes . . ." — Keene,
       p. 28 ("Matsukaze," "retranslated" by WTV).

345:   "So young! . . ." — Loc. cit. Not "retranslated."

346:   The sixteenth-century *juuroku* mask — Displayed at the Kanazawa Noh
       Museum, January 2008.

346:   Description of Matsukaze-do and environs — From a visit to Suma in
       2006.

347:   "It makes no sense whatsoever to imagine Matsukaze's height . . ." —
       Keene, *Twenty Plays*, p. 12.

347:   Specification of *waka-onna* mask for Matsukaze — Ibid., p. 22.

347:   Remarks of Ms. Nakamura on "Matsukaze" — Interview of October
       2006.

347:   Former specification of *fukai* for the same part — Tyler, p. 188 (introduc-
       tion to "Matsukaze").

349:   Employment of *fushikizo* in "Matsukaze" — Nakanishi and Komma,
       p. 123.

349:   "*Yuki* style with the nose tilted to the right . . ." — Hori, Masuda and Miyano,
       trans. for WTV by Yasuda Nobuko and slightly rev. by WTV; p. 49. My
       visual description of this mask derives from the accompanying plate.

349:   Footnote: "Kanzesoke has the beautiful *tsuki* . . ." — Ibid., p. 64. Another
       example of the specific meanings which can be attached to Japanese beauty:
       "A woman in a *yukata* (light kimono) after a bath, turning around while
       wiping her hands with a towel thrown over her shoulder. Her plump face,
       slightly open lips, breast barely showing, and the way her hands lay on top
       of one another, all depict the rich sensuality of a middle-aged woman. Her
       upright posture brings delicate elegance to the scene. This is what Utamaro
       sees as 'the fickle type' woman. *Baimage*, which is arranged by wrapping the
       hair around the *kougai* (=hairpin) and *kanzashi* (=hairpin), is a temporary
       hair arrangement after a bath or during makeup. Using *kushi* (=comb) and
       *kanzashi* for this hair arrangement could be signs of womanliness or ficti-
       tiousness of an Ukiyoe. 'Fujinsougakujittai' is the earliest series of portraits
       of beautiful women by Utamaro, attempting to illustrate the different char-
       acters and expressions of women." — Utamaro book, trans. Yasuda Nobuko,

slightly rev. by WTV. Picture 5: Fujinsougakujittai (Ten Types of Physiognomic Studies of Women), Uwakinosou (The Fickle Type). Around Kansei 4–5 (1792–93). Large Nishikie. New York Public Library.

350:    Remarks of Mr. Mikata on "Matsukaze" — Interview of October 2006.

350:    *Manyoshu* poem on the fisher-girls of Shika — Op. cit., p. 96 (poem 279: Ishikawa Kimiko, "The fisher-maids at Shika . . ."). A very similar poem in the *Tales of Ise* (p. 128; Dan LXXXVII) mentions the unloosed hair and also the fact that the combs were of boxwood.

350:    Hokusai illustration: burning seaweed — *One Hundred Poets*, p. 198.

350:    Tyler on fisher-girls as entertainers and prostitutes — Op. cit., pp. 185–86 (introduction to "Matsukaze").

350:    Lady Nijo's nuns — Op. cit., p. 228.

353:    *Marie Claire*, vol. 15, no. 4 (April 2008), p. 190 (Ning Chao, "Picture Perfect: The new makeup designed for high-definition television helps you look more flawless in real life").

353:    Description of the mask "Flower" — After Rath, color plates 3–4.

### 31: KAGEKIYO'S DAUGHTER

355:    "The Way of Heaven has no love for" the fighting man . . . — Blomberg, pp. 69–70.

355:    "The end is near . . ." — Waley, *No Plays*, p. 133 ("Kagekiyo").

355:    "Love of woman scarcely ever prevented the Japanese warrior from doing his duty as he saw it." — After Blomberg, p. 75.

355:    "Candle to my darkness . . ." — Waley, loc. cit.

355:    Dampened sleeve poem of pine tree wind — Brower and Miner, p. 314 (Ariie, "The Wind in the Pines").

355:    Poem of the dead wife under the moss — Ibid., p. 310 (Shunzei, "Mare ni kuru . . .").

355:    Remarks of Mr. Mikata — Interview of October 2006.

356:    Kagekiyo's shame in front of his daughter, and compassion at her shame in being known as a beggar's daughter — Waley, op. cit., p. 130 ("Kagekiyo").

356:    "No remembrance other," etc. — Op. cit., p. 133.

357:    "A swordsman should prepare a mind of mirrorlike emptiness" — Blomberg, p. 69.

357:    The way that Noh is "in absolute harmony with the *bushi* ethos . . ." — Ibid., pp. 196–97.

357:    Otsu's two mentions in *The Taiheiki* — Op. cit., pp. 61, 70. On p. 38 this work refers to "Biwa's saltless sea."

358:    Drawing of Semimaru — Hokusai, *One Hundred Poets*, pp. 44–45 (poem 10, untitled poem by Semimaru).

360: Description of Yasha's *masukami* — Kanze, Hayashi and Matsuda, paperback commentary vol., p. 35; hardcover plates 62–63.

361: Zeami's definition of fascination — Op. cit., p. 133 ("Shugyoku tokka").

361: Footnote: "You become really absorbed at a play . . ." — Denby, pp. 146–47 ("How to Judge a Dancer," 1943).

362: "Denied the moon . . ." — Tyler, p. 249 ("Semimaru," slightly "retranslated" by WTV).

363: The demented mother as entertainment — In "Miidera" also the madwoman dance is straightforwardly presented as fun ("for entertainment, bring her into the outer garden and have her dance insanely"). Bethe and Emmert, *Noh Performance Guide 3*, p. 26.

363: Description of the Edo period *fukai* mask — Kanazawa Noh Museum, on display in January 2008. I wish I could remember what the mask's eyelids looked like, because in a carver's description of one *fukai* believed to be by Zekan I read: "This *fukai* has no work on the eyelids. This is fine for the role of mothers searching for the child, as in the mother who lost her child in 'Sumidagawa.'" — Hori, Masuda and Miyano, p. 69, trans. for WTV by Yasuda Nobuko and slightly rev. by WTV. — Danyu-san, the musician who played for Konomi-san and Kofumi-san when I met those three together in Gion, told me that she had once performed in a play called "Shizu-hata." She said: "There was a dance in which a child was kidnapped and killed. The mother went insane. And I was supposed to play the insane woman's role. It was very difficult. To play an insane person you must not move your eyes."

363: Description of the fan — This is a certain Hosho School fan employed for roles of such madwomen as the grief-stricken mothers in "Sumidagawa" or the much happier "Miidera." (It is never used to play Sakagami in "Semimaru.") This fan expresses strength through golden mist-patterns; it also offers a spray of white plum-blossoms, white chrysanthemums, irises, etcetera. Also seen at the Kanazawa Noh Museum.

363: Sumida River poem — *Tales of Ise*, pp. 47–48 (Dan IX). Lady Nijo (pp. 199–200) could not resist making matters even sadder when she stood on this spot, remarking: "I recalled how Narihira had put a question to a capital bird here, but I did not see any birds at all." Meanwhile, "Sumidagawa" has given birth to many allusions of its own — e.g., Kafu, p. 177.

363: "Sumida in Autumn" by Chobunsai Eishi — Ota Ukiyo-e Museum, on display in October 2006.

363: Woodblock by Isoda Koryusai — Uhlenbeck and Winkel, p. 100.

366: Zeami's thoughts on the child actor in the mound — Op. cit., p. 188 ("Sarugaku dangi").

366: "What appeared to be a dear child . . ." — Tyler, p. 263 ("Sumida-gawa," slightly "retranslated" by WTV).

367: Epigraph: "Once a man met, courted, and won a woman . . ." — McCullough, p. 49.

367: Excerpt from *Taketori Monogatari* — McCullough, p. 57.

368: Hanago's remark on the sting of love (these words were actually chanted in her name by the Noh chorus) — Keene, *Twenty Plays*, p. 137 ("Hanjo").

368: Description of Mr. Mikata Shizuka and other actors in "Michimori" — Performed in Jumenji Temple, Kyoto, October 2006.

370: Kawabata: "For me, love more than anything else . . ." — Quoted in Keene, *Dawn to the West*, p. 795.

370: "Even in the provinces . . ." — McCullough, p. 45.

371: Kawabata's red weeping cherry trees — *The Old Capital*, p. 8.

371: One poet of the *Manyoshu* who pretends that sight of Kyoto would bring back his youth — Op. cit., p. 242 (poem 736: "If I could see the capital . . .").

372: Genji's fear that he will never glimpse the capital again — *Tale of Genji*, p. 253.

372: "Suma's image is loneliness." — Interview with Mr. Mikata of October 2006.

372: "Born at Akashi! What a hideous thought!" — *Tale of Genji*, p. 637.

372: Effects of the *Kokin Shu* anthology on subsequent centuries of poetic diction — Keene, *Seeds in the Heart*, pp. 256–57.

372: Woodblock of the courtesan-turned-letter-writer — Saikaku, p. 155 (illustration to "The Life of an Amorous Woman").

373: Symbolism of the three pines on the stage bridge — Pound and Fenollosa, p. 36.

374: "Clutching this transient life . . ." — *Manyoshu*, p. 23 (poem 63, by the exiled Prince Omi; "retranslated" by WTV).

374: The increasing loneliness of Semimaru's palanquin-bearers — Tyler, p. 240 ("Semimaru").

374: "I was not intended for a world in which women shackle themselves . . ." — Proust, p. 460 ("Place-Names: The Name" part of *Swann's Way*).

375: "Trend Watch: Metallics." — *InStyle*, vol. 15, no. 1, p. 83 ("Style File").

375: "The sea her world . . ." — *Tales of Ise*, p. 143 (Dan CIV; "retranslated" by WTV).

375: Departure of the *tsure* and others through the small stage door — Keene, p. 44 ("The Sought-for Grave").

375: Teika's thirteenth-century tanka — Brower and Miner, p. 308 (Teika, "Tabibito no . . .").

376: "Thither I go, / . . ." — *Manyoshu*, p. 44 (poem 109: "In the days when my wife lived . . .").

376: Extract from *The Taiheiki* — Op. cit., p. 355.

376: Protracted entrances and exits in Noh and Kabuki — Gunji, pp. 22–23.

376: "Matching the feelings to the moment." — Zeami (Rimer and Yamazaki), p. 82 ("Kakyo").

377: "And Lord Suketomo they banished to the land of Sado . . ." — *The Taiheiki*, p. 27.

377: Haiku on Sado and the Milky Way — Ueda, *Basho*, p. 30.

377: Loud and coarse rustling of a plebeian woman's gowns — Lady Nijo, p. 84, in reference to a fanmaker's daughter.

378: "Wait awhile . . ." — Brazell, p. 190 ("Shunkan," trans. Eileen Kato).

378: Description of Shunkan mask — After Nakanishi and Komma, p. 55 (plate 58).

378: "Please put aside / the River of Heaven . . ." — McCullough, p. 67.

378: "Sekare sekarete" — Dalby, p. 77 ("Longing").

379: "A dreadful island . . ." — *The Taiheiki*, p. 45.

379: "The cutting is like a gust of wind . . ." — Ibid., p. 47.

379: Footnote on the natives of Devil's Island — *The Tale of the Heike*, vol. 1, p. 186.

379: Same footnote: "When I learned that we were passing Suma . . ." — Lady Nijo, p. 227.

380: Description of *wabi* — De Mente, pp. 33–35.

380: Zeami's recollection of Kyoto's flowers — Interview with Mr. Mikata, October 2006.

380: "I can't help thinking about the capital . . ." — McCullough, p. 77 (*A Tosa Journal*). In the same source, on the twenty-seventh day of the eleventh month, "a certain person" composes a poem about sadness for a dead child, a little girl who will never go home to the capital (p. 75).

380: Proust on the sounds within an egg — Vol. 1, p. 482 ("Madame Swann at Home" section of *Within a Budding Grove*).

381: "Thus by living in the capital. . ." — Zeami (Rimer and Yamazaki), p. 96 ("Kakyo").

382: The three pictures of Nancy — Allen, pp. 99–101.

383: "A man's true feeling for a woman does not arise from the bodily contact . . ." — Owen, p. 918 (Li Yu, "Silent Operas" [seventeenth cent.]).

384: Zeami's definition of fulfillment — Op. cit., p. 137 ("Shugyoku tokka").

385: The famous moon poem in the *Tales of Ise* — McCullough, p. 60, noting that it was referred to years later in the poems of skillful courtiers in *A Tosa Journal*.

385: "For many are the pleasant forms which exist in numerous sins . . ." — Robinson, p. 303 ("The Thunder: Perfect Mind").

385: The once-a-year frequency of theater-going in Edo — *Guide to Edo-Tokyo Museum*, p. 8.

385: The geisha song about butterflies — Dalby, pp. 40–42 ("In the Right Now of Now").

386: Mr. Umewaka: "It's more difficult to always do the same thing than to change . . ." — Jeff Clark corrections, to ms. p. 3.

387: "To see with the spirit is to grasp the spirit . . ." — Zeami (Rimer and Yamazaki), p. 71 ("Shikado").

387: The square lacquered box with white butterflies — Nakamura Museum in Kanazawa, box *ca.* 1982.

387: "Those who dedicate themselves to pleasure . . ." — Makuzu, p. 31.

387: "An allegory carried too far or too low . . ." — Milton, p. 515 (extracts from Voltaire's *Essay Upon the Civil Wars of France . . . And also Upon the Epick Poetry of the European Nations from Homer to Milton* [London, 1727]).

387: Footnote: "I feel as if a mask kissed me . . ." — Mishima, *Five No Plays*, p. 103 ("Kantan").

388: Description of unfinished *ko-omote*s as wooden crystals — After illustrations in Hori, Masuda and Miyano, p. 148.

389: Description of the geisha Kikuyo — Kafu, p. 98 ("Decay of the Angel").

389: Footnote: Sei Shonagon on the etiquette of souvenirs accompanying letters to and from the capital — McCullough, p. 162.

393: Plot of "Nishikigi" — Keene, *Twenty No Plays*, pp. 89ff. ("The Brocade Tree").

393: The deathbed poem of Ki no Tsurayuki — Translated and briefly discussed in Keene, *Seeds in the Heart*, p. 267. This sentiment one comes across any number of times in the classical literature. For instance, the neglected wife of a highbred womanizer writes these eponymous lines in her *Gossamer Journal* (McCullogh, p. 155): "When I reflect on the perpetual uncertainty in which I exist, it seems to me that this is a journal of a woman whose fortunes have been as evanescent as the gossamer shimmer of a heat wave in the sky."

393: "We had been fussing about with our dress and powder since early dawn." — Murasaki, *Diary*, p. 23.


### POSTSCRIPT TO APPENDIX B

411: Descriptions out of Sigrid Undset — *The Bridal Wreath*, pp. 56–57, 111, 112–20, 16–17; *The Cross*, pp. 348, 44, 182–85; *The Mistress of Husaby*, pp. 292–93; *The Cross*, p. 403.


### APPENDIX E: NOH PLAY GROUPS, AND PLAYS MENTIONED

424: "Only a few hundred plays" — Rath, p. 201.

424: Eight hundred pre-1868 plays survive — Waley, *The No Plays of Japan*, p. 37.

424: Jeff Clark's estimate — From his corrections, on p. 2 of my ms.

## GLOSSARY

425: Definition of the Floating World: Ancient Egyptian love poem — Simpson, p. 333 ("The Song of the Harper", slightly "retranslated" by WTV).

426: Definition of *hikime kagibana*: Description of Hokusai's sketch of a court beauty — *Men and Women*, p. 35, no. 4 (court lady).

428: Definition of Shinto: Mr. Mikata's remarks — Interview of October 2006.

429: Definition of *tsuki*: description of *fushikizo*: Hori, Masuda and Miyano, trans. for WTV by Yasuda Nobuko and slightly rev. by WTV; p. 42 (quoting Kanze Kiyokazu).

## CHRONOLOGY

434: 1780s — "The ideals of the Floating World" — Peabody Museum, p. 124 (Money Hickman, "Geisha to the Fore: *Niwaka* Festivals and the New Luminaries of Edo"). One *niwaka* was derived from "Takasago" (ibid., p. 129).

435: 1952 — "Today, the Umewaka school may be forced to cease its performances . . ." — Bowers, p. 19.

# BIBLIOGRAPHY

Names of authors are *cited* here as they appear on their respective title pages, with resulting variation in the order of family and given names. But they are *listed* by family name.

I have categorized books by their area of relevance to *Kissing the Mask*, not by their own purported subject matter. Thus David Strauss's *Percival Lowell* appears in category C, relating to geishas, because it is only the geisha material in it which is cited here.

Texts as translated for this book by the four translators whom I commissioned (Sumino Junko, Keiko Golden, Yasuda Nobuko and Kawai Takako) will be placed in my archive in Ohio State University.

Especially beautiful pictorial sources relating to Noh masks and to geishas are bulleted (•). See sections A. and C.

## A. PUBLISHED SOURCES ON NOH THEATER

1. William Theodore de Bary, Donald Keene, George Tanabe and Paul Varley, comp., *Sources of Japanese Tradition*, vol. 1: From Earliest Times to 1600 (New York: Columbia University Press, 2001; orig. comp. 1950s).

2. Monica Bethe and Richard Emmert, with the assistance of Joni Koehn and Gustav Heldt, *Noh Performance Guide 7: Aoinoue* (Tokyo: National Noh Theatre, 1997; printed by Shobunsha Printing Co.).

3. Monica Bethe and Richard Emmert, with the assistance of Gus Heldt, *Noh Performance Guide 3: Miidera* (Tokyo: National Noh Theatre, 1993; printed by Shobunsha Printing Co.).

4. Monica Bethe and Richard Emmert, with Karen Brazell, *Noh Performance Guide 5: Atsumori* (Tokyo: National Noh Theatre, 1995; printed by Shobunsha Printing Co.).

5. Faubion Bowers, *Japanese Theatre* (New York: Hermitage House, 1952).

6. Karen Brazell, *Traditional Japanese Theater: An Anthology of Plays* (New York: Columbia University Press, 1998).

7. Ronald Cavaye, Paul Griffith, Akihiko Senda, *A Guide to the Japanese Stage from Traditional to Cutting Edge* (New York: Kodansha International, 2004).

8.  Reiko Chiba, ed., *Painted Fans of Japan: 15 Noh Drama Masterpieces* (Rutland, Vermont: Charles E. Tuttle Co., Inc., 1993 repr. of 1962 1st printing).

9.  Thomas Blenham Hare, *Zeami's Style: The Noh Plays of Zeami Motokiyo* (Stanford, California: Stanford University Press, 1986).

10. Hikawa Mariko, *Umewáka Rokuro Noh no Shinseiki* [Umewaka Rokuro, New Century of Noh: From Classics to New Works: Introduction to Noh] (Tokyo: Shogakukan, 2002).

11. • Shodai Yasuemon Hori, Shozo Masuda and Masaki Miyano, *Noh-men: Kansho to Uchikata* [Noh Masks: Appreciation and Making], 4th ed. (Kyoto: Tankosha, 2001 repr. of 1998 ed.).

12. • Kanze Kiyozaku, Hayashi Yoshikatsu and Matsuda Shozo, trans. Ian MacDougall, *Omote: The Kanze Soke Noh Collection*, 1 hardbound vol. of color plates and one pbk. vol. of commentary (Tokyo: Hinoki-shoten, 2002).

13. Donald Keene, ed., with the assistance of Royall Tyler, *Twenty Plays of the No Theatre* (New York: Columbia University Press, Translations from the Asian Classics ser. / UNESCO Collection of Representative Works: Japanese ser., 1970).

14. Kodama Shoko, *The Complete Guide to Traditional Japanese Performing Arts* (Tokyo: Kodansha / Bilingual Books, 2000).

15. Daiji Maruoka and Tatsuo Yoshikoshi, *Noh*, 15th ed., trans. Don Kenny (Osaka: Hoikusha Publishing Co. Ltd., Color Books ser. no. 15, 1992; orig. ed. 1969).

16. Yukio Mishima, *Five Modern No Plays*, trans. Donald Keene (Tokyo: Charles E. Tuttle Co., 1969 pbk repr. of 1967; orig. Knopf ed. 1957; plays in collection written 1950–55).

17. Toru Nakanishi and Kiyonori Komma, *Noh Masks*, trans. Don Kenny (Osaka: Hoikusha, Hoikusha's Color Book ser. no. 40, 1992 3rd ed.; 1st ed. 1983).

18. Ezra Pound and Ernest Fenollosa, *The Classic Noh Theatre of Japan* (New York: New Directions, 1979; orig. pub. 1917).

19. Eric C. Rath, *The Ethos of Noh: Actors and Their Art* (Cambridge, Massachusetts: Harvard University Press. Harvard University Asia Center, Harvard East Asian Monographs, no. 232, 2004).

20. • Sharon Sadako Takeda, in collaboration with Monica Bethe, *Miracles and Mischief: Noh and Kyogen Theater in Japan* (Los Angeles: Los Angeles County Museum of Art, 2002).

21. Kazuya Takaoka, Mutsuo Takahashi [text] and Toshiro Morita, *Noh*, trans. Emiko Miyashita (Tokyo: PIE Books, 2004).

22. Tokugawa Art Museum, *Noh Masks and Costumes: Treasures from the Tokugawa Art Museum No. 9* (Nagoya: Tokugawa Art Museum, 1995).

23. Royall Tyler, ed. and trans., *Japanese No Dramas* (New York: Penguin, 1992).

24. [Waley, *No Plays*.] Arthur Waley, *The No Plays of Japan, with Letters by Oswald Sickert* (New York: Grove Press, n.d., *ca.* 1920).

25. Ze-ami [Motokiyo], *Kadensho* [*Fushi Kaden*], trans. Chuichi Sakurai, Shuseki

Hayashi [Lindley Williams Hubbell], Rokuro Satoi, Bin Miyai (Tokyo: Sumiya-Shinobe Publishing Institute, 1968; orig. ed. Oei 25 [1442]).

26. [Zeami Motokiyo], *On the Art of No Drama: The Major Treatises of Zeami*, trans. J. Thomas Rimer and Yamazaki Masakazu (Princeton, N.J.: Princeton University Press, 1984; orig. treatises thirteenth century). Cited: Zeami (Rimer and Yamazaki),

### Noh Articles, Ephemera and Unpublished Manuscripts

27. Jeff Clark, comments and corrections on "The Mask Is Most Important Always" (letter to WTV + marked draft), 2003.

28. 44th Osaka International Festival 2002, Festival Noh brochure (April 10 — April 24, Festival Hall, Osaka).

29. [Kanze Sakon.] *The 25th Kanze Sakon's 13th Memorial Noh*, hosted by Kanze Soke (4/7/2002). Show program (in Japanese).

30. *"Kawamura Teiki Noh" Kawamura Nobushige Tuitou.* ["Kawamura Periodical Noh" in memory of Kawamura Nobushige.] Show performed in Kyoto, 3/12/2004, hosted by Kawamura Teiki Kennoh Kai and Kawamura Kyodai (sponsors). Show program (in Japanese).

31. Michael J. Lyons, Ruth Campbell, Andre Plante, Mike Coleman, Miyuki Kamachi and Shigeru Akamatsu, "The Noh Mask Effect: Vertical Viewpoint Dependence of Facial Expression Perception," in an offprint of the Royal Society, 2000, pp. 2239–2245.

32. [Mikata Shizuka.] *Noh "Kakitsubata": Koi no Mai* [Noh "Kakitsubata (Iris)": Dance of Love]. Performed in Kyoto, 5/15/2004, by Mikata Shizuka (Kanze style actor). Show program (in Japanese).

33. [Mitsui family.] *Mitsuike Denrai no Noh Shouzoku ten* [Mitsui Family's Ancestral Noh Costumes Exhibition, Mitsui Memorial Museum Opening Memorial] (Tokyo: Nihonkeizaishinbunsha, 2005; exhibition dates 10/4–10/16/2005). Selected captions trans. for WTV by Yasuda Nobuko, 2007.

34. [Nakamura Mitsue.] Postcards of Noh masks made by Nakamura Mitsue, Kyoto: Ko Omote (*girl in late teens*), Eko-Doji, Yamadori (*Mountain Bird*), Kanmurigata-Doji, Chujo (*general*), Wakai Onna (*young woman*), Uba (*Old Woman*), Zo Onna (*goddess or divine woman*).

35. *Noh "Dojyo-ji"* [Noh "Dojo Temple"], show program. The 10th memorial of Theatre Noh, 12/13/2003, at Kyoto Kanze Hall.) Performed by Mikata Shizuka.

36. Takigi-Noh, Nara City cultural asset. Show program (in Japanese). Performed 5/11–12/2005). Hosted by Takigi-Noh Hozon Kai.

37. Umewaka Rokuro, "On the 45th Anniversary of My Stage Career." One-page photocopy furnished to me by interpreter. Evidently the introduction to a collection of photographs by Takahashi Noboru, *ca.* 2006.

38. [Uryusan School.] The 17th Uryusan Taki-Noh. Show program, performed 5/9/2005 in Kyoto. Hosted by Uryusan School.

39. Yokoyama Taro, Ph.D. Candidate and the Department's assistant, the Gradu-
ate School of Arts and Sciences (Department of Culture and Representation),
the University of Tokyo; unpublished ms. communication to author, 2003.
Translated by Sato Yoshiaki. I have been told that he has since received his
Ph.D., so in the text I refer to him as Dr. Yokoyama.

## B. JAPANESE CLASSICS (INCLUDING *GENJI* PICTURE-SCROLLS)

40. ____, *Genji Monogatari Emaki, 2* [Picture-Scroll of the Tale of Genji], rev.
ed. (Nagoya: Tokugawa Museum, *Shinban Tokugawa Bijutsukan Zouhin Shou*
[Treasures from the Tokugawa Museum ser., no. 2], 1998, orig. ed. 1995).
41. ____, *Genji Monogatari, Gouka Genjie no Sekai* [The Tale of Genji: Deluxe
World of Genji Paintings] rev. ed., ed. Tsuyoshi Anzai (Tokyo: Gakushu
Kenkyusha, 2000: reissue of 1999 ed.).
42. ____, *One Thousand Poems from the Manyoshu: The Complete Nippon Gakujutsu
Shinkokai Translation*, trans. Japanese Classics Translation Committee (Min-
eola, New York: Dover Publications, Inc., 2005 slightly abbr. repr. of 1940
ed.; orig. poems eighth cent. and before).
43. ____, *The Taiheiki: A Chronicle of Medieval Japan*, trans. and abbr. Helen
Craig McCullough (Boston: Tuttle Publishing, 2003 repr. of 1953 ed.; orig.
classical Japanese version fourteenth cent.).
44. ____ [Arihira no Narihira and his unknown successors], *The Tales of Ise {Ise
Monogatari}*, trans. H. Jay Harris (Boston: Tuttle Publishing, 1972; orig.
classical Japanese version early tenth cent.; Arihira's poems wr. bef. his death
in 880).
45. ____ [The courtier Yukinaga?], *The Tale of the Heike (Heike Monogatari)*,
trans. Hiroshi Kitagawa and Bruce T. Tsuchida, 2 vols. (Tokyo: University
of Tokyo Press, 1975; orig. Japanese text *ca*. 1330).
46. Robert H. Brower and Earl Miner, *Japanese Court Poetry* (Stanford, California: Stanford University Press, 1997 pbk. repr. of 1961 ed.).
47. Donald Keene, *Seeds in the Heart: A History of Japanese Literature, vol. 1: Japanese Literature from Earliest Times to the Late Sixteenth Century* (New York:
Henry Holt & Co., 1993).
48. Helen Craig McCullough, comp. & ed., *Classical Japanese Prose: An Anthology*
(Stanford, California: Stanford University Press, 1990).
49. Miyeko Murase, ed., *The Tale of Genji: Legends and Paintings* (New York:
George Braziller, 2001; illustration originals from the seventeenth cent.
Burke album).
50. Lady Murasaki [Shikibu], *The Tale of Genji: A Novel in Six Parts*, trans.
Arthur Waley (New York: Modern Library, 1960; date of original English
ed. not given; *Genji* was composed *ca*. 1008).
51. [Lady Murasaki Shikibu.] *The Diary of Lady Murasaki*, trans. Richard Bow-
ring (New York: Penguin, 1996).

52. [Lady Nijo.] *The Confessions of Lady Nijo*, trans. Karen Brazell (Stanford, California: Stanford University Press, 1976 repr. of 1973 Doubleday ed.; orig. Japanese ms. [*Towazugatari*] wr. 1307).

53. Ihara Saikaku, *The Life of an Amorous Woman* and other writings, ed. and trans. Ivan Morris (New York: New Directions, UNESCO Collection of Representative Literary Works, 1963; orig. works seventeenth cent.).

54. Lady Sarashina "(as she is known)", *As I Crossed a Bridge of Dreams: Recollections of a Woman in Eleventh-Century Japan*, trans. Ivan Morris (New York: Penguin Books, 1975 repr. of 1971 Dial ed.; orig. untitled memoir *ca.* 1058).

55. Hiroaki Sato and Burton Watson, trans. and ed., *From the Country of Eight Islands: An Anthology of Japanese Poetry* (New York: Columbia University Press, 1986).

56. Haruo Shirane, *The Bridge of Dreams: A Poetics of the Tale of Genji* (Stanford, California: Stanford University Press, 1987).

57. *The Pillow Book of Sei Shonagon*, trans. and ed. Ivan Morris (New York: Columbia University Press, 1991 abr. of 1967 trans.; orig. Japanese text after A.D. 1000).

58. Makoto Ueda, comp. and ed., *Light Verse from the Floating World: An Anthology of Premodern Japanese Senryu* (New York: Columbia University Press, 1999).

59. Makoto Ueda, *Matsuo Basho: The Master Haiku Poet* (Tokyo: Kodansha International, 1982; orig. [English?] ed. 1970).


### C. RELATING TO GEISHAS

60. Dominique Buisson, *Japan Unveiled: Understanding Japanese Body Culture* (London: Hachette Illustrated UK, Octopus Publishing Group, 2003; orig. French ed. n.d.).

61. *Horace Bristol: An American View*, eds. Ken Conner and Debra Heimerdinger (San Francisco: Chronicle Books, 1996).

62. • Jodi Cobb, *Geisha: The Life, the Voices, the Art* (New York: Knopf, 1997).

63. Liza Dalby, *Little Songs of the Geisha: Traditional Japanese Ko-Uta* (Boston: Tuttle Publishing, 2000; repr. of 1979 ed.).

64. Martha Feldman and Bonnie Gordon, eds., *The Courtesan's Arts: Cross-Cultural Perspectives* (New York: Oxford University Press, 2006).

65. • John Gallagher, *Geisha: A Unique World of Tradition, Elegance, and Art* (London: PRC Publishing Ltd., 2003).

66. Iwasaki Mineko, with Rande Brown, *Geisha of Gion: The Memoir of Mineko Iwasaki* (New York: Simon and Schuster, 2002).

67. Sayo Masuda, *Autobiography of a Geisha*, trans. G. G. Rowley (London: Vintage Books East, 2006).

68. Kafu Nagai, *Geisha in Rivalry (Udekurabe)*, trans. Kurt Mesiner and Ralph Friedrich (Rutland, Vermont: Charles E. Tuttle Co., UNESCO Collection of Representative Works, Japanese Series, 1981 repr. of 1963 ed.; orig. Japanese ed. 1918).

69. • The Peabody Essex Museum, ed., *Geisha: Beyond the Painted Smile* (Salem, Massachusetts: The Peabody Essex Museum, in conjunction with George Braziller, Inc., 2004).

70. David Strauss, *Percival Lowell: The Culture and Science of a Boston Brahmin* (Cambridge, Massachusetts: Harvard University Press, 2001).

### Geisha Ephemera; Periodical

71. *Gion*, No. 179, summer edition (Kyoto: Gion Kobu Kumiai 7/10/2004).

72. *Gion*, No. 182, spring edition (Kyoto: Gion Kobu Kumiai 4/10/2004).

73. Theodore W. Goossen, ed., *The Oxford Book of Japanese Short Stories* (Oxford, U.K.: Oxford University Press, 1997).

74. *Kamogawa Odori*, Program for the 168th Kamogawa Odori show, performed from 5/1 to 5/24/H17 in Kyoto.) Hosted by the Kyoto City Tourist association, Sento-Cho Kabuki Group.

75. *Miyako Odori*, Program for the 133rd Miyako Odori show. Show performed from 4/1/ to 4/30/H17 in Kyoto.) Hosted by the *Gion kobu kabukai* [Kyoto City Tourist Association]. Trans. for WTV by Sumino Junko.

76. *Monumenta Nipponica: Studies in Japanese Culture* [Sophia University, Tokyo], vol. 55, no. 2 (summer 2000) (Emmanuel Pastereich, "The Pleasure Quarters of Edo and Nanjing as Metaphor: The Records of Yu Huai and Narushima Ryuhoku," the latter concerning itself with Edo's Yanagibashi quarter beginning in 1859).

## D. UKIYO-E, WOODCUTS AND PAPERCUTS

77. Timothy Clark, Anne Nishimura Morse and Louise E. Virgin, with Allen Hockley, *The Dawn of the Floating World: Early Ukiyo-e Treasures from the Museum of Fine Arts, Boston* (London: Royal Academy of Arts, 2001).

78. [Hokusai.] *Encyclopedia of Hokusai Sketches — Volume of Men and Women* (Tokyo: Tokyo Bijutsu, Inc., 1999).

79. Hokusai, *One Hundred Poets*, ed. Peter Morse, poems trans. Clay MacCauley (New York: George Braziller, 1989; orig. woodblocks 1839–1849).

80. [Miyata Masayuki.] *Miyata Masayuki, Kirie no Sekai* [Miyata Masayuki, World of Paper Cutout Art], in a special issue of *Bessatsu Taiyo, Nihon no Kokoro* [Taiyo, the Heart of Japan], no. 92, winter 1995 (Tokyo: Heibon Sha, 2003, 4th printing of 1996 ed.).

81. Munakata Shiko, *Munakata Shiko ~Wadaba Gohho ni naru* [I'm Becoming Van Gogh: A Centennial Exhibition, Celebrating the 100th Anniversary of the Artist's Birth], ed. by the Munakata Museum / The Miyagi Museum of Art / NHK Sendai Station (Sendai: NHK Sendai Station / NHK Tohoku Planning, 2003).

82. *Moronobu to Shoki Ukiyoe* [Moronobu and Early Days of Ukiyoe], comp. and ed. Tadashi Kobayashi (Tokyo: Shibundo, *Nihon no Bijutsu* 8, No. 363 [Japa-

nese Art ser., vol. 8, no .363], 1996). Selected captions trans. for WTV by Yasuda Nobuko, 2007.

83. [Ota Memorial Museum of Art], *Masterpieces of the Ota Memorial Museum of Art* (Tokyo: Ota Memorial Museum of Art, 2006).

84. [Ota Memorial Museum of Art], *Ukiyo-e Masterpieces in the Collection of the Ota Memorial Museum of Art* (Tokyo: no publisher or printer listed [probably the museum itself], 1988).

85. Chris Uhlenbeck and Margarita Winkel, with Ellis Tinios, Cecelia Segawa Seigle and Oikawa Shigeru, *Japanese Erotic Fantasies: Sexual Imagery of the Edo Period* (Amsterdam: Hotei Press, 2005).

86. *Ukiyo-e "Meisho Edo Hyakkei" Fukkoku Monogatari* [Ukiyo-e "100 Scenic Beauties of Edo" Reproduction Story], ed. Tokyo Dento Mokuhanga Kougei Kyokai; supervisor Tadashi Kobayashi (Tokyo: Geisodo, 2005).

87. Kitagawa Utamaro, Shincho Japanese Art Library No. 16, *Kitagawa Utamaro*, comp. and text Takanobu Sato, ed. Nihon Art Center (Tokyo: Shinchosha, *Shincho Nihon Bijutsu Bunko* [Shincho Japanese Art Library], 1997). Selected captions trans. for WTV by Yasuda Nobuko, 2007.

88. Kitagawa Utamaro, *Portraits from the Floating World*, text by Tadashi Kobayashi, trans. Mark A. Harbison (Tokyo: Kodansha International, 2000).

## E. JAPANESE *MANGA* AND CONTEMPORARY EROTIC PICTORIALS

89. Monthly Hot Hot May issue, *Gekkan hotto hotto* (*ca.* 1998).

90. Mio Murano [manga artist], *Women*, vol. 9 (Tokyo: Shueisha, 2000: repr. of *Business Jump* magazine, issues 14–22).

91. Rikitake Yasushi, photographer, *Surinukeru Kaze no youni* [As the Wind Blows]; model: Okamoto Sayaka (Tokyo: Shinkosha, 2001).

92. Saiki Hiroyoshi, photographer, *Koi me no rippu* [Heavy+Love Lipstick]; model: Kudo Aya (Tokyo: Wani Magazine, 2003).

93. Shimizu Sitaro, photographer, *Yobi*, supervised by Dan Oniroku (Tokyo: Wani Magazine, 2000:).

94. Sugiura Norio, photographer, *Lame-Back Four: Bishojyo* [Beautiful Girls], *SM Special Edition;* models: Miura Aika, Aso Sanae, Nagase Ramu, Mochida Kaoru (Tokyo: Sanwashuppan, 2000).

## F. MISCELLANEOUS JAPANESE ITEMS

95. ___, *A Dictionary of Japanese Art Terms: Bilingual (Japanese and English) Popular Edition* (Tokyo: Tokyo Bijutsu Co. Ltd., 1990).

96. Shigeru Aoyama, *Nara*, trans. Don Kenny and Money L. Hickman (Osaka: Hoikusha, Hoikusha's Color Book ser. no. 7, 1999, 25th ed.; 1st ed. 1964).

97. Alice Mabel Bacon, *Japanese Girls and Women* (London: Gay and Bird, 1901).

98.  Catharina Blomberg, *The Heart of the Warrior: Origins and Religious Background of the Samurai System in Feudal Japan* (Sandgate, Folkestone, Kent: Japan Library, 1994).

99.  Boyé Lafayette De Mente, *Elements of Japanese Design: Key Terms for Understanding and Using Japan's Classic* Wabi-Sabi-Shibui *Concepts* (Rutland, Vermont: Tuttle Publishing, 2006).

100. *Guide to Edo-Tokyo Museum*, English ed. (Tokyo: Foundation Edo-Tokyo Historical Society, 1995).

101. Masakatsu Gunji, *The Kabuki Guide*, with photographs by Chiaki Yoshida, trans. Christopher Holmes (New York: Kodansha International, 1995 repr. of 1987 ed.).

102. *Fuchikami Hakuyo to Manshu Shashin Sakka Kyoukai* [Fuchikami Hakuyo and the Photographers in Manchuria], gen. ed. Shinichi Otsuka (Tokyo: Iwanami Shoten, *Nihon no Shashinka* 6 [Japanese Photographers ser., vol. 6], 1998).

103. Francis L. Hawks, D.D. L.L.D., *Narrative of the Expedition of an American Squadron to the China Seas and Japan, Performed in the Years 1852, 1853, and 1854, Under the Command of Commodore M. C. Perry, United States Navy* (New York: AMS Press, Arno Press, 1967 repr.; orig. ed. 1856 [Washington: Beverly Tucker, Senate Printer]).

104. Higashifushimi Jigo and Yokoyama Kenzo, *Shoren-In* (Kyoto: Tankosha, *Kyoto no Furudera kara* 27 [Old Temples in Kyoto ser., vol. 27], 1998).

105. Thomas Hoover, *Zen Culture* (New York: Random House, 1977).

106. Hiroko Ikeda, *A Type and Motif Index of Japanese Folk-Literature* (Helsinki, Suomalainen Tiedeakatemia, Academica Scieniarum Fennica, FF Communications no. 209, 1971).

107. Motoko Ito and Aiko Inoue, *Kimono*, trans. Patricia Massy (Osaka: Hoikusha, Hoikusha's Color Book ser. no. 37, 1993 10th ed.; 1st ed. 1979).

108. Ayako Kano, *Acting Like a Woman in Modern Japan: Theater, Gender, and Nationalism* (New York: Palgrave, 2001).

109. Yasunari Kawabata, *Beauty and Sadness*, trans. Howard Hibbett (San Francisco: North Point Press, 1987; orig. Japanese ed. 1962).

110. Yasunari Kawabata, *The Old Capital,* trans. J. Martin Holman (New York: Putnam's; a Wideview/ Perigee Book, after 1981; repr. of 1975 Knopf ed.; orig. Japanese serializations 1961–65).

111. Yasunari Kawabata, *Snow Country*, trans. Edward G. Seidensticker (New York: Vintage, 1996).

112. Donald Keene, *Dawn to the West: Japanese Literature in the Modern Era: Fiction* (New York: Henry Holt & Co. / An Owl Book, 1987 pbk. repr. of 1984 hdbk. ed.).

113. Philip Lopate, ed., *The Art of the Personal Essay: An Anthology from the Classical Era to the Present* (New York: Anchor, 1995 pbk. repr. of 1994 Doubleday hdbk.; orig. Japanese version wr. bef. 1965). [For Tanizaki's essay "In Praise of Shadows."]

114. [Makuzu Tadano.] Janet R. Goodwin, Bettina Gramlich-Oka, Elizabeth A. Leicester, Yuki Terazawa and Anne Walthall, "Solitary Thoughts: A Translation of Tadano Makuzu's *Hitori Kangae*," in *Monumenta Nipponica*, 56:1–2 (spring and summer 2001), pp. 21–193 (orig. ms. 1818).

115. Yukio Mishima, *Runaway Horses*, trans. Michael Gallagher (New York: Simon and Schuster / Pocket Books: Washington Square Press, 1975 repr. of 1973 ed.; orig. Japanese ed. 1969).

116. Yukio Mishima, *Spring Snow*, trans. Michael Gallagher (New York: Simon and Schuster / Pocket Books: Washington Square Press, 1975 repr. of 1972 ed.; orig. Japanese ed. 1968).

117. Yukio Mishima, *Sun and Steel*, trans. John Bester (New York: Grove Press, n.d.; orig. Japanese ed. 1970).

118. *Nakayama Iwata*, gen. ed. Shinichi Otsuka (Tokyo: Iwanami Shoten, *Nihon no Shashinka* 7 [Japanese Photographers ser., vol. 7], 1998).

119. *Nojima Yasuzo*, gen. ed. Shinichi Otsuka (Tokyo: Iwanami Shoten, *Nihon no Shashinka* 4 [Japanese Photographers ser., vol. 4], 1998).

120. Maurice Pinguet, *Voluntary Death in Japan*, trans. Rosemary Morris (Cambridge, Massachusetts: Polity Press, 1993; orig. French ed. 1984).

121. *Suda Issei*, gen. ed. Shinichi Otsuka (Tokyo: Iwanami Shoten, *Nihon no Shashinka* 40 [Japanese Photographers ser., vol. 40], 1998).

122. Junichiro Tanizaki, *The Makioka Sisters*, trans. Edward G. Seidensticker (New York: Random House: Vintage International, 1995; repr. of 1957 Knopf ed.; orig. Japanese publs. 1943–48.)

123. Junichiro Tanizaki, *Seven Japanese Tales*, trans. Howard Hibbett (New York: Putnam; a Wideview/Perigee Book, 1981 repr. of 1963 Knopf ed.; orig. Japanese publs. 1910–59). [For another Tanizaki item, see Lopate in this section.]

124. Taishu Komatsu, *Otoko no Soshin-gu* [Men's Accessories] (Tokyo: Shibundo, *Nihon no Bijutsu* 4, no. 395 [Japanese Art ser., vol. 4, no. 395], 1999).

125. Yasuji Toita and Chiaki Yoshida, *Kabuki*, trans. Don Kenny (Osaka: Hoikusha, Hoikusha's Color Books ser., no. 11, 1992 11th ed.; 1st ed. 1967).

126. Marc Treib and Ron Herman, *A Guide to the Gardens of Kyoto*, rev. ed. (New York: Kodansha International, 2003; orig. ed. 1980).

127. *Ueno Hikoma to Bakumatsu no Shashinkatachi* [Ueno Hikoma and the Photographers of the Last Days of the Tokugawa Era], gen. ed. Shinichi Otsuka (Tokyo: Iwanami Shoten, *Nihon no Shashinka* 1 [Japanese Photographers ser., vol. 1], 1997).

128. *Yamahata Yosuke*, gen. ed. Shinichi Otsuka (Tokyo: Iwanami Shoten, *Nihon no Shashinka* 6 [Japanese Photographers ser., vol. 6], 1998).

### Miscellaneous Ephemera

129. ___, *Kofuku-Ji: Sanjyu no toh Shosoh • Kitaendou Naijin • Chukondoh Hakkutsu Genba* [Kofuku Temple: The first layer of the Three Layered Tower • The Chancel of the North Circled Hall • Chu-Kon Hall Excavation Site] (*ca.* 2000).

130. ___, *Sho-Ren-Nin* [printed for Shoren-in Temple, *ca.* 2005).

131. ___, Small porn pamphlet offering "sophisticated wives' secret time," *ca.* 2005, trans. for WTV by Keiko Golden.

132. Rainbow Channel 2 Hour Adult Channel, schedule no. 5 for 2005; 2-sheet pamphlet whose upper fold displays a seminude view of the actress Akari Hoshino.

### G. CHINESE ITEMS

133. Ernest Fenollosa, *The Chinese Written Character as a Medium for Poetry*, ed. Ezra Pound (San Francisco: City Lights Books, 1968; orig. ed. 1936; Fenollosa died in 1908).

134. Hsueh Tou Ch'ung Hsien (980–1052) and Yuan Wu K'e Ch'in (1063–1135), comp., *The Blue Cliff Record*, trans. Thomas Cleary and J. C. Cleary (Boston: Shambhala, 1992; preface dated 1128).

135. Li Ch'ing-chao, *Complete Poems*, trans. and ed. Kenneth Rexroth and Ling Chung (New York: New Directions Publishing Corp., 1979, 3rd pr.; life of Li Ch'ing-chao 1081–*ca.* 1141).

136. Stephen Owen, ed. and trans., *An Anthology of Chinese Literature: Beginnings to 1911* (New York: W. W. Norton & Co., 1996).

137. Pu Songling, *Strange Tales from a Chinese Studio*, trans. and ed. John Minford (New York: Penguin Classics, 2006; orig. tales wr. *ca.* 1660–1715; this trans. includes only 104 tales out of almost 500).

138. Eliot Weinberger, ed., *The New Directions Anthology of Classical Chinese Poetry* (New York: New Directions Publishing Corp., 2003).

### H. OLD NORSE, OLD GERMAN, ANGLO-SAXON, OLD WELSH AND OLD FRENCH ITEMS

139. ___, *The Earliest English poems*, trans. Michael Alexander, 3rd ed. (New York: Penguin Books, 1991 ed.; orig. ed. 1966; poems wr. A.D. 700–1000).

140. ___, *The Mabinogion*, trans. Gwyn Jones and Thomas Jones (London: Everyman, 1949, rev. 1993).

141. ___, *The Nibelungenlied*, trans. A. T. Hatto (New York: Penguin, 1969 repr. of 1965 ed.; original German ed. *ca.* 1200).

142. ___, [Snorri Sturluson?], *Egil's Saga*, trans. Hermann Palsson and Paul Edwards, rev. ed. (Middlesex, U.K.: Penguin Books, 1978 repr. of 1976 ed.; original Icelandic text *ca.* 1230).

143. ___, *Eyrbyggja Saga*, trans. Hermann Palsson and Paul Edwards, rev. ed. (Middlesex, U.K.: Penguin Books, 1989 rev. repr. of 1972 ed.; original Icelandic text *ca.* 1250).

144. ___, *Hrafnkel's Saga*, trans. Hermann Palsson (Middlesex, U.K.: Penguin Books, 1976 repr. of 1971 ed.; stories wr. thirteenth cent.)

145. ____, *Laxdaela Saga*, trans. Magnus Magnusson and Hermann Palsson (Austin: University of Texas Press, 1975 pbk. repr. of 1969 ed.; original Icelandic text *ca.* 1245).

146. ____, *The Poetic Edda*, trans. Lee M. Hollander, 2nd ed., rev. (Austin: University of Texas Press, 1987 pbk. repr. of 1962 ed.; original lays *ca.* 800 — *ca.* 1400).

147. ____, *The Saga of Grettir the Strong*, ed. Diana Whaley, various trans. (New York: Penguin Classics, 2005; orig. Icelandic text late fourteenth cent.).

148. ____, *The Saga of the Volsungs: The Norse Epic of Sigurd the Dragon Slayer*, trans. Jesse L. Byock (New York: Penguin Classics, 1990; orig. Icelandic text thirteenth cent.).

149. ____, *Sagas of Warrior-Poets*, trans. Bernard Scudder, ed. Ornólfur Thorsson (New York: Penguin Classics, 2002; orig. Icelandic texts thirteenth & fourteenth cent.).

150. ____, *Two Viking Romances*, trans. Hermann Palsson and Paul Edwards (New York: Penguin Books, 1995; orig. trans. 1985; orig. tales *ca.* 1300).

151. Chrétien de Troyes, *Cligès*, trans. Burton Raffel (New Haven: Yale University Press, 1997; orig. French ed. soon after 1169).

152. H[ilda] R[oderick] Ellis Davidson, *Gods and Myths of Northern Europe* (London: Penguin, 1964).

153. John Lindow, *Norse Mythology: A Guide to the Gods, Heroes, Rituals and Beliefs* (New York: Oxford University Press, 2001).

154. Snorri Sturluson, *Edda* [The Prose Edda or Younger Edda], trans. Anthony Faulkes (Rutland, Vermont: Charles E. Tuttle Co., Inc. / Everyman's Library, 1992 repr. of 1987 ed.; orig. Icelandic ed. *ca.* 1220–30).

155. Sigrid Undset, *Kristin Lavransdatter*, vol. I: *The Bridal Wreath*, trans. not credited (New York: Random House / Vintage Books, 1987 repr. of 1923 Knopf ed.; orig. Norwegian ed. 1920).

156. Sigrid Undset, *Kristin Lavransdatter*, vol. II: *The Mistress of Husaby*, trans. not credited (New York: Random House / Vintage Books, 1987 repr. of 1925 Knopf ed.; orig. Norwegian ed. 1921).

157. Sigrid Undset, *Kristin Lavransdatter*, vol. III: *The Cross*, trans. not credited (New York: Random House / Vintage Books, 1987 repr. of 1927 Knopf ed.; orig. Norwegian ed. 1922).

## I. TRANSGENDER ITEMS

158. Mariette Pathy Allen, *The Gender Frontier* (Heidelberg: Kehrr Verlag, 2003).

159. Jonathan Ames, ed., *Sexual Metamorphosis: An Anthology of Transsexual Memoirs* (New York: A Vintage Original, 2005).

160. Amnesty International, *Torture Worldwide: An Affront to Human Dignity* (New York: Amnesty International Publications, 2000).

161. Charles Anders, *The Lazy Crossdresser* (Emeryville, California: Greenery Press, 2002).

162. Jennifer Finney Boylan, *She's Not There: A Life in Two Genders* (New York: Broadway Books, 2003).

163. Kate Bornstein, *My Gender Workbook: How to Become a Real Man, a Real Woman, the Real You, or Something Else Entirely* (New York: Routledge, 1998).

164. Rachel Ann Heath, *The Praeger Handbook of Transsexuality: Changing Gender to Match Mindset* (Westport, Connecticut: Praeger Publishers / Sex, Love and Psychology ser., 2006).

165. Michel Hurst and Robert Swope, eds., *Casa Susanna* (New York: power-House Books, 2005).

166. Samantha Kane, *A Two-Tiered Existence*, ed. Sarah Harding (London: Writers and Artists PLC, 1998).

167. Mattilda, a.k.a. Matt Bernstein Sycamore, *Nobody Passes: Rejecting the Rules of Gender and Conformity* (Emeryville, California: Seal Press, 2006).

168. Catherine Millot, *Horsexe: Essay on Transsexuality,* trans. Kenneth Hylton (Brooklyn: Autonomedia, 1993; orig. French ed. 1983).

169. Lannie Rose, *How to Change Your Sex: A Lighthearted Look at the Hardest Thing You'll Ever Do*, 3rd ed. (No place of publication given: Lulu, 2008 rev. of 2004 ed.).

170. Deborah Rudacille, *The Riddle of Gender: Science, Activism, and Transgender Rights* (New York: Random House / Anchor Books, 2006 rev. repr. of 2005 ed.).

171. Julia Serano, *Whipping Girl: A Transsexual Woman on Sexism and the Scapegoating of Femininity* (Berkeley, California: Seal Press, 2007).

172. Susan Stryker, *Transgender History* (Berkeley, California: Seal Press, 2008.)

173. Susan Stryker and Stephen Whittle, eds., *The Transgender Studies Reader* (New York: Routledge, 2006).

174. Veronica Vera, *Miss Vera's Cross-Dress for Success: A Resource Guide for Boys Who Want to Be Girls* (New York: Random House / Villard, 2002).

175. *I Am My Own Woman: The Outlaw Life of Charlote von Mahlsdorf, Berlin's Most Distinguished Transvestite*, trans. Jean Hollander (Pittsburgh: Cleis Press, 1995; orig. German ed. 1992).

## Periodicals and DVDs

176. Danae Doyle Productions, "Feminine Movement Basic Vol. 1," disk copyright DDP & Feminage, 2007.

177. Deep Stealth Productions, "Finding Your Female Voice" (2 disks, manufactured by CreateSource, South Valley, California, 2007). The unidentified narrator may be the same person as the one on the older video "Melanie Speaks." But a third party (Rose, p. 127) believes her to be Andrea James.

178. *Transgender Tapestry* magazine, published by the International Foundation for Gender Education, www.ifge.org.

## J. ANDREW WYETH

179. Wanda M. Corn, ed., *The Art of Andrew Wyeth*, with contributions by Brian O'Doherty, Richard Meryman and E. P. Richardson (San Francisco: pub. for the Fine Arts Museums of San Francisco by the New York Graphic Society Ltd., Greenwich, Connecticut; exhibited at the M. H. de Young Museum of the Fine Arts, San Francisco, June 16 – September 15, 1973).

180. Richard Meryman, *Andrew Wyeth: A Secret Life* (New York: HarperPerennial / A Division of HarperCollins, 1998 repr. of orig. 1996 ed.).

181. Andrew Wyeth, *Autobiography*, intro. by Thomas Hoving, with commentaries by Andrew Wyeth as told to Thomas Hoving (Boston: A Bullfinch Press Book / Little, Brown & Co., in assoc. w/ the Nelson-Atkins Museum of Art, Kansas City, 1998).

182. *Andrew Wyeth: The Helga Pictures*, text by John Wilmerding, Deputy Director, National Gallery of Art, Washington (New York: Harry N. Abrams, Inc., 1987; paintings executed 1971–85).

## K. OTHER ITEMS

183. ___, *The Epic of Gilgamesh*, trans. N. K. Sandars (New York: Penguin, 1972; Akkadian Semitic text based on Sumerian from early 2nd. millennium B.C.).

184. Kevyn Aucoin, *Making Faces* (New York: Little, Brown & Co., 1997).

185. Erich Auerbach, *Mimesis: The Representation of Reality in Western Literature*, trans. Willard R. Trask (Princeton, New Jersey: Princeton University Press, 1953; orig. Swiss [German-lang.] ed. 1946).

186. Willis Barnstone, comp. and trans., *Sappho and the Greek Lyric Poets* (New York: Schocken, 1988 rev. & expansion of 1962 ed.).

187. Hans Bellmer, *Little Anatomy of the Physical Unconscious, or, The Anatomy of the Image*, trans. Jon Graham (Waterbury Center, Vermont: Dominion, 2004; orig. French ed. 2001).

188. Heinrich Böll, *Adam and the Train*, trans. Leila Vennewitz (New York: McGraw-Hill, 1970).

189. Marcus Tullius Cicero, *Letters to Atticus* (works in 28 vols., vols. XXII–XXIV), trans. E. O. Winstedt (Cambridge, Massachusetts: Harvard University Press, Loeb Classical Library, 1980–87 reprs. of 1912–18 eds.; orig. letters B.C. 65–44).

190. Kenneth Clark, *The Nude: A Study in Ideal Form* (Princeton, New Jersey: Princeton University Press, Bollingen Series XXXV 2; 1990 repr. of 1972 pbk; orig. text of A. W. Mellon Lectures 1953, augmented *ca.* 1956).

191. Dominique Collon, *The Queen of the Night* (London: The British Museum Press / British Museum Objects in Focus ser., 2005).

192. Edwin Denby, *Dance Writings*, ed. Robert Cornfield and William Mackay (New York: Alfred A. Knopf, 1986; original essays 1936–65).

193. Bérénice Geoffroy-Schneiter, *Greek Beauty* (New York: Assouline, 2003; orig. French ed. n. d.).

194. The J. Paul Getty Museum, *Handbook of the Antiquities Collection* (Los Angeles: J. Paul Getty Trust, 2002).

195. Pat Getz-Gentle, *Personal Styles in Early Cycladic Sculpture*, with a chapter by Jack de Vries (Madison: University of Wisconsin Press, 2001).

196. Marija Gimbutas, *The Language of the Goddess* (New York: Thames and Hudson, 2001; orig. ed. 1989).

197. Judith Lynne Hanna, *Dance, Sex and Gender: Signs of Identity, Dominance, Defiance, and Desire* (Chicago: The University of Chicago Press, 1988).

198. [Jayadeva.] *Love Song of the Dark Lord: Jayadeva's Gitagovinda*, ed. and trans. Barbara Stoler Miller, 20th anniversary ed. (New York: Columbia University Press / Columbian Asian Studies ser. [Translations from the Asian Classics], 1997 rev. repr. of 1977 ed.; orig. Sanskrit text *ca.* 1205).

199. David Kunzle, *Fashion and Fetishism: Corsets, Tight-Lacing and Other Forms of Body Sculpture* (Phoenix Mill / Sparkford, U.K.: Sutton Publishing Ltd., 2006 repr. of 2004 rev. ed.; orig. ed. 1982).

200. Georg Christoph Lichtenberg, *The Waste Books*, trans. and sel. with intro. by R. J. Hollingdale (New York: New York Review Books, 2000; orig. Penguin ed. 1990; orig. German notebooks wr. bef. 1800).

201. André Malraux, *The Voices of Silence*, trans. Stuart Gilbert (Princeton, New Jersey: Princeton University Press, Bollingen Series XXIV A; 1990 repr. of 1978 reissue; orig. 3-vol. ed. 1949–50).

202. Henri Matisse, *Frauen: 32 Radierungen* (Munich: Im-Insel Verlag, Insel-Bücherei Nr. 577, n. d., inscribed in flyleaf 1956).

203. William Maxwell, *Early Novels and Stories* (New York: Library of America, 2008).

204. John Milton, *Paradise Lost: A Norton Critical Edition*, ed. Scott Elledge (New York: W. W. Norton & Co., 1975; orig. poem 1674).

205. Alexander Nehamas, *Only a Promise of Happiness: The Place of Beauty in a World of Art* (Princeton, New Jersey: Princeton University Press, 2007).

206. Novalis [Georg Friedrich Philipp von Hardenberg], *Henry von Ofterdingen*, trans. Palmer Hilty (New York: Frederick Ungar, 1974 repr. of 1964 ed.; orig. posthumous German ed. 1802).

207. Boris Pasternak, *Dr. Zhivago*, trans. Max Hayward and Manya Harari; "The Poems of Yurii Zhivago" trans. [from the Russian] by Bernard Guibert Guerney, revs. to trans. by Pantheon Books, 1958 (New York: New American Library of World Literature, Inc., Signet Books, 7th pr. 1961; orig. Italian ed. 1957; Russian ed. was later).

208. Giovanni Giovano Pontano, *Baiea*, trans. Rodney G. Dennis (Cambridge, Massachusetts: Harvard University Press, the I Tatti Renaissance Library, 2006; orig. poems fifteenth cent.).

209. Marcel Proust, *Remembrance of Things Past*, trans. C. Scott Moncrieff and Terence Kilmartin (New York: Vintage, 1982; orig. French ed. 1954); 3 vols.

210. James M. Robinson, gen. ed., *The Nag Hammadi Library*, 3rd rev. ed., trans. and introduced by members of the Coptic Gnostic Library Project of the Institute for Antiquity and Christianity, Claremont, California (San Francisco: HarperSanFrancisco, 1990).

211. Saadi [Sheikh Muslihuddin Saadi Shirazi], *The Rose Garden (Gulistan),* trans. Omar Ali-Shah (Reno, Nevada: Tractus Books, 1997; orig. Persian ed. *ca.* 1260).

212. William Kelly Simpson, ed., *The Literature of Ancient Egypt: An Anthology ofr Stories, Instruction, Stelae, Autobiographies, and Poetry*, 3rd ed. (New Haven: Yale University Press, 2003).

213. *The Variorum Edition of the Poems of W. B. Yeats*, ed. Peter Allt and Russell K. Alspach (New York: Macmillan Publishing Co., Inc., 1977 7th repr.; orig. copyright 1940).

214. Stefan Zweig, *The World of Yesterday* (Lincoln: University of Nebraska Press / Bison Books, 1964; orig. Viking ed. 1943).

### Periodicals and DVDs

215. *Allure* magazine. New York: Condé Nast Publications.

216. *Harper's Bazaar* magazine. New York: harpersbazaar.com.

217. *InStyle* magazine. Group publisher, The Style Collection, Lynette Harrison Brubaker. New York: instyle.com.

218. *Marie Claire* magazine. New York: Hearst Communications and Comary, Inc.

219. *New Beauty* magazine. Boca Raton, Florida: Sandow Media Corporation.

220. *San Francisco Chronicle*.

221. *Sophisticate's Black Hair Styles and Care Guide* magazine. Chicago: Associated Publications, Inc.

222. *Vogue* magazine. www.vogue.com.

# NOTE ON THE ILLUSTRATIONS

Never winning permission to photograph any Noh performances or rehearsals, I made sketches instead. Hopefully these will give some indication of stage layout and choreography.

The geishas who danced for me were more permissive. You will find their performances documented here, even if inadequately.

Even a high-quality color photograph of a Noh mask, printed on the best glossy stock, would fail to serve, given the subtleties of mask painting, and, more important, the power that these works of art possess of seeming to alter expression with angle. I refer you to the bibliography for several beautifully illustrated works on this topic; likewise for portraits of geishas.

As for Kabuki, that is scarcely represented here in either text or images. My apologies.

I would have liked to reproduce images of Stiff White Ladies, Genji Picture-Scrolls, Andrew Wyeth's Helga paintings, Noh fans, cosmetic advertisements and the like, but "commercial considerations" advised against it.

Finally, I want to assure you that even though my made-up face appears in a couple of illustrations herein, I lack illusions as to my attractiveness. It seemed germane to show how different makeup artists addressed the same problem. Smeary reproductions on rough paper stock may well improve the originals.

# Note on the Orthography

For the first few years I diligently collected macrons (those bars which in Japanese transliterations so often bask over the letters "u" and "o"). One sometimes meets "Noh" without its "h," and then with or without a macron. Dogen's thirteenth-century "Genjo Koan" may glide onstage wearing three macrons, one of them roofing Dogen himself. But no romanization is consistent; and so, reader, I took pity on you and on myself. You will see no macrons here.

All Japanese proper names are given, as is customary for them (not for us), with the family name first.

# ACKNOWLEDGMENTS

My great gratitude to the following Noh actors (and actress): Mr. Umewaka Rokuro (whose kind wife I also wish to thank for her kindness), the late Mr. Kanze Hideo, Mr. Mikata Shizuka, and Ms. Yamamura Yoko. Learning a little about Noh has been one of the most thrilling experiences of my life.

Mr. Yoshio Kou introduced me to some of the above, to several other people mentioned here, and, as ever, to various secret islands of the floating world aesthetic. He has been a great teacher, a fatherly guide and a superhuman night owl who could always drink more and stay up later than I. Mr. Kou, I will always admire you.

Dr. Sato Yoshiaki, Dr. Yokoyama Taro, formerly of the University of Tokyo, Mr. Jeff Clark, Professor Nishino Haruo, Director of the Nogami Memorial Institute for Noh Studies at Hosei University, Tokyo, and Ms. Hagashi Sumiko, curator of the Kanazawa Noh Museum, gave me much Noh information and corrected more mistakes than I can bear to think of.

I am deeply indebted also the geishas and ochaya-sans mentioned in this book: Kofumi-san, Konomi-san, Danyu-san, Imamura-san, Masami-san, Suzuka-san, Fukutaro-san and Hachishige-san. I will never forget the ephemeral beauties, each unique, of the handful of geisha dances which it has been my privilege to see.

The mask carvers Mr. Otsuka Ryoji and Ms. Nakamura Matsue were a great help. I met the sweet Ms. Nakamura on enough occasions to fall under her spell. Both of these people, who, being among the most renowned exemplars of their craft now living, must have better things to do than chat with me, were patient with my ignorance. Ms. Nakamura corrected the captions to the mask photographs which appear in this book.

The onnagata Mr. Ichikawa Shunen gave me an openhearted introduction to Kabuki's performance of femininity. My sincere thanks to him.

Katy, Jennifer and other Los Angeles transformers trusted me, taught me and drank with me, all at the same time. Yukiko did what she could with unpromising material.

I gratefully thank Hilary Nichols, "Sachiko" and Marina Vulicévic for expressing their tripartite femininities to me.

Regarding Kawai Takako (one of whose many other names is Silver Flower Star Goddess), the dedication says it all.

Tochigi Reiko (also known as Precious Moon Goddess) went painstakingly over a draft of the manuscript, resolving orthographic inconsistencies and saving me from any number of errors. Still better, she continued to be a considerate friend who was usually up for a bowl of grilled eel and a shot of booze in Kabukicho. Interpreter, translator, go-between and answer lady in a number of disciplines, Reiko is also the politest person I have ever met.

Mrs. Keiko Golden (the Jade Empress of the Innermost Diamond) and the other translators she found for me, Ms. Sumino Junko and Ms. Yasuda Nobuko, were all excellent. Keiko, thank you for being so kind to me all these years.

I would like to thank Dan Halpern, Ginny Smith, David Koral, Mary Austin Speaker, Bruce Giffords and Miranda Ottewell for their various contributions to this book. Mary went many extra miles to make the illustrations reproduce as nicely as possible.

Richard Grossman did me the great favor of sending me *The Blue Cliff Records* as a present. This book helped me understand a little more about snow in a silver bowl. Prof. Chris Martin gave me a copy of Pontano's *Baiea*, from which I quote in the chapter "What Is Grace?" Declan Spring and Thomas Keith at New Directions furnished me with some great books, including the anthology of Chinese poetry, which I cite in the chapter on perfect faces. Thank you all, my friends.

Ben Pax, Michael Markowitz, Jake Dickinson, Mary Swisher and my sister Ann all helped me in various personal ways. Mr. Joseph Mattson always knew which bars to go to when. And I wish to thank Katie Peterson, for reasons best known to her (they may have something to do with Anne Gregory's yellow hair). Teresa McFarland was, as ever, solace, help, interlocutor, inspiration and makeup consultant.

My Norwegian editor, John Erik Riley, and Gina Granum, who directed the Norsk Litteraturfestival in Lillehammer, made it possible for me to present a preliminary version of the chapter on Norse beauty to a knowledgeable audience. I thank them in all friendship.

Ms. Susan Golomb of her eponymous agency dazzled me with her feminine beauty, not to mention her business qualities. I am equally grateful to her two assistants from that period, Mr. Casey Pannell and Ms. Terra Chalberg.

The American Academy of Arts and Letters and Ohio State University (in the later institution I think especially of Geoff Smith and Lisa Iacabellis) helped subsidize this book. (The advance I received will recoup at best one-third of the money I laid out.) My thanks to both institutions for supporting these few frivolous swims into the floating world. The students of staff of Deep Springs College gave me a beautifully isolated home and perfect company for a month while I was working on this book. Since Noh is so slowed down, and geisha dance so brief, and all human beauty so temporary, there is no place better to consider such matters than the desert, whose solitudes are deep, slow, yet ever altering.